The Wizard of Oz
Vocabulary Builder

Books by Mark Phillips

Metallica Riff by Riff
Guitar for Dummies
Honeymooners Trivia
Sight-Sing Any Melody Instantly
Sight-Read Any Rhythm Instantly
The Pinocchio Intermediate Vocabulary Builder

The Wizard of Oz Vocabulary Builder

Mark Phillips

A. J. Cornell Publications
New York

The Wizard of Oz Vocabulary Builder

For information address:
A. J. Cornell Publications
18-74 Corporal Kennedy St.
Bayside, NY 11360

Cover illustration by Debbie Phillips
Cover design by Jonathan Gullery

Library of Congress Control Number: 2002096752

ISBN: 0-9727439-0-1

Printed in the Unites States of America

How to Use This Book

In the story, all the vocabulary words appear in **bold type**. Read with a pencil in hand. As you go, underline any word you already know. If you think you know a word but aren't 100 percent sure about it, check the definition. For any word that's new to you, read the definition carefully. By the time you get to the end of the story, you will have learned many of the words (because you learned them in context). Your next step is to go back to Chapter 1 and read the entire story a second time, again with pencil in hand. This time through, you'll be able to underline many more words than you did the first time. As you go, re-check the definitions of any words you've forgotten. Every time you re-read the story you not only learn new words, but you reinforce the meanings of the words you've already learned. You'll probably need to re-read the story several times, each time underlining more and more words until they all have been accounted for.

By the way, if you see any words in *plain* type whose meanings you don't know, look those up in any standard dictionary. But generally, for all the boldface words, use the definitions included here rather than those in a dictionary. Why? A dictionary might show five different meanings for the same word, yet four of those might rarely be used by anyone. And there's no little sign pointing to the fifth one that says: *This is the one you really want.* And dictionaries aren't always user-friendly. You might read a definition in a dictionary and *still* not understand what a word means because the definition might contain other difficult words or because the dictionary doesn't show you *how* the word is used— it doesn't use it in context.

Once you're familiar with the special words presented in this book, you'll probably start noticing them everywhere— in newspapers, in other books, on TV shows, or in movies. You might even become possessive of them— every time you come across one, you'll proudly think to yourself: *Hey! That's one of my words!*

Introduction

Why I Wrote This Book

When I was a student, I had a terrible vocabulary. That's because I didn't like to read— and, as parents and teachers have always told us, reading is the only effective way to build a vocabulary. Once I tried to improve my vocabulary by memorizing the definitions of 1000 words (that appeared on little flash cards that came in a pretty box). I was able to memorize the meanings of *abase*, *abash*, and *abate*, but by the time I got to *abdicate*, my mind became fuzzy— and I still had 996 words to go! The unpleasant alternative was to do a lot of reading. But how many books would I have had to read to learn all of the words I needed to know? And what guarantee was there that the books I chose would even contain the words I needed— assuming I even knew what those words were?

When I was in the seventh grade, I did feel duty bound to read one particular book because it was written by a relative of mine. I learned something about the study of vocabulary by reading that book: If you learn a word in context you'll remember what it means. For example, in one scene it said that an eleven-year-old boy "brandished" a toy sword. Well, at that time, I had never heard of the word *brandish* (but I looked it up and found that it meant "to wave in a threatening manner"). What a vivid mental picture I had! Of course that's what it meant. What else would an 11-year-old boy do with a toy sword?

Because I didn't want to have to read a lot of books, I wished there existed one good book of fiction that was fairly short and just happened to contain all the words I'd ever need to know (for my SATs or just for intelligent-sounding conversation). That way, I could learn the necessary words in context and remember what they meant. But no such book existed.

As an adult, after having finally built a vocabulary through reading— hey, you have to do something to get through those boring hours of commuting to work on public transportation!— I decided to create the book I wished for as a teenager. Because the story of *The Wizard of Oz* is known and loved by everyone, and because it's rich in characters and situations, I decided it would make the perfect vehicle for the book I had in mind. I made a list of the best vocabulary words— about 1850 of them— and, reworking and rewriting L. Frank Baum's classic story from beginning to end (but maintaining the overall plot), I sprinkled the words— in contexts as meaningful as I could make them— throughout.

Chapter 1 "The Tornado"

Once upon a time, a **winsome**[1] young orphan named Dorothy lived with her Aunt Em and Uncle Henry on a bleak, **hardscrabble**[2] Kansas farm. Located about fifty feet from their **Spartan**[3] little house was a small underground room called a cyclone cellar, where the family could go in case one of those mighty, house-crushing whirlwinds arose.

Dorothy's one real joy came from playing with Toto, her little black dog. Toto had long silky hair and small black eyes that twinkled merrily on either side of his funny little nose. Together they frittered away many an afternoon, frolicking among the haystacks in perpetual delight, far beneath the **pellucid**[4] Kansas

---

[1] **winsome** If you're *winsome*, you're naturally charming, engaging, adorable, winning, etc., and you probably have a childlike innocence, too. The word is used more often to describe a female than a male. *When I told Phil that the new film comedy starred Meg Ryan, he said, "Let me guess; she plays a winsome young woman who finds love, but not until the last five minutes of the movie."*

[2] **hardscrabble** This word describes things (towns, farms, land, etc.) that provide very little in return (crops, for example) for much effort. People who live a *hardscrabble* existence (mountainside farmers, for example) barely subsist. *In 1985 Pulitzer Prize–winning columnist Russell Baker said, "Goat cheese produced a bizarre eating era when sensible people insisted that this miserable cheese produced by these miserable creatures [raised] on miserable hardscrabble earth was actually superior to the magnificent creamy cheeses of the noblest dairy animals bred in the richest green valleys of the earth."*

[3] **Spartan** If something is *Spartan*, it's severely simple or restrained. Note: The word is usually capitalized because it refers to the ancient Greek city of Sparta, famous for its strict discipline and strict way of life. *When she saw how the house was decorated (no rugs, no knickknacks, and bare floors), she exclaimed, "This place is as Spartan as a monk's bedroom!"*

[4] **pellucid** If something is *lucid* (in the sense of being transparent), it allows light to pass through. But when you refer to something as *pellucid*, you mean that it allows the *maximum possible* amount of light to pass through. *The anti-pollution campaign featured a teary-eyed American Indian standing on a hill beside a pellucid brook.*

skies.

One day, while **hunkered**[1] down to milk a **mottled**[2] cow, Uncle Henry kept an anxious eye toward an increasingly **ominous**[3] sky above. Suddenly seeing the long grass ripple before him, he froze. Now there came a sharp whistling from behind him, and as he turned his head he saw **undulations**[4] in the grass in that direction also. The usually **phlegmatic**[5] farmer bolted straight up in alert attention. "There's a twister coming, Em," he shouted to his wife.

---

[1] **hunker (hunkered)** To *hunker* is to squat or crouch down. Thus, if you're hunkered down, you're squatting down, close to the ground. *The water-skier generally maintained an upright position but hunkered down at each curve and before each jumping ramp.*

[2] **mottled** If something is *mottled*, it's spotted or blotched with different colors or shadings. *Our calico cat's coat was mottled with shades of brown, black, and white.*

[3] **ominous** If something is *ominous*, it gives you a feeling that something bad is about to happen. It comes from the word *omen*, which means "a sign that foretells a (usually bad) future event." *In the 1975 film* Jaws, *the shark's appearance is usually signaled (to the audience) by low, ominous music.*

[4] **undulate (undulations)** If something *undulates*, it moves with smooth, wavelike motions. *Undulations* are these wavelike motions. *Bill avoided dancing at parties because he didn't like to be seen undulating— or making any uncouth motions, for that matter— in public.*

[5] **phlegmatic** In the days before modern medicine, it was believed that if you had *phlegm*— that thick mucus that sometimes gets annoyingly stuck in your throat— it caused you to not care too much about things and to be slow or sluggish. Today, if you say someone is *phlegmatic*, you mean that he doesn't get excited too easily; he's rather unemotional and indifferent. Note: Dictionaries will tell you that the word is pronounced with a hard g, but many people pronounce it with a silent g. *On Halloween eve, 1988, journalist David Streitfeld wrote, "According to stereotype, the English are phlegmatic and [imperturbable] souls, which hardly explains the attraction of places like the Chamber of Horrors in Madame Tussaud's Wax Museum or the London Dungeon, [which] combines the technology of Disneyland with the spirit of, well, Jack the Ripper."*

THE WIZARD OF OZ VOCABULARY BUILDER

Ever **solicitous**[1] of his livestock, he bolted toward the barn. With uncommon **alacrity**[2], Aunt Em dropped her work and ran to the door. One glance at the **lowering**[3] sky told her of the coming danger. "Quick, Dorothy!" she shrieked. "Run for the cyclone cellar!"

Galvanized[4] into action by Aunt Em's **strident**[5] **exhortation**[6], Dorothy grabbed Toto and followed her aunt to the metal trap

---

[1] **solicitous** When you're *solicitous* of (or about) someone, you're thoughtfully concerned (often anxiously concerned) about his welfare, health, or safety. *Most Americans were solicitous of Lindbergh's safety during his solo 1927 nonstop flight from New York to Paris.* Note: Don't confuse this with the word *solicit* that you sometimes see on signs (on buildings) that say "No soliciting." Those signs basically mean that door-to-door salesmen are not permitted to seek business there.

[2] **alacrity** When you do something with *alacrity*, you do it right away and speedily (and often with a cheerful willingness). *Our boss said that to him, the perfect employee was one who responded to his orders with politeness and alacrity.*

[3] **lowering** This word is a tricky one because it *looks* like it might pertain to being low (as in *low down, close to the ground*). But, in fact, the first syllable *(low)* doesn't rhyme with "know"; it rhymes with "now." To *lower* (rhymes with "shower") is to be dark and threatening. Thus, a *lowering* sky is a dark and threatening one. *American artist Winslow Homer's most famous painting,* The Gulf Stream *(1899), shows a man in a small boat struggling against a raging sea beneath a lowering sky.*

[4] **galvanize (galvanized)** The literal meaning of this word is "to stimulate with an electric current" (and you can imagine how startling that would feel). But people usually use the word figuratively. If something *galvanizes* you, it suddenly arouses you to act. *The Soviets' successful launch of* Sputnik *in 1957 galvanized the American government into accelerating its own space program.*

[5] **strident** A sound described as *strident* is loud and shrill. *While Russian composer Sergei Prokofiev's early pieces were often harsh and strident, his later works were often pleasing and lyrical.*

[6] **exhort (exhortation)** When you *exhort* someone, you give him an urgent warning or an urgent piece of advice. An *exhortation* is an act of exhorting or the urgent message itself. *During World War I, Herbert Hoover, then U.S. Food Administrator, exhorted housewives to observe "meatless Mondays" and "wheatless Wednesdays" as food conservation measures.*

3

door that led to the **sanctuary**[1] of the underground room. But just as she was about to enter, Toto jumped from her arms and scampered back into the house. After running this way and that, he found what seemed to be a safe **haven**[2]— a spot under the center of Dorothy's bed.

Not yet appreciating the full power of the storm, and despite her aunt's hurried **admonitions**[3], Dorothy started back to retrieve the little dog from the house, which, framed against the **eerie**[4], electrified sky, lost its **prosaic**[5] outlines and became mysterious and threatening. After she had taken only two steps, the tornado descended violently, **decimating**[6] everything in sight. The wind,

---

[1] **sanctuary** Originally, a *sanctuary* was a church or a part of a church. But now the word can describe any place that offers protection from harm. It can also refer to the immunity from harm the place offers. *Some experts believe that when we sleep curled up in a fetal position, we're exhibiting an unconscious longing for the sanctuary of the womb.*

[2] **haven** A *haven* originally meant "a natural harbor used to keep ships safe." Now the word can be used to refer to any place of safety. *While some of the 13 original colonies gave protection to persecuted religious groups, Georgia was conceived as a haven for English debtors!*

[3] **admonition (admonitions)** An *admonition* is a warning or a piece of cautionary advice. The verb is *admonish*. *Most cookbooks admonish the reader to avoid overcooking pasta and vegetables.*

[4] **eerie** If something is *eerie*, it makes you feel fearful or uneasy, as if some sinister power or mysterious (or even supernatural) force were at work. *At 4:30 a.m. the foggy, deserted metropolis was eerie and fantastic to behold.*

[5] **prosaic** Prose (ordinary writing) is supposedly less beautiful and imaginative than poetry. So if something (not just writing, but *anything*) is described as *prosaic*, it's commonplace, ordinary, and run-of-the-mill. *Most UFO sightings have boringly prosaic explanations— reflected sunlight from airplanes, weather balloons, or meteorological phenomena, for example.*

[6] **decimate (decimating)** This word *originally* referred to the killing (as a punishment for mutiny) of one out of every ten soldiers (chosen by lot). (Note the root *deci*, which refers to "ten.") But today the word is used to refer to any great loss of life or large-scale destruction. *Experts say that the smoking population will be decimated by lung cancer.*

tearing past her at ninety miles an hour, seized a sharp-edged shingle from the roof and flung it downward through the air like a guillotine that missed Dorothy's neck by mere inches.

Now the wind took hold of the girl and knocked her down. All around her, flying flowerpots, **denuded**[1] branches, and pieces of fence smashed to bits as they struck the ground. She slowly raised herself to her feet, and, **inclining**[2] her body sharply forward, set out again toward the house. But her flapping dress **hobbled**[3] her as it clung to her legs at every step.

With her head down and arms stretched out before her, she stumbled on, feeling her way like a blind girl. After every few steps some unseen flying object appeared from the darkness and struck her. But when she screamed out in fear and pain, her own voice was **obliterated**[4] by the deafening, insane music of the swirling storm.

With great difficulty she had now crossed the yard, and as she was about to enter the house, the storm made a final **malevolent**[5]

---

[1] **denuded** If something has been *denuded*, it has been stripped bare (of its natural or usual covering). (Note the similarity to the word *nude*.) *Earthquakes and landslides have long ago denuded Italy's Apennines mountains of their original forest cover.*

[2] **incline (inclining)** An *incline* is a slanted surface. To *incline* something is to slant or angle it. *A helicopter is steered in a particular direction by inclining the axis of the main propeller in that direction.*

[3] **hobble (hobbled)** If you've ever tried to walk with your pants around your ankles, you know what it feels like to be *hobbled*. If something *hobbles* you, it doesn't prevent you from walking; it just makes walking difficult. Sometimes a horse's legs are fastened together to prevent free motion; when that happens, the horse has been *hobbled*, and the piece of rope is called a *hobble*. The word can be used figuratively to refer to anything that restrains or hinders. *In 1904 catcher Branch Rickey, hobbled by injuries and by his religious objections to playing on Sundays, was dropped by the Cincinnati Reds.*

[4] **obliterate (obliterated)** If something is *obliterated*, it's completely wiped out so that there's no trace of it. *Most of the London slums described in Charles Dickens' novels were obliterated by bombing raids during World War II.*

gesture. Two sharp metal gutters, stripped from the roof by a single blast of wind, came flying toward her like parallel spears. Before she knew what had happened, she saw them stick themselves deeply into the ground at her feet!

Now inside the house, she desperately looked for Toto. The wind, which outside the house had maintained a constant course, now swirled around the furniture in a hundred directions and made it impossible for Dorothy to walk in a straight line. She was tossed and battered like a ship in a **maelstrom**[1] until an **erratic**[2] **vortex**[3] caught her and flung her upon her bed, where she lost consciousness.

Then something strange **ensued**[4]. The house, now at the center

---

[5] **malevolent** Someone (or something) *malevolent* usually has a natural evilness or ill will and will cause (or would like to cause) harm or injury to others. *When she replied that she was on her way to her grandmother's house, Little Red Riding Hood never suspected that the wolf was actually holding malevolent intentions.*

[1] **maelstrom** A *maelstrom* is any large or powerful whirlpool. It's named after an actual whirlpool (named *Maelstrom*) located off the coast of Norway. The word can also be used figuratively to describe any violent or turbulent situation, as in *the maelstrom of war* or *the maelstrom of morning traffic. During the 2000 presidential election, the state of Florida became caught in a maelstrom of competing definitions of "clear intent of the voter."*

[2] **erratic** If something is *erratic*, it lacks consistency, uniformity, or regularity. If something moves *erratically* it doesn't follow a fixed or regular course; it jumps from place to place. *A 1984 article in the* London Times *said that Academy Award-winning American actress Helen Hayes' "education was erratic, though she learned to add by counting the nightly box office takings."*

[3] **vortex** A *vortex* is a swirling mass or column of water or air (especially one that has the power to draw into it whatever surrounds it). The word also can be used figuratively to describe anything (other than swirling water or air) that draws into its center all that surrounds it. *The Broadway actor was eventually swept into the vortex of Hollywood.*

[4] **ensue (ensued)** To say that some action or activity *ensues* is to say that it happens or takes place (often immediately) as a result or consequence of some prior action or activity. *After Abraham Lincoln was elected President (1860), the South seceded from the Union and the Civil War ensued.*

of the tornado, where the air is somehow strangely still, whirled around two or three times, then started to rise slowly through the air like a balloon. Once at the **pinnacle**[1] of the twister's funnel, it was whisked across the boundless **firmament**[2].

When Dorothy finally regained consciousness she saw that the air in her room was still, but she lay on the bed with Toto beside her until her shattered nerves began to compose themselves. Then she looked out the window and was horrified to see that her house was airborne! It was terribly dark outside, and the wind, which refused to **abate**[3], howled horribly.

Dorothy found that in spite of the surrounding **turbulence**[4], the house was riding quite easily. When several hours had passed without a catastrophe, she settled down a bit, and then, examining

---

[1] **pinnacle** The *pinnacle* of something is its highest point. The word can refer to a physical high point, but is often used to refer to a figurative high point (as of an achievement, for example). *In his 1963 book* The Quiet Crisis, *U.S. Secretary of the Interior Stuart Udall said, "We stand today poised on a pinnacle of wealth and power, yet we live in a land of vanishing beauty, of increasing ugliness, of shrinking open space, and of an overall environment that is diminished daily by pollution and noise."*

[2] **firmament** The word *firmament* can be used as a synonym for *sky* when *sky* is thought of as "the expanse (or great arch) of the heavens." The word can also be used figuratively to mean "highest plane." *Plato, Aristotle, Buddha, and Confucius are stars in the firmament of thought.*

[3] **abate** If something (bad weather, conflict, pain, enthusiasm, interest, for example) *abates*, it becomes less intense; it dies down. *The years-old ethnic conflict in areas of the former Yugoslavia showed no signs of abating.*

[4] **turbulent (turbulence)** If something (air or water movement, or an era, for example) is *turbulent*, it's stormy, agitated, violent, etc. The noun is *turbulence*. *With its civil rights protests, antiwar protests, and assassinations, the decade from 1960–1969 is often referred to by historians as "the turbulent sixties."*

her situation, began to seriously **lament**[1] her **plight**[2]. After all, when the house fell again, she and Toto could be smashed to pieces. With a brave but **spurious**[3] **insouciance**[4], she decided to wait and see what would happen next. But the gentle swaying of the house was a **soporific**[5], and Dorothy finally became drowsy and fell asleep.

---

[1] **lament** If you *lament* something, you feel or express grief or sorrow over it (as in *she lamented her mother's death*). But you don't have to lament *over* something; you can just plain lament (as in *ever since her puppy ran away, all she does is lament*). *In April 1999 journalist Rachel Alexander, speaking of "The Great One," said, "Showing the grace and poise that marked his 20-year NHL career, Wayne Gretzky today made official the retirement hockey fans have been lamenting for days."*

[2] **plight** A *plight* is a bad or unfavorable condition or situation. The word is used especially if the situation is trying or unfortunate, as in *the plight of the homeless*. *During the 18th and 19th centuries, many poverty-stricken rural families responded to their plight by migrating to cities.*

[3] **spurious** To describe something as *spurious* (pronounced *SPYUR-ee-is*) is to say that it lacks authenticity; it's not the genuine article; it's counterfeit, fake, bogus. A *spurious* argument is an illogical one; it leads to a false conclusion. *In March 1990, the* Los Angeles Times *reported that at a British museum "a spurious 6th-century [stone coffin] was exposed only after someone noticed that it depicted a female figure wearing 19th-century underwear."*

[4] **insouciant (insouciance)** Someone who's *insouciant* (prounounced *in-SOO-see-ent*) is carefree, unconcerned, without anxiety. If you remember that the French word *souci* means "care" and that the prefix *in-* means "without," it's easy to remember that *insouciant* means "without care." *Insouciance* is the noun. *According to the* Cambridge Biographical Encyclopedia, *British actor Roger Moore "brought a lightweight insouciance to the role of [fictional secret service agent] Jame Bond."*

[5] **soporific** As a noun, a *soporific* is something (a drug or boring speech, for example) that causes you to feel sleepy. As an adjective it means "causing sleepiness." *Cold medicines containing alcohol and antihistamines have a soporific effect.*

Chapter 2 "The Munchkins"

A sudden shock jolted Dorothy awake. She noticed that she was back on the ground **unscathed**[1], and she gratefully patted the **pliant**[2] mattress she and Toto had been lying upon. Brilliant sunshine **suffused**[3] the house with light. Dorothy, feeling restored and refreshed, leaped from her bed and ran to the door. Then, as a wave of uncertainty came over her, she **gingerly**[4] pushed it open.

As she stepped outside, a little cry of amazement escaped from her lips. As her pupils contracted to adjust to the bright sunlight, her eyes simultaneously widened at the unbelievable **vista**[5] she beheld.

Sparkling brooks **meandered**[6] through **verdant**[1] fields, and

---

[1] **unscathed** This word means "unhurt, unharmed, uninjured." *When the Space Shuttle Endeavour landed at Cape Canaveral in September 1995, it was the first time in months that the O-ring seals came back unscathed.*

[2] **pliant** Something that's *pliant* will bend, flex, or yield readily; it won't be stiff. *Sculptors find it easier to manipulate pliant clay than clay that has hardened.*

[3] **suffuse (suffused)** To *suffuse* is to completely spread through or over (something); to saturate (as with liquid, color, feeling, etc.). *In Victor Hugo's 1831 novel* The Hunchback of Notre Dame, *(deformed bell ringer) Quasimodo's heart becomes suffused with love whenever he sees (the beautiful gypsy girl) Esmeralda.*

[4] **gingerly** To do something *gingerly* is to do it carefully or cautiously (and therefore sometimes even delicately), so as to avoid danger or risk. *While renovating the barn, we chased raccoons from the stalls, cleared bird nests from the rafters, and very gingerly shooed snakes out into the yard.*

[5] **vista** A *vista* is a view (usually of a natural setting), especially a far-reaching or panoramic one. *The Italian island of Capri, known for its deep caves, mild climate, and beautiful vistas, has been a famed resort for over 2000 years.*

[6] **meander (meandered)** If something (a river, for example) doesn't follow a straight course, but instead follows a turning and winding course, it *meanders*. If you talk about people or language (conversations, stories, etc.) *meandering*, you mean that they wander aimlessly. *The fellow who wrote a novel while cruising down the Mississippi admitted that his story was written by the river— when it meandered, so did his plot.*

variegated[2] profusions of flowers sprang **copiously**[3] from **luxuriant**[4] banks. Friendly trees **proffered**[5] **cornucopias**[6] of

---

[1] **verdant** If you say that land is *verdant*, you mean that it's green with vegetation, or that it's covered with grass or plants. The word can also simply mean "green in color." *Early settlers named Vermont's Green Mountains from the verdant forests of evergreens that covered them.*

[2] **variegated** If something is *variegated* it's marked by patches or spots of many different colors; often it's dappled or has a patchwork effect. *Every fall, many New Yorkers drive to New England to view the variegated autumn leaves.* Note: The word can also mean "diversified, diverse, varied, etc."

[3] **copious (copiously)** To describe something as *copious* is to say that it's large in quantity or amount; it's plentiful. *The Marshall Plan (proposed in 1947 by Secretary of State George C. Marshall) was a program by which the United States gave copious economic aid to European countries to help them rebuild after the devastation of World War II.*

[4] **luxuriant** Don't confuse this word with *luxurious* (which means "characterized by luxury"). The word *luxuriant* is usually used to describe land—land that's excessively fertile and productive, land that produces abundant, even superabundant, vegetation. *The Hawaiian Islands are largely covered with luxuriant vegetation.*

[5] **proffer (proffered)** This word means "to offer; to put before someone for acceptance or rejection." You might use the word *proffer* (as opposed to *offer*) if the context is literary or to imply that the offering in question has been motivated by generosity or courtesy. (Note that the *o* sound in the first syllable is the sound of *o* in *on*, not *off*.) *When, in the movie, the wicked Queen proffered a shiny but poisoned apple to Snow White, we all silently screamed, "Don't take it!"*

[6] **cornucopia (cornucopias)** You've probably seen a picture of a curved, cone-shaped basket (or hollowed-out goat's horn) overflowing with fruit (and sometimes flowers and grain, too). That's known as a *horn of plenty* or a *cornucopia*. But figuratively, the word signifies any great abundance or overflowing supply of something. *He opened the paper to the "help wanted" section and was greeted by a cornucopia of employment opportunities.*

luscious fruits, and singing birds of brilliant, **iridescent**[1] plumage fluttered from bush to bush.

All this was so different from the **arid**[2], gray prairies she had known, that Dorothy **surmised**[3] she was no longer in Kansas. She promptly divulged her little **epiphany**[4] to Toto.

For a while, she stood, mouth **agape**[5], in a state of **transfixed**[6]

---

[1] **iridescent** If something is *iridescent* it has or displays shining, glowing colors, like those of a rainbow. *Six-year-old Billy was afraid to admit to his teacher that the reason he was five minutes late for school was that he'd just spent that much time standing in front of the building staring in wonder at the iridescent streaks of an oil slick.*

[2] **arid** This word means "dry" or "very dry" and is usually used in describing land. The implication is that the land so described is unproductive, parched, or barren. *The Hoover Dam and its reservoir, Lake Mead, supply irrigation water to many areas of the arid Southwest.*

[3] **surmise (surmised)** To *surmise* something is to take an educated guess about it. If you don't have any concrete proof of something, but you do have some slight evidence of it, the best you can do is *surmise*. *The ancient astronomer Ptolemy incorrectly surmised that the planets, along with the sun and stars, revolved around the earth.*

[4] **epiphany** If you have a sudden revelation, comprehension, insight, or understanding about something (especially something considered important or far-reaching), you've had an *epiphany*. The implication is that as a result of this revelation your life will somehow be different or better. *After (blind and deaf girl) Helen Keller's epiphany that words represent objects, her learning progressed rapidly.*

[5] **agape** If you say that someone's mouth is *agape* you mean that it's open in wonder or amazement. If you say that a person is *agape* you mean that he has his mouth open in wonder or amazement. *In the 1982 film E.T.— The Extra-Terrestrial, when Elliott's older brother first sees E.T., he stands frozen with mouth agape.*

[6] **transfixed** If you see something amazing, scary, awesome, captivating, etc., and your attention is fixed on it to the point that you become motionless, you're *transfixed*. *In December 2000 journalist Mary Quattlebaum, speaking of snow days, said, "When snow begins to fall, adults may foresee stranded cars and impassable roads, but kids are transfixed by a shimmering vision: Sleds! Snowmen! School closed for days!"*

incredulity[1]. As she finally came out of her **stupor**[2], she noticed a **knot**[3] of strange little people approaching her. They were only as tall as children, but they looked to her much older.

There were several men, but only one woman. The **bewhiskered**[4] men Dorothy thought to be about as old as Uncle

---

[1] **incredulous (incredulity)** If you're *incredulous* (pronounced *in-KREJ-uh-lis*) about something, you don't believe it or you find it difficult to believe. The noun *incredulity* (pronounced *in-krih-DOO-lih-tee* or *in-krih-DYOO-lih-tee*) means "the state of being incredulous." *In a 1493 letter (translated to English in* American History Leaflets*) to the Treasurer of (the Spanish region of) Aragon announcing his discovery of America, Christopher Columbus wrote, "Although these lands had been imagined and talked of before they were seen, most men listened incredulously to what was thought to be but an idle tale."*

[2] **stupor** When you're in a daze, or when your mental faculties have been deadened or greatly diminished (often by shock, drugs, or disease), you're in a *stupor*. *According to a May 2001* Washington Post *article, "Dolphin sightings are not unusual on the beaches of the Delaware shore; sunbathers are periodically roused from their reptilian stupor by excited shouts, and pull themselves onto their elbows as everyone else on the beach races toward the surf and squints into the waves as dolphins pass by, often surprisingly close to shore, the shining curves of their backs visible above the waves."*

[2] **knot** A *knot* of people is a (not large) group of people, somewhat tightly clustered together, as in *a knot of onlookers*. Sometimes the word can refer to things (instead of people), as in *a knot of trees*. *Speaking of Richard Nixon to a knot of reporters after a 1977 press conference, President Jimmy Carter said, "I personally think that he did violate the law, but I don't think that he thinks he did."*

[4] **bewhiskered** The meaning of quite a few words starting with the prefix *be-* can be figured out simply by looking past the prefix (here, look at *whiskered*). *Bewhiskered* means "having whiskers" or "bearded." Likewise, if you're *bespectacled*, you're wearing spectacles (eyeglasses). *In social studies class, nearly everyone recognized the photo of a bewhiskered cigar-smoker in combat uniform as Cuban leader Fidel Castro.*

THE WIZARD OF OZ VOCABULARY BUILDER

Henry. But the woman, **wizened**[1] and **hoary**[2], with a stiff, deliberate **gait**[3], was doubtless much older.

When these **diminutive**[4] creatures drew near to where Dorothy was standing, they suddenly paused, as if afraid to come any closer.

---

[1] **wizened** To *wizen* is to dry up or shrivel (as with age); thus, if someone is *wizened*, he (or at least his face) is shriveled, wrinkled, and looks old. Likewise, *wizened* fruit is shriveled, old fruit. The word can also imply a shrinking in size. Note: The first syllable is pronounced *wiz* (not *wise*). *In 1985 journalist Heidi Berry, speaking of a whaling expedition about to depart from Nantucket (the first such since the 19th century), said, "The pursuit of these magnificent mammals has long been an integral part of Nantucket's history, but both the distance and purpose of the upcoming venture— whale sightings— would no doubt seem tame to the wizened captains and young lads who comprised the island's famed 19th-century whaling fleet, for they hunted whales far into the Atlantic Ocean as early as 1715."*

[2] **hoary** If someone is described as *hoary (or hoary-haired or hoary-headed)*, it means he has white or gray hair as a result of being old. Sometimes the word means simply "old," as in *hoary jokes* or *hoary show tunes*. Because respect often comes with age, the word can also mean "old and respected," as in *the hoary halls of Harvard University. In May 2000, journalist William Booth reported that "in his final months in the White House, using the powers vested in him by the Antiquities Act of 1906, President Clinton [made] a series of proclamations to ensure that America's magnificent landmarks are preserved; so far, [he] has protected hoary groves of giant [redwood trees], otherworldly volcanic spires, [and] grand canyons in the painted deserts."*

[3] **gait** Your *gait* is your manner of style of walking— what your walking looks like. A man with one leg shorter than the other, for example, would have a clumsy, awkward *gait. In January 1998, speaking of a meeting between Pope John Paul II and Cuban president Fidel Castro, the* Washington Post *said, "For a few moments, they were just two old men, talking of the aches and pains that come with age; Castro walked with a stiff-kneed gait [and] the pope relied on a cane as he labored down the halls for their private talk."*

[4] **diminutive** Something *diminutive* is small or smallish, below average in size. The word sometimes implies that the smallness is exceptional or abnormal. *Overly aggressive men of diminutive stature are sometimes said to have a "Napoleon complex."*

THE WIZARD OF OZ VOCABULARY BUILDER

Then, while the men **timorously**[1] held back, the woman **emboldened**[2] herself to walk up to Dorothy and say, "Welcome to the Land of the Munchkins. Thank you for killing the Wicked Witch of the East and for freeing our people from her **heinous**[3] **hegemony**[4]."

Dorothy, an **ingenuous**[5] little girl who had never killed anything

---

[1] **timorous (timorously)** To describe someone as *timorous* is to say that he's fearful or timid. He lacks self-confidence and is afraid to take action or assert himself. *In 1985 Canadian novelist Robertson Davies said, "The average politician goes through a sentence like a man exploring a disused mine shaft— blind, groping, timorous, and in imminent danger of cracking his shins on a subordinate clause or a nasty bit of subjunctive."*

[2] **embolden (emboldened)** At the center of this word is the word *bold*. To *embolden* yourself is to make yourself bold, to give yourself courage— enough courage to overcome whatever timidity you might be feeling in a certain situation. *She emboldened herself to play the piano for her parents' friends.*

[3] **heinous** If something is *heinous* (pronounced *HAY-nus*), it's outrageously, atrociously bad or wicked. The word is often heard in the phrase "heinous crimes," which refers to crimes (such as murder, rape, torture, etc.) that are so horrible that just hearing about them fills you with shock and horror. *In 1990 presidential speechwriter Peggy Noonan interpreted the meaning of the insanity verdict handed down to John Hinckley (would-be assassin of President Ronald Reagan in 1981), as follows: "If you commit a big crime then you are crazy, and the more heinous the crime the crazier you must be; therefore, you are not responsible, and nothing is your fault."*

[4] **hegemony** *Hegemony* is total dominance or control of one country (or group, or person) over others. You often see the word in the phrase "world hegemony," which means "domination and control of the whole world." Note: In pronouncing the word, the accent is on the second syllable *(he–GEM-o–ny)* and the g is soft, as in *gem*. *Adolf Hitler's strategy for world hegemony can be found in his book* Mein Kampf.

[5] **ingenuous** *Ingenuous* people are unsophisticated, naïve, and innocent, and, when dealing with others, are open and honest, sometimes with a childlike directness. They're free of deceit and deception; they can't mask their feelings. (Sesame Street's Big Bird is an example of someone who is *ingenuous*.) *When asked if it was her bad luck that discouraged her from playing poker, she answered, "No, it's my ingenuousness."*

in her life, was taken aback. She wondered what the little woman could possibly mean. "I didn't kill anyone," Dorothy protested. "There must be some mistake."

"Your house fell on her, and therefore, however **unwittingly**[1], you killed her just the same," **rejoined**[2] the little woman. The Wicked Witch's two feet, sticking out from under the corner of the house, **evinced**[3] the **veracity**[4] of the little woman's claim.

The woman then told Dorothy that she herself was a witch! Sensing the girl's sudden alarm, she quickly reassured her. "Not all witches are wicked," she explained. "In the Land of Oz there were four witches. Two of them, the ones who live in the North and the

---

[1] **unwitting (unwittingly)** If you do something *unwittingly*, you do it without realizing it, without knowing you're doing it—you don't do it on purpose. *In November 1997 the Associated Press reported that "so-called light cigarettes are just as dangerous as regular ones, in part because smokers unwittingly cover the air holes around the filters that are supposed to dilute the cancer-causing agents."*

[2] **rejoin (rejoined)** A *rejoinder* is a (generally contradictory and sharp) answer or counter-reply (a reply to a reply). To *rejoin* is to make (to say) a rejoinder. *Legend has it that when a flight attendant asked boxing champ Muhammad Ali to fasten his seatbelt before takeoff, Ali replied, "Superman don't need no seatbelt," to which the flight attendant rejoined, "Superman don't need no airplane, either."*

[3] **evince (evinced)** To *evince* something is to show it clearly. Sometimes the thing being evinced is a person's desire, character, or feeling, which had been previously hidden or unexpressed. In that case the showing takes the form of some outward sign. *His sudden smile evinced his satisfaction.* Other times, the thing being evinced is evidence of something (usually in order to prove something). *During the trial, the wounds on the victim's back were evinced as proof the assault had taken place.*

[4] **veracity** This word means "truth" (or "truthfulness"). When a person has *veracity*, he's habitually truthful (he's honest through and through), and you can always depend on him to speak the truth. If a statement has *veracity*, it's true (or accurate). You'll see this word used especially when a person's (or statement's) truthfulness is doubtful or called into question. *On Christmas day, 1980, the Washington Post reported, "Although some readers may doubt the veracity of this report, our reporter assures us that all witnesses have verified the incidents described below. We leave it to the reader. Nine reindeer that were part of a live animal exhibit at the National Pageant of Peace were reported missing soon after dark last night, but returned on their own early this morning, according to a park police spokesman."*

South are good. I should know this is true because I am the Witch of the North."

Elucidating[1] further, the Witch of the North continued, "There were two wicked witches— the ones who lived in the East and West. But of course, now that the Witch of the East is **patently**[2] dead, there remains only one wicked witch— the Witch of the West."

Just then, the Munchkins, who had been silently standing by, began shouting and **gesticulating**[3]. They were pointing toward the corner of the house where the Wicked Witch had been lying. Amazingly, her legs and feet began to disappear! The good Witch explained, "This is a case of what we call spontaneous **desiccation**[4]. The Witch of the East was so old that, now that she is dead, the sun

---

[1] **elucidate (elucidating)** To *elucidate* something (usually an explanation) is to make its meaning clearer. When you *elucidate*, you shed light (through further explanation, clarification, illustration, etc.) on something that was previously not completely clear or understandable. *Psychiatrist Carl Jung elucidated the concepts of extroversion and introversion in a book entitled* Psychological Types *(1921)*.

[2] **patent (patently)** To refer to something as *patent* is to say that it's obvious; that is, it's open to view and understandable by everyone. Often the word is used (instead of "obvious") when someone is drawing attention to a readily seen negative quality (as in *patent defects in workmanship, patent lack of preparation, patent disrespect,* etc.). *A July 1992 op-ed piece in the* Washington Post *said, "One of the most popular clichés during election years is: 'Government should be run like a business.' What a patently absurd statement. It is equivalent to saying, 'Armies should be run like day care centers' or 'Football should be played like golf.'"*

[3] **gesticulate (gesticulating)** When you *gesticulate* you make gestures (movements of the arms and hands) to emphasize what you're saying (or to express something without speaking). Waving, pointing, signaling, and motioning are all forms of gesticulation. *In March 1995 journalist Tony Kornheiser noted that "basketball coaches come in different sizes, shapes and temperaments— some sit quietly, with a program rolled up in their hands, [while others] roam the sideline, shouting and gesticulating wildly."*

[4] **desiccate (desiccation)** When something becomes *desiccated* it becomes completely dried up. The noun is *desiccation*. *The skin of a snake is primarily a protective structure, guarding it against injury and desiccation.*

can quickly dry her up!"

All that remained was a pair of beautiful, gleaming, Silver Shoes that so **belied**[1] the wickedness of the Witch. The good Witch reached down and picked them up, then handed them to Dorothy. "These Silver Shoes are yours to keep and to wear," she said, **beneficently**[2] **waiving**[3] the **putative**[4] claim she had on them herself.

"The Witch of the East was especially proud of the Silver Shoes," one of the Munchkins chimed in, "because of their **reputed**[5] magical powers. But so far, no one has discovered what the Shoes' powers are or how they're used. Over the years, a few ideas have

---

[1] **belie (belied)** Notice that the word *lie* is part of *belie*. To *belie* something is to show it to be false; to show that it's a misrepresentation or contradiction. Note: The word rhymes with *lie* and has the accent on the second syllable *(bee–LIE)*. *The picturesque tropical appearance of Devil's Island (a small Caribbean isle off the coast of South America's French Guiana) belies its past as one of history's most brutal prison camps.*

[2] **beneficent (beneficently)** Notice the similarity of this word to *benefit*. If you're *beneficent*, you like to do good (give benefits); you're kindly in your actions or intentions. Usually this word is used to describe people who are in a position to do (great) good (such as kings or other people of power). *In their darkest hour, the soldiers hoped not only that a divine power exists, but that it has a beneficent interest in human affairs.*

[3] **waive (waiving)** To *waive* a claim or right is to voluntarily give it up. *If you take your bike to Italy, you must put it in a box (airlines will take your unboxed bike only if you waive your right to claim damages).* To *waive* a rule or penalty is to refrain from insisting upon it. *In October 1996 the U.S. government waived a ban on direct flights from the United States to Cuba to let a Roman Catholic Church charity send a planeload of aid for victims of Hurricane Lili.*

[4] **putative** To refer to something as *putative* is to say that it's accepted as being true by everyone, even though it has never actually been proved. *Lee Harvey Oswald is the putative assassin of President John F. Kennedy.*

[5] **reputed** Sometimes something is thought to be true merely because people have spoken of it as true, or because it's rumored to be true. It acquires a "reputation" for being true. Its truth is *reputed* (supposed, accepted without proof). *A sea monster is reputed to inhabit the waters of Scotland's Loch Ness.*

17

been **bandied**[1] about, but so far no one has **postulated**[2] a **credible**[3] theory. It's a **conundrum**[4] that may never be solved.

Dorothy suddenly became aware that Aunt Em and Uncle Henry were probably beginning to worry about her by now, so she asked how she might get back to Kansas. But knowing the Land of Oz was surrounded on all sides by vast deserts, the good Witch regretfully told her, "There is no way back to Kansas, so you will have to remain with the Munchkins forever."

---

[1] **bandy (bandied)** To *bandy* a ball is to throw, strike, or pass it back and forth. To *bandy* words (insults or compliments, for example) is to give and receive them; to trade or exchange them. To *bandy* ideas is to discuss them in a casual manner. *In 1987, in his review of a new NBC TV series, journalist Tom Shales said, "Should cosmetic surgery be available to ugly dogs? Will the seeing-eye cat and the artificial tonsil become realities? Questions like that are bandied about and then stomped into submission on* Our Planet Tonight, *a mirthful sendup of [CBS's]* 60 Minutes.*"*

[2] **postulate (postulated)** To *postulate* something (an idea, a hypothesis, a theory) is to set it forth as being true (even though it might not be) so that it can be used as a starting point for further study or experimentation. *The existence of the neutrino (a subatomic particles with no mass and no electric charge) was postulated by Austrian theoretical physicist Wolfgang Pauli in 1931—a quarter century before one was actually observed in the laboratory.*

[3] **credible** To refer to something (a statement, explanation, etc.) as *credible* is to say that it's believable. To refer to a person as *credible* (as in *credible witness*) is to say that he's believable or trustworthy. *In 1987 journalist P. D. James said, "In 1930s mysteries, all sorts of motives were credible which aren't credible today, especially motives of preventing guilty sexual secrets from coming out—nowadays, people sell their guilty sexual secrets."*

[4] **conundrum** A *conundrum* is technically a riddle whose answer is a pun (a play on words). But the word is more generally used to mean "any difficult-to-solve problem, or any problem that seems insolvable or paradoxical." *How to achieve full employment without inflation is a conundrum still unanswered.*

THE WIZARD OF OZ VOCABULARY BUILDER

Dorothy was **crestfallen**[1]. She wondered if this could be her **comeuppance**[2] for her **inadvertent**[3] act that had caused the Wicked Witch's **demise**[4]. Soon she began to cry because she felt lonely among such strange people. Her tears seemed to grieve the kindhearted Munchkins, who became **lachrymose**[5] and began pulling out handkerchiefs.

It suddenly occurred to the Witch of the North that perhaps the great Wizard of Oz himself might help Dorothy find her way

---

[1] **crestfallen** If you're *crestfallen* you're greatly unhappy or depressed (especially if those feelings are the result of some great disappointment). *The student, expecting an A on his term paper, was crestfallen when he received a C minus.* Note: If you look carefully at the smaller words that make up this compound word (*crest* meaning "the head, or the top of something"), you'll realize that if you're crestfallen, you have (perhaps figuratively) a drooping head (fallen crest).

[2] **comeuppance** A *comeuppance* is a deserved punishment, especially an overdue (or even long overdue) punishment. Saying that one received his *comeuppance* is the same as saying that he received his just desserts. *The noisy teenager received his comeuppance when he was physically ejected from the movie theater.*

[3] **inadvertent** If you do something *inadvertently*, you do it unintentionally or accidentally. *Many dolphins have been killed inadvertently by commercial tuna fishermen using nets.*

[4] **demise** This word means "death (usually of a person)," but it can also mean "the end of the existence, operation, or activity of something," as in *the demise of silent films* or *the demise of trolley cars. In 1986, in a speech made a few hours after the demise of seven astronauts in the explosion of the space shuttle* Challenger, *President Ronald Reagan said of them, "They had that special grace, that special spirit that says: Give me a challenge and I'll meet it with joy."*

[5] **lachrymose** Sometimes this word is used as a synonym for *sad* or *mournful,* but more specifically (because in the human body the *lachrymal glands* are the glands that produce tears), it means "tearful" or "weepy." A *thing* described as *lachrymose* tends to cause tears. Note that the first syllable (which receives the accent) is pronounced *lack* and that the last syllable rhymes with *dose. It wasn't until after she finished her lachrymose confession that the suspect realized her carefully applied makeup was destroyed.*

home. "The Land of Oz is ruled by a **benevolent**[1] but **redoubtable**[2] **potentate**[3] known as the Great Wizard, who lives in the Emerald City," explained the good Witch. "His immense power is often **touted**[4] as being more powerful that that of all the witches put together. Perhaps he might help you find a way back to Kansas."

Dorothy immediately seized upon this opportunity and asked how she might get to the Emerald City. The good Witch answered, "The Emerald City is located far off, in the exact center of the Land of Oz. The only way to get there is to hike along the road paved with yellow bricks." Then the Witch of the North kissed Dorothy on the forehead, leaving a shiny, round mark. "This kiss," the good

---

[1] **benevolent** If you're *benevolent*, you want to do good for people; you're kind, humane, and generous. Often (but not always), you'll see this word used to describe kings, queens, or other powerful rulers. *We thought it was pretty obvious from their names that Frederick the Great (of Prussia) was a benevolent ruler and Peter the Cruel (of Spain) was not.*

[2] **redoubtable** If someone is described as *redoubtable*, it means he arouses fear (or dread) or inspires awe (or wonder), especially if that awesomeness is worthy of respect. The word is often used to describe an opponent. *In the world of chess, there has never been an opponent more redoubtable than Bobby Fisher.*

[3] **potentate** The word *potent* means "powerful" or "mighty." A *potentate* (pronounced with the accent on the first syllable) is a powerful or mighty person. Often the word refers to a ruler (a king, for example), but it can refer to any person of power, as in *an industrial potentate. At the February 1945 Yalta Conference, a meeting of U.S. President Franklin D. Roosevelt, British Prime Minister Winston Churchill, and Soviet Premier Joseph Stalin to plan the final phase of World War II, the potentates agreed to require Germany's unconditional surrender.*

[4] **tout (touted)** If you *tout* something, you speak about it flatteringly (often publicly or energetically), to (or as if to) convince others of its positive attributes. Likewise, if something is *touted*, it's favorably spoken of; it's praised. *After winning a gold medal in the 1984 Olympics (at Los Angeles), gymnast Mary Lou Retton became the first female athlete to be pictured on the front of a box of Wheaties (long touted as the "Breakfast of Champions").*

Witch explained, "will **forestall**[1] any injuries and protect you from harm during your travels."

---

[1] **forestall** To *forestall* something is to prevent it from happening by taking some kind of precautionary action ahead of time. *After the Watergate affair, Richard Nixon forestalled possible prosecution by accepting President Gerald Ford's pardon.*

Chapter 3 "The Scarecrow"

Dorothy went back inside her house to prepare for the long journey. But suddenly feeling hungry and thirsty, she took Toto outside with her to a little brook that flowed behind the house. There she filled a pail with cool, clear water. While drinking it she spotted some **savory**[1]-looking fruit, hanging like so many colored **pendants**[2] from a nearby branch. As **ambrosial**[3] as the fruit tasted, she **judiciously**[4] ate only until she was pleasantly **sated**[5]. With such

---

[1] **savory** Anything that tastes (or smells) good can be described as *savory*. The more delicious, mouth-watering, or flavorful it is, the more *savory* it is. *She made her lentil soup even more savory by adding a bit of lemon juice.*

[2] **pendant (pendants)** A *pendant* is something that hangs (from something) or is suspended from something— especially a charm (or any piece of jewelry) suspended on a chain (necklace). The adjective *pendulous* means "loosely hanging or suspended," as in *pendulous folds of flesh*. *In his March 1996 article entitled "If You Rib Hudek, He'll Take It," journalist Robert Fachet said, "Major league [baseball] players are known to wear [gaudy] gold chains and flashy pendants during games, [but] Houston Astros reliever John Hudek has taken that custom to a new level. Hudek, who had a rib removed last year to allow better circulation in his pitching arm, has fashioned a necklace out of the detached bone; the rib, about three inches long, hangs on a chain."*

[3] **ambrosia (ambrosial)** In Greek and Roman mythology, *ambrosia* is the food of the gods. In addition to being extra-delicious, it gave the gods immortality. Today anything that is especially delicious can be referred to as *ambrosia* (noun) or *ambrosial* (adjective). *In 1981 tennis player John McEnroe tasted the sweet ambrosia of his first Wimbledon title.* Note: *Ambrosia* is also the name of a particular dessert— a mixture of orange, coconut, and marshmallow.

[4] **judicious (judiciously)** To be *judicious* (in handling some matter) is to act wisely or to show sound judgment or common sense. *Their judicious use of pesticides allowed them to control the insects without violating any environmental regulations.*

[5] **sate (sated)** To *sate* an appetite (for food or anything else) is either to completely satisfy it or to overly satisfy it (to the point of a loss of desire). *In May 1999, after basketball's New York Knicks defeated the Miami Heat in a 97-73 game that included a 32-2 spurt, New York Newsday said, "How rare that Madison Square Garden's hungry beast of a crowd is so well fed, so sated."*

a long walk facing her, she knew that she had to avoid the uncomfortable, sick feeling a **surfeit**[1] of eating would surely cause.

Now it was time to dress for her trip. Dorothy was not a **vain**[2] little girl, so she never wasted time **primping**[3] or **preening**[4]. She had one other dress to wear, a blue-and-white checkered **gingham**[5] frock, which she **donned**[6] **unceremoniously**[1]. Then, spying her

---

[1] **surfeit** As a noun this word means "an excessive amount of something (often food)," or "an overindulgence in eating," or "the sick feeling you get from overeating." As a verb it means "to overeat to the point of nausea or disgust." *The two brothers, after surfeiting themselves with cookies, spent the rest of the afternoon holding their stomachs and moaning.*

[2] **vain** If you're *vain* you're overly concerned about your appearance and accomplishments. The implication is that you're a rather shallow, self-centered person. The noun is *vanity* ("the state or quality of being vain"). *In 1933 Russian revolutionary Leon Trotsky said of bicycles, "Let a man find himself, in distinction from others, on top of two wheels with a chain— at least in a poor country like Russia— and his vanity begins to swell out like his tires; in America it takes an automobile to produce this effect."*

[3] **primp (primping)** Sometimes teenaged girls (or other people) spend lots of time in front of the mirror grooming themselves with great care and attention to detail so they'll look *just right*. This is known as *primping*. *In the movie, when Betsy's mother yelled, "Why are you primping so? You're only going to the corner store," it was pretty obvious to us that Betsy was meeting someone.*

[4] **preen (preening)** When a bird *preens*, it smoothes its features with its beak, and when a cat *preens*, it cleans its fur with its tongue. But usually you'll hear this word in connection with a person. When a person *preens*, she carefully grooms herself in front of the mirror. *In 1997 a study on chimpanzees reported, "Female chimps, once thought to be passive and above the chest-pounding contests of the males, appear to be as obsessed by status as any debutante preening in a Paris original."*

[5] **gingham** This is a type of fabric used in making clothes— it's dyed cotton yarn woven into stripes or checks, or sometimes solid colors or plaids. *In May 1999, a New York Times fashion show review said, "Gingham is no longer restricted to country picnics but has taken on a sophisticated look for spring."*

[6] **don (donned)** To *don* an article of clothing is to put it on. *In the 1998 children's book* Harry Potter and the Sorcerer's Stone, *Harry becomes invisible when he dons a magic cloak.*

old, **lackluster**[2] shoes, she quickly grabbed the shiny Silver Shoes
the Witch of the North had given her. These fit as if they had been
made for her. And so, with her hunger **appeased**[3] and thirst
slaked[4], and with a fresh change of clothes, shiny, magical, new
Shoes, and a protective kiss on her forehead, one guaranteed to
stave[5] off anything and everything **untoward**[6], Dorothy set off on

---

[1] **unceremonious (unceremoniously)** If you do something *unceremoniously* you do
it in a simple, matter-of-fact way, without formality, ritual, or ceremony. *In July
1984, journalist Loren Jenkins, speaking of U.S. Marines leaving Lebanon, said, "The
last combat troops, [the remains] of the 1,800-man force sent as peace-keepers in 1982,
began a final withdrawal today. The departure was unceremonious; it got under way
with no official announcements and at an hour when most of Beirut was still asleep."*

[2] **lackluster** If you understand that to *lack* something is to be without it and that
luster is a glow (as of reflected light), then you can see that something *lackluster* has
no shine or glow (it lacks luster); it's drab, dull, lifeless, colorless, or ordinary. *The
candidate wasn't sure whether it was his lackluster personality or his lackluster
campaign that was responsible for his losing the election.*

[3] **appease (appeased)** When you *appease* a thing (such as hunger or thirst), you
satisfy it or relieve it. When you appease a person you calm or quiet his anger or
agitation (by giving him something or giving in to him). *I sent my landlord a
written apology and a gift, but his anger was still not appeased.*

[4] **slake (slaked)** To *slake* your thirst is to quench it or satisfy it. *In Greek mythology,
Tantalus was tortured (for having offended the gods) with continual thirst and forced to
stand up to his chin in water; whenever he bent to slake his thirst, the water receded.*

[5] **stave** To *stave* off something (something undesirable) is to keep it away or to
prevent it from happening. *They agreed to close the nuclear power plant to stave off
any possibility of disaster.*

[6] **untoward** Any situation or event that's *untoward* is unfavorable or unfortunate.
*In September 1992, journalist Alison Muscatine noted, "It is a rare first day at the U.S.
Open when nothing untoward happens, when the sun doesn't melt a few players and the
humidity doesn't leave a steamy haze over the National Tennis Center."* A behavior or
action that's *untoward* is one that's troublesome or improper. *In March 1994,
journalist Thomas DiBacco said, "One of the latest medical trends is research into the
biochemical and genetic characteristics of the brain that may explain untoward social
behavior such as violence."*

her journey.

She located the yellow brick road with no problem, and soon found herself walking through some pretty countryside. There were **natty**[1] little blue fences along the side of the road, and beyond them were miles of **fecund**[2] fields. As she and Toto passed by each little, round, blue house, she noticed that the Munchkins who lived there came out to **genuflect**[3] to her. Because she was both a child and a **rank**[4] outsider, their **deification**[5] of her seemed strange, but then she realized that these people knew it was she who had freed them from bondage.

After walking several miles, Dorothy stopped for a short rest.

---

[1] **natty** To describe something (clothing, for example) as *natty* is to say that it's neat, trim, and stylish. *In September 1989 journalist Art Harris, speaking of a well-known TV evangelist who had been involved in an extramarital sex scandal and was accused of diverting millions of dollars of donations for his own use, said, "Declared mentally fit to stand trial one week after he was found cowering under a couch in his lawyer's office, Jim Bakker was back today in federal court, exhausted but natty in a blue double-breasted pin-striped suit brought him by his wife, Tammy Faye."*

[2] **fecund** Land that is *fecund* (pronounced *FEK-ind* or *FEEK-ind*) is fertile and productive. Lots of vegetation grows there. But things other than land can be *fecund*, such as parents or someone's imagination. *The sunfish (which derives its name from its practice of floating on its side, as if sunning itself) is perhaps the must fecund of all fish— a female lays up to 300 million eggs!*

[3] **genuflect** To *genuflect* is to bend the knees or to touch the knee or knees to the ground in (or as in) worship, prayer, or devotion. *In 1829, when telegraph and Morse code inventor Samuel Morse visited Rome, a soldier knocked him down when he failed to genuflect before a Catholic procession.*

[4] **rank** As an adjective, this word means "total," "absolute," or "utter," as in *rank beginner*. *Automated "point and shoot" cameras are so easy to use that even rank beginners can take satisfactory pictures.*

[5] **deify (deification)** To *deify* (pronounced so that the first syllable is accented and rhymes with *bee*) someone is to elevate him to the level of a god. *After winning the Oscar for Best Actor, he was suddenly deified by his former critics.*

THE WIZARD OF OZ VOCABULARY BUILDER

Sitting on a fence that **skirted**[1] a large cornfield, she noticed in the field, attached to a tall pole, a Scarecrow, **ostensibly**[2] placed there to frighten away any **marauding**[3] crows. The Scarecrow's head was nothing more than a straw-filled sack with painted eyes and nose. And its body, a **sartorial**[4] disaster, was a threadbare, tattered, old blue suit, also stuffed with straw.

The Scarecrow's queer, painted **visage**[5] attracted Dorothy's attention. As she stared at it, she saw one of the eyes wink at her! She thought that during her **hiatus**[6] she might have dozed off and

---

[1] **skirt (skirted)** To *skirt* something (an area, for example) is to go around the outside (the border) of it, as opposed to going through the middle of it; or to lie along or form the edge of it. To *skirt* an issue (or difficult problem or question) is to sidestep (evade) it. *The high plateau skirting Arizona's Grand Canyon was once the home of the Paiute Indians.*

[2] **ostensibly** This word means "apparently" or "seemingly," or "for the apparent (or seeming) purpose of." The apparent purpose may or may not be the real purpose. *The senator conducted his investigations ostensibly to uncover anti-government sentiment, but later he admitted his real purpose was to harass those whose views differed from his.*

[3] **marauding** To *maraud* is to roam about looking for goods or property to steal, then to take those goods or property by force. *Marauders* often travel in bands. *When asked why she refused to enter the stagecoach, the girl explained she was afraid they might encounter marauding bands of outlaws.*

[4] **sartorial** This word means "pertaining to clothing or tailoring" (in terms of style or manner of dress), as in the phrase "sartorial elegance." *The hippies' American Indian–style dress represented a sartorial rebellion against the late-sixties establishment.*

[5] **visage** This word means "face," but it's often used instead of "face" when the shape, proportions, features, or expression of the face is important. *According to Compton's Encyclopedia, in Norse mythology, (supreme God) Odin's "visage could change with the viewer: He appeared so [kind] among his friends that they rejoiced at the sight of him, but to his enemies he would appear fearsome and terrible."*

[6] **hiatus** A hiatus is a break, pause, interruption, or gap in something (some work or activity, for example). *A key settlement of the Washington Conference (1921–1922), an attempt at naval disarmament made after World War I, was the Five Power Naval Armament Treaty (between the U.S., Britain, Japan, France, and Italy), which provided for a ten-year hiatus in building warships of more than 10,000 tons.*

was only dreaming, because no scarecrows she'd ever seen in Kansas had ever winked. But now, fully awake, she saw the **tatterdemalion**[1] figure **genially**[2] nod his head at her.

Normally, Dorothy would have been **chary**[3] of speaking to such an oddity as a **sentient**[4] Scarecrow, but because he seemed such an **affable**[5] sort, Dorothy approached him without **trepidation**[6]. Toto ran around and around the pole, barking gleefully.

"Good day. How do you do?" said the Scarecrow.

"Very well. How do you do?" answered Dorothy.

"Not well at all," said the Scarecrow, who, in a most polite

---

[1] **tatterdemalion** A person dressed in tattered or ragged clothes is known as a *tatterdemalion*. As an adjective the word means "tattered, ragged." *In a famous fairy tale, a tatterdemalion stepdaughter named Cinderella escapes from a life of drudgery by marrying a handsome prince.*

[2] **genial (genially)** If you're *genial*, you're friendly, agreeable, cheerful, and pleasant, perhaps even a bit jolly. The noun is *geniality*. *An unbeatable combination of talent and geniality made Louis Armstrong everyone's favorite trumpet player.*

[3] **chary** If you're *chary* (of some suspected danger or risk) you're wary, cautious, or carefully watchful, and you're reluctant to act or proceed. *In March 1982 journalist William Claiborne said, "Nearly three years after Egypt and Israel signed their historic [March 1979] peace treaty, normalization of relations remains hesitant; Israel, [ecstatic] in those initial days of peace fever, gradually has become chary— bordering on disillusioned."*

[4] **sentient** To describe something as *sentient* (pronounced *SEN-shint*) is to say that it has the capacity for sensation or feeling; it has consciousness. *In a famous children's story, a sentient puppet named Pinocchio longs to become a real boy.*

[5] **affable** If you're *affable* you're friendly, warm, easy to approach, and easy to talk to. *Historians say that though President Ronald Reagan was affable to all, he felt close only to his wife and a few friends.*

[6] **trepidation** This word means "fear," especially when that fear implies a nervous reluctance to face someone or something, or when it implies a trembling kind of fear. *Even though he completed a "fear of flying" treatment program, Jim can't board a plane without some degree of trepidation.*

manner, began to **bemoan**[1] his fate. The underlying problem was that the pole forced his body into an unnatural position. He hoped he might become **inured**[2] to the discomfort, but that didn't seem to be happening. On top of that, he felt **listless**[3], no doubt from staying in one position all day. Certainly, the **enervating**[4] tedium of his life was enough to subject anyone to feelings of **languor**[5], even depression. He told Dorothy that he would be much obliged if she would remove him from the pole. She was able to lift him off easily because, being made of straw, the Scarecrow was quite light.

Once on the ground, the Scarecrow asked Dorothy who she was and where she was going. Dorothy told him her name and

---

[1] **bemoan** To *bemoan* something is to complain about it, moan over it (note that *bemoan* contains the word *moan*), or express grief about it. *In his campaign speeches of 1988 and 1992, Republican vice-presidential candidate Dan Quayle bemoaned the decline of family values.*

[2] **inured** To become *inured* to something undesirable is to become used to it; to become accustomed to it by being subjected to it over time. *After two years he had still not become inured to his mother-in-law's whining voice.*

[3] **listless** If you lack vitality and spirit or if you simply feel like you don't have the energy or the interest to do anything, you're *listless*. *According to reporter William Branigin, in July 1998 "Border Patrol agents in Del Rio, Texas, were checking a train bound for San Antonio when they came across air holes punched in the top of a sealed boxcar; inside, they found 11 listless men from Mexico, baking in 150-degree heat with no food or water."*

[4] **enervate (enervating)** This is a tricky word because it looks like it may mean the opposite of what it really does. Something that's *enervating* doesn't give you energy; rather, it takes energy (or strength or vitality) away from you; it tires or exhausts you. *The trip to the zoo was exhilarating for the child but enervating for his grandparents.*

[5] **languor** This word means "a lack of energy, spirit, or vitality," and it's often used when this lack is caused by one of the following: a life of easy luxury, hot or humid weather, illness, a natural laziness, or love. The adjective is *languorous* or *languid*. *After the teenager spent an entire April weekend on the couch numbly flipping channels, his mother suggested a trip to the doctor; however, his father insisted their son's languor was induced by nothing more than spring fever.*

explained that she was going to the Emerald City to ask the Great Wizard to find a way to send her back to Kansas. But then she discovered that the Scarecrow had never heard of the Emerald City or the Great Wizard or even Kansas! Her surprise was so apparent that the Scarecrow felt it necessary to explain. "Because I'm made of straw, I have no brains, and so I don't know anything at all," he said sadly. Then, in a sudden fit of **lucid**[1] forethought, especially for one made of straw, he asked, "Do you think the Great Wizard might be able to give me some brains?"

"I don't know," said Dorothy, "but you may come with me if you like. Even if the Great Oz won't give you any brains, you'll be no worse off than you are now."

The Scarecrow sensed that this was a chance, however **tenuous**[2], to get some brains and thereby **preclude**[3] the **mortification**[1] of

---

[1] **lucid** This word has three meanings, all related and all having to do with the concept of being clear. First, it means "clear" in the sense of allowing light to pass through; transparent. But you'll usually see this word used as described in either of the next two definitions. Second, it means "clear" (as of language or speech) in the sense of being intelligible or easily understood. *Author Isaac Asimov (1920–1992) was known for his lucid explanations of complex scientific principles.* Third, it means "clear" in the sense of being characterized by rational thought or understanding. *When my wife returned from the hospital and I asked if her grandmother was okay, she answered, "There were a few lucid moments, but mostly she just ranted incoherently."*

[2] **tenuous** Something *tenuous* is thin, flimsy, or weak. But more often than describing a substance (such as thread or an atmosphere, for example) the word is used to describe a thin, flimsy, or weak situation or relationship. *The students believed their professor was one of the university's permanent fixtures, but his wife knew well that his relationship with the history department was tenuous at best.*

[3] **preclude** To *preclude* something is to make it impossible to happen. This impossibility can be the result of either something you do (in advance to prevent something) or something that occurs or exists naturally. *The truck's height precluded it from using roads with low overpasses.* Often the word is used in negative sentences. *My going to dinner with her at 6:00 doesn't preclude my going to the theater with you at 8:00.*

being thought a fool—his great fear, second only to his fear of a lighted match! And the thought of a **convivial**[2] **triumvirate**[3] intrigued him, especially after the overwhelming **lassitude**[4] he'd suffered in the **desolate**[5] **purgatory**[6] of the cornfield.

---

[1] **mortification** This word means "extreme embarrassment or humiliation." The first syllable, *mor*, is related to the word *death* (as in *mortician* or *mortuary*). So when you're *mortified*, you feel like you're dying of embarrassment. *When the play ended I let my parents know in no uncertain terms that I was mortified when they waved and called my name from the audience.*

[2] **convivial** If you're *convivial*, you enjoy friendly companionship; you're merrily sociable. In a *convivial* group, all the people are friendly and have a good time enjoying each other's company. The noun is *conviviality*. *When asked when he would retire, British Prime Minister Winston Churchill replied, "One does not leave a convivial party before closing time."*

[3] **triumvirate** This word means "any group of three (people); a threesome." Originally, in ancient Rome, the word referred to a governing or ruling board of three men (Caesar, Pompey, and Crassus, for example, were known as "the first triumvirate" of the Roman Republic). *"All for one and one for all" is the motto of Alexandre Dumas' fictional triumvirate, the Three Musketeers.*

[4] **lassitude** This word describes a condition of unpleasant weariness (of body or mind) or a condition of lazy indifference, especially when these conditions are brought on by fatigue, illness, or depression. *We all noticed the gorilla's lassitude and agreed that zoos with cages should be outlawed.*

[5] **desolate** A place described as *desolate* is uninhabited, deserted, lonely, stark, barren. *We all wondered what Neil Armstrong was thinking when he first set foot on the moon's desolate surface.*

[6] **purgatory** According to Roman Catholics, after a (good) person dies, but before he goes to heaven, his soul is in *purgatory*—a temporary place where the soul makes amends for still-unpunished minor sins. But in general usage, the word means "any place or condition of temporary punishment or suffering." *We arrived at the airport seriously jet-lagged, then were forced to suffer the purgatory of customs inspection!*

THE WIZARD OF OZ VOCABULARY BUILDER

And so, with Toto following **desultorily**[1] in their wake, the two of them—a would-be **interloper**[2] turned **lionized**[3] savior and a **despondent**[4], **benighted**[5] sack of straw turned **jovial**[6] **wayfarer**[7]—started along the yellow brick road for the promise of the Emerald City.

---

[1] **desultory (desultorily)** When you proceed (move, act, or talk) in a *desultory* way, you don't follow a constant, consistent, methodical course—you jump about, from here to there. *I've never heard conversations as desultory as those that take place in Internet chat rooms.* When you do something in a *desultory* way, you don't give it your full attention or effort—you do it in fits and starts. *He made a few desultory attempts to find a job, but nothing panned out.*

[2] **interloper** An *interloper* is a person (usually an outsider) who thrusts himself into other peoples' affairs without invitation (sometimes for selfish reasons). *The criminal was about to hand his weapon to the police but suddenly changed his mind when an interloper screamed at the top of his lungs, "Shoot him! He's got a gun!"*

[3] **lionize (lionized)** To *lionize* someone is to treat him (or look upon him) as a celebrity. *When a 1919 solar eclipse confirmed his light-deflection theory, scientist Albert Einstein was lionized by the press.*

[4] **despondent** When you're *despondent* (about something), you feel depressed, gloomy, dispirited, or discouraged, especially when these feelings are accompanied by a feeling of hopelessness. *Lyndon Johnson, despondent over the no-win Vietnam situation, announced that he would not seek or accept a second term as President.*

[5] **benighted** When it's night, it's dark. If a person is *benighted*, he's figuratively in the dark (or kept in the dark); in other words, he's unenlightened, uneducated, ignorant. *"When it comes to the current dating scene, my parents are as benighted as a couple of Neanderthals," she complained.*

[6] **jovial** If you're *jovial*, you're merry and jolly and have a hearty good humor. The noun is *joviality*. *At the beginning of his shift, the department store Santa felt appropriately jovial, but by the time the last kid climbed off his lap he was ready to scream.*

[7] **wayfarer** A *wayfarer* is a person who travels, especially on foot. You're apt to see this word (or *wayfaring*) pop up in titles of songs or poems more often than you'll hear people actually use it in conversation. *From the 13th to the 19th century, a religious sect devoted to the goddess Kali and known as the Thugs wandered India robbing and killing wayfarers.*

Chapter 4 "The Tin Woodman"

Dorothy, the Scarecrow, and Toto walked for a long while, past the suburbs and **exurbs**[1], to the **hinterlands**[2] of Oz. Here, the yellow brick road became rough and irregular, with increasingly widening gaps between the bricks. Dorothy and Toto easily jumped over these **interstices**[3], but, with crack-jumping apparently beyond the **purview**[4] of his understanding, the Scarecrow continued walking as though the road were still smooth and regular. Over and over he fell flat on his face and Dorothy repeatedly had to straighten him up. Being made of straw, these falls never hurt the

---

[1] **exurb (exurbs)** Suburbs, as you know, are a city's outlying residential areas. *Exurbs* are small communities lying beyond the suburbs of a city. *With the exception of commuter lines connecting major cities with their suburbs and exurbs, all city-to-city passenger rail service today is supplied by Amtrak.*

[2] **hinterlands** The *hinterlands* of a region are its undeveloped or less developed areas; its backcountry, backwoods, etc. *In the 18th century, grain and fruit flowed from the hinterlands, down the Hudson and Delaware rivers, to New York and Philadelphia.*

[3] **interstices** Narrow spaces or gaps that occur between things or parts of a thing (especially when these spaces look alike and occur at regular intervals) are known as *interstices*. *Jimmy ran his stick only along slatted fences— never solid ones— because he loved the "rat-tat-tat" sound generated by the interstices.*

[4] **purview** This word means "range" or "scope" in two senses. If you're discussing a person, his *purview* is his range of understanding, insight, or vision. *I wonder why she asked me to help her with her calculus homework when she knows very well that even algebra is beyond the purview of my mathematical comprehension.* If you're discussing a thing, its *purview* is its range of authority, control, or power. *The Centers for Disease Control and Prevention operates under the purview of the Department of Health and Human Services.*

Scarecrow, who smiled **blithely**[1] at each mishap.

Around noon, Dorothy was **famished**[2], so she stopped to eat by a **placid**[3] pond. She noticed a pretty little **promontory**[4] jutting out into the water but was too **ravenous**[5] to bother walking out on it.

She offered some bread from her basket to the Scarecrow, but he declined. His show of **asceticism**[6] seemed unreasonable to her, so she gave him a questioning look. "I never get hungry," he told her, "because I have no stomach; only straw." Then he said that he was lucky he never became hungry. If he were to eat, he explained, he would swallow the straw where his mouth was, distorting the shape of his head. Disfigurement added to ignorance would be a burden

---

[1] **blithe (blithely)** This word can mean "merry" (or "cheerful," "happy"), and it can mean "lightheartedly carefree" (or "unconcerned," "indifferent"). But it especially means "merry" *and* "carefree" (at the same time). Note: In pronunciation, the *i* sounds like the *i* in *blind*, the *th* can be pronounced either as in *then* or *thin*, and the *e* is silent. *I was all ready to scold her for being late, but her blithe spirit somehow made me forget all about doing that.*

[2] **famished** If you're *famished*, you're very hungry, starving. *We were famished after our all-night study session, so we stopped for breakfast on the way to the final exam.*

[3] **placid** This word means "calm." A *placid* person isn't easily disturbed. He has an even temperament and a tranquil expression. *Placid* water is regular, smooth, quiet, and undisturbed. *Compared to the turbulent sixties, the fifties seem rather placid.*

[4] **promontory** A *promontory* is a piece of high land (or rock) that juts out from the coast into a body of water. *The Rock of Gibraltar is a well-known promontory extending from southwest Spain into the Mediterranean Sea.*

[5] **ravenous** To be *ravenous* is to be very (often uncontrollably) hungry; to be starving. Note: The word can also mean "greedy," as in *ravenous for power*. *The Colosseum (the large outdoor theater of ancient Rome) was the site of combat between gladiators and battles between men and ravenous lions.*

[6] **ascetic (asceticism)** As a noun, an *ascetic* is a person who lives a simple life, practices self-discipline and self-denial, and, in so doing, denies himself normal pleasures (such as material comforts and eating for enjoyment). As an adjective, the word describes that way of life. *Asceticism* is the practice of that way of life. *The son of a wealthy merchant, Saint Francis of Assisi at the age of 22 rejected his inheritance and began living an ascetic life.*

too **onerous**[1] to bear. Dorothy **ruminated**[2] on this awhile; then, realizing that what the Scarecrow said was true, nodded and continued her **repast**[3] in silence.

Finally **satiated**[4], Dorothy handed the basket to the Scarecrow and said, "Let's go."

As they walked along the road, the Scarecrow tried to think of something interesting to say to show the girl that he was not quite as empty-headed as she might suppose. Then it struck him— some witty **repartee**[5] would be just the thing! But when he tried to think of something clever to say, nothing came to him except an

---

[1] **onerous** Any burden, task, responsibility, or situation described as *onerous* is troublesome and burdensome. When you're dealing with something *onerous* you feel like you have a heavy load (figuratively or literally) that can test your strength. *He remained a bachelor because the onerous task of supporting a family frightened him.*

[2] **ruminate (ruminated)** When you *ruminate* about something you think about it, turning it over and over in your mind; you chew it over, so to speak, as a cow chews its cud. Note: "To chew the cud" is the literal meaning of the word. *I didn't want to admit that I was lying on the couch doing nothing, so I said that although it looked that way I was actually ruminating on the purpose of the universe.*

[3] **repast** This is another word for meal (a single session of eating) or for the food eaten at a meal. *We ate a late breakfast, so at lunchtime we had a light repast of two kinds of melon.*

[4] **satiate (satiated)** When you're *satiated* with something you have an appetite or desire for (food, for example), you're full to the point of being totally satisfied. The word may imply (but not necessarily) that you're overly full (of whatever you've taken in). *Little Bobby believed that no amount of cartoon watching could be too much, but after five hours he was satiated.*

[5] **repartee** Conversation full of quick, witty replies is called *repartee* (pronounced so that the last syllable is accented and rhymes with either *bay* or *bee*). *In the late 1960s, singing comedy team the Smothers Brothers often began their weekly TV variety show with some clever repartee that was actually written by comedy writer (and future comedian and film star) Steve Martin.*

THE WIZARD OF OZ VOCABULARY BUILDER

inchoate[1] jumble of **trite**[2] **clichés**[3]. Oh, how he cursed himself for being such a **dolt**[4]! Now he felt it **incumbent**[5] upon himself to relieve the **constraint**[6] quickly descending upon him, and his straw

---

[1] **inchoate** If something is in an early or developing stage, it can be referred to as *inchoate* (pronounced *in-KOH-it*). Or if something is disorganized, jumbled, or lacking order, it can be referred to as *inchoate*. But if something is both at an early stage *and* lacks organization, then it's especially referred to as *inchoate*. *It's amazing to think that our solar system began as nothing more than an inchoate mass of swirling gas and dust.*

[2] **trite** If something (a word, expression, or idea in speech or writing) is *trite*, it lacks freshness and effectiveness because it has been used or repeated too often. *In her review of the 2001 film* Pavilion of Women, *a cross-cultural romance set in 1938 China, critic Rita Kempley said, "[It's] as bland as a fortune cookie and as trite as the message inside."*

[3] **cliché (clichés)** A *cliché* is a phrase or sentence that, because of long overuse, has lost its impact or freshness. *He had an uncanny talent for freshening up old clichés by slightly altering one of the words, as in "where there's a whip [instead of "will"] there's a way"!*

[4] **dolt** A *dolt* is a dull, stupid person. *During the 2000 presidential campaign, the TV show* Saturday Night Live *portrayed Republican nominee George W. Bush as a dolt who couldn't pronounce the names of foreign leaders.*

[5] **incumbent** If you say that a task or duty is *incumbent* on (or upon) you, you mean that you have an obligation to perform that task or duty. *It's incumbent on all parents to provide for their children.* Another meaning of this word refers to political office. A person who already holds a particular political office is referred to as the *incumbent. Though, in a presidential election, the incumbent often wins a second term, Bill Clinton's defeat of George H. Bush in 1992 showed that that isn't always the case.*

[6] **constraint** If you're with an other person and neither of you is saying or doing anything, you may begin to feel uncomfortable, embarrassed, or awkward. That feeling is called *constraint. For a while my new roommate and I stared at each other awkwardly; then, when we began to argue over who gets the top bunk, all constraint vanished.* Another, more common, meaning of the word is "confinement" or "restriction," as in *the constraints of the monastery.*

mind **compelled**[1] him to break the silence. In a desperate, **jejune**[2] attempt at high wit, he blurted out the **banal**[3] declaration, "Nice weather we're having." When she just looked at him curiously, he said, "I'm sorry."

"What for?"

"For being so stupid and such dull company," he answered **dejectedly**[4], convinced he was nothing but a pathetic **cipher**[5].

---

[1] **compel (compelled)** If you're *compelled* to do something, you're forced to do it. The implication is that the thing doing the forcing is either some kind of authority (who has the power to compel) or some overpowering force or uncontrollable inner urge (such as your conscience). The noun is *compulsion. After seeing the TV documentary about crippled children, Hank felt compelled to make a donation.*

[2] **jejune** This word (pronounced *ji-JUNE*) can mean "dull" (not interesting, plain, uninspired), as in *a jejune novel*, or it can mean "childish" (immature, amateurish, uninformed, inexperienced), as in *jejune attempts to create a business plan*, or it can mean one ("dull" or "childish") with the added implication of the other. *When Sheldon asked his girlfriend why she was breaking up with him, she answered, "Because of all the stupid, jejune activities you suggest— like staring at your ant farm!"*

[3] **banal** If something is *banal*, it lacks freshness or is uninspired; it's ordinary or commonplace and therefore dull and uninteresting. The preferred pronunciation of this word has the accent on the second syllable (rhyming with *canal*), but it can also be placed on the first (rhyming with *anal*). The noun is *banality* (accent on the second syllable). *It has been said that pop art— as exemplified by its most famous image, Andy Warhol's Campbell's Soup Can— celebrates the banal.*

[4] **dejected (dejectedly)** If you're *dejected*, you're in low spirits; you're downcast; you're depressed. Usually this word is used (instead of *depressed*) if these feelings are sudden but temporary. The noun is *dejection. His teammates couldn't decide whether the quarterback's dejection was caused by their losing the game or by his girlfriend's absence.*

[5] **cipher** Technically, a *cipher* is a zero (the mathematical symbol or quantity). But if you describe something as a *cipher*, you mean it's unimportant or it has no value. If you describe a person as a *cipher*, you mean he's a nobody, a nothing. *She had always suspected her son was a cipher; then, when he attained the office of Vice President of the United States, she wondered if her suspicion was negated or confirmed!* Note: Another meaning of this word is "code" (a set of symbols for transmitting secret messages).

THE WIZARD OF OZ VOCABULARY BUILDER

"My heavens! You shouldn't put yourself down like that." Then she continued kindly, "I'm enjoying walking with you. I'm enjoying every minute of it."

The Scarecrow felt his self-consciousness slowly melt into a kind of **euphoria**[1]. Did she really like him?

Now they walked in silence until they reached the point where the little, blue fences ended. Here they found the surrounding land rough and unplowed.

Toward evening, they came to a spot on the yellow brick road where the trees that **straddled**[2] it were so large that their branches intertwined above, **occluding**[3] most of what remained of the **waning**[4] sunlight. **Undaunted**[1], they continued into the

---

[1] **euphoria** A feeling or state of extreme happiness or well-being is known as *euphoria*. This feeling can be induced by events in your life or by drugs. The adjective is *euphoric*. *Steve actually enjoys going to the dentist because of the euphoric feeling the laughing gas gives him.*

[2] **straddle (straddled)** If you *straddle* something, you're on both sides of it at the same time. For example, if you straddle a line on the ground, you have one leg on each side of it. If you straddle an issue (a controversy), you seem to favor both sides at the same time. If a thing (not a person) straddles something, it's on both sides of it and it extends over or across it. *Not many people are aware that with some very early bicycles, instead of pedaling, you pushed your feet along the ground while straddling the vehicle!*

[3] **occlude (occluding)** When something is *occluded*, it's partially or completely blocked, obstructed, or closed. The noun is *occlusion*. *Heart attack or stroke may result from occlusion of a major artery.*

[4] **wane (waning)** When something (light, enthusiasm, or popularity, for example) *wanes*, it gradually becomes less (in intensity, power, importance, size, degree, etc.). *After the Watergate affair, public confidence in the Presidency waned.*

forbidding[2] woods, until, after about an hour, they found themselves enveloped by a **foreboding**[3] darkness.

Luckily, dogs and scarecrows can see well in **crepuscular**[4] light, so Dorothy took hold of the Scarecrow's arm, and they managed to proceed at a reasonable pace. She instructed the Scarecrow to watch for a place to sleep, and he soon spotted an empty cottage made of logs and branches.

He led the child through the trees and into the cottage, where she found a soft bed of dried leaves. With Toto beside her, she soon fell fast asleep. The Scarecrow, who was unaffected by the

---

[1] **undaunted** If something (a task, responsibility, etc.) is *daunting*, it's difficult, scary, or overwhelming to the point that you become discouraged about it; you want to give up. But if you're *undaunted* (not daunted), you're *not* discouraged; you proceed in spite of difficulties. *In September 2001 journalist Sebastian Malla, speaking of a 20-pound bomb that exploded (1984) in the Grand Hotel (Brighton, England), where most of the British cabinet was lodged, said, "It blew out the windows in the Napoleon suite, where Margaret Thatcher was staying, and the bathroom that she had been in just two minutes earlier was demolished; but the Prime Minister was undaunted— less than an hour later, she appeared before the television cameras in her earrings."*

[2] **forbidding** We all know what the verb *forbid* means, as in *I forbid you to leave the house.* But the adjective *forbidding* is used to describe something that appears threatening, scary, disagreeable, menacing, dangerous, hostile, etc. Most often, the word is used to describe landscapes, buildings, or the weather. *In a message from Apollo 8 in 1968, astronaut Frank Borman described the moon as "a vast, lonely, forbidding expanse of nothing."*

[3] **foreboding** To describe something as *foreboding* is to say that it possesses a quality that causes you to feel as if something bad or unfortunate is about to happen. A synonym is *ominous.* As a noun, a *foreboding* is that feeling (that something bad is going to happen). *Gothic novels (which flourished in England from the late 18th to the early 19th century) usually involve evil characters, enchantments, castles, and a sense of foreboding.*

[4] **crepuscular** This adjective refers to that time of day when the sun is going down— when it's twilight or dusk. By extension, the word can also mean "dim" or "indistinct." If you refer to animals (bats or owls, for example) as *crepuscular*, you mean that they become active in the twilight. *The meadow's crepuscular charm was suddenly heightened by the flashing lights of thousands of fireflies.*

circadian[1] rhythms of humans, stood all night in the corner of the room with nothing to do but listen to the soft, **susurrant**[2] sounds of the **ambient**[3] wind.

The next morning, the sun was shining brightly. Dorothy, feeling hungry and grimy, led the Scarecrow to a small brook, where she washed. Then, casting the **ablution**[4] in all directions with a few careless flicks of her wrists, she took some bread from her basket. While she ate, the Scarecrow **opined**[5] that being human

---

[1] **circadian** The word *circa* means "about," and a *day* is a 24-hour period. Knowing that, it's easy to remember that the word *circadian* refers to a 24-hour cycle. Specifically, *circadian rhythm* refers to your cycle of activity— including both your daily functioning (eating, sleeping, etc.) and your body's chemistry (changes in blood pressure, urine production, etc.)— that lasts for and recurs approximately every 24 hours. *The natural circadian rhythms of the astronauts were maintained by keeping the Americans on Houston time and the Russians on Moscow time.*

[2] **susurrant** To describe a sound as *susurrant* is to say that it's continuous and indistinct; it's softly whispering, murmuring. *Even when it's not very hot I like to go to bed with the air conditioner on because its susurrant sound lulls me to sleep.*

[3] **ambient** If something (sound, air, etc.) is *ambient*, it completely surrounds or encompasses (something). *In 1994, 21 fragments of a comet tore through Jupiter's ambient clouds and bombarded its surface.* As a noun, *ambience* is the overall quality, character, mood, or atmosphere of something. People especially use the word to refer to the overall atmosphere of a restaurant. *On a scale of one to ten, I give the new restaurant a nine for food, an eight for ambience, and a three for service.*

[4] **ablution** This word can mean "the washing of the hands or body," or it can refer to the liquid itself that's used in the washing. Often (but not always) the word is used when the washing is part of some religious ritual. *A mosque (a place of public worship in the Muslim religion) must point toward Mecca (Mohammed's birthplace) and have a place for ritual ablutions.*

[5] **opine (opined)** Notice how similar this verb is to the noun *opinion*. To *opine* is to state (or have) an opinion (about something). *Their material is old hat, critics opined— but (mid-20th century American comedy team) Abbott and Costello's expert delivery made the oldest jokes seem fresh.*

must be a great deal of trouble, what with all the **concomitant**[1] hunger, thirst, and fatigue. But then he speculated that having a brain would make all that discomfort worth a lot of bother. Dorothy considered this awhile, but just as she was about to respond, she was startled to hear a deep, **plaintive**[2] groan.

"What was that?" Dorothy asked, looking a little afraid.

"I can't imagine. But let's go see," replied the Scarecrow.

Just then, coming from the same place as the previous sound, they heard a desperate, **keening**[3] wail. The **celerity**[4] of their

---

[1] **concomitant** When something exists with or occurs with something else (especially in a lesser way or as the result of the other), it's referred to as *concomitant* (meaning "concurrent and accompanying"). *The lawyer knew from the outset that raising his hourly fee might result in a concomitant decrease in demand for his services.* As a noun the word means "something that accompanies (goes along with, results from) something else." *One of the concomitants of childhood is short pants.*

[2] **plaintive** If a sound is *plaintive*, it expresses sorrow; it's mournful, sad (as in *the plaintive cry of a trapped, hungry animal*). Note: Don't confuse this adjective with the noun *plaintiff*, which means "a person who institutes a lawsuit." Also note: The noun *plaint* means "complaint." *In 1999 journalist Warren Brown said, "Winter mornings [in Washington, D.C.] are urban symphonies played in the dark. There is the distant rumbling of garbage trucks, the plaintive wailing of a car alarm, the whoosh of wind between tall buildings, and, to the careful listener, the squeaking, rattling sound of an automatic garage door going up."*

[3] **keening** A *keen* is a loud, wailing expression of grief (often like a chant) for the dead. To *keen* is to make these loud wails. A sound described as *keening* resembles the sound of a keen. *I realize my son whines, but I was more than a bit dismayed to learn that his pre-school teachers had nicknamed him "the keening banshee."*

[4] **celerity** To do something with *celerity* is to do it swiftly or quickly. *When I assured him the months he had to spend in jail would pass with celerity, he didn't appear especially comforted.*

response surprised Toto, who followed **apace**[1] as Dorothy and the Scarecrow raced through the woods toward the person or thing from which these hideous sounds **emanated**[2].

Through the trees, a brilliant glint of light sharply struck Dorothy's eye, and she saw that it was reflected from a piece of shiny tin! Toto barked wildly, as if disturbed by the **anomaly**[3] of shiny metal in a **pristine**[4] forest. As Dorothy and the Scarecrow moved closer, they were amazed to see a man made entirely of tin standing perfectly still, like a statue!

"Did you groan?" asked Dorothy.

"I did," answered the Tin Woodman. "I've been standing here groaning like this for over a year, but until now, no one has come to help me."

---

[1] **apace** To do something (proceed, continue, move, etc.) *apace* is to do it swiftly, rapidly, speedily, etc., or to do it at a necessary or required speed (to keep up with the momentum of a particular thing). *In a March 1997 article entitled "New City Law Virtually Bans Smoking Even in Bars, but Many Are Still Lighting Up," the* Washington Post *reported that "Toronto joined the big leagues of the anti-smoking movement with one of North America's strictest tobacco [laws, but] life in Toronto's nightclub district continued apace with late nights, loud music, and a slowly accumulating haze."*

[2] **emanate (emanated)** If something *emanates* (from a source), it flow out (from it); it comes from it. An *emanation* (noun) is a thing that flows out (from a source). *The 1922 Nobel Prize for physics went to Niels Bohr for his investigation of the structure of atoms and the radiations that emanate from them.*

[3] **anomaly** An *anomaly* is something that's out of place, an exception or deviation from a general rule. Any abnormality, irregularity, or peculiarity (a birth defect, for example) can be seen as an *anomaly*. *In an era when Republicans dominated the Presidency, Jimmy Carter's Democratic victory in 1976 was a historical anomaly.*

[4] **pristine** When something is *pristine*, it's in its original, natural state; it has its original purity; it hasn't become dirty or corrupted by civilization. *Teddy Roosevelt was a passionate conservationist, and by the end of his administration, pristine forest reserves totaled nearly 200 million acres.*

THE WIZARD OF OZ VOCABULARY BUILDER

Dorothy and the Scarecrow were moved by the **melancholy**[1] tone of the Tin Woodman's voice, so they wanted to help him in any way they could.

"How can we help you?" asked Dorothy.

Now, oil was an **anodyne**[2] that never failed to **allay**[3] the Tin Woodman's discomfort. He asked Dorothy, "Can you please pick up the oilcan on the ground and oil my joints, starting with my neck?" Dorothy applied the **balm**[4] at once, and as the neck joint was badly rusted, the Scarecrow gently moved the tin head from side to side until the Tin Woodman could do this on his own.

Next Dorothy oiled the arms and legs, which the Tin Woodman,

---

[1] **melancholy** As an adjective, this word means "sad" or "depressed." It's often used (instead of "sad") to imply that the sadness might be habitual (as of someone's nature) or prolonged, or to imply that serious thought accompanies the sadness. As a noun, the word means "a state of sadness or depression." *After hearing Hank Williams sing "Swing Low, Sweet Chariot," we argued about which was more melancholy— the song or his voice!"*

[2] **anodyne** An *anodyne* is anything (sometimes a medicine) that relieves or lessens pain. The word has more of a literary than a medical connotation. (In medicine a word like *analgesic* or *anesthetic* is usually used). *Our aerobics instructor confessed that she listens to heavy metal music at full volume as an anodyne for depression.*

[3] **allay** This word has two meanings, both having to do with relieving or lessening (something). If you *allay* pain (or some other medical condition), you lessen it or relieve it (at least for a short time). *In science class we learned that certain eucalyptus trees are called "fever trees" because their leaves and bark are actually used to allay fever.* If you *allay* an unpleasant emotion (fear, suspicion, anxiety, concern, anger, depression, doubt, etc.), you calm it or put it to rest. *To allay the doubts of the general public, the President volunteered to be the first to receive a swine flu shot.*

[4] **balm** Technically, a *balm* is an oily, fragrant substance that comes from a plant and has some medicinal value. But any aromatic or soothing ointment can be called a *balm*. Also, anything that soothes, heals, or comforts (even if it's not a ointment) can be called a *balm*. *After the entire divorce process finally ended, he told us it wasn't his therapist but the balm of our friendship that sustained him through the toughest times.* Note: If something (weather, for example) is *balmy*, it's mild, gentle, or soothing.

sighing with relief, slowly bent and unbent. The **salutary**[1] effect of the **efficacious**[2] treatment was immediately apparent as the Tin Woodman, now in much higher spirits, repeatedly thanked Dorothy and the Scarecrow, who were touched by his politeness and gratitude.

"How did you happen to be here?" asked the Tin Woodman.

Dorothy explained all about how she and the Scarecrow were on their way to see the Great Oz to ask him to send her back to Kansas and to give him some brains. The Tin Woodman seemed to **cogitate**[3] deeply for a while, then said suddenly, "Because I'm made of tin, I have no heart. But I want one ever so badly. Do you suppose Oz could give me one?"

"I don't see why not," answered Dorothy. "It would be just as easy as to give the Scarecrow brains."

"That's true," said the Tin Woodman. "If you'll allow me, I'll join you on your trip to the Emerald City."

---

[1] **salutary** If something (usually some product or activity) is *salutary*, it promotes health or well-being (of body or mind); it's healthful; it's good for you. (But note that if you're talking about a climate or air as being healthful, it's more common to use the word *salubrious*.) *In the late 1950s, many parents believed that listening to rock-and-roll was harmful to teenagers and that listening to "good" music— Beethoven, for example— would actually have a salutary influence.*

[2] **efficacious** This word is similar to *effective* in that they both mean "able to produce a desired result." But while *effective* means "having the ability to produce a result whether or not that ability is actually used," as in *aspirin is an effective remedy for pain*, the word *efficacious* is often used when the ability has been used and the desired effect attained, as in *the aspirin was efficacious in lowering the patient's temperature. Dairy farmers must find the most efficacious and economical feed for their cows.*

[3] **cogitate** When you *cogitate* about (or on) something, you think about it carefully or intently; you turn it over in your mind. The noun is *cogitation. As my five-year-old daughter stared intently at the dead ladybug, I assumed she was deep in cogitation over the meaning of life— but, I found out later, she was merely counting the spots on its back!*

THE WIZARD OF OZ VOCABULARY BUILDER

Dorothy and the Scarecrow heartily welcomed the **amiable**[1] Tin Woodman to join them on their **pilgrimage**[2]. As the Tin Woodman shouldered his axe, a **prescient**[3] Dorothy took a quick look at the oilcan and **prudently**[4] placed the **panacea**[5] in her basket. Then they all walked merrily through the woods until they were back on the yellow brick road headed for Oz.

---

[1] **amiable** If you're either friendly (social, gracious, warm) or pleasant (agreeable, good-natured, sweet-tempered) you're *amiable*. *In 1998 journalist Lloyd Grove said of Sonny Bono, "As a television entertainer in the early 1970s, [he] perfected the persona of an amiable loser; alongside the tall and stunning Cher, who regularly zapped him with put-downs, he looked like a grinning simpleton with mouse-brown hair."*

[2] **pilgrimage** A *pilgrimage* is a long journey or quest, especially one undertaken for some important purpose (originally, to show devotion, as in *a pilgrimage to Mecca,* or *a pilgrimage to the Wailing Wall*). *The most memorable part of my New York State vacation was our pilgrimage to the Baseball Hall of Fame in Cooperstown.*

[3] **prescient** If you're *prescient*, you have foresight; you have knowledge of things before they happen. The word can refer to either a supernatural foreknowing (as in *fortunetellers in fairy tales are prescient about future events*) or to a natural foresight (as in *a good financial advisor is prescient about coming stock market trends*). The noun is *prescience*. *Jules Verne's prescient 19th-century science fiction novels anticipated many aspects of 20th-century technology.*

[4] **prudent (prudently)** To describe someone as *prudent* is to say that he's careful and cautious about his conduct. The noun is *prudence*. *With no cure in sight, our best defense against the AIDS virus is prudence.* In another sense, someone who's *prudent* shows good judgment or forethought (in protecting against future problems). *French mathematician, scientist, and philosopher Blaise Pascal believed it was prudent to believe in God's existence because little can be lost if there is no God, and eternal happiness can be gained if there is one.*

[5] **panacea** If you refer to something as a *panacea* (pronounced *pan-uh-SEE-uh*), you mean that it's a cure-all, a universal remedy (for either medical problems or societal problems). But since there's no such thing as a cure-all, people also use this word (in a negative way) to describe something that pretends or claims to be a cure-all but really isn't. *In May 1983 former Idaho senator Frank Church (1924–1984) said, "The United Nations is a reflection of the world as it is; [it] is no panacea for the world's problems, but a necessary institution."*

THE WIZARD OF OZ VOCABULARY BUILDER

If not for their **serendipitous**[1] encounter with the Tin Woodman, the travelers would have soon been at a standstill, for they were now standing at a place where a thick overgrowth of trees and long branches made the road impassable. But the Tin Woodman tirelessly worked his axe, **truncating**[2] limb after limb, until a passage was finally cleared.

As they walked along again, the Scarecrow and the Tin Woodman, **espousing**[3] opposite points of view, debated the relative importance of brains and hearts. Meanwhile, Dorothy, noticing that there was enough bread left in her basket for only one more meal, and anxiously envisioning **abstemious**[4] days ahead, **pragmatically**[5] **propounded**[1] the theory that access to food was

---

[1] **serendipitous** To refer to something (a fortunate discovery or encounter, for example) as *serendipitous* is to say that it occurred both by luck and by accident. The noun is *serendipity* (the lucky, accidental making of a fortunate discovery or encounter). *While searching for a westward route to India, Columbus serendipitously discovered America!*

[2] **truncate (truncating)** When you *truncate* something, you shorten it by cutting off a part of it. You can *truncate* both physical objects (tree branches, countries, etc.) and non-physical objects (speeches, conversations, etc.) The noun is *truncation*. *The word "taxi" is a well-established truncation of "taxicab."*

[3] **espouse (espousing)** One meaning of this word is "to marry (a person)." But usually, when people use this word they're referring to the "marrying" of a person to an idea; that is, the taking of an idea (or principle) and embracing it as one's own, taking it to heart. *In the early 1950s, many public figures who were suspected of espousing communism— or any leftist causes— were ruined by blacklisting.*

[4] **abstemious** If you're *abstemious*, you're restrained in eating and drinking (of alcohol); you eat and drink sparingly or moderately. *When she saw the painting of the fat monk, she exclaimed, "I thought those guys were supposed to be abstemious!"*

[5] **pragmatic (pragmatically)** If you're *pragmatic*, you approach things from a practical, realistic point of view (as opposed to an emotional, idealistic, or visionary point of view). *In February 2000, journalist Teresa Wiltz, speaking of a challenge that confronts clothing designers, said, "It's always there, the tension between the pragmatic and the artistic, between the bottom line of retail and the [showiness] of the runway, between clothing as shelter and clothing as expression."*

45

perhaps most important of all!

---

[1] **propound (propounded)** When you *propound* an idea (or concept, theory, etc.), you put it forward for consideration (in speech or writing). There is sometimes (but not always) the implication that the person putting forth the idea accepts it as true. *While nearly everyone praises Shakespeare for writing brilliant plays, many criticize him for failing to propound any particular philosophy.*

Chapter 5 "The Cowardly Lion"

Walking with her companions through thickening, darkening woods, Dorothy began to feel a gnawing **disquietude**[1] in her gut. She had a vague **premonition**[2] of danger, but she wasn't sure why. Maybe it was because in this part of the woods the birds no longer chirped. Or perhaps it was because here all the yellow bricks that made up the road were covered by dried branches and leaves. She nervously clutched the Scarecrow's sleeve. In his mind he **extrapolated**[3] that the darkening sky was merely a **precursor**[4] to total darkness, but he didn't announce this for he knew it would probably frighten the girl.

"How much longer until we're out of the forest?" asked Dorothy

---

[1] **disquietude** If you think of the word *quiet* as meaning "restful peace," then *disquiet* is "a *lack* of restful peace." So, if you experience *disquietude* (a state or condition of *disquiet*), you lose your peace of mind; you feel anxious, concerned, worried, or uneasy (you've been *disquieted*). *When the message on the airport's "Arriving Flights" display suddenly changed from "on time" to "to be announced," an overwhelming disquietude shot through him.*

[2] **premonition** If you have a *premonition* about something, you have a (usually uneasy, anxious) feeling that something (usually bad) is about to happen. *In 1963, in spite of a premonition expressed by Adlai Stevenson, President Kennedy flew to Dallas (where he was assassinated).*

[3] **extrapolate (extrapolated)** To *extrapolate* is to use information that you already know to make estimates or educated guesses about what you don't know. *We knew that the square root of 16 is 4 and that the square root of 25 is 5; by extrapolation we estimated the square root of 20 to be about 4.5.*

[4] **precursor** Although this word sometimes means simply "predecessor," as in *the adding machine was the precursor of the modern electronic calculator,* the word usually means "something (or someone) that goes before and somehow indicates the approach of something (or someone) else." *Many doctors consider a high cholesterol level a precursor to heart disease.*

47

in a **tremulous**[1] little voice.

With a natural, **avuncular**[2] affection, the Tin Woodman tried to **assuage**[3] the child's **burgeoning**[4] panic by reminding her that no harm could come to her because she still carried on her forehead the protective mark of the good Witch's kiss. "And you don't need to worry about me or the Scarecrow either," he told her, "because I'm made of tin and the Scarecrow of straw, so we can't be hurt."

"But what about Toto?" asked Dorothy anxiously. "What will protect him?" She knew she had always **cosseted**[5] her dog— at least that's what Uncle Henry claimed— but now she didn't care if she

---

[1] **tremulous** This word can mean either "trembling, quivering, shaking" or "timid, fearful, cowardly," but it's especially used to mean "trembling as a result of fear." *I cursed myself for volunteering as, with tremulous fingers, I picked up the spider and carried it outside.*

[2] **avuncular** The middle part of this word looks a little like the word *uncle*, and, in fact, the word means "uncle-like"; in other words, kindly, compassionate, generous, etc. *In the 1988 film* Big, *actor Robert Loggia plays the avuncular boss of a toy company.*

[3] **assuage** To *assuage* something (pain, hunger, anger, or fear, for example) is to make it less intense; to relieve it, reduce it, satisfy it, or calm it. *Years later Karen admitted she'd joined the Peace Corps only to assuage the guilt she felt about her overprivileged childhood.*

[4] **burgeoning** Technically, a plant *burgeons;* that is, it begins to grow, to sprout, to blossom, to flourish. But generally, when people describe something (besides a plant) as *burgeoning,* they mean that it's (usually suddenly or quickly) growing, expanding, developing, increasing, thriving, etc. *In the 1960s both industrial expansion and burgeoning truck and automobile use worsened the air pollution problem.*

[5] **cosset (cosseted)** When you *cosset* someone (a child, celebrity, or pet, for example), you pamper him (indulge him, exclusively cater to his desires, etc.). *In 1981 Pulitzer Prize-winning journalist Mary McGrory, speaking of the funeral of assassinated Egyptian president Anwar Sadat, said, "Richard Nixon, Gerald Ford, and Jimmy Carter were entirely gratified to go to Cairo— to ride again on* Air Force One, *to feel wanted, to be cosseted, consulted, interviewed, and photographed as of old."*

coddled[1] him; in fact, she was glad of it!

"We will protect him ourselves," said the Tin Woodman, still hoping to **placate**[2] the little girl.

Just as he was about to offer a few **bromidic**[3] reassurances, he heard a terrifying roar and an enormous Lion jumped onto the road! With one swipe of his paw, the great beast sent the Scarecrow head over heels to the side of the road. With another blow, he easily knocked the Tin Woodman to the ground. They both began to get back up but then **quailed**[4], apparently **cowed**[5] by the Lion's

---

[1] **coddle (coddled)** If you *coddle* someone you excessively tend to his needs or feelings; you treat him in an overly tender or indulgent manner. The implication is that by doing so you weaken his character. *She confessed to us that she secretly enjoyed when her children had colds because it was the only time she got to coddle them without guilt!*

[2] **placate** If you *placate* someone, you lessen or ease his anger, agitation, disturbance, etc. Often you do this by making some concession or by offering something so that his feelings of anger or resentment are actually changed to feelings of goodwill. *When in public— and only when in public— they placate their screaming toddler with cherry lollipops.*

[3] **bromide (bromidic)** A *bromide* is an often-repeated expression, phrase, or saying that has lost its freshness and originality. You'll often see the word *old* before the word, as in *the old bromide that you are what you eat*. The adjective, *bromidic*, means "of or like a bromide." *The song "A Wonderful Guy" (from Rodgers and Hammerstein's South Pacific) is filled with corny, old expressions and contains the line "I'm as trite and as gay as a daisy in May, a cliché coming true; I'm bromidic and bright as a moon-happy night pouring light on the dew."*

[4] **quail (quailed)** If you *quail*, you suddenly lose courage and shrink back in fear, usually because you've been somehow intimidated. *He was just about to finally tell his wife that he would no longer tolerate the nasty looks she always gave him, but he quailed when he saw the nasty look on her face.*

[5] **cow (cowed)** To *cow* someone is to intimidate or frighten him, usually by threats or a show of force. Often, once you've been *cowed* (by someone or something), you lose spirit and courage. *Cowed by the overwhelming odds against getting rich by writing poetry, Arnold decided to sell his typewriter and use the money to buy lottery tickets.*

size and **pugilistic**[1] pose.

Little Toto **intrepidly**[2] ran barking toward the Lion, whose gaping **maw**[3] was ready. Dorothy, looking like a mother rushing to save her child from an oncoming train, raced forward and whacked the Lion on his nose as hard as she could!

Incredibly, the Lion started to cry, and **blubbered**[4], "What did you do that for? I didn't hurt him."

"No, but you tried to," said Dorothy **indignantly**[5], gently **dandling**[6] Toto in her arms. "You should be ashamed of yourself, a big beast like you trying to bite a poor little dog. Why, you're nothing but a great big coward!"

---

[1] **pugilism (pugilistic)** *Pugilism* is just a fancy word for "boxing." Joe Louis and Muhammad Ali, for example, were famous *pugilists*. As an adjective, *pugilistic* means "pertaining to boxing." *There was little law or order in pugilism until 1743, when English boxing champion Jack Broughton drew up a set of rules for the game (which included no hitting below the belt).*

[2] **intrepid (intrepidly)** If you're *intrepid*, you're boldly or daringly fearless (when faced with something dangerous or scary). *The intrepid Mercury astronauts (Alan Shepard, John Glenn, and others) paved the way for the later Apollo astronauts.*

[3] **maw** A *maw* is the mouth (or jaws) of an animal, especially a large, meat-eating one. You'll see this word more often in writing than you'll hear it spoken. Figuratively, the word can be used to denote the opening of anything that has or seems to have a large appetite, as in *he was sucked into the gaping maw of hell*. *In general, there is little chewing of food among lizards; many simply seize their prey, place it in their sharp-toothed maw, bite it, then swallow it.*

[4] **blubber (blubbered)** When you cry (out loud) and talk at the same time, so that what you say is broken, inarticulate, or incoherent, you're *blubbering*. *The young mother ignored her child's blubbering about not being allowed a second ice cream cone.*

[5] **indignant (indignantly)** If you're *indignant*, you're angry about something you consider unfair. The noun is *indignation*. *In 1995 many Americans, especially white Americans, were indignant when a jury found O.J. Simpson not guilty of murder.*

[6] **dandle (dandling)** When you lightly or playfully move someone (a baby, a small child, etc.) up and down on your knee (or in your arms), you're *dandling* him. *When he told me he had once been dandled on Teddy Roosevelt's knee, I did some quick math and figured him to be at least 90 years old.*

THE WIZARD OF OZ VOCABULARY BUILDER

"I know it," said the Lion, hanging his head in shame. He went on to explain that his **craven**[1] behavior was **inherent**[2] in his nature, most likely **congenital**[3]. "I learned early on," he continued, "that my loud roar scared the other animals, so I've always used it to frighten them away. That way I avoided fights. Until now it had always worked."

"It's not right that the King of Beasts should be afraid," said the Scarecrow.

"I know," said the Lion, wiping a tear from his eye. "But what can I do? I don't have the nerve to act brave. I'm even afraid of my own shadow." An embarrassing **paroxysm**[4] of sobbing, briefly **presaged**[5] by quivering shoulders, forced him to turn away from

---

[1] **craven** If you're *craven*, you're cowardly. The word is especially used if great timidity, faintheartedness, or fear accompanies your cowardice. *As boys, even the most craven among us, in an attempt to prove we were "regular guys," jumped off the high diving board.*

[2] **inherent** Something that exists as an essential, permanent, and inseparable part of something else is said to be *inherent* (in that something else). An *inherent* trait in a person is one that's hereditary and existing since birth. *After reading Darwin we debated about whether the "struggle to survive" inherent in every species is the same thing as the "will to live" inherent in every human.*

[3] **congenital** This word means "existing since birth but not hereditary." It's generally used to describe some medical defect that was acquired during fetal development, as in *a congenital heart malformation*. *Scientists are still not sure whether homosexuality is congenital or acquired.*

[4] **paroxysm** Technically, this is a medical term that refers to either a sudden attack (or intensification or recurrence) of a disease or to a convulsion (or spasm). But people often use the word to mean "any sudden, extreme outburst of emotion." *She didn't enjoy the new comedy because her boyfriend's paroxysms of laughter drowned out half the lines.*

[5] **presage (presaged)** To *presage* is to foreshadow (indicate or suggest beforehand) or foretell (predict), as in *dark clouds presaged the downpour*. As a noun, a *presage* is something that foreshadows or foretells. *The emotional intensity of (19th century German composer) Robert Schumann's orchestral works presaged his later nervous breakdown.*

51

the group.

In **sotto voce**[1] tones, the travelers agreed that, rather than **chastise**[2] the Lion further, they should try to **succor**[3] him in some way. Agreeing on a plan, they approached the Lion, told him about their trip, and invited him to join them in the hope that the Great Oz would give him some courage.

The Lion seemed afraid of meeting the Wizard, but with great **resolve**[4] he said, "I must go with you, for living a life without

---

[1] **sotto voce** In Italian this phrase (pronounced *sot-oh VOH-chee*) literally means "under (the) voice." When you speak *sotto voce*, you speak in a soft, low voice so as not to be overheard. *From a bit of a distance, in sotto voce tones, we shamelessly ridiculed her outfit; then when she was introduced to us we smiled and told her how nice she looked!*

[2] **chastise** When you *chastise* someone, you either scold him or spank him for having done something wrong (usually as a means of bringing about an improvement in his behavior). *When the freshman boys returned to their dorm after their first panty raid, the faculty resident chastised them loudly.*

[3] **succor** To *succor* someone is to give him aid or assistance (or relief or help) at a time of need. As a noun, the word refers to the aid or assistance itself. The implication is that when you *succor* someone, you rescue him from some distress. *In his November 1978 article entitled "Buccaneers No Longer Needy," journalist Robert Fachet said, "When the [Tampa Bay] Buccaneers battle the Buffalo Bills today, [football] fans are asked to bring cans of food to succor the needy on Thanksgiving; it is something that would not have been attempted the last two seasons— it would have inspired too many jokes about that neediest of all football teams, the Tampa Bay outfit that lost its first 26 games in the NFL."*

[4] **resolve** If you have *resolve*, you have firm determination (to follow some fixed purpose or course of action). *It was when he heard what life was like on a reservation that Sioux leader Sitting Bull formed his resolve to never sign a treaty with the white man.*

courage is simply unbearable." Dorothy was especially **sanguine**[1] about having the Lion along because she knew that with his great roar he could keep away other wild beasts.

Once again the little company set off upon the journey to the Emerald City. All the rest of that day there was no other adventure to **mar**[2] the peace of their travels—no other, that is, except when the Tin Woodman accidentally stepped on a tiny bug and killed it! He felt so bad that he cried until he rusted himself with his tears.

"You people with hearts," the Tin Woodman said, after the Scarecrow had applied some oil to his mouth, "are lucky because you have something to guide you, and you'll never do wrong. But I have no heart and so I have to be very careful." And thereafter, the Tin Woodman, in an effort to **expiate**[3] his offense, **vigilantly**[4] looked down at the road as he walked and carefully stepped over every little bug he encountered along the way.

---

[1] **sanguine** If you're *sanguine* about something, you're hopeful, confident, or cheerily optimistic about it. *He was so in love with Microsoft that he remained sanguine about the company's future even as his shares fell to less than half of what he'd paid for them.* Note: Most dictionaries give "bloody" as one meaning for this word. While it's true that "sanguine" derives from a Latin word meaning "bloody" or "full of blood," nobody today uses it in that sense. The connection is that in medieval times it was (erroneously) believed that if your prevalent body fluid were blood (as opposed to phlegm or bile) you would have a ruddy complexion and therefore be of good humor.

[2] **mar** To *mar* something is to damage or spoil it to some extent or in some way; to make it less than perfect. *His brilliant essay was marred by numerous typographical errors.*

[3] **expiate** To *expiate* something (a sin, an offense, a misdeed) is to make up for it, to make amends for it. *In Charles Dickens' A* Christmas Carol *(1843), after Ebenezer Scrooge reforms, he expiates his miserliness by offering help to a crippled boy.*

[4] **vigilant (vigilantly)** If you're *vigilant*, you're keenly watchful; you're carefully and continuously looking out for possible danger (or opportunity). *With his vigilant eye, the tax examiner detected (and deleted) every non-allowable deduction.*

Chapter 6 "The Kalidahs"

As night fell, our little group decided to **bivouac**[1] under a large tree in the forest. The Tin Woodman chopped a pile of wood with his axe and Dorothy built a fire, which warmed her. After she ate the last remaining **smidgen**[2] of bread, she confided to the Scarecrow that she was thirsty and still a little hungry.

Assigning himself the task of **procuring**[3] **sustenance**[4] for the girl, he began **foraging**[5] in the surrounding area for food and **potable**[6]

---

[1] **bivouac** To *bivouac* is to camp out; that is, to set up improvised, temporary shelter in an unprotected outdoor area (for the purpose of resting or sleeping). As a noun, a *bivouac* is such a camp. *In the Civil War's bloody Battle of Shiloh (April 1862), Confederate troops surprised the Union army, bivouacked near Shiloh Church (in Pittsburg Landing, Tennessee); the following day the Union took the offensive and gained the final victory.*

[2] **smidgen** A *smidgen* of something is a very small amount of it (or, if speaking of food, a very small portion of it). *In January 1995 the* Washington Post *reported that "police are searching for a motorist who they say showed just a smidgen of compassion after he ran over a 60-year-old woman and drove away; the woman told police that the man returned a few minutes later, drove her home, dumped her at the curb, and sped off."*

[3] **procure (procuring)** To *procure* something is to get it (or obtain or acquire it). The implication is that some effort or difficulty is involved (in getting it). *His great claim to fame is that back in the sixties he managed to procure a backstage pass for a Beatles concert.*

[4] **sustenance** This word means "food (or nourishment), especially if the food is thought of as life-sustaining." *The homeless are often seen picking through garbage cans because they're in desperate need of sustenance.* But the word can also refer to anything (other than food) that preserves (or seems to preserve) life. *The missionary found sustenance in his decision to devote his life to winning souls for Christ.*

[5] **forage (foraging)** To *forage* is to wander about in search of food (or sometimes other provisions). *He theorized that animals in the wild never become bored because they're too busy foraging for food.*

[6] **potable** If you refer to water as *potable*, you mean that it's drinkable (fit or safe to drink). *The astronaut's life-support system contained breathable air, potable water, and nutritious food.*

54

water. After not too long he spotted, next to a clear brook, a tree full of nuts. He **culled**[1] the largest of them to fill Dorothy's basket, then filled the hollow of a small, curved piece of tree bark with water.

When he returned and handed the food and drink to the child, she noticed that the nuts looked strange and prickly. Though normally not particularly **fastidious**[2] about food, she was rather afraid to try them. She sipped some of the water; after a while she sipped some more. Then, with hunger winning out over caution, she cracked open one of the strange-looking shells. Taking a **tentative**[3] taste of the kernel inside, she found it to be surprisingly **palatable**[4].

---

[1] **cull (culled)** To *cull* something is to pick out (or select) only the best parts of it (and reject the rest). *Radio comedian Fred Allen (1894–1956) once observed, "The American arrives in Paris with a few French phrases he has culled from a conversational guide or picked up from a friend who owns a beret."*

[2] **fastidious** People who are *fastidious* are difficult to please (they're fussy, particular, critical, etc.), often because they're excessively attentive to detail or appearance (they're overly refined, delicate, dainty, correct, etc.). *According to Compton's Encyclopedia, "Most cats never need a bath; a cat is naturally fastidiously clean and spends much time grooming."*

[3] **tentative** To describe something as *tentative* is to say either that it's done on an experimental or provisional basis (it's not final or definite), as in *they made tentative plans to meet for dinner,* or that it's done in a hesitant, uncertain manner, as in *she tentatively petted the snake. In his 1960 book* The Process of Education, *American psychologist and Harvard professor Jerome Bruner said, "The shrewd guess, the fertile hypothesis, the courageous leap to a tentative conclusion— these are the most valuable coins of the thinker at work; but in most schools guessing is heavily penalized and is associated somehow with laziness."*

[4] **palatable** Your *palate* is the roof of your mouth. If food is described as *palatable,* it's pleasing or agreeable to your palate (your taste)— or it's at least agreeable enough to be eaten. If an idea is described as *palatable,* it's agreeable (or at least acceptable) to your mind. *The director of the new production of Gilbert and Sullivan's Mikado, in order to make the songs more palatable to today's politically correct audience, deleted from the lyrics anything that might be considered offensive to minorities.*

THE WIZARD OF OZ VOCABULARY BUILDER

When Dorothy lay down to sleep, the Scarecrow covered her with dry leaves that kept her snug and warm. Toto and the Lion **lolled**[1] near the fire awhile, then fell fast asleep. The Tin Woodman and the Scarecrow, not needing sleep, stood awake all night **plying**[2] the burning **pyre**[3] with fresh logs and trying hard not to laugh at the Lion's **stertorous**[4] breathing.

The next morning, the little group started off again toward the Emerald City. But within an hour they came to a great ditch that crossed the road and divided the forest as far as they could see to their left and right. Walking to the edge, they saw the sides of the ditch were **precipitous**[5] and that the deep bottom was filled with

---

[1] **loll (lolled)** If you're half sitting and half lying (on your couch, for example) in a relaxed, comfortable way, you're *lolling*. *He called in sick to work and then spent the day in his bathrobe, lolling on the sofa, watching TV.*

[2] **ply (plying)** When you *ply* something, you repeatedly supply it with something (or apply something to it). *All through dinner, hoping to loosen up his uptight date, he plied her with alcohol.* Note: The word also has two other meanings: (1) "to work with or use busily," as in *the seamstress plied her needle.* (2) (referring to boats) "to follow a course on a regular basis," as in *ferries that ply the route between Cape Cod and Martha's Vineyard.*

[3] **pyre** A *pyre* is a pile of wood (or other combustible material) for burning. The word is often used in the phrase "funeral pyre," which is a *pyre* used for burning dead bodies. *In Egyptian mythology, when a phoenix reaches 500 years of age, it burns itself on a pyre, later to rise renewed from its own ashes.*

[4] **stertorous** Breathing described as *sterterous* is breathing accompanied by heavy snoring sounds. (In medicine, a *stertor* is a heavy breathing sound that accompanies respiration in certain diseases.) *I couldn't enjoy the movie because of the stertorous breathing of the old guy in the seat next to mine.*

[5] **precipitous** A *precipice* is a very steep cliff. Something described as *precipitous* (a mountain or road, for example) is very steep. But the word can also describe non-physical things (as in *a precipitous drop in stock prices*). *The precipitous rise in rents that many areas of the U.S. experienced in the 1980s has lead to increased homelessness.* Note: People also often use the word—though some language experts feel this is an error—as a synonym for the adjective *precipitate* (last syllable rhymes with *bit*), which means "headlong," "abrupt," or "rash" (as in *I would have said good-bye, but we left rather precipitiously*).

large, jagged rocks.

For a while it seemed their journey must end. Then the Lion had a thought, but he felt too **diffident**[1] to voice it. Finally forcing himself, he proclaimed, "I think I can jump across the ditch!"

"Then we can continue," said the Scarecrow in another exhibit of **perspicacious**[2] insight. "You can carry us over on your back, one at a time. Take me first, because if I fall, I won't get hurt."

"I'm terribly afraid of falling myself," said the Lion, "but what else can we do? Get on my back and I'll give it my best." So the Scarecrow climbed upon his mighty **mount**[3] and the large beast, giving a great spring, shot through the air and landed safely on the other side. The Scarecrow dismounted and the Lion sprang back across the ditch for the next passenger.

Dorothy decided she would be next, and since Toto weighed very little, she carried him in her arms. She climbed on the Lion's back, and in a moment she found herself on a brief but **harrowing**[4]

---

[1] **diffident** If you lack self-confidence (and don't really trust your own opinions or abilities), and as a result act timid, restrained, or hesitant (in speaking or acting), you're *diffident*. *On the cafeteria line he luckily found himself standing right behind the prettiest girl in the school; unfortunately, he was suddenly too diffident to say one word to her.*

[2] **perspicacious** If you're *perspicacious* you have keen perception and sound judgment; you're insightful; you're able to see into things in a way that let's you penetrate them and understand them. *Jonas Salk's perspicacious insight that viral vaccines do not need to infect in order to immunize led to his development of the first polio vaccine.*

[3] **mount** As a noun, a *mount* is something that you ride— especially a large animal; more especially, a horse. *As soon as Zorro finished drawing the letter "Z" with his sword, he climbed his mount and rode off.*

[4] **harrowing** An experience described as *harrowing* is one that is distressing, agonizing, nerve-wracking, upsetting, disturbing, etc. *The classic film* The Snake Pit *(1948) is a harrowing look at life inside a mental institution.*

flight over the **treacherous**[1] ditch. After landing safely on the other side, the Lion went back a third time for the Tin Woodman.

After they had all safely crossed the ditch, and once the **haggard**[2] Lion had had a chance to rest awhile, they all set out again along the yellow brick road. On this side of the ditch, the thick, **Cimmerian**[3] woods frightened the travelers, and each wondered, in his own mind, if they would ever reach the **refuge**[4] of the Emerald City.

Now Dorothy started to hear strange noises coming from deep within the forest, and the Lion whispered to her, "This is the part of the country where the Kalidahs live." Then he thought to himself: *And I'm scared to death of them!* The Kalidahs, he went on to explain, were large, **rapacious**[5] beasts with heads like tigers and

---

[1] **treacherous** Something described as *treacherous* is dangerous or hazardous, as in *the treacherous ascent to the top of Mount Everest* or *the treacherous waters off North Carolina's Cape Hatteras. Work on the Panama Canal began in 1881, but malaria, yellow fever, and treacherous terrain led most engineers to believe that a canal could not be built.* Note: If a person is described as *treacherous*, the word has a different meaning; it means "unfaithful" or "disloyal."

[2] **haggard** If you have a worn-out and exhausted appearance (and especially if you look thin or distressed) from (or as if from) exertion, anxiety, hunger, or disease, you're *haggard. The destructive effects of the Civil War were visible in Abraham Lincoln's haggard face.*

[3] **Cimmerian** In Greek mythology, *Cimmerians* were people who inhabited a land of perpetual darkness. Hence, a place described as *Cimmerian* is very dark (or gloomy). *Countless bats inhabit the deep, Cimmerian caves of New Mexico's Carlsbad Caverns National Park.*

[4] **refuge** A *refuge* is any place of safety, shelter, or protection (from danger or trouble). *In the children's story "The Three Little Pigs," the first and second pig take refuge (from the Big Bad Wolf) in the third pig's brick house.*

[5] **rapacious** A *rapacious* animal is one that exists by eating other animals. People who are rapacious are hungrily greedy; they take what they want. *Army ants are rapacious tropical ants that move in large swarms and devour anything in their path.*

bodies like bears, and with long, sharp claws that could easily **sever**[1] a limb. Suddenly hearing a **tocsin**[2] of alarm sound in his mind, he began anxiously obsessing about his dreaded *bête noire*[3]. That's when he **avowed**[4] his great fear of them to Dorothy.

Now, terrified that some Kalidahs might detect their presence, they moved onward as **stealthily**[5] as possible.

Suddenly they saw before them another gulf across the road. This one was so big that the Lion knew he couldn't possibly leap over it. As they all sat down to consider what to do, the Scarecrow quickly surveyed the surrounding area. With reasoning surprisingly **cogent**[6] for one with no brains, he determined that if the Tin Woodman could chop down a nearby tree so that if fell across the

---

[1] **sever** To *sever* (something) is to cut it off (from the whole). The word can apply to physical things or non-physical things. *By June of 1861, 11 Southern states had severed their ties with the Union.*

[2] **tocsin** A *tocsin* is a signal (especially of alarm), usually sounded on a bell. *When I smelled smoke coming from the airplane's engine, a tocsin of alarm rang in my head.*

[3] **bête noire** This is a French phrase that literally means "black beast" and is used to describe whoever or whatever you especially dread or dislike. *In our school production of* Peter Pan, *I played Captain Hook's bête noire— the crocodile who'd bitten off his hand.*

[4] **avow (avowed)** To *avow* something is to say it or acknowledge it frankly and openly (and usually without shame); to admit it, to confess it. *Avowed* can be a verb (past tense of *avow*) or an adjective meaning "declared" or "acknowledged," as in *George Wallace was an avowed segregationist. In 1966 Huey Newton and Bobby Seale formed the Black Panther Party for Self-Defense with the avowed intention of protecting the black community of Oakland, California, from police brutality.*

[5] **stealth (stealthily)** To do something *stealthily* is to do it quietly, cautiously, secretly, etc. (so as not to attract notice). As a noun, *stealth* is the practice of moving or acting in such a manner. *During the TV nature show, we were afraid to look as the crocodile stealthily swam toward the drinking antelope.*

[6] **cogent** If an explanation or argument is *cogent*, it's convincing, believable, or compelling (because it's clearly presented and logical). *Interestingly, Gregor Mendel's cogent explanation of inherited traits in plants was ignored until after his death.*

ditch, they could all easily cross to the other side!

And so, with an axe-blade as **trenchant**[1] as the Scarecrow's perception, the Tin Woodman mightily set to work, and soon the tree trunk was nearly chopped through. Now the Lion pressed his strong front paws against the tree and pushed hard until the tree slowly tipped over. With a **cacophonous**[2] crash it fell across the ditch, its **benumbed**[3] leaves and top branches resting on the other side.

They had just started to cross this queer bridge when they heard behind them a loud snarl that made them stop and turn around. Racing toward them were two large beasts with heads like tigers and bodies like bears! Dorothy, Toto, the Scarecrow, and the Tin Woodman immediately scrambled to the other side. But the Lion, shaking with fear, stayed behind to face the **abhorrent**[4] brutes.

Feigning[5] **truculence**[1], the Lion roared so loudly that even

---

[1] **trenchant** This word originally meant "sharp" or "sharp-edged" (as of a blade), but today refers to sharpness of mind or language. Anything described as *trenchant* (criticism, arguments, wit, etc.) is incisive and cutting; it gets to the heart of the matter in a sharp, clear way. *Sinclair Lewis's trenchant satires about middle-class America won him a Nobel Prize for literature (1930).*

[2] **cacophonous** A sound described as *cacophonous* is harsh, dissonant, unpleasant, or chaotic sounding. The noun is *cacophony*. *We visited the forest because we heard how peaceful it was; then when we arrived we were greeted with an unbearable cacophony of bird calls and insect noises.*

[3] **benumbed** To *benumb* something is to make it numb (deprive it of sensation). Something described as *benumbed* has been made numb (stiff, lifeless). *The frostbite victim's benumbed fingers had turned grayish-yellow and felt doughy.*

[4] **abhorrent** If you find something *abhorrent*, you find it hateful (or disgusting or repellent). The word is especially used (instead of simply "hateful") if the object of your hatred is considered truly horrible or outrageous. *Right-to-life groups find the idea of abortion abhorrent.* Note: The verb *abhor* means "to hate" (usually something horrible or outrageous), as in *I abhor any kind of animal cruelty.*

[5] **feign (feigning)** To *feign* (something) is to put on a false appearance of it, to deceptively imitate it. *In the 1986 film* Ferris Bueller's Day Off, *the title character feigns illness in order to avoid going to school.*

THE WIZARD OF OZ VOCABULARY BUILDER

Dorothy and her friends were momentarily frightened. The Kalidahs stopped a moment in startled surprise, but then, realizing they were bigger that the Lion and that there were two of them and only one of him, easily saw through his empty **bravado**[2] and again rushed forward.

Knowing he was only moments away from **excoriation**[3] or worse, the Lion, responding more to **visceral**[4] than intellectual motivation, crossed the bridge like something shot from a slingshot.

Now the Kalidahs were crossing the tree, and the Lion **impetuously**[5] said to Dorothy, "They're going to tear us to pieces, but stand behind me and I'll fight them as long as I'm alive." With

---

[1] **truculent (truculence)** If you're *truculent*, you're aggressively hostile; you're naturally disposed to fight. *In that staged entertainment known as professional wrestling, a "hero" often battles a truculent "villain."*

[2] **bravado** A false or pretended show of courage or bravery is known as *bravado*. Often there's an implication that this show is swaggering or boastful. *When I go to the dentist alone, I tremble with fright; but whenever I take my young son with me, I force myself to put on a convincing show of bravado.*

[3] **excoriate (excoriation)** To *excoriate* something is to rip (or strip or tear) its skin off. *The castaways trapped a rat; then they excoriated it, cooked it, and ate it.* Often the word is used figuratively to mean "criticize severely" (rip apart), as in *in his review, the drama critic excoriated the new playwright.*

[4] **visceral** The word *viscera* denotes your internal organs, especially your intestines, your guts. So if you feel something *viscerally*, you feel it in your guts; you feel it instinctively and naturally (not intellectually). If you refer to something (a form of artistic expression, for example) as *visceral*, you mean that it's earthy and characterized by natural urges. *When the teenage punk-rock guitarist's father told him he should study music theory, the boy answered, "I avoid musical knowledge; it would only inhibit my visceral explorations."*

[5] **impetuous (impetuously)** If you're *impetuous*, you act abruptly, hastily, or rashly, without due consideration or deliberation. Often there's an implication that the action you're undertaking has some element of risk or danger to it. *New York Yankees principal owner George Steinbrenner is known for his impetuous firings and hirings of team managers (he's changed managers nearly 20 times).*

palpable[1] apprehension, he **girded**[2] himself for the **fray**[3].

Meanwhile, the Scarecrow had been furiously **ratiocinating**[4]. With the **sapient**[5] strategy of a **seasoned**[6] general, he told the Tin Woodman to chop away the end of the tree that rested on their side of the ditch. The Tin Woodman set to work at once, and just as the

---

[1] **palpable** If something is *palpable*, it can be touched or felt. Often the word is used to refer to something abstract (a feeling, an idea) that is so intense that you feel as if you can touch it, as in *the tension in the room was palpable. The mystery's settings and characters together conveyed a palpable sense of evil.*

[2] **gird (girded)** When you *gird* yourself for something (a battle, a test, etc.), you prepare yourself for it (by drawing on your resources of strength and power). *Finding himself face to face with a drooling, snarling German shepherd, he forced himself to smile and say, "Nice dog, nice dog"; meanwhile, he was girding himself for the fight of his life.*

[3] **fray** A *fray* is a noisy or heated fight; a brawl, a scuffle. *Because of Switzerland's strict neutrality, the city of Geneva sits "beyond the fray" and thus provides an impartial meeting ground for representatives of other nations.*

[4] **ratiocinate (ratiocinating)** To *ratiocinate* (pronounced *rash-ee-OS-ih-nate*) is to reason logically, to deduce. *My favorite mystery stories are ones in which the detective uses pure ratiocination to solve the crime.*

[5] **sapient** If you're *sapient*, you're wise and you show good judgment or discernment. *All of the sapient observations made by Dr. Benjamin Spock in his 1946 book* Baby and Child Care *might be summarized by one statement he made in 1950: "What good mothers and fathers instinctively feel like doing for their babies is usually best after all."*

[6] **seasoned** Everyone knows that when food is *seasoned*, its flavor is (supposedly) enhanced through the adding of spices. But if you say that a person is *seasoned*, you mean that he's competent and mature; he's been around a long time and has learned a lot from his experience. *In 1928 Herbert Hoover, a former mining engineer from Iowa, decided to run for the Presidency against the seasoned New York Democratic governor, Al Smith.*

THE WIZARD OF OZ VOCABULARY BUILDER

voracious[1] **predators**[2] were nearly across, the tree fell with a horrifying **din**[3] into the gulf, carrying the Kalidahs with it. Both were neatly **impaled**[4] on the sharp, jagged rocks below. Understandably, the travelers now felt even more threatened by the **baleful**[5] atmosphere of the **tenebrous**[6] woods, and they walked as fast as they could. They were delighted to see that the trees became thinner as they advanced. But suddenly they stopped, for before them was a broad, swiftly flowing river.

---

[1] **voracious** If you're *voracious*, you greatly crave something (usually food); your appetite (for it) is hard to satisfy. You'll often hear the phrase *voracious reader*, which refers to someone who loves to read (he can't get enough). *Looking over a published list of animals considered voracious, I was surprised to find that the sharp-toothed piranha was not included but that Cookie Monster was!*

[2] **predator (predators)** A *predator* is an animal that lives by seizing and eating other animals. The adjective is *predatory*, as in *wolves are predatory animals*. But if you refer to a person as *predatory* (or as a *predator*), you don't mean he eats live animals; you mean he greedily takes whatever he wants. *When disturbed, octopuses eject a dark ink, which hides them from predators.*

[3] **din** A *din* is any (usually prolonged) noisy jumble of sound— the kind of loud but indistinct sound you might hear in a crowded restaurant or a machine shop, for example. *The noon whistle pierced the din of the factory.*

[4] **impale (impaled)** To *impale* someone (or something) is to pierce through his body with something long and pointed (like a sharpened stake or spike). *In the last scene of the movie, the villain fell from the roof and was impaled on the sharp, spiked fence below.*

[5] **baleful** Anything that's *baleful* in some way (either intentionally or unintentionally) threatens or foreshadows evil or harm (which may or may not actually occur). *The vampire Count Dracula was played in films by actor Bela Lugosi, whose Hungarian accent and baleful eye have become associated with the character.*

[6] **tenebrous** This word, which derives from the Latin word for darkness, means "dark and gloomy." *As seen in his masterpiece* The Descent from the Cross, *Rembrandt was able to increase the dramatic impact of his paintings by setting partially illuminated figures against tenebrous backgrounds.*

Chapter 7 "The River"

On the other side of the river they could see brilliant sunshine, **azure**[1] skies, and beautiful, green meadows studded with brightly colored flowers. And **wafting**[2] across the water was the delightful aroma of the delicious fruits that hung from the trees that bordered the yellow brick road.

"How will we cross the river?" Dorothy asked.

"That's easy," said the Scarecrow. "The Tin Woodman can chop logs and fasten them together to make a raft. We'll float across."

So the Tin Woodman set to work by chopping down small trees. But it takes a long time to build a raft, even when one is as **assiduous**[3] as the Tin Woodman. By nightfall, the work was still not done, and Dorothy, now comfortably **ensconced**[4] in a bed of dry leaves, fell asleep.

The next morning the raft was finished, and Dorothy and her

---

[1] **azure** This word means "light blue"; specifically, the color of the sky on a clear, cloudless day. *Speaking of the Egyptian sunset, British photographer Cecil Beaton once said, "More varied than any landscape was the landscape in the sky, with islands of gold and silver, peninsulas of apricot and rose against a background of many shades of turquoise and azure."*

[2] **waft (wafting)** To *waft* is to float gently through (or be carried through) the air (as an aroma, for example). *She told us she finally succeeded in getting her teenage son out of bed before noon— by allowing the aroma of cooking bacon to waft through the house at about 10:30!*

[3] **assiduous** This word means "persevering," especially when combined with "attentive." In other words, if you work hard and continuously (at some task or toward some goal), and especially if you do this work carefully (with attention to detail), you're *assiduous* (or your effort is *assiduous*). *The publication in 1928 of the massive, multivolume Oxford English Dictionary required decades of assiduous reading, writing, and editing.*

[4] **ensconce (ensconced)** To *ensconce* yourself in something (an armchair, for example) is to comfortably and securely settle yourself in it. *We finally found the cat in the bedroom, ensconced among the pillows.*

THE WIZARD OF OZ VOCABULARY BUILDER

friends awakened feeling refreshed and full of hope. The **halcyon**[1] landscape across the river seemed to **herald**[2] an **auspicious**[3] new chapter in their **peregrinations**[4].

Dorothy sat at the middle of the raft with Toto in her arms. When the massive Lion stepped on, the raft **listed**[5] so severely to **starboard**[6] that it appeared the vessel might **founder**[1]. The

---

[1] **halcyon** This word (pronounced *HAL-see-in*) can mean "peaceful, calm, tranquil" as in *halcyon weather*, but more often it means "happy and carefree" (especially when referring to past times), as in *halcyon days of youth*. The word derives from the name of a mythical bird (halcyon) which was said to have the power to calm the wind and waves as it bred in a nest floating on the sea. *In Alfred Hitchcock's 1943 film* Shadow of a Doubt, *a girl's halcyon existence is destroyed when she suspects that the visiting uncle she loves is really the Merry Widow Murderer.*

[2] **herald** To *herald* something (that's about to come) is to announce it, give a sign or indication of it, or usher it in. As a noun, a *herald* is something (or someone) that gives a sign or indication of something (that's about to come). *Robin redbreasts herald the coming of spring.*

[3] **auspicious** If something (an occasion, event, situation, etc.) is *auspicious*, its circumstances are favorable and a successful or happy outcome is thus indicated or suggested. *In October 1908, on the auspicious occasion of the birth of the Model T, Henry Ford said, "I will build a motor car for the great multitude."*

[4] **peregrination (peregrinations)** A *peregrination* is a traveling or journeying (from one place to another), especially on foot. The word is usually used in the plural. *During his peregrinations in the Ohio River valley, Johnny Appleseed planted apple seeds, pruned apple trees, and encouraged settlers to start orchards.*

[5] **list (listed)** This is a verb that usually applies to boats (or any water vessels). When a boat *lists*, it leans (or tilts or slants) to one side. *In most movies about the December 7, 1941, surprise Japanese air attack on Pearl Harbor, you can see American ships listing, burning, or sinking.*

[6] **starboard** When speaking of a ship (or aircraft), *starboard* refers to the right side, as you face the front from within. (The left side is called *port*.) *I requested a starboard cabin on our southbound cruise ship because I wanted to watch the sun set from our stateroom window.*

THE WIZARD OF OZ VOCABULARY BUILDER

Scarecrow and the Tin Woodman quickly positioned themselves on the **port**[2] side, one near the **bow**[3] and the other near the **stern**[4], and this way they were able to steady the wobbly craft.

With long poles held in their hands, the Scarecrow and the Tin Woodman, pushing against the river bottom, began propelling the raft across the river. They moved along quite well at first, but when they reached the middle of the river, the strong, **inexorable**[5] current swept them downstream, further and further away from the yellow brick road.

In an effort to stop the **errant**[6] raft, the Scarecrow pushed hard

---

[1] **founder** When a ship *founders*, it sinks (or fills with water and sinks). *Over 1500 people drowned when, on its maiden voyage in April 1912, the* Titanic *foundered after colliding with an iceberg.* The word is also used figuratively to mean "to fail utterly, collapse." *After his second marriage to Elizabeth Taylor foundered, Richard Burton said, "Our love is so furious that we burn each other out."*

[2] **port** When speaking of a ship (or aircraft), *port* refers to the left side, as you face the front from within. (The right side is called *starboard*.) *She requested a port cabin on our southbound cruise ship because she wanted to watch the sun rise from our stateroom window.*

[3] **bow** The *bow* (rhymes with *now*) is the front part of a ship (or any water vessel). (The rear part is called the *stern*.) *Ancient warships were often equipped with "beaks": metal projections on the bow to ram enemy vessels.*

[4] **stern** The *stern* is the rear part of a ship (or any water vessel). (The front part is called the *bow*.) *Many warships are equipped with "stern chasers": special backward-pointing guns or cannons mounted on the stern for firing at pursuing vessels.*

[5] **inexorable** If something is *inexorable*, it cannot be swayed or diverted from its (usually inevitable) course; it's relentless, unyielding, unalterable. *Unwilling to submit to the inexorable forces of weather and time that break down mountains, Japan, in 1982, erected a wall to halt erosion of the perfectly formed, snow-capped cone of their sacred Mount Fuji.*

[6] **errant** This word has two meanings. The first is "wandering or moving about aimlessly." *The errant calves were quickly lassoed and brought back into the herd.* In another sense, if you're *errant*, your action or behavior deviates from the proper course, or it deviates from accepted standards. *Every profession (medicine, law, journalism, politics, etc.) must have some means for excluding or punishing errant members.*

on his pole and it stuck fast in the **viscous**[1] mud. Before he could pull it back out or even let go, the raft was swept away from under his feet, and the **hapless**[2] Scarecrow was left clinging to the pole in the middle of the river!

Soon the **careering**[3] raft was far downstream, and the Lion, realizing something must be done to save them, said to the Tin Woodman, "I'll jump into the water and swim to shore. If you hold on to the end of my tail, the raft will be pulled along behind me."

The Lion swam **tenaciously**[4], but the **implacable**[5] current was hard to overcome. Eventually he managed to draw the raft out of the flow, and Dorothy, taking the long pole from the Tin

---

[1] **viscous** If a liquid is *viscous*, it's thick and sticky; it doesn't flow easily. Tar and honey, for example, are viscous liquids. The noun is *viscosity*. *Some volcanic lava is too viscous to flow very far; consequently, it piles over the volcano's open top, forming a dome over it.*

[2] **hapless** If you're *hapless*, you're unlucky or unfortunate; bad things seem to happen to you for no apparent reason. *On their way out, the bank robbers smacked the hapless guard across the face.*

[3] **career (careering)** Everyone knows that as a noun, your *career* is your chosen occupation or profession. But as a verb, to *career* is to move along at top speed (or at least to move rapidly, to rush). *When its brakes failed, the 18-wheeler careered down the hill.* Note: Don't confuse this word with *careen*, which means "to swerve or lurch while in motion," or (of ships) "to slant to one side."

[4] **tenacious (tenaciously)** If you're *tenacious* (about achieving some goal, clinging to an idea or object, or upholding some principle), you're persistent and enduringly stubborn about it; you won't give up or admit defeat. The noun is *tenacity*. *According to Disney movies, nobody fought more tenaciously at the historic battle of the Alamo than Davy Crockett.*

[5] **implacable** People who are *implacable* can't be soothed or satisfied; they refuse to change (a behavior or an opinion). *Some historians believe that what really ended the Civil War in 1965 was Ulysses S. Grant's implacable policy of concentrating all his efforts on dividing and destroying the Confederate armies.* Things that are implacable are relentless and unalterable. *Floods and mudslides from implacable rains caused widespread property damage in Southern California in January 1969.*

THE WIZARD OF OZ VOCABULARY BUILDER

Woodman, **conned**[1] the craft to shore.

With the rafting **fiasco**[2] behind them, it was now time to find their way back to the Scarecrow and the yellow brick road. The Lion thought the best plan would be to simply walk along the riverbank toward where they had started. So, with their **flagging**[3] energy restored by a short rest, they began their journey upstream.

As they walked they couldn't help but **imbibe**[4] the beauty of the scenery. **Myriads**[5] of **motes**[1], **hitherto**[2] invisible, now flitted

---

[1] **con (conned)** To *con* (also spelled *conn*) a ship is to steer it (or direct the steering of it). (The enclosed, raised area from which a warship is steered is called a "conning tower.") *We knew that a "pilot" is a person who flies an airplane; then we learned that "pilot" is also the word for a person who, though not belonging to a ship's company, is licensed to con the ship into and out of port or through dangerous waters.*

[2] **fiasco** Something referred to as a *fiasco* is a complete failure in which everything goes wrong. *The 1961 Bay of Pigs fiasco, in which about 1400 CIA-trained Cuban exiles tried to overthrow Castro but were killed or taken prisoner, was probably the most embarrassing episode in the Presidency of John F. Kennedy, who had approved the mission.*

[3] **flag (flagging)** When something *flags*, it decreases in energy, vitality, strength, activity, or interest. *In 1976 New Jersey legalized casino gambling in Atlantic City to help revive the city's flagging economy.*

[4] **imbibe** Depending on the context, this word can mean "to drink," or "to take in or absorb (in the mind), as if by drinking." When the word means literally "to drink" and it's used without an object, alcoholic beverages are implied, as in *I imbibe only once a year— on New Year's Eve.* When your mind *imbibes*, it absorbs some concept or idea (knowledge, beauty, etc.). *With the enthusiastic encouragement of her Spanish-born husband (actor José Ferrer), singer Rosemary Clooney imbibed the music, art, and culture of Europe on her very first trip to the continent.*

[5] **myriad (myriads)** This word derives from a Greek word for "ten thousand." But today the word refers to any large or uncountable number (of something). As an adjective it means either "countless," as in *myriad fish in the sea*, or "composed of numerous, diverse elements," as in *American cookery is the product of myriad influences.* As a noun the word can be used in the singular ("a myriad of") or the plural ("myriads of.") *In building the first atomic bomb, researchers worked furiously to solve a myriad of scientific problems.*

evanescently[3] as the wind whisked them through parallel bars of sunlight. And beyond them Dorothy saw a copse[4] of pretty trees festooned[5] with multicolored fruits. If not for her deep concern for the Scarecrow, Dorothy could have been very happy on this side of the river.

All at once the Tin Woodman pointed and cried out "Look!" Dorothy and the Lion saw the Scarecrow still perched on his pole in the middle of the river, his usual cheerful countenance[6]

---

[1] **mote (motes)** A *mote* is a tiny speck or particle. Specifically, people usually use this word to refer to tiny specks of floating dust that become visible when struck by direct sunlight. *I thought that by buying a bedroom air purifier I would solve my allergy problem; but in the morning when I opened the shades and the sunlight poured in, I saw that the room was filled with dust motes!*

[2] **hitherto** This word means "until now; formerly." *After the Watergate affair, Democrats elected the hitherto unknown Jimmy Carter as President.*

[3] **evanescent (evanescently)** If something is *evanescent*, it lasts for only a very short time; it's fleeting; it tends to disappear quickly, like vapor. *According to my friend Bruce's "moments" theory, all the really good parts of your life add up to nothing more than a series of pleasurable but evanescent moments.*

[4] **copse** A *copse* of trees is a clump (group, thicket) of trees standing by itself. *In 1964 New York's Fire Island (a sandy, narrow, 30-mile-long island off the southern coast of Long Island) was made a national seashore; as such, it's animals, beaches, dunes, and copses of pine trees are protected by federal law.*

[5] **festoon (festooned)** A decorative string, chain (sometimes of flowers or leaves), ribbon, etc., that's suspended in a curve between two points is called a *festoon.* As a verb, to *festoon* is to hang such a decoration (or something similar). *He knew he'd walked into his own surprise party, because, even before everyone shouted "surprise," he saw, festooned on the wall, a long piece of colored paper with the words "Happy Birthday, Bill."*

[6] **countenance** Your *countenance* is your facial expression. *After a 1960 meeting with David Ben Gurion, French president Charles de Gaulle described the Israeli Prime Minister as "a lion with a lion's countenance."*

metamorphosed[1] into a **scowl**[2]. They tried to think of a way to help him but couldn't, so they just sat on the riverbank and gazed at him **commiseratively**[3].

After a while, a Stork happened to fly by and, seeing Dorothy and her friends, stopped to rest near them. When the large bird gazed at them **quizzically**[4], Dorothy introduced herself and her friends and told the Stork about their trip to the Emerald City. "The only problem," Dorothy finished, looking **wistfully**[5] toward the river, "is that we've lost the Scarecrow."

The Stork eyed the Scarecrow thoughtfully and said, "If he weren't so big, I would get him for you."

---

[1] **metamorphose (metamorphosed)** To *metamorphose* is to change into a completely different form or appearance. (The word is related to *metamorphosis*, which, you may remember from biology class, is the term for the change in form of an animal during normal development after the embryonic stage; for example, through metamorphosis a caterpillar changes into a butterfly and a tadpole becomes a frog.) *In Robert Louis Stevenson's classic tale, the good Dr. Jekyll, after drinking a potion, metamorphoses into the cruel, sadistic Mr. Hyde.*

[2] **scowl** A *scowl* is a facial expression that, usually accompanied by a drawing in of the eyebrows, expresses anger or displeasure. As a verb, to *scowl* is to put on a dark, threatening, angry, or displeased expression. *When he asked his fiancée if she'd like to go camping on their honeymoon, she scowled and said, "What are we, chipmunks?"*

[3] **commiserate (commiseratively)** When you *commiserate* with someone (who suffered some misfortune), you sympathize with him; you express your sorrow (to him); you act like you share his pain. *In 1990, speaking of heroes, British author Jeanette Winterson said, "It's true that heroes are inspiring, but mustn't they also do some rescuing if they are to be worthy of their name? Would Wonder Woman matter if she only sent commiserating telegrams to the distressed?"*

[4] **quizzical (quizzically)** To describe something (a facial expression, for example) as *quizzical* is to say that it's questioning or puzzled. *When Bruce Springsteen took the stage, she turned to me with a quizzical look and asked, "Why is everyone booing him?" (I explained that they weren't yelling "boo," they were yelling "Bruce!").*

[5] **wistful (wistfully)** If you're *wistful*, you're sadly thoughtful; you're longing or yearning (for something). *In his "Prayer for Animals," French theologian and medical missionary Albert Schweitzer (1875–1965) prayed for "all wistful creatures in captivity that beat their wings against bars."*

"But he's very, very light because he's made of straw," urged Dorothy **beseechingly**[1], hoping this **riposte**[2] would convince the bird to at least try.

"I'll try," said the Stork, "but if he's too **cumbersome**[3], I'll have to drop him in the river." And with that the bird suddenly flew to the Scarecrow.

She tried to lift him, but he desperately clung to the still-stuck pole. "Pull up if I pull up," she coached him **palindromically**[4]. Then with her strong, sharp **talons**[5] she pulled on his shoulders as he did on the pole, and she easily carried him, pole still in hand, to the shore.

---

[1] **beseech (beseechingly)** To *beseech* is to beg, or to earnestly request. Sometimes the word carries with it an implication of eagerness or anxiety. *In the Leopold-Loeb "thrill killing" murder case of 1924, criminal attorney Clarence Darrow introduced psychiatric evidence and beseeched the court to have mercy on the defendants; the result was a verdict of life imprisonment rather than the death penalty.*

[2] **riposte** A *riposte* is a quick, sharp reply (sometimes in response to an insult or challenge). (The term comes from the sport of fencing, where a *riposte* is a quick thrust in response to an opponent's lunge.) *When Lady Astor, first female member of the British Parliament, said to Winston Churchill, "If I were married to you, I'd put poison in your coffee," Churchill answered with this riposte: "If I were married to you, I'd drink it!"*

[3] **cumbersome** Something that's *cumbersome* is awkward or difficult to carry, move, manipulate, deal with, or handle because it's heavy, large, or clumsy. *The medieval suit of armor, while cumbersome, was an effective protective covering.*

[4] **palindrome (palindromically)** A *palindrome* is a word, phrase, or sentence that reads the same backwards as forwards, such as "A man, a plan, a canal, Panama!" *A humorous palindrome we heard was "Kay, a red nude, peeped under a yak."*

[5] **talon (talons)** A *talon* is the claw of a bird (especially a bird of prey). *In the Great Seal of the United States, the American eagle holds an olive branch (of peace) in its right talon and arrows (of war) in its left.*

THE WIZARD OF OZ VOCABULARY BUILDER

The Scarecrow was so happy to be on dry land with his **cronies**[1] again that, after flinging away the pole, he **capered**[2] about **ebulliently**[3], stopping only to momentarily hug each of them. Finally, exhausted from his own **revelry**[4], he quit the **histrionics**[5], sat down, and said with sincere gratitude to his rescuer, "If I ever get any brains, I'd like to do some kindness for you in return." But

---

[1] **crony (cronies)** A *crony* is a long-time close friend, especially one whose company you often keep. Sometimes the word has political implications; for example, the term *cronyism* refers to the practice of favoring one's friends in political appointments. *The 1988 film* Married to the Mob *is about a Mafia widow trying to escape the clutches of her husband's cronies.*

[2] **caper (capered)** To *caper* is to playfully (and usually happily) leap (skip, hop, etc.) about. (The word comes from the Latin word for "male goat," and, as you know, males goats playfully leap about.) *In a famous fairy tale, every time Rumpelstiltskin's name is guessed incorrectly, he gleefully capers about.*

[3] **ebullient (ebulliently)** If you're *ebullient*, you're bubbling up with enthusiasm, excitement, or spirit. *On the first day of summer vacation the children were ebullient; by the second day they were bored.*

[4] **revel (revelry)** As a verb, to *revel* is either to take delight or great pleasure (in something), as in *he reveled in his sudden wealth*, or to indulge in noisy, unrestrained partying or celebrating, as in *on New Year's Eve they reveled for hours*. As a noun, a *revel* is noisy, unrestrained merrymaking. *Revelry* is the act of *reveling. According to* Compton's Encyclopedia, *"the earligest celebrations of Mardi Gras in New Orleans began in 1766 with masked balls and [indecent] street processions. By 1806 the annual revelry had gotten so out of hand that Mardi Gras celebrations were forbidden, but the law was widely ignored."*

[5] **histrionics** Exaggerated, artificial, or theatrical emotional behavior (arm waving, yelling, etc.) done for effect is known as *histrionics*. The adjective is *histrionic* ("excessively emotional or dramatic"). *In her review of the 1987 film* Orphans *(which concerns a gangster who befriends two homeless young men), critic Rita Kempley said, "Not since Shelley Winters sank with the* Poseidon *have we seen such histrionics."*

the Stork, politely **deprecating**[1] what she had done, **altruistically**[2] assured the Scarecrow that no repayment was expected, and with that the bird wished them luck and flew off.

---

[1] **deprecate (deprecating)** To *deprecate* something (an accomplishment, for example) is to minimize it (to make it seem less important). *Because he didn't want to seem conceited, he deprecated his heroism by saying, "Oh shucks, it was nothing."* Note: The word can also mean "to express disapproval of (something)." *Although a slaveholder, statesman Henry Clay (1777–1852) deprecated slavery as a system.*

[2] **altruistic (altruistically)** If you're *altruistic*, you're unselfishly concerned for the welfare of others; you're generous, charitable. The noun is *altruism*. An altruistic person is called an *altruist*. *The Marshall Plan (also known as the European Recovery Program), which channeled over $13 billion to finance the economic recovery of Europe between 1948 and 1951, was seen by most historians as a representation of American altruism.*

73

Chapter 8 "The Poppies"

As they all walked further upstream, they heard the **dulcet**[1] songs of birds and the gentle **plash**[2] of the river waves as they **lapped**[3] the shoreline. Their eyes were drawn by brilliantly colored flowers that dotted the **bucolic**[4] landscape. Yellow, white, blue, and purple ones were scattered about, but it was the great clusters of brilliant, **scarlet**[5] poppies that dazzled Dorothy's eyes. The further they walked, the thicker the flowers became, until they formed a carpet beneath their feet.

As they continued walking, all the while breathing in the spicy scent of the flowers, they began to notice a **plethora**[6] of red poppies

---

[1] **dulcet** A sound that's *dulcet* is pleasing to the ear; it's appealing, soothing, or melodious. *Examining the lyrics to the song "The Sound of Music," we found several images of dulcet sounds: a church chime flying on a breeze, a brook laughing, and a lark singing while learning to pray (though we seriously doubted that larks learn how to pray!).*

[2] **plash** A *plash* is a light (gentle, small) splash (of water). It can also mean the sound of a light splash. *Though it was pitch dark, we knew we were approaching the fountain by its distinctive, repetitive plash.*

[3] **lap (lapped)** When water *laps* something, it washes or slaps against it with soft splashing sounds. *The waves lapped the side of the dock.*

[4] **bucolic** Land that's *bucolic* is rustic or rural; it's out in the country. *As evidenced by his most famous work,* The Blue Boy, *British painter Thomas Gainsborough (1727–1788) often set the subjects of his portraits in bucolic landscapes.*

[5] **scarlet** *Scarlet* is a color; it's bright red or reddish orange. *In a famous novel by Nathaniel Hawthorne (1804–1864), a woman who commits adultery is forced to wear a scarlet letter A on her dress as a symbol of her guilt.*

[6] **plethora** A *plethora* (of something) is either a large amount or an overabundance (of it). Note: In pronunciation, the accent is on the first syllable *(PLETH-o-ra)*. *The large number of Davy Crockett books that appeared in the mid 1800s was nothing compared to the plethora of Davy Crockett merchandise that appeared in the 1950s.*

and a **paucity**[1] of the other blossoms. Soon they found themselves in the center of a vast meadow of poppies. Now, nearly everyone knows that when you have great numbers of poppies, their fragrance is so **potent**[2] that anyone who breathes it falls asleep. And if the sleeper isn't carried away from the **cloying**[3] perfume, he'll sleep on forever!

But Dorothy didn't know this, and soon the **somniferous**[4] effect of the poppies caused her eyes to grow heavy, and she announced that she must lie down. But the Tin Woodman and the Scarecrow, who, not being human, were unaffected by the poppies, wouldn't permit this. They took the **somnolent**[5] little girl by the arms and

---

[1] **paucity** A *paucity* (of something) is a smallness or insufficiency of number or amount (of it); a scarcity. *In December 1983 journalist Warren Brown reported that "eight of the 15 people who work at the Center for Auto Safety don't own cars [and that the Center's director] says the paucity of cars reflects the paucity of pay."*

[2] **potent** Something that's *potent* is strong; it has power; it's capable of producing or exerting a strong effect or influence. *After the 19th Amendment guaranteed women the right to vote, Carrie Chapman Catt (founder of the League of Women Voters) sought to make women voters a potent force in national politics.*

[3] **cloy (cloying)** Something that *cloys* (or that's *cloying*), starts out as sweet or pleasant (such as a taste, smell, or sentiment), but becomes unpleasant or even disgusting when too much (of it) has been supplied. *I never knew how cloying sweets could be until I first moved out of my parents' house and made a meal of 12 chocolate donuts and two root beers.*

[4] **somniferous** Something *somniferous* (a drug or a boring speech, for example) makes you feel sleepy; it induces sleep or drowsiness. *I never understood the point of drinking Irish coffee (a mixture of sweetened hot coffee and Irish whiskey); after all, wouldn't the somniferous effect of the whiskey and the arousing effect of the coffee cancel each other out?*

[5] **somnolent** This word, when used to describe a person or thing, means "sleepy" or "drowsy," as in *the somnolent child who stayed up past her bedtime*, or *the somnolent little Southern town*. The word can also be used (though not as often) to describe something (a drug or hot weather, for example) that causes you to feel sleepy, as in *the somnolent tropical air*. *From its beginnings as a somnolent pueblo of only 44 people, Los Angeles has become a bustling international metropolis.*

goaded[1] her along, lest she **succumb**[2] once and for all to the **insidious**[3] spell of the flowers.

With her friends supporting her by the arms, Dorothy **somnambulated**[4] awhile. But then her lifeless form suddenly collapsed to the ground. "What shall we do?" asked the Tin Woodman, **ruefully**[5] gazing at the pathetic, **prostrate**[1] figure at

---

[1] **goad (goaded)** Technically, a *goad* is a long, pointed stick used for prodding animals. But when you *goad* someone (into doing something) you strongly urge, prod, prompt, or drive him. *In a famous play by Shakespeare, Scottish nobleman Macbeth, misled by the predictions of three witches and goaded on by his wife, seizes the throne by murdering his cousin, King Duncan.*

[2] **succumb** To *succumb* to something (usually an overpowering force or desire) is to give in to it, to yield to it. Often there's an implication of helplessness on the part of the one who *succumbs*. *In his last film, actor John Wayne played an aging gunfighter dying of cancer, an illness the actor himself succumbed to three years later.*

[3] **insidious** If something is *insidious*, it's in some way harmful, but it works (or spreads, proceeds, operates, etc.) in a subtle or inconspicuous manner; it sneaks up on you, so to speak. *Syphilis, which occurs in four stages, is a particularly insidious disease: the symptoms of the first three stages, even when left untreated, are either mild or non-existent; but in its final stage the disease can cause blindness, deafness, paralysis, or insanity.*

[4] **somnambulate (somnambulated)** To *somnambulate* is to sleepwalk. The word derives from the Latin words for "sleep" (somnus) and "walk" (ambulatus). *In our favorite episode of the 1950s TV series* The Honeymooners, *Ralph believed that Norton somnambulated because he was searching for his lost dog, Lulu.*

[5] **rueful** When something (a look, expression, etc.) is *rueful*, it shows or expresses sorrow or pity. When a person is *rueful*, he feels or shows sorrow or pity. Sometimes you'll see the phrase "rueful smile," which seems contradictory but refers to a smile that somehow expresses sorrow, pity, or remorse. *According to an article in* Time *magazine, "[paperback books], as older collectors have ruefully discovered, fade and fall apart even more rapidly than their owners."*

their feet.

The Lion's energy, too, was now seriously beginning to **ebb**[2]. At best he would remain **ambulatory**[3] for only a few minutes more. And poor Toto was already deeply asleep.

"Run fast," said the Scarecrow to the Lion. "Get out of the poppy field as fast as you can. If you fall asleep here you'll die. We can carry Dorothy and Toto, but you're too big to carry." So with great determination of will, and despite a nearly incapacitating **torpor**[4], the great beast somehow managed to **shore**[1] himself up; he

---

[1] **prostrate** If someone is *prostrate*, he's lying down flat, at full length, as on the ground. A condition of physical incapacity is sometimes implied. Some people use the word to mean "lying flat, face down"; others use it to mean simply "lying flat" (facing either way). The word is usually used to describe people but can also describe objects, as in *prostrate trees*. Don't confuse this word with "prostate," which is a gland (near the bladder) in males. *No matter how many times I visit Manhattan, I can't get used to the sight of homeless people prostrate on the sidewalk.*

[2] **ebb** When something *ebbs*, it declines, recedes, or fades away; it becomes less. The phrase "ebb tide" refers to the receding or outgoing (ocean) tide. The phrase "ebb and flow" refers to alternating periods of decrease and increase (of something), as in *the ebb and flow of the economy.* As a noun, an *ebb* is a low point. *Columnist Art Buchwald once observed, "Every time you think television has hit its lowest ebb, a new program comes along to make you wonder where you thought the ebb was."*

[3] **ambulatory** If you're *ambulatory*, you're capable of walking (as opposed to, say, being bedridden or in a wheelchair). *An institution that provides medical diagnosis and treatment for ambulatory patients is usually called a "clinic," not a "hospital."*

[4] **torpor** A state of physical (or mental) inactivity, inertness, or sluggishness is known as *torpor*. The word can refer to a state of suspended animation, like hibernation, but more often it merely suggests a state of physical sluggishness (usually with an implication of accompanying indifference). The adjective is *torpid*. *In the daytime hummingbirds can be seen darting through the air at 60 miles an hour, or hovering with their wings beating 75 times per second; maybe that's why at night they lapse into a state of torpor!*

bounded forward and was soon out of sight.

Now the Scarecrow and the Tin Woodman picked up Toto and placed him in Dorothy's lap. They crisscrossed their hands to form a seat, and with a deep sense of purpose, they **steadfastly**[2] carried the sleeping child between them through the flowers' sweet but **noxious**[3] fumes.

They walked on and on, following the river upstream, and it seemed as if the great carpet of poppies would never end. Finally they came upon the Lion, lying asleep among the **baneful**[4] flowers. He had at last given up, only a short distance from the end of the

---

[1] **shore** As a noun, a *shore* (in addition to being land along the edge of a body of water) is a post (or beam) propped against a structure to provide support. As a verb, to *shore* (up) is to give (added) support (to something), as if with a *shore*. So when you "shore yourself up," you pull yourself together and give yourself strength (in preparation for some crisis, battle, or other trying or difficult situation). *Marie Antoinette's marriage to Louis XVI, made only to shore up France's ties with Austria (where she was born), was not consummated for seven years.*

[2] **steadfast (steadfastly)** If you're *steadfast* (about something, such as a loyalty, principle, purpose, conviction, or course of action), you're firm, fixed, steady, or unwavering (about it). *According to the Bible, a man named Job steadfastly praised God, even when all his possessions were destroyed, his children were killed, and his body became covered with sores.*

[3] **noxious** If something (a fume, odor, etc.) is *noxious*, it's bad for your health; it causes you harm; it makes you sick, as in *noxious chemical waste*. Similarly, a concept (idea, plan, etc.) described as *noxious* is morally harmful. *Though we didn't know very much about science, we assumed that the black smoke we saw coming out of a truck's exhaust pipe was noxious— or at least more noxious than white smoke would have been.*

[4] **baneful** Something *baneful* is poisonous, destructive, or exceedingly harmful; it can cause death, sickness, or ruin. (The noun *bane* refers to a deadly poison or to something that causes death, destruction, or ruin.) Usage note: While the word *baleful* is used to describe something that foreshadows harm or evil (*a baleful atmosphere*), *baneful* is used to describe something that actually causes harm or destruction. *Sometimes you know right away if a plant is baneful because it actually contains the word* bane *as part of its name; for example, wolfsbane.*

flowerbed. Beautiful, green meadows **loomed**[1] just beyond.

The Scarecrow and the Tin Woodman looked down at the sleeping beast and knew at once there was nothing they could do for him. With wretched anguish they agreed that they would have to leave him to sleep on forever, for he was much too massive to lift. They both now tried to think of some **felicitous**[2], **epitaphic**[3] remarks to make but were unable to. **Dolefully**[4], the **bereft**[5] but **stalwart**[6] pair walked on until they reached a pretty spot next to

---

[1] **loom (loomed)** When something (especially something massive or indistinct) *looms* (into view), it becomes visible or rises before you. *We turned the corner at 34th Street, and the Empire State Building suddenly loomed before us.*

[2] **felicitous** Something *felicitous* is fitting and appropriate; it's well suited (for the occasion). *In his eulogy for George Washington, soldier and political leader Henry Lee felicitously described our first President as "First in war, first in peace, and first in the hearts of his countrymen."*

[3] **epitaph (epitaphic)** An *epitaph* is a commemorative phrase inscribed on a tombstone. It can also be a short piece of writing (not on a tombstone) that praises someone who died. *In 1986 blue-eyed actor Paul Newman imagined what his own epitaph might say: "Here lies Paul Newman, who died a failure because his eyes turned brown."*

[4] **doleful (dolefully)** If you're *doleful*, you're sorrowful or mournful. The implication is that you're also gloomy. *Because of its doleful call, the turtledove is sometimes called a "mourning dove."*

[5] **bereft** As an adjective, this word usually means "suffering the death of a loved one," as in *bereft parents crying over the loss of their daughter;* but it sometimes simply means "deprived (of something)," as in *bereft of his dignity.* As a verb, the word (also *bereaved*) is the past tense of *bereave,* which means "to deprive (especially by death)," as in *a sudden heart attack bereaved them of their father. In 1884, after his wife and mother died within a few hours of each other, a bereft Teddy Roosevelt temporarily retired to his ranch in the Dakota territory.*

[6] **stalwart** If you're both strong (physically or morally) and determined (unwaveringly fixed in purpose), you're *stalwart.* As a noun, a *stalwart* is a strong supporter (of some organization or cause), as in *Republican Party stalwarts. With the help of Annie Sullivan, her stalwart companion and teacher, Hellen Keller (who'd lost her sight and hearing at the age of 19 months) was graduated from Radcliffe College with honors.*

the river, far enough away from the flowerbed to prevent any more of the **deleterious**[1] vapors from affecting their **insensate**[2] passenger. Here they lay Dorothy down on the soft grass and patiently waited for the cool, fresh air to revive her.

---

[1] **deleterious** If something is *deleterious*, it's harmful (usually to your health or your body). *In science class we learned that our lymph nodes are little reservoirs that collect bacteria and other deleterious agents and prevent them from entering our blood.*

[2] **insensate** If you're *insensate*, you lack sensation; you're unaware or unconscious. The word can also mean "lacking sensitivity or feeling," as in *an insensate society. In a famous fairy tale, the insensate Sleeping Beauty is awakened by a prince's kiss.*

Chapter 9 "The Mice"

As they waited for Dorothy to awaken, the Scarecrow and the Tin Woodman were suddenly startled by the sound of a low growl. Running toward them at **breakneck**[1] speed was a large, **tawny**[2] wildcat. It must be chasing something, reasoned the Tin Woodman, because its ears were flat against its head, its mouth was **slavering**[3], and its eyes glowed liked fireballs.

As the cat came near, the Tin Woodman saw that before the **feral**[4] **feline**[5], running for its life, was a tiny mouse. Now, even though the Tin Woodman had no heart, he knew it was wrong for

---

[1] **breakneck** To move at *breakneck* speed is to move dangerously fast. *In hindsight, it seemed somehow ironic that what had forced the driver to race toward the emergency room at breakneck speed was the nature of the patient's injury— a broken neck!*

[2] **tawny** *Tawny* is a color; it's yellowish-brown. *The well-known children's story* Tawny Scrawny Lion *is about a lion who's yellowish-brown (like most lions) and skinny (unlike most lions).*

[3] **slaver (slavering)** To *slaver* (pronounced so that the first syllable rhymes with *have*), is to have saliva drooling from your mouth. *I felt sorry for Pavlov's dogs who, at the end of the famous experiment, heard a bell ring even when they weren't fed; I can just picture them: slavering in eager anticipation, then confused, disappointed, and miserable.*

[4] **feral** To describe something (a facial expression, for example) as *feral* is to say that it's suggestive of a wild animal (that is, it's ferocious, brutal, savage, etc.). A *feral* plant or animal is one that exists in its natural or wild state (that is, it's not cultivated or domesticated). *First brought to the New World by 16th-century Spanish explorers, mustangs are small, feral horses of the American West.*

[5] **feline** As an adjective, *feline* means "belonging or pertaining to the cat family (which includes domestic cats, lions, tigers, etc.)" or "catlike." As a noun, a *feline* is an animal of the cat family. *In 1986 author Erica Jong, speaking of Venice, said, "The stones themselves are thick with history, and those cats that dash through the alleyways must surely be the ghosts of the famous dead in feline disguise."*

81

the wildcat to kill such a harmless creature. With his finely **honed**[1] axe, he found himself in a perfect position to **mete**[2] out a little justice. Just as the **odious**[3] brute ran by, the Tin Woodman lifted his blade, and with one sharp, perfectly aimed blow, cleanly **decapitated**[4] him.

Now that the mouse was safe, it stopped short, turned around, and walked slowly back to the Tin Woodman. "Thank you for saving my life," it said in a high, squeaky voice.

"Because I have no heart," the Tin Woodman explained, "I must always be extra careful to help all those in need, even if they are only mice.

---

[1] **hone (honed)** When you *hone* something (a knife, for instance), you sharpen it. Sometimes the word is used to mean "sharpen" in the sense of making something more perfect, as in *he honed his skills. Theatrical agent Robert Kass once told a group of actors how to hone their talent, how to market their talent, how to discipline their talent, and how to type their talent; then he told them they might as well forget about talent.*

[2] **mete** When you *mete out* something (usually punishment or justice) you administer it; you distribute or allot it. *It's the function of a judge to mete out a punishment that fits the crime; knowing that, we didn't envy whoever had to decide the fate of the Mets fan who tried to spur his team on by parachuting into Shea Stadium during the sixth game of the 1986 World Series.*

[3] **odious** Someone (or something) *odious* arouses or deserves intense dislike or hatred; he (or it) is detestable, hateful, repellent, offensive, objectionable, etc. The noun is *odium* (state or quality of being *odious*). *Harriet Beecher Stowe's pre–Civil War novel* Uncle Tom's Cabin *shocked many northerners into a hatred for the odious institution of slavery.*

[4] **decapitate (decapitated)** To *decapitate* someone is to cut off his head. *Not many people know that the guillotine, a machine that uses a large, heavy, falling blade to decapitate people, was devised by a humanitarian French doctor—Joseph Guillotin (1738–1814).*

THE WIZARD OF OZ VOCABULARY BUILDER

The mouse **bristled**[1] and said, "Only mice! Why, I am the Queen— the Queen of all the mice!"

With sincere **reverence**[2], the Tin Woodman bowed and **humbly**[3] said, "Yes, Your Majesty."

"You have done a great and brave thing in saving my life," the Queen said. And as she said this, many other mice came running up. Without leaving out the **lurid**[4] details, the Queen told them how the Tin Woodman had saved her life, and they all listened with **morbid**[5] fascination. Then, in an **imperious**[1] tone, she

---

[1] **bristle (bristled)** When someone *bristles*, he reacts in an angry, irritated, or offended manner (as if his hair were standing or rising stiffly, like the bristles on a brush). *It seemed to us that during the televised hearings (1991) of his appointment to the Supreme Court, Clarence Thomas silently bristled whenever Anita Hill's accusation of sexual harassment was mentioned.*

[2] **reverence** *Reverence* is a feeling of deep respect (for someone or something). The implication is that feelings of awe or devotion are intermingled with that respect. As a verb, to *revere* means "to respect deeply." *In 1985 Pulitzer Prize–winning author James Michener complained, "Russia, France, Germany, and China— they revere their writers; America is still a frontier country that almost shudders at the idea of creative expression."*

[3] **humble (humbly)** Acting or being *humble* is the opposite of acting like you're a big shot. You're modest, unassuming, even perhaps a bit lowly or meek. The noun is *humility* (state or quality of being *humble*). The word can also mean "low in rank, position, or quality," as in *humble origins. Noticing that many highly competent people were also annoyingly arrogant or conceited, we decided that to be truly successful one needed to combine competence with humility.*

[4] **lurid** Something *lurid* is shockingly sensational (or gruesome, ghastly, or horrible). The word is usually used to describe accounts, as in *a lurid account of the murder*, or periodicals, as in *lurid supermarket tabloids. Just by looking at the names of some of those 1930s pulp mystery magazines, such as* Strange Detective Mysteries, Thrilling Mystery, *and* Black Mask, *we knew they would be full of lurid accounts of ghastly crimes.*

[5] **morbid** When you say someone has a *morbid* interest in something (usually in death, disease, or anything gruesome or ghastly), it means he has an unwholesomely gloomy, overly sensitive interest in it. *Many of Alfred Hitchcock's films explore the morbid and macabre elements of human emotion.*

instructed her **minions**[2] to forever after serve the Tin Woodman and obey his slightest wish! In giving **obeisance**[3] to the Queen, the tiny subjects bowed so low that they appeared to be standing on their heads!

"Is there anything we can do to repay you for saving our Queen?" one of the bigger mice **deferentially**[4] asked the Tin Woodman.

"Nothing that I can think of," he answered.

But the Scarecrow, who was trying to think but couldn't because he had no brain, said, "Yes. You can save our friend the Lion who is asleep in the poppy field." And when the mice heard the word "Lion," their little bodies convulsed **apoplectically**[5] and their faces

---

[1] **imperious** Someone who's *imperious* is bossy (in the way a ruler, who's accustomed to commanding, might be); he's arrogantly domineering, overbearing, dictatorial. *We didn't agree with what she said, but her imperious tone ruled out any possibility of argument.*

[2] **minion (minions)** A *minion* is a servile follower or subordinate (of a person in power). *In the 1971 Sharon Tate murder trial, Charles Manson and his minions spent much of the time sitting with their backs to the judge.*

[3] **obeisance** A movement or gesture of the body that shows courteous respect or homage (to a superior) is known as *obeisance* (pronounced *oh-BAY-since*). *Legendary Swiss archer and hero William Tell was forced to shoot an apple off his son's head as punishment for refusing to give obeisance (by bowing to a hat) to an Austrian official.*

[4] **deference (deferentially)** When you courteously yield or submit to someone else's wishes, opinion, judgment, will, etc., you're showing *deference* (you're being *deferential*). *Although he considered it unnecessarily fussy, in deference to his editor he changed "he" to "he or she" throughout the book.*

[5] **apoplectic (apoplectically)** *Apoplexy* is a medical condition marked by a sudden loss of bodily function (as from a stroke). The word is also used to mean "a sudden fit (of anger or rage)". If you're *apoplectic*, you act as if you have *apoplexy*— you have a fit. *Her normally laid-back husband became apoplectic when she told him she'd spent $700 on a fancy mirror.*

turned **ashen**[1].

"L-L-L-Lion?" they all stammered, **quavering**[2] with fear.

The Scarecrow made a **quelling**[3] motion and said, "This Lion is a coward, and he would never hurt you."

His words seemed to **pacify**[4] them somewhat. The mice huddled together and, using their peculiar mouse **patois**[5], discussed the situation. The Scarecrow strained to hear what they were saying, but their squeaky, **argotic**[6] speech was all but **indecipherable**[1].

---

[1] **ashen** Something *ashen* is the color of ashes: grayish-white. If you say that someone's face is *ashen*, you mean that it's very pale or drained of color. *After she identified the body, she turned toward me, her face ashen and overwrought.*

[2] **quaver (quavering)** When something (usually your voice or body) *quavers*, it shakes or trembles (as from fear, nervousness, or weakness). Note: The word can also be applied to birdcalls that trill and quiver. *In hopes of winning the public speaking contest, she rehearsed her speech over and over; then when the big night came, her hopes were dashed by an uncontrollable quavering in her voice.*

[3] **quell (quelling)** When you *quell* an unpleasant emotion (fear, anxiety, worry, etc.), you quiet or calm it. Consequently, if you make a *quelling* motion, you make some gesture that says, in effect, "calm down; it's okay." If you *quell* a disturbance (a disorder, revolt, mutiny, etc.) you put it down forcibly; you suppress it. *In May 1970 at Kent State University, Ohio National Guardsmen, trying to quell an anti-Vietnam War demonstration, shot and killed four students.*

[4] **pacify** When you *pacify* someone, you calm or quiet him; you soothe his anger or agitation; you bring him to a state of peace or tranquility. *A rubber nipple attached to a piece of plastic is so effective in pacifying a crying baby that the device is actually called a "pacifier."*

[5] **patois** A *patois* (pronounced *pa-TWAH*) is a form of nonstandard speech—a regional dialect, an ungrammatical mixture of languages, or the special jargon of some group. *In the South American country of Suriname, the official language is Dutch, but most people speak Sranang Tongo, a native patois.*

[6] **argot (argotic)** The (sometimes almost secret) special vocabulary and expressions of a particular closely knit group (a profession, social class, clique, etc.) is called *argot*. Note: The word can be pronounced so that it rhymes with either *Margo* or *target*. *At the diner we found ourselves one booth away from a group of drug dealers; but because they spoke in the argot of the underworld, we couldn't make sense of what they were saying.*

THE WIZARD OF OZ VOCABULARY BUILDER

Finally, the Queen came forward and said, "Very well. What can we do to help?"

Encouraged by her **acquiescence**[2], the Scarecrow quickly answered, "Do you have many subjects who will obey you?" And when the Queen told him there were thousands, the Scarecrow asked the Queen to summon all her followers and have each one bring a long piece of string.

Immediately, the Queen **peremptorily**[3] ordered her **acolytes**[4] to spread the word. Now, with the **conscription**[5] **decreed**[1], the

---

[1] **indecipherable** If you *decipher* something (something ambiguous, obscure, illegible, etc.), you interpret it or make sense of it. Consequently, if something is *indecipherable*, it can't be deciphered; it's illegible, incomprehensible, etc. *Hieroglyphics (strange symbols and pictures used in ancient Egyptian writing) were so difficult for scholars to decipher that today, indecipherable handwriting is sometimes jokingly referred to as "hieroglyphics."*

[2] **acquiesce (acquiescence)** When you *acquiesce* (to something proposed), you agree or submit (to it) without protest. Often, the implication is that originally you were opposed to it, or at least had some reservations about it. *When we gently urged my strong-willed grandmother to move into a nursing home, she strongly objected, going so far as to say that she'd rather destroy herself; then, a day later, for reasons we never understood, she quietly acquiesced.*

[3] **peremptory (peremptorily)** When you do or say something in a *peremptory* way, you do it in a commanding, self-assured, and decisive way that leaves no opportunity for anyone to resist or argue. *A November 1990 editorial in the* Washington Post *said of Britain's Margaret Thatcher, "Prime Minister since 1979, like many people long in power she had become increasingly peremptory, remote, and dictatorial."*

[4] **acolyte (acolytes)** Originally, an *acolyte* was an altar boy (a priest's attendant). Today the word is used to mean "a follower or attendant (of an important person)." Sometimes the word is used sarcastically or as a put-down to describe servile, boot-licking followers. *Unification Church founder Sun Myung Moon, who is regarded by his acolytes as God's messenger, was convicted (1982) of conspiracy to evade taxes.*

[5] **conscription** *Conscription* is another word for *draft* (compulsory enrollment for military service). *During the Vietnam War, future President Bill Clinton intended to avoid conscription by joining the Reserve Officers Training Corps; he canceled his plans when draft calls were reduced.*

Scarecrow turned his attention to the Tin Woodman. With military precision he said, "Go with your axe to the trees by the river and build a truck that will carry the Lion."

The Tin Woodman worked as quickly as he could, chopping away leaves and branches, making wheels out of short pieces of tree trunk, and **adroitly**[2] fastening all the pieces together with wooden pins. When he finished, he looked down and saw a curious **pullulation**[3] at his feet. The **multitudinous**[4] army had arrived with their strings!

The Scarecrow and the Tin Woodman now began attaching the mice to the truck. One end of each string was tied around the head of a mouse, and the other end was tied to the truck. Of course, the

---

[1] **decree (decreed)** When something (an order, policy, etc.) is *decreed*, it's formally pronounced or put into effect (by some authority). As a noun, a *decree* is an authoritative order (having the force of law). *In 1941 Congress decreed that Thanksgiving should fall on the fourth Thursday of November.*

[2] **adroit (adroitly)** This word (pronounced *uh-DROYT*) can mean "expert or nimble in the use of the hands," as in *an adroit seamstress,* or "skillful, clever, ingenious, adept (in dealing with challenging situations)," as in *an adroit negotiator. Harry Houdini's (1874–1926) adroit maneuvering allowed him to escape from chains, handcuffs, straitjackets, and padlocked containers.*

[3] **pullulate (pullulation)** To *pullulate* is to gather or move in great numbers; to swarm or teem. *While bedridden from a nasty cold during my Caribbean vacation, I reached down to pick up what I thought was my black T-shirt and was horrified to discover I was holding a chain of mucus-covered tissues pullulating with tiny black ants!*

[4] **multitudinous** A *multitude* is a great number (of something). Consequently, to describe something as *multitudinous* is to say that it's very numerous (it exists or is present in great numbers). *The major unit of the multitudinous Roman army was the "legion," consisting of thousands of men.*

truck was a thousand times bigger than any of the **Lilliputian**[1] soldiers who were to draw it, but when all the mice had been harnessed, they were able to pull it quite easily.

When the truck had been drawn alongside the sleeping Lion, the Scarecrow and the Tin Woodman tried to push the beast aboard. This took a **prodigious**[2] effort because the Lion was so **ponderous**[3]. The moment they finally accomplished the **Herculean**[4] task, the Queen ordered her people to start pulling the truck, for she knew

---

[1] **Lilliputian** In Jonathan Swift's 1726 satire *Gulliver's Travels*, the first land Gulliver visits is Lilliput, where the people are only six inches tall. (The most famous image from this book is of the tiny Lilliputians having tied down the sleeping giant, Gulliver.) Consequently, something described as *Lilliputian* (pronounced *lil-i-PYEW-shin*) is very tiny (like the inhabitants of Lilliput). *In February 1993, speaking of drugstores of the future, journalist Jay Mathews said, "The pills bump along on conveyor belts in their little blue, orange, green, or yellow trays like rides at a Lilliputian Disneyland, up and down and across the huge, brightly lit room full of people in white coats. Welcome to your favorite (and perhaps only) drugstore, circa 2010— where prescriptions are filled only by mail."*

[2] **prodigious** This word means "extraordinary or impressive in size, force, amount, extent, degree, etc." *Rembrandt's prodigious output included 600 paintings, 300 etchings, and nearly 2,000 drawings.*

[3] **ponderous** Something *ponderous* is heavy or massive and therefore difficult to move or carry. *Since the 16th century, pictures of the Greek god Atlas and his ponderous burden (the earth on his shoulders) have been used as decorations on maps.* Figuratively, the word is used to mean "lacking in grace, dull, labored" (as of speech or writing). *Many music critics find Leonard Bernstein's Broadway music delightful but his symphonies ponderous.*

[4] **Herculean** Hercules was a mythological hero known for his great strength. If you describe something (a difficult task, for example) as *Herculean*, you mean that it requires the strength of Hercules, or that it's extremely difficult (to accomplish). The word can also simply mean "very strong." *Scholars tell us it was slaves who accomplished the Herculean feat of building the colossal Egyptian pyramids.* Note: The word can also be spelled with a lower case *h* (herculean).

that if the mice **tarried**[1], they, too, would be overcome by the poppies' deadly **miasma**[2].

Here is where the Queen proved her **mettle**[3] as a monarch. Knowing her troops would **perish**[4] if they didn't give their all, and knowing that even a single **goldbricker**[5] could **scuttle**[6] the mission,

---

[1] **tarry (tarried)** To *tarry* is to delay or be slow (when it's time to come, go, start, act, etc.); to linger, wait, pause. *In November 2000 journalist Kevin Merida, calling America a "hurried nation," said, "We are a drive-thru-window culture, an instant-gratification society. Express lanes at the supermarket— no time to tarry. Miracle weight loss belts. Online shopping. Twelve-minute oil changes. Crave long nails? Don't wait for them to grow, just glue them on. This is America— the America of microwaved mashed potatoes."*

[2] **miasma** Thick, vaporous air filled with harmful, dangerous, poisonous, polluting, or foul-smelling material (as air rising from swamps or decaying organic matter, or air in a smoke-filled room) is called a *miasma*. *We decided the cleaning crew did "too good" a job because for the next eight hours or so our eyes stung and our throats burned from a miasma of bleach, ammonia, and powerful (so-called) air fresheners.* Figuratively, the word can be used to describe a pervasive psychological atmosphere (of corruption, danger, harm, etc.), as in *a miasma of deceit.*

[3] **mettle** Your *mettle*, an aspect of your character, is your natural capacity for being strong, courageous, tough, persevering, etc. *In the 1976 film* Rocky, *an underdog's mettle is severely tested when he boxes the world champ.*

[4] **perish** To *perish* is to die. Sometimes the word implies violence, as in *perish in battle;* other times it implies a gradual passing away, as in *perished from starvation. In July 1996, 230 people perished when TWA's Paris-bound Flight 800 exploded in midair off the south shore of Long Island.*

[5] **goldbricker** A *goldbricker* is a person, especially a soldier, who avoids duty or work (usually by pretending to be ill). *We agreed that, throughout American military history, the army general least likely to have tolerated goldbricking was the stern, demanding one they nicknamed "Old Blood and Guts," George Patton.*

[6] **scuttle** When you *scuttle* a ship, you intentionally sink it (usually by cutting or opening holes in its bottom). *Knowing the Coast Guard was approaching, the boat thieves scuttled the ship to get rid of the evidence.* The word also can be used figuratively to mean "to (or cause to) abandon, destroy, discontinue (as plans, hopes, missions, ideas, etc.)." *A sudden storm scuttled the launch of the Space Shuttle.*

she became a **martinet**[1], threatening **draconian**[2] punishments for all who didn't perform.

The truck started to move, and the Queen, unwilling to **brook**[3] any sign of **sloth**[4], **meticulously**[5] watched over the proceedings. Any mouse without **fervor**[6] in his eyes she **hectored**[1] mercilessly.

---

[1] **martinet** A *martinet* is a strict disciplinarian, especially a military one (named after a 17th-century French army general, Jean Martinet). *Demanding legendary orchestra conductor Leopold Stokowski once said, "On matters of intonation and technicalities I am more than a martinet— I am a martinetissimo."*

[2] **draconian** Draco, a statesman of ancient Athens, was known for the severity of his code of laws (for example, imposing the death penalty for a trivial offense). So when you describe penalties, rules, laws, etc., as *draconian*, you mean they are very strict, severe, or harsh, sometimes unreasonably so. *At a 1985 UN ceremony honoring his work against the draconian racist policies of apartheid, singer Stevie Wonder referred to South Africa as "the land with tears in her eyes."* Note: The word *draconic* can mean either "draconian" or "of or like a dragon."

[3] **brook** As a verb, to *brook* something is to tolerate it, to put up with it. People always use this word in the negative; they say they won't (or refuse to) *brook* something or other. *I didn't even bother saying that my dog ate my homework because I knew our teacher wouldn't brook any excuses.*

[4] **sloth** This word means "laziness" or "habitual aversion to work or exertion." *Sociologists have concluded that poverty is more likely to be caused by unsteady employment than by sloth.*

[5] **meticulous (meticulously)** When you're *meticulous* about something (or about doing something) you're extremely careful about it, especially about the minute details of it; you're fussy, painstaking. *The Walt Disney studios are known for meticulous craftsmanship in full-length animated features, such as 1938's* Snow White and the Seven Dwarfs *and 1940's* Pinocchio.

[6] **fervor** When you do something with *fervor*, you do it with intensity of feeling, with warmth, passion, earnestness, eagerness, etc. *When gospel music is performed in church, correct vocal technique is usually not as important as religious fervor.*

THE WIZARD OF OZ VOCABULARY BUILDER

Malingerers[2] were yanked to their feet by their ears. With the Scarecrow and the Tin Woodman pushing the truck from behind, they soon rolled it out of the deadly flowers and onto the sweet, green grass.

The mice were unharnessed, and they all ran off to their homes. The Queen was the last to remain. The Tin Woodman sincerely thanked her for saving their companion, while the Scarecrow enthusiastically praised her leadership skills. Not one to rest on her **laurels**[3], she said, "If you ever need our help again, just call and we shall come to your assistance. Good-bye." Then she was gone. Now the Scarecrow and the Tin Woodman, **recumbent**[4] on the cool grass, waited for Dorothy and the Lion to awaken.

---

[1] **hector** To *hector* someone is to persistently, domineeringly, or annoyingly intimidate, scold, harass, badger, hound, or torment him (often to break him down or break his spirit). *In March 2001 journalist Robert Kagan noted that "when John Kennedy entered the White House in 1961, Nikita Khrushchev wanted to find out right away what the young, inexperienced American President was made of; so at a summit in Vienna that year, the Soviet leader hectored and bullied Kennedy on the question of Berlin and other [controversial] issues."*

[2] **malinger (malingerers)** To *malinger* is to pretend illness to avoid work or duty. *Finally fed up, the army doctor threatened to take the suspected malingerer's temperature orally— with a rectal thermometer!*

[3] **laurels** In ancient times a wreath of leaves from the *laurel* (a Mediterranean evergreen tree) was bestowed (upon poets, heroes, athletes, etc.) as a mark of honor. Today, any honor or glory won (as for achievement in a particular field or activity) can be referred to as *laurels*. *In February 1992 journalist William Drozdiak reported, "When Vegard Ulvang captured three gold medals in cross-country skiing at the 1992 Winter Olympics, he did not rest on his laurels; while fellow Norwegians were celebrating his victories, he decided to wind down by climbing the highest peaks on four continents."*

[4] **recumbent** When you're *recumbent*, you're lying down or leaning back in a restful, comfortable position. *When I saw my girlfriend recumbent on the couch doing absolutely nothing, I asked, "Would you like me to feed you grapes?"*

Chapter 10 "The Guardian of the Gates"

When Dorothy and the Lion finally woke up, they felt refreshed and were very glad to find themselves still alive and safe from the floral **effluvium**[1]. The Scarecrow told them how the mice saved the Lion's life, and the large beast inwardly marveled that such small things as flowers could almost kill him and such tiny animals as mice could save him.

They started walking upstream again, greatly enjoying the **salubrious**[2] effects of the clean, fresh air. Soon they reached the yellow brick road that led to the Emerald City. As they walked they noticed that on this side of the river the road was smooth and well paved, and the surrounding countryside was especially beautiful. Once more they could see neat, little fences along the side of the road; but whereas those in Munchkinland were blue, these were green.

They walked for a while listening to nature's **counterpoint**[3]— a

---

[1] **effluvium** An *effluvium* is a (usually slight or invisible) vapor, gas, or exhalation, especially one that is harmful or odorous. *My aunt knew that the cesspool was buried somewhere under her front lawn, but she wasn't sure exactly where; so, sniffing daintily but continuously, and with her hand steadily waving back and forth in front of her nose, she slowly walked across it, trying to detect the telltale effluvium.* Note: The plural is *effluvia.*

[2] **salubrious** If something (often a certain climate) is *salubrious*, it's favorable to (or promotes) health; it's healthful. *In the movie, the vampire just rolls his eyes when a naïve young woman says to him, "You look kind of pale; a few weeks in the salubrious sunshine of Miami Beach would do wonders for you!"*

[3] **counterpoint** This is a technical term in music that means "the combining of two or more distinct melodies (such that they sound good together but at the same time retain their individuality)," as in much of the music of J. S. Bach. Figuratively, the word can be used to indicate the combining of any contrasting but related elements (in art, discussions, ideas, etc.). The adjective is *contrapuntal. Unlike ballroom dancing, where you gracefully sweep across the floor, in contemporary modern dance you pretty much remain in one spot; your feet stomp and slide while your arms punch and swing in counterpoint.*

softly hissing wind competed with songbirds for the **treble**[1], while distant, **bovine**[2] **lowing**[3] dominated the bass. Suddenly they noticed in the distant sky a beautiful green glow. "That must be the Emerald City!" cried Dorothy **exultantly**[4].

As they walked on, the heavenly, green **nimbus**[5] became brighter and brighter, and it seemed that their journey was at last over. Still, it wasn't until an hour later that they finally arrived at the huge, emerald-studded gate to the City. There was a bell beside it, and when Dorothy pushed it, they heard exquisite, silvery

---

[1] **treble** In music, the *treble* part is the high part (as distinguished from the low part, which is called the *bass*). But the word can also denote any high (or shrill) sound. *In boogie-woogie piano playing, your left hand plays a repeated "boogie" pattern in the bass while your right hand improvises melodies in the treble.*

[2] **bovine** This word means "pertaining to or resembling a cow." (Technically, the word can be used to refer to any animal of the genus *Bos*, such as the ox, buffalo, or yak.) The word is also used figuratively to mean "dull, sluggish." *My mother is afraid to buy milk from cows that have been given bovine growth hormone (a naturally occurring or genetically engineered hormone that increases milk production).*

[3] **lowing** This word rhymes with *knowing* and means "mooing" (the sound cows make). (To *low* is to moo.) *The second verse of the famous Christmas carol "Away in a Manger" begins "The cattle are lowing; the Baby awakes."*

[4] **exultant (exultantly)** When you're *exultant*, you feel great joy, jubilation, or elation (sometimes mixed with a feeling of triumph). As a verb, to *exult* is to rejoice, delight, etc. *Photographer Alfred Eisenstaedt's most famous picture shows a sailor kissing a nurse in the middle of an exultant "end of World War II" victory celebration in Times Square.*

[5] **nimbus** In art and mythology, a *nimbus* is a halo (a radiant light, usually in the form of a circle, that appears above or around the head of someone sacred, such as an angel, a god, or an emperor). But in general use, the word means a visible or invisible aura or atmosphere (like a halo) that surrounds someone or something splendid, glamorous, or important. *We imagined that in any painting of Joan of Arc being burned at the stake, some sort of nimbus would encircle her dying face.*

tintinnabulations[1] that made them smile.

The great **portal**[2] swung open, revealing the Emerald City in all its glittering glory. Awe-struck, the travelers stared at the **coruscating**[3] wonderland until they heard a voice ask, "What do you wish in the Emerald City?"

Before them stood a little man about the same size as the Munchkins. When Dorothy told him they had come to see the Great Oz, the little man told Dorothy that the Wizard usually **shunned**[4] the company of strangers, and that, in particular,

---

[1] **tintinnabulation (tintinnabulations)** This long and fancy word means "the ringing or sound of bells." *In music, "chimes" (also called "tubular bells") are a portable set of bells whose tintinnabulations are tuned to the intervals of the major scale.*

[2] **portal** A *portal* is a door (or doorway, gate, or entrance). But the implication is that if you're talking about an actual door, it's a large and impressive one (such as that of a castle). And if you're talking about a (physical or conceptual) entryway, it's to some important or impressive place or realm (such as the Internet). *The west side of Paris's Cathedral of Notre Dame is famous for its portals, sculptures, and huge rose window.*

[3] **coruscate (coruscating)** When something *coruscates*, it intermittently gives off glints or flashes of light; it sparkles or glitters (as in *the silvery tinsel coruscated as the Christmas tree lights twinkled*). The word can be used figuratively to mean "exhibiting or displaying brilliance or virtuosity (as if giving off glints of light)." *In his review of a June 1991 piano recital at the University of Maryland, music critic Mark Adamo said, "In scores by Chopin, Rachmaninoff, and Prokofiev on the coruscating Steinway, the young Soviet pianist [Alexei Sultanov] made the bass register bite and threaten and obsess, and made melodies in the highest octaves echo and chime like ghosts in the chandeliers."*

[4] **shun (shunned)** When you *shun* something (or someone or someplace), you deliberately (and often habitually) avoid it; you keep away from it. The implication is that you don't like it or are wary of it. *Whereas the AFL (American Federation of Labor) craft unions tended to shun women, blacks, immigrants, and unskilled workers, the IWW (Industrial Workers of the World) welcomed them.*

curiosity seekers, members of the **fourth estate**[1], and people with foolish requests greatly angered him. "And if Oz detects even a trace of **guile**[2], he will destroy you in an instant!" finished the man **complacently**[3], staring directly into Dorothy's face.

The Scarecrow decided he had nothing to lose by **interceding**[4]. "But our request isn't foolish," he said. "And we were told that Oz is a good wizard."

"I'm the Guardian of the Gates, and since you demand to see the Great Oz, I must take you to his Palace," said the man, **obviating**[5] the need for any further debate. Relieved, and with a high sense of

---

[1] **fourth estate** This is a phrase (sometimes capitalized) that refers to the press (people involved in writing or reporting the news). *In 1961 writer Gene Fowler observed: "News is history shot on the wing; the huntsmen from the fourth estate seek to bag only the peacock or the eagle of the swifting day."*

[2] **guile** This word means "craftiness, deceitfulness, deceptiveness, sneakiness, trickery, underhandedness, etc." If you're without guile, you're *guileless* (honest, forthright, frank, genuine, natural, innocent, naïve, etc.) *In the 1958 movie comedy* No Time for Sergeants, *Andy Griffith plays a guileless, well-intentioned farm boy who creates mayhem when he gets drafted into the army.*

[3] **complacent (complacently)** If you feel *complacent* about something (such as your situation or advantage), you feel smugly self-satisfied about it. Sometimes the implication is that you're too self-satisfied (and therefore unconcerned) and that some hidden danger will somehow cause your defeat. The noun is *complacency*. *In 1985, speaking of academic competition, the president of Yale University said, "To take the measure of oneself by reference to one's colleagues leads to envy or complacency rather than constructive self-examination."* Note: Don't confuse this word with *complaisant* (which is pronounced the same); see *complaisant.*

[4] **intercede (interceding)** When you *intercede*, you intervene (on behalf of someone in some difficulty or trouble); you try to mediate or reconcile differences (between people). *The Virgin Mary is honored by all Christians because they believe strongly in her mercy and her power to intercede with God.*

[5] **obviate (obviating)** When something is *obviated*, it's made unnecessary (or made no longer necessary). *I'm thrilled that he quit, because that obviates the unpleasant task of firing him.*

expectancy, Dorothy and her little **retinue**[1] followed the Guardian of the Gates into the streets of the Emerald City.

---

[1] **retinue** A *retinue* is a group of followers or companions (usually accompanying a high-ranking person). *In ancient Egyptian mummification (embalming and tight wrapping of a corpse), royal figures— along with their retinue and even their food!— were preserved.*

Chapter 11 "The Emerald City"

Dorothy and her friends were dazzled by the brilliancy of Oz. Glittering emeralds studded the beautiful houses that lined the streets. Even the sidewalk sparkled because between the green marble blocks that formed it lay **interposing**[1] rows of closely set emeralds glinting in the sunlight.

Now, most little girls **reared**[2] in the modest, **austere**[3] surroundings of rural Kansas might have found the **ornate**[4] City **garishly**[5] **ostentatious**[1], but Dorothy thrilled to its magnificence.

---

[1] **interpose (interposing)** Something that *interposes* (between two things), comes (is located or put) between those things; for example, an interposing wall might be placed between two fighting pet hamsters. *By interposing cold solder and then heating it, he was able to join together the two metal parts.* Note: The word can also mean "interject" (throw a comment into a conversation) or "intervene" (come between two parties to help negotiate).

[2] **rear (reared)** To *rear* a child is to raise it; to bring it up; to care for (and support) it. *Born into a Quaker family in Iowa in 1874, President Herbert Hoover was orphaned at the age of nine and reared by relatives in Iowa and Oregon.*

[3] **austere** A place or an artistic style described as *austere* has no ornamentation or adornment; it's bleak, barren, cold, naked, or stark. *Composer Roger Sessions' early music is romantic and harmonic, but his later works are austere and complex.* A person described as *austere* is severe in either his manner (he's strict and stern) or in his self-discipline (he's self-denying and restrained). The noun is *austerity*. *The phrase "Trappist monk" brings to mind a vow of silence and a life of austerity.*

[4] **ornate** If something (architecture, clothing, artistic style, etc.) is *ornate*, it's either very intricate (elaborately detailed) or it's highly ornamented (flowery, flashy, showy). *Legend has it that once when they were both guests at a wedding party, British novelist E. M. Forster (1879–1970) mistook Queen Mary for an ornate wedding cake.*

[5] **garish (garishly)** Something (clothing or ornamentation, for example) described as *garish* is excessively and tastelessly showy, bright, colorful, or flashy; it's gaudy, loud, tacky. *In the early part of his career, singer Elton John was known for his intentionally garish costumes.*

THE WIZARD OF OZ VOCABULARY BUILDER

The Guardian of the Gates **squired**[2] Dorothy through the streets, and her friends followed closely behind. The **hoi polloi**[3], looking mostly happy and prosperous, were milling about, and they stared at the travelers in wonder.

Many of the younger women had one or two **docile**[4] youngsters in tow, but one poor woman **suffered**[5] an **obstreperous**[6] little girl,

---

[1] **ostentatious** If something's *ostentatious*, it draws attention to itself; it's boastfully showy; it means to impress people. *Denying that his family's Parisian luxury hotel was ostentatious, Charles Ritz once paradoxically remarked, "The Ritz is not ritzy."*

[2] **squire (squired)** To *squire* (a woman) is to escort (her), as to a social gathering, for example. *After his blind date, he complained to us, "I squired her all over town for three hours and spent all kinds of money, then she picks up her jacket, shakes my hand, and says 'Thank you for a lovely evening'!"*

[3] **hoi polloi** This phrase, which in Greek literally means "the many," refers to the common people, the ordinary people, the masses. Sometimes it has the derogatory connotation that common people are unsophisticated or ignorant. *While the vulgar comedy sickened the film critic, around him the hoi polloi laughed uproariously.* Note: The phrase is pronounced so that both words rhyme with *boy* and the second word has the accent on the second syllable.

[4] **docile** If you're *docile*, you're easy to handle, manage, or control; you willingly or readily follow orders and take directions; you're submissive (agreeably obedient) and mild-mannered. *At the petting zoo we saw mostly farm animals, such as goats, ducks, and sheep, but we also saw a few of the more docile wild animals, such as turtles and deer.*

[5] **suffer (suffered)** We all know that when you *suffer*, you feel pain or distress. But if you *suffer* a particular thing, you tolerate it, allow it, or put up with it (as in the famous idiom "suffer fools gladly"). *It has been said that in marriage you study each other for three weeks, you love each other for three months, you fight for three years, and you suffer the situation for thirty.*

[6] **obstreperous** If you're *obstreperous*, you resist control in a noisy way; you're unruly and loud. *President Nixon believed that the obstreperous demonstrators who opposed the involvement of the U.S. in Vietnam were in the minority and that the great body of Americans, whom he referred to as the "silent majority," supported his policies.*

THE WIZARD OF OZ VOCABULARY BUILDER

a **refractory**[1], **sassy**[2]-mouthed little boy, a **fractious**[3] bulldog, and a **recalcitrant**[4] cat. When they saw the huge Lion, they all silently scampered behind the woman's skirt.

Dorothy noticed that the City was made up mostly of cute little shops and **tony**[5] restaurants. Splendid **statuary**[1] adorned the front

---

[1] **refractory** If you're *refractory*, you're hard to manage; you're stubbornly disobedient or resistant (to control or authority). *When the third grader again stubbornly refused to get in his seat, his teacher wondered if there existed in their town any special schools for refractory children.*

[2] **sassy** If you're *sassy*, you say rude, disrespectful things. The word is often used to describe children who speak disrespectfully to adults. The noun is *sass* (rude, disrespectful talk; back talk). *In the 1984 film* Beverly Hills Cop, *comedian Eddie Murphy plays a sassy, wisecracking, streetwise Detroit policeman who goes to Beverly Hills to track down the men who killed his best friend.* Note: The word can also mean "lively; spirited" (as in *a sassy performance*) or "stylish, chic" (as in *a sassy hat*).

[3] **fractious** If you're *fractious*, you're peevish (irritable, complaining, quarrelsome, disagreeable, cranky) or unruly (difficult to control, apt to cause trouble). Or you're both (peevish and unruly). *Fractious* machines are ones that tend to break down a lot. *Fractious* animals are ones that haven't been properly trained. *I thought it might help to take my whining little troublemaker to the amusement park, but then the thought of having to stand on line with a fractious child put a quick end to that.*

[4] **recalcitrant** If you're *recalcitrant*, you're hard to manage or control; you determinedly resist or oppose authority. The implication is that you're apt not only to resist, but somehow to rebel against authority. *In April 1968, over 200 recalcitrant Columbia University student demonstrators (opposed to U.S. involvement in the war in Vietnam) were injured by New York City police when they refused to vacate the campus buildings they had occupied.*

[5] **tony** If you describe a place (such as a restaurant or nightclub) as *tony*, you mean it's fashionable, elegant, stylish, exclusive, chic, etc. *In 1986, to make room for a new entrance to the Rainbow Room and Rainbow and Stars (the tony restaurant and nightclub located at the top of the GE building in New York City's Rockefeller Center), an observation deck, described in the* New York Times *as "an unusually tranquil skyscraping vantage— a kind of front porch 850 feet in the air," had to be closed.*

of one especially pretty restaurant, and Dorothy stopped to gaze through its window. Inside she saw snow-white **napery**[2] and gleaming, silver **cutlery**[3] far more exquisite than any she'd ever seen in Kansas. An **obsequiously**[4] bowing, **saccharinely**[5] smiling maître d' **fulsomely**[6] flattered each **opulently**[1] dressed, **bejeweled**[2]

---

[1] **statuary** A group or collection of statues is known as *statuary*. *Speaking in 1962 of the lost role of saints in the Christian tradition, the vicar of a New York City chapel said, "We have relegated the saints to a pink and blue and gold world of plaster statuary that belongs to the past; it is a hangover, a relic, of the Dark Ages, when men were the children of fantasy's magic."*

[2] **napery** Table linen (napkins, tablecloths, etc.) is known as *napery*. *The bride's only complaint with her wedding reception concerned the napery— she was convinced that the particular off-white shade of the napkins didn't precisely match that of the tablecloths.*

[3] **cutlery** Tableware for eating and serving (knives, forks, and spoons) are collectively known as *cutlery*. *When my mother first told me to put the vase on top of the "sideboard," I didn't realize she was referring to that thing in the dining room with drawers and shelves where she keeps the linens and cutlery.*

[4] **obsequious (obsequiously)** If you're *obsequious*, you're submissive (agreeably obedient) and flattering (usually in an attempt to win someone's favor); you bootlick; you brown-nose; you "suck up" (to someone). *We loved to watch our nasty boss turn suddenly obsequious whenever his overbearing wife visited the office.*

[5] **saccharine (saccharinely)** People and things that are *saccharine* are sugary sweet (in attitude, tone, character, etc.). The implication is that they're overly sweet. The word can also mean "excessively sentimental" (as literature, for example). *You'd think that by now Disney cartoon heroes and heroines would learn not to trust anyone with a saccharine smile.* Note: *Saccharin* (without an e at the end) is the name of the artificial sweetener dieters use.

[6] **fulsome (fulsomely)** If something (praise, flattery, apologies, introductions, language, etc.) is *fulsome*, it's excessive (overdone, over-full) to the point of being offensive or insincere. *The comments people wrote to me in my high school yearbook run the gamut from fulsome gushes of praise ("you're the greatest guy in the world") to meaningless nothings ("good luck").* The word can also mean "sickening, disgusting," especially when it refers to an excess in the quantity or richness of food.

THE WIZARD OF OZ VOCABULARY BUILDER

customer, and **fawning**³, **unctuous**⁴ waiters hovered **officiously**⁵, ready to pounce on any water glass that was less than full.

At a small table at the back, two **inebriated**⁶, **rambunctious**¹

---

¹ **opulent (opulently)** People who are *opulent* possess great wealth; they're rich. Things that are *opulent* (mansions, weddings, jewelry, etc.) exhibit great wealth or spending (often in a showy display). *In 1978, in a reference to the opulence of Radio City Music Hall, the Commissioner of the New York City Department of Cultural Affairs said, "It is the theater God would have built if he had the money."* The word can also mean "richly abundant," as in *opulent sunshine* or *opulent use of color.*

² **bejeweled** Someone or something that's *bejeweled* is decorated with (or wearing) jewels or jewelry. *Russian goldsmith and jeweler Peter Fabergé (1846–1920) was particularly well known for the bejeweled, enameled Easter eggs he created for the Russian royal family.*

³ **fawning** If you're *fawning* (if you *fawn* over someone) you seek favor through insincere flattery, exaggerated attention, or servile submission; you butter (someone) up. *After seeing Elizabeth Taylor play Cleopatra in a movie, we wondered who, in reality, had more people fawn over her— the character or the actress.*

⁴ **unctuous** This word literally means "oily," but people who are *unctuous* (pronounced *UNK-chew-is*) are smarmy and overly smooth or slick; they pretend to be sincere or earnest (in their concern or attention, for example), but they generally have some ulterior motive (financial gain, for example). *The funeral director's unctuous smile suddenly disintegrated when the widow insisted upon a plain, plywood casket for her husband's burial.*

⁵ **officious (officiously)** People who are *officious* annoyingly interfere in your affairs by giving you unwanted help, advice, or attention; they're meddlesome. *Shedding some light on whether or not mothers-in-law are officious meddlers, anthropologist Margaret Mead noted: "Of all the peoples whom I have studied, from city dwellers to cliff dwellers, I always find that at least 50 percent would prefer to have at least one jungle between themselves and their mother-in-law."*

⁶ **inebriated** People who are *inebriated* are drunk, intoxicated (from alcohol). Sometimes the word is used figuratively to mean "mentally or emotionally intoxicated (as from something exhilarating, confusing, etc.)" *With so many colorful synonyms to choose from, we pity the poor writer who needs to refer to someone's inebriated state; why, considering just the "s" words alone, his possibilities include sloshed, smashed, soused, stewed, stoked, stoned, and stupid (not to mention a few vulgarisms!).*

young men giggled uncontrollably as they **quaffed**[2] beers and **taunted**[3] their **crimson**[4]-faced young waitress. At the front, a **queue**[5] of **palavering**[6] **patrons**[1] waited to pay the cashier.

---

[1] **rambunctious** If you're *rambunctious*, you're rowdy, noisy, disorderly; you're difficult to manage. *After her rambunctious five-year-old ruined her formal dinner party, Donna whispered to her husband, "Next time remind me to invite W. C. Fields."*

[2] **quaff (quaffed)** To *quaff* is to drink (a beverage, especially an alcoholic one) heartily. *When she said she liked "lost generation" writers, like Hemingway and Fitzgerald, I said, "Yeah, the thought of quaffing ale in a 1920s Parisian café appeals to me, too."*

[3] **taunt (taunted)** To *taunt* someone is to tease, insult, ridicule, or mock him (often to make him an object of laughter). *In 1985, explaining why he shot four youths on a New York City subway, Bernard Goetz said: "When you are surrounded by four people, one of them smiling, taunting, demanding, terrorizing, you don't have a complete grasp or perfect vision."*

[4] **crimson** *Crimson* is a color; it's red or purplish red. (Someone who's *crimson-faced* is blushing, red in the face.) *In the Thanksgiving snowstorm, leaves of crimson and gold turned to white.*

[5] **queue** A *queue* (pronounced the same as *cue*) is a line of people waiting their turn (as at a ticket window, bank, post office, etc.). To *queue up* is to form such a line. Though more commonly used in England, the word is also used in the U.S. *British playwright Noel Coward (1899–1973) once said that the description of his 1930 comedy* Private Lives *as "delightfully daring" suggested to the public mind references to sex, "thereby causing a gratifying number of respectable people to queue up at the box office."*

[6] **palaver (palavering)** As a noun this word (pronounced with the accent on the second syllable) means "idle or trivial talk; chatter." As a verb it means "to engage in idle or trivial talk; to chitchat." *In his review of Frank Bianco's 1991 book* Voices of Silence: Lives of the Trappists, *critic Colman McCarthy wrote, "Among the world's finest hotels— quiet, no palaver from the desk clerk, low cost— are the guest houses at Trappist monasteries."*

THE WIZARD OF OZ VOCABULARY BUILDER

Finally arriving at the exact center of the City, our group stood before a great building, which was the Palace of the Great Wizard. A soldier stood before the door, and Dorothy noticed that a green **epaulet**[2] adorned each shoulder of his **resplendent**[3] green uniform.

"Here are strangers," said the Guardian of the Gates, "and they demand to see the Wizard."

The soldier led the little party into a **capacious**[4], green-carpeted waiting room that boasted green leather armchairs and small **teak**[5]

---

[1] **patron (patrons)** A *patron* is a paying customer (especially a regular one) of a store, hotel, restaurant, etc. Your *patronage* of a business is your economic support of it (by buying or spending there), and when you *patronize* a business, you economically support it (by shopping there). *I had to explain to him that when a restaurant has "valet parking," patrons leave their cars at the entrance, and attendants park and retrieve them.*

[2] **epaulet** An *epaulet* is a shoulder piece (usually a rectangular strap) worn on uniforms (usually of army and navy officers) as a decoration or to signify rank. *The uniforms of the toy soldiers were accurate in every detail, from the epaulets all the way down to the boots.*

[3] **resplendent** Something *resplendent* is splendid (extraordinary, impressive, etc.) and dazzling (shining, gleaming, brilliant, glowing, blazing, etc.). *New York City's Rockefeller Center boasts the 70-story GE Building, Radio City Music Hall, and (at Yuletide) a huge, resplendent Christmas tree.*

[4] **capacious** Something described as *capacious* is large or roomy; it can hold a large amount (of something). *In 1963 Ralph Nader abandoned his private law practice in Hartford, Connecticut, and with one capacious suitcase hitchhiked to Washington, D.C., to begin a career as a public crusader.*

[5] **teak** *Teak* is a hard, strong, yellowish-brown wood used in making furniture, ships, and floors. It comes from the teak tree, a tall evergreen found in southeast Asia. Sometimes the word is used to describe a grayish yellowish brown or grayish brown color. *In his 1962 book* The Anatomy of Britain, *Anthony Sampson noted that that from boarding school to law school to Parliament, upper crust British boys "retain the same male world of leather armchairs, teak tables, and nicknames."*

tables inset with emeralds. **Wainscoting**[1] divided the walls into two **discrete**[2] yet complementary shades of green, the lighter shade toward the top. "Make yourselves comfortable while I go to the Throne Room to tell Oz you are here," said the soldier politely.

While waiting for the soldier to return, the travelers had their first chance to relax and discuss the **vicissitudes**[3] of their long journey. **Waxing**[4] philosophical, the Scarecrow attributed everything that had happened to nothing more than the **vagaries**[5]

---

[1] **wainscoting** Sometimes the wall of a room has a different treatment or finish on its lower portion than its upper (for example, the lower part might be wood paneling with the upper part wallpaper). *Wainscoting* is the word used to describe either this type of wall or the material (usually wood) used on the lower portion. *When I complained to my decorator that the knotty pine wainscoting had way too many knots, she had it painted to imitate oak.*

[2] **discrete** If you say that (two or more) things are *discrete,* you mean that they're separate and distinct (from each other). *In the U.S. government, power is separated among three discrete branches: executive, legislative, and judicial.* Note: Don't confuse this word with *discreet* (see *discreet*).

[3] **vicissitudes** The unexpected, uncontrollable, shifting changes (especially difficulties) that occur in your life, fortune, or activities (the "ups and downs" of life) are known as *vicissitudes* (pronounced *vi-SIS-i-tudes*). *In her 1935 novel* Little House on the Prairie, *Laura Ingalls Wilder chronicles the vicissitudes of life on the American frontier.*

[4] **wax (waxing)** As a verb, to *wax* is to grow or become (a particular emotion), as in *wax sentimental* or *wax nostalgic. We wondered how many members of the San Francisco Symphony Orchestra waxed enthusiastic at the prospect of performing with the heavy metal band Metallica.* Note: Another meaning of the verb *wax* (as the opposite of *wane*) is "to gradually increase" (see *wane*).

[5] **vagaries** Unpredictable, irregular occurrences (in life, weather, business, or any other area that might experience a sudden turn of events) are called *vagaries. In an attempt to protect himself from the vagaries of the stock market, he invested half his money in gold.*

of fate. The Tim Woodman, sounding somewhat **Calvinistic**[1], **conjectured**[2] that whatever happened was simply "meant to be." And at one point, the Lion, at the risk of sounding **solipsistic**[3], asked if he might merely be dreaming.

Their reflections were interrupted by the sudden return of the soldier. Dorothy noticed for the first time that a single-striped **chevron**[4] was sewn onto each of his sleeves. "Have you seen the Wizard," she **queried**[5] expectantly.

"I've never seen him," answered the soldier, "but I spoke to him

---

[1] **Calvinistic** People who are *Calvinistic* (named after the religious doctrines of 16th-century Protestant theologian and reformer John Calvin) believe that all events have been predetermined by an all-powerful God. *Throughout the war, the young soldier believed with Calvinistic certainty that he would survive and that his country would eventually win.*

[2] **conjecture (conjectured)** To *conjecture* is to form or state an opinion based on guesswork or incomplete evidence. As a noun, a *conjecture* is such an opinion. *He said that when he first begins solving a crossword puzzle he uses nothing but conjecture; then he assured us that as he nears the end he's able to fill in all the words with certainty.*

[3] **solipsistic** If you're *solipsistic*, you believe in *solipsism*, the philosophical theory that everything (other than you) is only imagined (by you); that the only thing (in the universe) that truly exists (or that can be proven to exist) is yourself. Sometimes the word is used figuratively to describe someone who's very self-centered, who acts as if he's the only person in the world who matters. *Because former Haitian dictator "Papa Doc" Duvalier once declared himself "president for life" and once said "I know the Haitian people because I am the Haitian people," our social studies teacher called him a solipsist.*

[4] **chevron** A *chevron* is a badge consisting of (usually) inverted V–shaped stripes sewn onto the upper part of the sleeve of a military (or police) uniform to indicate rank or years of service. *We knew he was a corporal because his chevron had two gold stripes.*

[5] **query (queried)** As a verb, to *query* is to ask (to put a question to someone), especially as a means of settling doubt (about something). As a noun, a *query* is a question or inquiry. *Thanks to the Internet, local libraries can locate materials that are not among their holdings by querying the Online Computer Library Center (OCLC).*

as he sat behind his screen. He said that you should all come back tomorrow and he will grant you an audience. Tonight you shall sleep in the Palace."

Their disappointment at not being received at once was somewhat **mitigated**[1] by the soldier's assurance that they would be heard tomorrow. Exhausted from their long day, they decided to go to bed at once and **adjourned**[2] to their **respective**[3] bedrooms.

Alone in her room, Dorothy gazed for a while through the window at the **taffeta**[4] backdrop of the night, wondering what tomorrow would bring. When she climbed into bed she found she was too keyed up to sleep. After a while she got dressed again and slipped out of the room to roam the halls of the great Palace.

---

[1] **mitigate (mitigated)** To *mitigate* a painful, unpleasant, or distressful condition or situation is to make it less severe or more tolerable (by somehow counteracting or reducing the intensity of whatever's causing the problem). *My doctor told me that symptoms of low blood sugar, such as weakness, shakiness, and irritability, can be mitigated by sucking on a lollipop.*

[2] **adjourn (adjourned)** To *adjourn* is to move from one place to another (especially a room). The implication is that you'll be in the new room for some time. *After dinner, we adjourned to the den to watch some TV.* Note: In another, more common sense, this word is used in official meetings (such as those that follow parliamentary procedure) and means "to end or postpone to another time," as in *I move to adjourn.*

[3] **respective** The adjective *respective* (or the adverb *respectively*) is used to assign, in the correct order, separate things to members of a group. For example, to say that a brother and sister inherited their father's boat and car is to imply that they now co-own each. But to say that a brother and sister inherited their father's boat and car *respectively* is to say that the (first-mentioned) brother now owns the (first-mentioned) boat and the (second-mentioned) sister owns the (second-mentioned) car. *In August 1945 a uranium bomb and a plutonium bomb were dropped, respectively, on Hiroshima and Nagasaki.*

[4] **taffeta** *Taffeta* is a fabric used in making clothing, especially women's. Made of various fibers (silk, nylon, or rayon, for example), it has a smooth, crisp texture and a slight sheen or luster. As an adjective, the word means "resembling or suggesting taffeta in appearance." *In 1968, wearing an off-white taffeta miniskirt, actress Sharon Tate married European director Roman Polanski in London.*

Chapter 12 "The Citizens of the Emerald City"

The **denizens**[1] of Oz, who, for the most part, were **gregarious**[2] and **garrulous**[3], were out in great number, and it seemed they had nothing to do but satisfy their **penchant**[4] for **colloquy**[5]. A feeling of downtown **bonhomie**[6] **pervaded**[1] the atmosphere. Dorothy

---

[1] **denizens** The *denizens* of a city, country, etc., are its residents or inhabitants (the people who live there). *In the 1800s, Dodge City, Kansas, was a rough, disorderly cowboy town whose denizens included such legendary law officers as Wyatt Earp and Bat Masterson.*

[2] **gregarious** If you're *gregarious*, you like to socialize; you seek and enjoy the company of others. If an animal is *gregarious*, it lives in a flock or herd. *The psychic told me that sometimes I feel like a loner and other times I feel gregarious— and I thought: Well, that covers just about every possibility.*

[3] **garrulous** If you're *garrulous*, you're talkative; you like to talk. Sometimes the implication is that the talk is excessive, rambling, or tiresome. *Eddie said that he hates to wind up sitting next to a garrulous neighbor on his evening commuter train because he knows that for the next 30 minutes his mind won't have a single chance to rest.*

[4] **penchant** To have a *penchant* for something is to have a strong liking for it or a strong inclination toward it; to be strongly attracted by it. *When my science teacher said that monkeys have a penchant for bananas, I said that maybe the only reason they eat them is because they're so readily available.*

[5] **colloquy** A *colloquy* is a conversation (or dialogue or discussion). Sometimes the word implies that the conversation is rather formal or high-level. *In 1956, when asked about his colloquy with Soviet leaders, UN Secretary-General Dag Hammarskjöld said, "I never discuss discussions."*

[6] **bonhomie** The quality of being friendly, cheerful, good-natured, good-hearted, warm-hearted, etc., is known as *bonhomie* (pronounced with the accent on the last syllable). *According to journalist William Drozdiak, when President George W. Bush visited Europe in June 2001, he "impressed most of his European peers with his confident manner and backslapping bonhomie."*

covertly² listened in on a few conversations.

A short, **corpulent³**, **swarthy⁴** fellow, whose colorful but somewhat **slovenly⁵ attire⁶** flirted with **bohemianism¹**, had

---

¹ **pervade (pervaded)** When one thing *pervades* another, it passes through it and fills every part of it (as in *mental health problems resulting from stress pervade the workplace*), or it causes it to be filled with a particular mood or tone (as in *a sixties flavor pervaded the high school reunion*). The adjective is *pervasive. In July 1990 journalist Blaine Harden noted, "Amid the gloom and grumbling that pervades Poland's post-Communist economy, there are two shining beacons of entrepreneurial success: sex and guns; in heated embrace of Western culture, Poles are buying life-size Wonder Wanda inflatable dolls [and] they are [lining] up for handguns that fire stun-gas bullets."*

² **covert (covertly)** Something *covert* is not openly shown; it's hidden or covered, as in *a covert glance*. When you do something *covertly*, you do it secretly, so that people don't know you're doing it. *According to legend, although the townspeople were asked to remain indoors and not look when the naked Lady Godiva, covered only by her long hair, rode by on horseback, a tailor named Tom covertly watched through his shutter (and was struck blind).*

³ **corpulent** If you're *corpulent*, you're fat, heavy, overweight. *Corpulence* used to be considered a sign of wealth; that (and because the word *corpulent* is not as insulting as the word *fat*) is why the word was often applied to overweight European kings (Henry VIII, for example). *In the 1961 movie* The Hustler, *Paul Newman plays a young pool shark and Jackie Gleason plays the corpulent champ, Minnesota Fats.*

⁴ **swarthy** A person who's *swarthy* is dark-complexioned (usually naturally, but also from exposure to the sun). *Vacationing in Greece, the blond, blue-eyed Swede felt more fair-skinned than ever among all the swarthy locals.*

⁵ **slovenly** People who are *slovenly* are habitually untidy, sloppy, dirty, disheveled, etc. A *slovenly* person is known as a *sloven. If you watch the 1970 film* Woodstock, *you'll see that hippies liked to project a slovenly image in their dress and grooming.*

⁶ **attire** Your *attire* is your clothing; it's what you wear. *In the 18th century, embroidery (ornamental needlework) was applied to both male and female attire, but today it's used mainly on women's clothes.*

buttonholed[2] a tall, thin, **taciturn**[3], conservatively dressed **towhead**[4] and was now forcing him to listen to a **bawdy**[5] joke. The story, which Dorothy didn't completely understand, concerned an especially **nubile**[6], **coquettish**[7], and **décolleté**[1] young woman who,

---

[1] **bohemian (bohemianism)** People who are interested in artistic or intellectual pursuits (more so than in money) and who disregard conventional standards of dress and behavior are called *bohemians* (or, to use the word as an adjective, their lifestyle, behavior, dress, etc., is *bohemian*). They sometimes live in poverty and dress sloppily. *New York City's Greenwich Village has been home to beatniks, hippies, and other bohemians.*

[2] **buttonhole (buttonholed)** To *buttonhole* someone is to stop him and detain him in conversation (when he'd rather be continuing on his way). *It was practically impossible for Fran to walk from her house to her car without being buttonholed by one of her lonely neighbors.*

[3] **taciturn** People who are *taciturn* don't talk much; they're quiet, reserved, uncommunicative. The implication is that they're even unsociable and might speak only when necessary. *In the movie, the young New Yorker became enraged with the taciturn Vermont farmer who answered every question with "yup" or "nope."*

[4] **towhead** A *towhead* (pronounced *TOE-head*) is a person with whitish blond hair. *We weren't sure if the movie actor who played Hitler's bodyguard was a natural towhead or if he'd bleached his hair for the role.*

[5] **bawdy** Talk, writing, people, amusements, etc., that are *bawdy* are (often humorously) obscene, indecent, dirty. *My younger brother wrote a bawdy limerick that began "There was a young lady named Cass."*

[6] **nubile** Technically, to say that a young woman or girl is *nubile* (usually pronounced *NEW-bile*) is to say that she's suitable for marriage (in the sense of being old enough or physically mature enough). But generally, if a fellow describes someone as a "nubile young woman," he means that she's young and sexy. *Some of those Calvin Klein ads feature nubile young women wearing boys' underwear.*

[7] **coquettish** A woman who's *coquettish* is flirtatious; she makes light, teasing, romantic overtures to men for her own gratification. (A coquettish woman is called a *coquette;* what she engages in is called *coquetry*.) *French actress Brigitte Bardot rose to stardom playing a sexy coquette in the 1957 film* And God Created Woman.

THE WIZARD OF OZ VOCABULARY BUILDER

while **sultrily**[2] **carousing**[3] at a **Bacchanalian**[4] New Year's Eve **fete**[5], met an **erstwhile**[6] **uxorious**[1] **milquetoast**[2], recently **cuckolded**[3],

---

[1] **décolleté** If you describe a dress (or other garment) as *décolleté*, you mean that it has a low neckline. If you describe a woman as *décolleté*, you mean that she's wearing a dress (or other garment) with a low neckline. (The noun *décolletage* is the name for a dress with a low neckline or for the low neckline itself.) *The students at the junior prom were shocked to see the school librarian décolleté.*

[2] **sultry (sultrily)** Weather that's *sultry* is hot and humid. A woman who's *sultry* is sensual or voluptuous; she arouses heated passion. *In a 1965 TV Guide article about interviewing film legend Mae West, the once-sultry sex symbol was said to have worn a loose gown of beige lace "with a blonde wig above false eyelashes— a kind of Mount Rushmore of the cosmetician's art."*

[3] **carouse (carousing)** To *carouse* is to drink (alcohol) and (loudly) make merry; to whoop it up, to party. *Carson City is the official capital of Nevada, but Las Vegas is its gambling and carousing capital.*

[4] **Bacchanalian** In Roman mythology, Bacchus was the god of wine and fertility (his Greek name was Dionysus). A festival held in his honor, a *Bacchanalia*, was marked by drunken orgies. Today a *Bacchanalia* is any noisy, rowdy, drunken party (or feast or celebration). The adjective *Bacchanalian* refers to such a party. *We found out that Mardi Gras, that Bacchanalian celebration that literally means "fat Tuesday" and occurs the day before Ash Wednesday, takes place not only in New Orleans, but in Biloxi (Mississippi) and Mobile (Alabama) as well.*

[5] **fete** A *fete* (also spelled *fête*) is an elaborate party, a celebration, a feast. Note: The word rhymes with *bait*, but the French pronunciation rhymes with *bet*. As a verb, to *fete* is to celebrate or honor with such a party. *Customary activities at a Fourth of July fete include picnics, parades, band concerts, and fireworks displays.*

[6] **erstwhile** As an adjective, this word means "former," as in *erstwhile enemies*. As an adverb it means "formerly." *After his death in 1992, author Isaac Asimov's erstwhile uncollected letters were edited by his brother and published in a book entitled* Yours, Isaac Asimov.

who was now an **overweening**[4], **roistering**[5] **roué**[6]. The listener never actually laughed, but kept rolling his eyes in larger and larger

---

[1] **uxorious** A man who's *uxorious* is overly devoted, submissive (agreeably obedient), or attentive to his wife. *In his 1990 review of the book* Loving Letters from Ogden Nash, *critic Jonathan Yardley wrote, "It may seem a pity that this collection of [20th-century American poet] Ogden Nash's private correspondence comes with such a sappily off-putting title, but the truth had just as well be told: The title is absolutely accurate. On the evidence of the letters herein published, all but a handful written to his wife and daughters, Nash appears to have been the most uxorious and paternal of men."*

[2] **milquetoast** Derived from the name of a comic strip character (Caspar Milquetoast in *The Timid Soul*), a *milquetoast* is a person (generally a man) who is timid, meek, unassertive, spineless, etc.; a wimp. *Timmy, the middle management milquetoast whose assistant demanded a raise, was in quite a pickle— he couldn't say no without a fight but was afraid to say yes because his own boss might not approve.*

[3] **cuckold (cuckolded)** As a noun, a *cuckold* is a man who's wife has been unfaithful (by sleeping with another man). As a verb, to *cuckold* a man is to turn him into a *cuckold* (by sleeping with his wife). *We imagined that if supermarket tabloids existed in the time of Henry VIII (famous for his six wives, more than one of whom was unfaithful), his obituary headline, instead of reading "King Dies," would have read "Cuckolded King Conks."*

[4] **overweening** People who are *overweening* are overconfident, arrogant, assertive, conceited, pushy, overbearing, etc. *In a January 1995 op-ed piece in the* Washington Post, *Pulitzer Prize–winning commentator William Raspberry spoke of speaker of the House Newt Gingrich's "[sharp] tongue, general nastiness, and overweening self-righteousness."*

[5] **roister (roistering)** To *roister* is to party or celebrate noisily or unrestrainedly, especially in a boastful or arrogant manner. *Surprisingly, the first to leave the high school dance was the roistering quarterback, and the last to leave was that skinny, withdrawn guy from the math club.*

[6] **roué** A *roué* is a man who's lewd and immoral. *In the Rodgers and Hammerstein musical* The Sound of Music, *a 17-year-old boy advises a 16-year-old girl to be careful about facing a world of men by singing, "You are sixteen going on seventeen; fellows will fall in line. Eager young lads and roués and cads will offer you food and wine."*

arcs. The story became increasingly **salacious**[1] as it continued, and Dorothy, feeling embarrassed, walked away before the punch line. Still, from a slight distance, she heard "... so the sister-in-law said, 'and if you think he's a **misogynist**[2], you should see his cousin Harold!' " Then, only the fat one laughed.

Listening now to a group of **slatternly**[3] women in heavy makeup and **tawdry**[4] clothes, Dorothy heard another **ribald**[5] tale, this time

---

[1] **salacious** Things (stories, pictures, etc.) that are *salacious* appeal to or stimulate sexual desire; they're indecent, obscene, dirty, etc. *Writer Norman Mailer's publisher originally rejected his 1955 book* The Deer Park *because of "six salacious lines Mr. Mailer would not remove."*

[2] **misogyny (misogynist)** *Misogyny* (pronounced *muh-SAHJ-uh-nee*) means "hatred of women." A *misogynist* is a person who hates women. *The subject of the classroom debate was whether or not record companies should continue releasing rap music, and my side, arguing against it, pointed out that rap lyrics often promote violence and misogyny.*

[3] **slatternly** A *slattern* is an untidy, dirty woman. People (or things) that are *slatternly* are sloppy, untidy, dirty, etc. The word can also suggest sordidness. *After watching the show we agreed that "bag ladies" depicted in TV comedies are never as slatternly as real-life homeless women.*

[4] **tawdry** Things (clothes, makeup, decorations, etc.) that are *tawdry* are gaudy (flashy, showy) and cheap; they're tacky; they appeal to people who have poor taste. The word also often suggests sleaziness, as in *a tawdry affair. On our tour of the city, we noticed that the saloons became increasingly tawdry as we moved toward the waterfront; in fact, the one all the way at the end, our guide told us, doubled as a brothel.*

[5] **ribald** Something (language, speech, a joke, a song, etc.) *ribald* is humorously off-color, vulgar, lewd, coarse, indecent, etc. *The song's ribald humor relied on the device of having an off-color ending rhyme double as the "clean" beginning of a new line; for example, "Send him straight to/Hello, everybody."* Note: In pronunciation, the first syllable is accented and rhymes with *bib*.

scatological[1] in content. Throughout the long story, to the listeners' delight but Dorothy's confusion, baby farm animals served **metaphorically**[2] for a group of Munchkins, the humor deriving from the City dwellers' unspoken but obvious **bias**[3] against the appearance of their pint-sized neighbors to the east. For additional comic effect, the speaker **bowdlerized**[4] this **conceit**[1] by

---

[1] **scatological** *Scatology* is the biological study of fecal excrement (solid waste material eliminated from the bowels after digestion). Jokes, stories, language, etc., referred to as *scatological* deal (usually humorously or sexually) with excrement and bathroom functions. *Because of all its scatological humor, I wouldn't have recommend the movie to anyone under 11 or over 12 (but go figure; it ended up as one of the highest-grossing pictures of the year).*

[2] **metaphor (metaphorically)** A *metaphor* is a literary device in which a word or phrase is used figuratively (to suggest some kind of comparison) rather than literally. For example, if you say of a beautiful, friendly girl "she was a cold drink of water on a hot summer day," you're speaking metaphorically. By the way, a literary comparison that includes the word *like* or *as* (for example, "she was like a cold drink of water," or "she was as irresistible as a cold drink of water,") is called a *simile* (not a metaphor). *On the way to the Red Sox game at Fenway Park, I had to reassure my young son that the "green monster" he'd heard about was only a metaphor for the high left field wall.*

[3] **bias** A falsely based dislike or suspicion of a particular group (especially when stemming from prejudice) is known as *bias*. People who show or feel *bias* are said to be *biased*. *Many people believe the 1921 murder convictions of Italian-born anarchists Sacco and Vanzetti (who six years later were electrocuted in Massachusetts despite widespread demonstrations of support) were based less on evidence (the trial testimony was contradictory) than on bias against their political views.*

[4] **bowdlerize (bowdlerized)** In 1818 a prudish English editor named Thomas Bowdler published an edition of Shakespeare's plays with the immodest passages removed (so it could be "read aloud in a family"). Today, to *bowdlerize* something (a novel or play, for example) is to remove (or modify) objectionable (vulgar or erroneous) passages before publication. *Because The Ed Sullivan Show was family oriented, when rock groups whose lyrics dealt with drugs or sex (the Door or the Rolling Stones, for example) appeared, Sullivan insisted they perform bowdlerized versions of their songs.*

intentionally omitting the vulgarisms, knowing for a certainty her listeners' imaginations would accurately fill in the **interlarding**[2] **lacunae**[3]. At every **expurgation**[4] she slowly and deliberately ran her long painted fingernails through her **blowzy**[5], dyed hair, giving her audience, all of whom appeared to Dorothy frighteningly

---

[1] **conceit** We all know one meaning of this word ("a very high opinion of oneself"). But *conceit* also means "a fanciful, far-fetched, or extended metaphor (literary comparison)." *Seventeenth-century English poet and clergyman John Donne is famous for his conceits, as in a poem in which he compares the souls of two lovers to the two legs of a drawing compass.*

[2] **interlard (interlarding)** To *interlard* something is to diversify it by inserting into it (here and there) some contrasting, foreign, unique, or striking element. For example, a list of boring, dry instructions might be *interlarded* with witty remarks; a thesis on the English legal system might contain *interlarding* Latin phrases, etc. Note: The word originally meant to mix fat (lard) with lean (as of meat). *The first truly Russian opera, Mikhail Glinka's A Life for the Tsar (1836), was written in the style of Russian folk songs but was interlarded with sections written in the popular Italian operatic style of the time.*

[3] **lacuna (lacunae)** A *lacuna* (the second syllable is accented and pronounced *cue*) is an empty space. Technically (in anatomy or botany, for example), it's a cavity, depression, or air space (as in bone substance or cellular tissue). In general usage it means "a missing part or gap (as in a manuscript or argument, for example)." The plural is *lacunae* (with the last syllable rhyming with *bee*) or *lacunas*. *In science class we learned that the lacunae between our nerve cells are called "synapses" and that signals are sent across them by special chemicals called "neurotransmitters."*

[4] **expurgate (expurgation)** To *expurgate* something (an unpublished manuscript, for example) is to remove (or sometimes change) objectionable or offensive words or passages; to clean it up. The noun is *expurgation,* which can refer to the act of *expurgating* or to a particular deletion. *We imagined that people who edit Bible stories for young children must be careful to expurgate all references to sex or violence.*

[5] **blowzy** This word (sometimes spelled *blowsy*) means "disheveled, unkempt, sloppy, untidy." It often carries with it a suggestion of coarseness, grossness, or crudity. *The punk rock band featured a blowzy, blue-haired female lead singer who began her act by sniffing her armpits and spitting on the floor.*

consumptive[1], time to giggle and snort as their imaginations ran wild. Dorothy's face reddened as the **frowzy**[2], **jocund**[3] women laughingly pointed at her and asked each other who the **prissy**[4] little stranger was. Our little **ingénue**[5], thoroughly **discomfited**[6], quickly backed away. Once at a safe distance, she wondered if all

---

[1] **consumptive** Another (especially former) name for the infectious lung disease tuberculosis (TB) is *consumption*. People referred to as *consumptive* are afflicted with tuberculosis. They appear thin, weak, and sweaty, sound hoarse, cough, and spit; they look as if they're wasting away. *Seven-year-old Joey couldn't sleep after watching the horror movie— not because of the 80-foot monster but because of a short hospital scene featuring four consumptive women.*

[2] **frowzy** This word (sometimes spelled *frowsy*) means "untidy, dirty." It sometimes implies, as well, an ill-smelling mustiness. *We weren't sure if our new employee's frowzy clothes were a reflection of low self-esteem or simply the unfortunate result of his circumstances (he couldn't afford to live anywhere, he said, except a basement apartment that often became flooded).*

[3] **jocund** People who are *jocund* are merry, jolly, cheerful, etc., especially in a lively and carefree way. *When they got back from the bar, the jocund conventioneers, laughing uncontrollably, began throwing water balloons out the hotel window.*

[4] **prissy** This word (originally formed by blending together the words *prim* and *sissy*) means "excessively (or affectedly) prim and proper" (see *prim*). People who are *prissy* are primmer than prim, so to speak. *We wouldn't have thought it possible, but when our elderly school librarian was called up to accept her "librarian of the year" award, she walked even more prissily than usual.*

[5] **ingénue** In the theatre, movies, etc., *ingénue* is the term for the leading young, unsophisticated female character. The word also refers to an actress who typically plays that type of role or to any (real-life) simple, honest, innocent girl or young woman. *When we heard that Whitney Houston was starring in Disney's 1997 TV remake of Rodgers and Hammerstein's musical* Cinderella, *we thought that she was too old to play the ingénue— sure enough, it turned out she played the fairy godmother.* Note: The word is pronounced as in French, with the accent on the last syllable.

[6] **discomfit (discomfited)** To *discomfit* someone is to (intentionally or unintentionally) make him feel embarrassed or uneasy; to unnerve or disconcert him. (The noun *discomfiture* means "a feeling of uneasiness, embarrassment, etc.") *The quiz show contestant was an attorney who became visibly discomfited when he couldn't answer an easy question concerning law.*

the **habitués**[1] of the Palace hallways were as **lewd**[2] as the first few she'd encountered. Then again, she thought, maybe those people were merely the city's **riffraff**[3].

Dorothy knew that her Kansas upbringing had been somewhat **prim**[4], but she didn't wish to be thought a prude. At the risk of **sullying**[5] her character, she decided to listen in on one more

---

[1] **habitué (habitués)** People who regularly or habitually frequent (pay frequent visits to) a particular place (usually one that offers some pleasurable activity, such as a restaurant, art gallery, or gambling casino) are known as its *habitués*. *He explained to us that "lounge lizards" weren't actually lizards but were habitués of cocktail lounges; then he added with a wink, "But, depending on how much they've had, some of them do turn green or breathe fire."* Note: The word is pronounced as in French, with the accent on the last syllable.

[2] **lewd** People who are *lewd* are preoccupied with sex or they behave in an obscene, indecent manner. *Lewd* language, literature, songs, pictures, etc., are obscene, indecent, dirty. *After the funeral we all acknowledged his lifelong inclination toward lewdness; then we agreed that we liked him better as a "red-blooded young male" than as a "dirty old man" (even though we weren't sure exactly when the change took place).*

[3] **riffraff** The people that make up the disreputable or worthless element of a society are known as its *riffraff*; they're the lowlifes, the trash. *He explained, "I really don't mind that the rents in my neighborhood are sky high; at least it keeps out the riffraff."*

[4] **prim** A person who's *prim* (or behavior that's *prim*) is excessively (or affectedly) formal, proper, strait-laced, precise, etc. The word, which can also suggest stiffness or prudishness, is often heard in the expression "prim and proper." *According to a 1983 article in* Reader's Digest, *"the parrot holds its food for prim consumption as daintily as any debutante."*

[5] **sully (sullying)** To *sully* something is to soil it (to make it dirty or stained). The word is used to apply both to objects (such as articles of clothing, which literally become dirty or stained) and to reputations (which become stained or blackened as the result of improper or immoral behavior). To say that something (an article of clothing or a reputation, for example) is *unsullied* is to say that it remains clean and pure. *In trying to decide which of Bill Clinton's misdeeds sullied his character the most, we had it narrowed down to two— his affair with a White House intern and his lying about it.*

conversation, however **licentious**[1]. **Wending**[2] her way through the crowd, she soon found herself standing near a distinguished-looking **septuagenarian**[3] in a well-tailored, green **serge**[4] suit who at first seemed a gifted and **charismatic**[5] **raconteur**[6]. Before him was a

---

[1] **licentious** Originally, this word was used to describe people who were unrestrained by law, who had no regard for universally accepted standards or rules. But today, people use this word to describe someone or something *sexually* unrestrained, someone or something lewd or indecent. *In our college course on the history of the feminist movement, the teacher asked, "Historically, have feminists encouraged or discouraged licentious sexuality?" and someone raised his hand and asked, "Do you mean before or after the 1960s?"*

[2] **wend (wending)** To "*wend* one's way" (through a crowd, for example) is to move about or through at random, from one place to another. *Hoping to stumble into a waiter carrying a tray of mini-franks, we began to wend our way through the crowd.*

[3] **septuagenarian** A *septuagenarian* is a person in his 70s (the prefix *sept* refers to the number seven). Similar words based on other familiar prefixes refer to other older people: an *sexagenarian* is a person in his 60s, an *octogenarian* is a person in his 80s, and an *nonagenarian* is a person in his 90s. *In 1984, speaking of President Andrew Jackson (1767–1845) to older volunteer workers at the White House (whom he addressed as "my fellow septuagenarians"), Ronald Reagan joked, "He was actually 70 years old when he left the White House— I know; he told me!"*

[4] **serge** *Serge* is a fabric used in making clothing, especially suits. Usually made of compactly twisted woolen yarn, it has a hard, smooth texture and is twilled (has a pattern of diagonal parallel ribs). *In 1984 New York magazine described the gangster characters in the musical* Guys and Dolls *as "tough-talking, double-breasted, blue-serged hoods."*

[5] **charisma (charismatic)** *Charisma* (pronounced *ka-RIZ-ma*) means "personal magnetism." People who are *charismatic* have an appeal (charm, energy, excitement, etc.) that naturally attracts others. *He argued, and honestly believed, that the primary reason the United States was the greatest country in the world was that it produced the world's most charismatic personalities; then, as examples, he named Elvis Presley, Marilyn Monroe, and Leonard Bernstein.*

[6] **raconteur** A *raconteur* (pronounced as in French, with the accent on the last syllable) is a gifted storyteller, a person who skillfully, interestingly, and often amusingly entertains others with (usually rather long) anecdotes or stories. *I invited my wife's Uncle Stanley (a raconteur who didn't exactly fit our age group) to our dinner party only to avoid disaster— all the other guests were painfully quiet and shy.*

117

sizable group.

He spoke **volubly**[1] and **grandiloquently**[2], using many **sesquipedalian**[3] words Dorothy had never heard. His **animated**[4] facial expressions and hand gestures served to emphasize his points. Unable to understand even the gist of his **prolix**[5] discourse, it

---

[1] **voluble (volubly)** People who are *voluble* speak fluently, freely, and easily; they have a ready and continuous flow of speech. Note: Don't be confused by the word's similarity (in the first four letters, at least) to the word *volume*—the word *voluble* doesn't refer to loudness; it refers to fluency (ease of speech) and talkativeness. *In March 2001 journalist Megan Rosenfeld said, "Reporters who cover the abortion wars quickly learn one thing—people on both sides are more than happy to talk to you; in my experience the [anti-abortionists] were particularly voluble, enjoying any opportunity to [lecture] a listener into exhaustion."*

[2] **grandiloquent (grandiloquently)** *Grandiloquent* speech is speech that's showy, self-important, full of big words, flowery, formal, etc. (the kind of speech apt to be used by a stuffy politician on the Fourth of July, for example). *In September 1997 a* Washington Post *editorial, speaking of an upcoming Senate vote on an amendment seeking to prevent the sale of cigarettes to minors, said, "This is a clear test of the instincts of the Senate on this issue, which over the years has inspired so many grandiloquent speeches and so little action."*

[3] **sesquipedalian** A word described as *sesquipedalian* is long or polysyllabic. (From Latin, *sesqui* means "one and a half" and *ped* means "foot"; so a *sesquipedalian* word seems like it's about a foot and a half long.) A person (or writing or speech) described as *sesquipedalian* tends to use long words. Note: The word (with the same spelling) can also be used as a noun to mean "a long word." *William F. Buckley, Jr., is an American writer and editor known as much for his sesquipedalian speech as for his wit.*

[4] **animated** This word describes things that are lively, active, spirited, in motion, etc. *Because the song started with a slow, out-of-rhythm introduction, the young dancers didn't know what to make of it; then, when the bass and drums kicked in (and the mirrored ball began to spin), they became suddenly animated.*

[5] **prolix** Writing, speech, or a person described as *prolix* (usually pronounced with the accent on the second syllable) is tediously wordy or long-winded. The noun is *prolixity* (state of being *prolix*). *In 1987, on his TV show* Nightline, *Ted Koppel interrupted a prolix guest to say, "I think we're glazing eyes all across America."*

occurred to her that this man might be as **lascivious**[1] as the others, but she couldn't tell.

With **abeyant**[2] distrust, she listened for about fifteen minutes to what sounded to her like a **skein**[3] of **unfathomable**[4] **circumlocution**[5] but was in reality a **caustic**[1], **pontificating**[2]

---

[1] **lascivious** People who are *lascivious* are inclined toward (or are expressive of) lustfulness, or they excessively indulge in sexual activity. *Lascivious* materials (books, pictures, etc.) excite sexual desire. *We felt sorry for Tammy Faye Bakker— not so much because her secretly lascivious TV evangelist husband had been exposed, but because her makeup looked so frightful.*

[2] **abeyance (abeyant)** To hold something (a discussion, a decision to be made, etc.) in *abeyance* is to temporarily set it aside, suspend it, make it inactive, put it "on hold," etc. The adjective is *abeyant*, meaning "temporarily held off or suspended." *In 1993 the search for a new Commissioner of Baseball (to replace the one who'd resigned the year before) was held in abeyance pending the resolution of a labor dispute between players and owners.*

[3] **skein** Technically, a *skein* (pronounced *skane*) is a loosely wound coil of yarn or thread. But anything resembling or suggesting such a coil (that is, anything coiled, tangled, or complex) can be referred to as a *skein,* as in *a skein or lies, a skein of winding streets,* etc. *At the conceptual art exhibit, none of us could tell whether the skein of wire sitting on top of old newspapers was litter or an example of post-minimalist sculpture.*

[4] **unfathomable** To describe something as *unfathomable* is to say that it's difficult or impossible to comprehend or understand, or that it's difficult or impossible to measure. *In Greek mythology, Chaos was the name given to the vacant, unfathomable space from which everything supposedly arose.*

[5] **circumlocution** From Latin, *circum* means "around" and *locution* refers to speech, so when you indulge in *circumlocution* you "talk around" a subject— you're wordy, indirect, or evasive. When you put the word "a" in front ("a circumlocution"), you're referring to a particular roundabout expression or phrase. *Pointing to the phrase "party of the first part" in the wordy legal document my lawyer handed me, I complained, "This is all gobbledygook," to which he pointed to the phrase "quid pro quo," and replied, "Not all of it's circumlocution— some of it's just Latin."*

polemic[3] on the Wizard's politics and character. She noticed that many of the listeners grew increasingly **aloof**[4] with each passing minute. Some just stood there with **bemused**[5] expressions, others with **vacuous**[6] stares.

---

[1] **caustic** This word can refer to either chemicals or to critical commentary. *Caustic* chemicals burn, corrode, or dissolve (something). (An example of a caustic chemical is sodium hydroxide, also known as "caustic soda" or "lye.") *Caustic* critical commentary (as you might find in a negative movie or book review, for example) stings— it's cutting or biting and often satirical or sarcastic. *With its caustic lyrics and pretty melody, Bob Dylan's "Blowin' in the Wind" became an anthem of the early 1960s civil rights movement.*

[2] **pontificate (pontificating)** To *pontificate* is to (often long-windedly) express judgments or opinions (about something) in an arrogant, authoritative, know-it-all, self-important, or showy way. Note: The word *pontiff* means "pope" (the Roman Catholic Pope); by extension, people who *pontificate* often act high and mighty. *At the Super Bowl party, just to sound like a regular, sports-minded kind of guy, Les (who knew nothing about football) began pontificating about why the team he'd bet on would win; then he gave himself away by asking, "What inning is it?"*

[3] **polemic** A *polemic* is a controversial verbal or written argument or attack against some belief, opinion, philosophy, principle, policy, etc. *Political philosopher Thomas Paine's 1776 pamphlet* Common Sense, *a polemic against British rule in the American colonies, helped convert George Washington to the cause of independence.*

[4] **aloof** As an adjective this word means "emotionally indifferent, detached, distant, disinterested, apart, etc. (often from feelings of superiority or shyness)." As an adverb it means "at a distance; standing apart." *Our team captain said, "Okay, now we're going to give that tattletale the silent treatment— and remember, that doesn't mean just maintaining silence; it means maintaining aloof silence."*

[5] **bemused** People who are *bemused* are (and usually appear, as by their facial expression) confused, bewildered, in a daze, perplexed, stupefied, etc. *We weren't sure if he was criticizing or complimenting his new girlfriend when he told us, "She has the happy, bemused expression of a baby animal."*

[6] **vacuous** A person or thing (a book or conversation, for example) that's *vacuous* (note the word's similarity to *vacuum*) is empty; it lacks intelligence, ideas, or substance. A *vacuous* look or stare is expressionless (empty of expression). *Jane, a dedicated amateur actress cast in the role of a blonde bimbo, prepared by acting simultaneously vacuous and sexy throughout the day (in spite of nasty looks from her boss and frequent marriage proposals from her male coworkers).*

THE WIZARD OF OZ VOCABULARY BUILDER

She tried to pay attention, but the **verbose**[1] speech was so **obfuscating**[2] that she couldn't. Absorbing only bits and pieces, she heard him say:

"Most of you don't remember, long ago, when our **eponymous**[3] leader first came to us, but I do—a **mercurial**[4] presence with an **intractable**[5] point of view. Is there any among us who can **vouch**[1]

---

[1] **verbose** Writing or speech that's *verbose* is wordy; it uses more words than necessary to express a thought; it goes on and on. *Depending on the situation, her husband's verbose frankness either made up for or accentuated her natural shyness.*

[2] **obfuscate (obfuscating)** To *obfuscate* something is to make it obscure or cloudy; to make it difficult to understand. Something (a book, instructions, etc.) that's *obfuscating* tends to confuse, bewilder, perplex, etc. *Most kids with boom boxes don't seem to care that when they turn the bass all the way up they run the risk of obfuscating the true musical pitches.*

[3] **eponymous** An *eponym* (pronounced with the accent on the first syllable) is a person (real or fictional) from whom something (a country, a philosophy, a medical procedure, a record album title, etc.) has taken its name (or is thought to have taken its name). The adjective *eponymous* (pronounced with the accent on the second syllable) refers to such a person. *Nineteenth-century German economist and revolutionary Karl Marx is the eponymous father of Marxism, a philosophy which predicts the inevitable triumph of the working class.*

[4] **mercurial** If you're familiar with the element mercury, you know that it exists as a silvery liquid at room temperature and that it flows, expands, and contracts easily (which is why it's used in thermometers and why it's sometimes called *quicksilver*). To describe a person's temperament (behavior, reactions, mood, etc.) as *mercurial* is to say that it's like mercury: changeable, unpredictable, variable, etc. *He said that from day to day he never could tell, when first walking into the house after work, whether his mercurial wife would greet him with a hug or a dirty look.*

[5] **intractable** To refer to a person as *intractable* is to say that he's either difficult to manage (he's uncontrollable, uncooperative, etc.) or that he inflexibly sticks to a particular position or purpose (he's headstrong, stubborn, willful, etc.). The word is also used to refer to things (problems, disputes, illnesses, for example) that are stubborn or difficult to control. The word's opposite is *tractable*, which means "yielding readily to external pressure." *Concerning the treatment of mental disorders, the psychiatrist said, "I recommend talk therapy for mild ones, medication for more severe ones, and brain surgery for truly intractable ones."*

THE WIZARD OF OZ VOCABULARY BUILDER

for this man's **rectitude**[2]? Why should we trust anyone with a **sobriquet**[3] as ridiculously unlikely as *Oz*? At every turn he **eschews**[4] publicity and **spurns**[5] all who try to befriend him. From his **exalted**[6] position, and under the **guise**[7] of charity, he **garners**[1]

---

[1] **vouch** To *vouch* for someone or something is to assure or prove its quality or validity (by guaranteeing it, standing behind it, corroborating it, backing it up, etc.). *The article he read entitled "How to Write an Effective Résumé" suggested adding, at the end, a list of references (people, such as former teachers or employers, who can vouch for your suitability for the particular job you're applying for).*

[2] **rectitude** Your *rectitude*, an aspect of your character, is your moral uprightness, decency, honesty, etc. *Watching the Western, it wasn't hard to for us to predict that the young cowboy known for his fearlessness and rectitude would become the town's next sheriff.*

[3] **sobriquet** This word (pronounced with the accent on either the first or last syllable and with the last syllable rhyming with either *bay* or *bet*) means "nickname." *Comedian Milton Berle's extremely successful early-'50s TV show earned him the sobriquet "Mr. Television."*

[4] **eschew (eschews)** To *eschew* something is to abstain from it, avoid it, keep away from it, etc. The implication is that it would be unwise or morally wrong to do otherwise. *When I offered my witty friend a piece of bubble gum, he shook his head and said, "Bubble gum is something I eschew, not chew."*

[5] **spurn (spurns)** When you *spurn* something (or someone), you reject it, snub it, refuse it, give it the brush off, etc. The implication is that you do so because you consider it unworthy or you look down upon it. *When the patient asked, "Why is it that the more she spurns my advances, the more infatuated with her I become?" the therapist answered, "Low self-esteem."*

[6] **exalt (exalted)** To *exalt* someone (or something) is to elevate his status or position, to glorify or honor him, to put him on a pedestal, etc. *We knew that in Greek mythology the most exalted of all the gods was Zeus, who lived atop Mount Olympus; but we didn't know that he had a weakness for women and that he fathered, among many others, Hercules, Apollo, and Helen of Troy.*

[7] **guise** A *guise* is an outward appearance (sometimes a style of dress) that's usually intended to deceive (or to conceal one's identity). *In the guise of a sheep, the Big Bad Wolf knocked on the third little pig's door.*

filthy **lucre**[2] by **exploiting**[3] the masses—with **impunity**[4]! He **kowtows**[5] to the **gentry**[1] while **sanctimoniously**[2] **extolling**[3] an

---

[1] **garner (garners)** To *garner* something is to gather it, collect it, acquire it, etc. (and sometimes to then amass it, store it, horde it, etc.). *In the 1992 U.S. presidential election, independent candidate Ross Perot, while not winning any electoral votes, managed to garner 19% of the popular vote.*

[2] **lucre** This word (pronounced *LEW-ker*) means "money" or "monetary gain." It often carries a negative connotation; as such, it's usually used to imply that greed or illegality is somehow connected (with the money or monetary gain). *Continental army general Benedict Arnold's motive for planning to surrendering West Point to the British for 20,000 pounds was personal rather than political: he was greedy and always on the lookout for lucre.*

[3] **exploit (exploiting)** To *exploit* something (or someone) it to (sometimes by indirect means) use it, control it, or take advantage of it, for one's own ends (especially for one's own financial gain). *The actress was thrilled to have a popular clothing line named after her; then she wondered if it was worth it when she was accused of exploiting Asian children (who supposedly sewed the garments for only pennies a day).* The word can also mean "utilize" or "employ to practical advantage" (without a connotation of selfishness or wrongdoing), as in *just as the Beverly Hillbillies had, we exploited the oil well we discovered in our yard.*

[4] **impunity** If you have *impunity* you have exemption (freedom) from punishment, penalty, or harm (especially where others might not have such immunity). *In a unanimous 1984 opinion that a man may be prosecuted for raping his wife, New York State Court of Appeals judge Sol Wachtler said, "A marriage license should not be viewed as a license for a husband to forcibly rape his wife with impunity."*

[5] **kowtow (kowtows)** When you *kowtow* to someone you give in to or support everything he requests or believes; you always say yes to him; you suck up to him. (In China this word literally means "knock head" and refers to the former custom of touching one's forehead to the ground while kneeling, as a sign of respect or worship.) *In 1953 Soviet diplomat Andrei Gromyko, speaking of America's sweeping influence throughout the world remarked, "Greece is a sort of American vassal; the Netherlands is the country of American bases that grow like tulip bulbs; Cuba is the main sugar plantation of the American monopolies; Turkey is prepared to kowtow before any United States proconsul, and Canada is the boring second fiddle in the American symphony."*

egalitarian[4] **ethos**[5]. There must be a **parity**[6] between what this **mercenary**[7] monarch gives and what he takes. The reason **alms**[1] for

---

[1] **gentry** When speaking of society's classes, the *gentry* is the upper class (people of good breeding and high social/economic position). *In Rodgers and Hammerstein's 1945 musical* Carousel, *a handsome, unruly merry-go-round operator named Billy Bigelow is adored by young girls but detested by the local gentry.*

[2] **sanctimonious (sanctimoniously)** People who are *sanctimonious* make an insincere or false show of devotion or righteousness. *The title character of Sinclair Lewis's 1927 satiric novel* Elmer Gantry *is a successful but sanctimonious Midwestern preacher.*

[3] **extol (extolling)** To *extol* something (or someone) is to praise it highly. *Though he was known for extolling the virtues of observing nature, writer Henry David Thoreau once declined membership in a scientific society, saying he was "a mystic, a transcendentalist, and a natural philosopher."*

[4] **egalitarian** As a noun, an *egalitarian* is a person who believes in the equality of all people; he believes everyone should have the same political, economic, social, and civil rights. As an adjective, the word refers to this belief. *Some scholars dismiss the phrase "Jacksonian Democracy" as a contradiction in terms because President Jackson's so-called egalitarian ideals applied to white men only.*

[5] **ethos** The particular underlying sentiment (basic beliefs, moral code, attitude, character, values) of a group (or of an individual, organization, institution, movement, subculture, culture, or society) is known as that group's *ethos*. *Sociologists have complained that the advertising industry encourages a materialistic approach to the world and promotes an ethos suggesting that what you possess is more important than who you are.*

[6] **parity** This word means "equality, sameness, equivalence (in amount, value, status, etc.)" *One task of a family court judge is to award alimony and child support in amounts that will ensure some degree of parity in the living standards of divorced men and women.*

[7] **mercenary** As a noun, a *mercenary* is a person who does a job merely for monetary gain, especially a professional soldier serving in a foreign army. As an adjective, the word means "motivated solely by a desire for money." *I could tell from the way the newspaper ad read that Joey was enthusiastic about his music: "Singer, bassist, and drummer wanted to form gigging blues band with guitarist; mercenaries need not apply; call Joey."*

the **indigent**[2] are **minuscule**[3] is the same as why government **subsidies**[4] and **endowments**[5] have been **abrogated**[6]— it's his **propensity**[7] for greed and **proneness**[1] to **parsimony**[2].

---

[1] **alms** Money or goods (such as food or clothing) given as charity to the poor are called *alms* (pronounced *ahmz*). *We asked the preacher if the box that's passed around in church for collecting alms for the poor has a special name, and he told us, not surprisingly, that it's called a "poor box."*

[2] **indigent** People who are *indigent* are poor, penniless, poverty-stricken, etc., often to the point of lacking the basic necessities of life (food, clothing, shelter). As a noun, the *indigent* are these people collectively. *In considering financial relief for the indigent, the government distinguishes between the "truly needy" (orphans, the elderly, the handicapped) and the merely "needy" (those whose poverty stems from laziness or wastefulness).*

[3] **minuscule** Something that's *minuscule* (sometimes spelled *miniscule*) is very small, tiny. *In 1905 physicist Albert Einstein suggested that light travels in minuscule bundles of energy called photons.*

[4] **subsidy (subsidies)** A *subsidy* is an (often governmental) contribution of money, usually to a private business or charitable organization in support of an activity or enterprise that serves the public interest. *In 1971 Congress created Amtrak, a railroad passenger service covering a 24,000-mile network; it was government subsidized, but by 1988 was paying 69 percent of its way.*

[5] **endowment (endowments)** An *endowment* is money or property donated to a person or institution to be used as a permanent fund or source of income. *Oil tycoon and art collector Jean Paul Getty bequeathed (left in his will) an endowment of $750 million to the art museum he founded (the J. Paul Getty Museum in Malibu, CA), making it the world's richest museum.*

[6] **abrogate (abrogated)** To *abrogate* something (a law, policy, treaty, agreement, contract, etc.) is to officially end it, abolish it, do away with it, etc. *A 1916 treaty that gave the United States the exclusive right to build a canal through Nicaragua was abrogated in 1970.*

[7] **propensity** If you have a *propensity* for something, you have a natural liking for it or an inclination toward it. Sometimes, but not always, the word implies that the thing you have a leaning toward is not admirable, as in *a propensity for gambling*. *To save space, the newspaper summarized the entire plot of the murder mystery in just one sentence, as follows: A small boy with a propensity for exaggeration tells his parents he's witnessed a murder, but they don't believe him.*

THE WIZARD OF OZ VOCABULARY BUILDER

He **purports**³ to be a man of **lofty**⁴ ideals, a **paradigm**⁵ of

---

¹ **prone (proneness)** To be *prone* to something is to have a natural inclination or tendency toward it. *In November 2000 the* Washington Post *reported that "a study suggests teen smokers are prone to anxiety disorders in adulthood, adding to a growing body of research implicating cigarette use as a cause rather than a result of emotional upheaval."* Note: Another, unrelated, meaning of the word is "lying down, with the face or front facing downward" (as in *the boxer's prone body*).

² **parsimonious (parsimony)** A person who's *parsimonious* hates to give or spend his money; he's stingy, penny-pinching, cheap, miserly, tightfisted, etc. The noun *parsimony* means "stinginess, cheapness, etc." *Because throughout his long, successful career he's maintained the same modest bachelor quarters, some people describe wealthy consumer advocate Ralph Nader as parsimonious.*

³ **purport (purports)** To *purport* (something) is to openly claim or declare it to be true when there is no proof of it. Sometimes the word implies that what is being *purported* is actually false. *Bigfoot is a large, hairy, humanlike creature purported to inhabit the Pacific Northwest and Canada.*

⁴ **lofty** This word is used in two senses, each of which concerns highness. Physical objects described as *lofty* are very high or tall, as in *lofty mountain peaks*. Things non-physical (ideas, ideals, sentiments, views, goals, conduct, language, etc.) described as *lofty* are on a higher (nobler, more virtuous, more decent, more serious, more intelligent, etc.) than usual plane. *Before the unethical practices of certain doctors began to be exposed in newspapers and on television, the public image of the medical profession was one of lofty devotion to the good of humanity.*

⁵ **paradigm** A *paradigm* is a perfect example (of something) that serves as a model or pattern from which imitations or variations can derive. *Rice companies often use pictures of African-American cooks and the word* Carolina *in their product names because the African-American way of cooking rice "Carolina style" has become the paradigm of rice cookery.*

126

effective leadership, but in truth he's a **pharisee**[1]. The beauty of this glittering City actually masks deep **systemic**[2] problems that are largely unknown to the public. Do you think that government **devoid**[3] of **graft**[4] and **collusion**[5] is a **quixotic**[1] notion? I say it is

---

[1] **pharisee** Originally, this word (but with a capital *P*) referred to a group of Jewish teachers who lived in Palestine at the time of Jesus and who followed religious laws very strictly. But because they added their own interpretations to these laws and added many of their own rules, Jesus called them hypocrites (phonies). Today, if you refer to someone as a *pharisee*, you mean he self-righteously pretends to have virtues or beliefs he doesn't really possess. *In the 1870s, women's rights activist Victoria Woodhull criticized preacher Henry Ward Beecher's pharisaism in sermonizing against free love while carrying on an affair with a married woman (ironically, shortly after revealing the details of the affair, Woodhull was arrested for sending obscene materials through the mail!).*

[2] **systemic** If you say that something (a problem, a disorder, etc.) is *systemic* (pronounced with the accent on the second syllable) you mean that it relates to or affects an entire system (such as the human body, a government, etc.), as opposed to only a part of it. *The manifestations of valley fever, a disease contracted by inhaling dust containing fungus, range from complete absence of symptoms to systemic infection and death.*

[3] **devoid** To be *devoid* of something is to be completely without it, completely lacking it. For example, a vacuum is space *devoid* of matter. *The center of the city had become a commercial area nearly devoid of residences.*

[4] **graft** The unethical, dishonest, or unfair use of one's position (in government or business, for example) to acquire profit or advantages (taking a bribe, for example) is known as *graft*. *In 1958 a congressional investigation of the FCC (Federal Communications Commission) led to the resignation of one commissioner over graft in the granting of television licenses.*

[5] **collusion** A secret agreement between two or more people or parties for a deceitful, evil, or illegal purpose is known as *collusion*. (People involved in collusion are sometimes informally referred to as being "in cahoots" with each other.) *Some people believe that the reason gasoline prices sometimes suddenly rise is that American oil companies are profiteering or working in collusion with OPEC (Organization of Arab Petroleum Exporting Countries).*

not; I say corruption can be **extirpated**[2].

"You may be asking yourself, Why is this **droning**[3] **dissident**[4] **haranguing**[5] us with this **loquacious**[1], **vituperative**[2] **invective**[3]?,

---

[1] **quixotic** This word (pronounced *kwik-SOT-ic*), meaning "idealistic or unrealistic to the point of impracticality," refers to the fictional character Don Quixote (pronounced *key-HOH-tee*), a dreamer who comes to believe he's a knight destined to right wrongs, from Miguel de Cervantes' humorous 1605 novel *Don Quixote de la Mancha*. *People who called Italian physicist Guglielnmo Marconi's 1894 experiments in wireless telegraphy (radio) quixotic changed their minds when, in 1909, his equipment helped bring rescue ships to a sinking ocean liner and he won the Nobel Prize in physics.*

[2] **extirpate (extirpated)** Technically, to *extirpate* something (a weed, for example) is to pull it out by the roots. But in general usage the word is used to mean "utterly remove, destroy, exterminate, rid, etc." *An August 1997 editorial in the* Washington Post *said that "the Redskins [will] play on natural grass in their new stadium; none of that artificial stuff that began to spread over American playing fields in the '60s and is only gradually being extirpated like so much stubborn crabgrass."*

[3] **drone (droning)** Technically, to *drone* is to speak in a monotonous tone (or a low, monotonous tone). But usually, when you speak about someone "droning on and on," you mean that he talks continuously and lengthily (and sometimes in a monotone) about something that is not interesting to you. *Our new computer has a feature called "speech," which allows you to hear text read aloud by a synthesized, strangely Swedish-sounding "computer voice"; we tested it by opening our longest text document and clicking on "speech," after which the "voice" droned on endlessly.*

[4] **dissident** A *dissident* is a person who dissents (disagrees) with the majority opinion about something (such as politics or religion). The implication is that this disagreement might divide people into rival groups and cause fighting or turmoil. *Yugoslavian king Alexander I (who, in 1929, had unified the peoples of Serbia, Croatia, and Slovenia) was assassinated in 1934 by Croation dissidents.*

[5] **harangue (haranguing)** As a noun, a *harangue* (pronounced *huh-RANG*) is a long, passionate (usually angry, denunciatory, or accusatory) speech. As a verb, to *harangue* is to make such a speech. *Patrick Henry's 1775 "Give Me Liberty or Give Me Death" speech was a harangue against British rule in the American colonies.*

and I tell you it's because we're all in danger—the man is evil
incarnate[4]. Now, you might think that opposing an **omnipotent**[5]
Wizard is **fruitless**[6]—but remember, history has shown that when
great numbers unite in their demand for change, they are a

---

[1] **loquacious** People who are *loquacious* are either talkative (chatty, ready to talk, easy and fluent with speech) or wordy (using too many words to express their ideas, longwinded). *Scolding loquacious audience members at a 1967 concert, famed orchestra conductor Leopold Stokowski remarked, "A painter paints his pictures on canvas, but musicians paint their pictures on silence; we provide the music and you provide the silence."*

[2] **vituperative** To describe speech or language as *vituperative* (pronounced with the accent on the second syllable) is to say that it's marked by harsh or abusive disapproval or criticism; it's deliberately harmful, nasty, insulting. As a noun, *vituperation* is such speech or language (or the act of using such speech or language). *In 1992, while campaigning for the re-election of President George H. Bush, Vice President Dan Quayle made numerous vituperative attacks against opponent Bill Clinton's character.*

[3] **invective** As a noun, *invective* is harshly abusive or denunciatory language; a tongue-lashing. As an adjective, it means "abusive, denunciatory, etc." *In the 1973 film* The Paper Chase, *veteran actor John Houseman portrays an awesome but stuffy Harvard Law School professor whose sarcastic invective humiliates unprepared students.*

[4] **incarnate** This adjective means "in human form (invested with a bodily form)," as in *the devil incarnate* or "personified (perfectly exemplified by a human being)," as in *Mother Teresa was goodness incarnate. A fundamental doctrine of Christianity is that God exists in three persons— the Father, the Son (who became incarnate as Jesus), and the holy ghost (which is usually represented in art as a dove).*

[5] **omnipotent** To describe someone as *omnipotent* (pronounced with the accent on the second syllable) is to say that he has unlimited or universal power or authority. The noun is *omnipotence. In Judaism and Islam, miracles are regarded as evidence of God's omnipotence.*

[6] **fruitless** If something (an attempt, a search, etc.) is *fruitless,* it produces no success or no result; it's useless, pointless, ineffectual, etc. *In August 1994, major league baseball players (mainly because they were opposed to a proposed player salary cap) went on strike; a month later, after negotiations had proven fruitless, the baseball owners canceled the rest of the season and the World Series.*

129

juggernaut[1]. Join me now and you'll stand in the **vanguard**[2] of—and I'm not being **hyperbolic**[3]— the greatest reform movement this land has ever known. Then, because increasing our numbers is **paramount**[4], we must go out and **pertinaciously**[5] **importune**[1] our

---

[1] **juggernaut** Something (a destructive force, an object, a set of beliefs, for example) that overwhelmingly, ruthlessly, or unstoppably advances forward (as a football team, a war, a large battleship, etc.) and crushes all opposition is referred to as a *juggernaut. Though individually puny, when tropical army ants move in a million-strong swarm, they are a juggernaut that overruns and devours any animal in their path.*

[2] **vanguard** To be in the *vanguard* of a trend or movement is to be at the forefront (leading position) of it; to be one of its driving forces. *It seems every time singer Madonna reinvents herself, she's in the vanguard of a new fashion trend.*

[3] **hyperbole (hyperbolic)** A statement or figure of speech that uses obvious or intentional exaggeration and is not necessarily intended to be taken literally (such as "I'm so hungry I could eat a horse") is known as *hyperbole* (pronounced *high-PER-ba-lee*). The adjective is *hyperbolic* ("using exaggeration; exaggerated"). *A few weeks after the 2000 presidential election (between George W. Bush and Al Gore), a* Washington Post *editorial, referring to the war of words surrounding the controversial Florida recount, said, "With luck, we'll reach Inauguration Day without a civil war; okay, that's a little hyperbolic, but it's no exaggeration to say that this election is growing uglier by the hour."*

[4] **paramount** If you refer to something (an objective, a concern, etc.) as *paramount,* you mean that it's first (chief, utmost, etc.) in importance or regard. *In February 1993 (in a speech on international trade), President Bill Clinton said, "Thirty years ago, in the last year of his short but brilliant life, John Kennedy [addressed] the paramount challenge of that time: the [pursuit of] peace in the face of nuclear confrontation."*

[5] **pertinacious (pertinaciously)** People who are *pertinacious* stubbornly stick to whatever they're trying to accomplish; they're persistent, insistent, persevering, determined, etc. However, the word often implies that this "stick-to-it-iveness" is somehow annoying or obnoxious (to others), as in *a pertinacious door-to-door salesman who wouldn't take no for an answer.* The noun is *pertinacity. Even though I told my cat she wasn't allowed to jump up on the supper table, she did so repeatedly (possibly as a display of pertinacity but more likely because she didn't understand English).*

friends and neighbors to join the **insurrection**[2]."

At this point a bearded, **bespectacled**[3] college student in the crowd, worried that this **subversive**[4] **radical**[5] might **foment**[1]

---

[1] **importune** To *importune* (pronounced with the accent on the third syllable) is to ask, request, or urge, especially repeatedly, persistently, or annoyingly (as a child might when asking a parent for candy). The adjective is *importunate* (pronounced with the accent on the second syllable and with the first *t* pronounced as *ch*). *Because he was constantly being harassed by importunate fundraisers from charities he'd never heard of, Stan almost wished he'd never won the lottery.*

[2] **insurrection** An *insurrection* is a rebellion (or revolt or uprising) against an established authority (a government, for example). The word sometimes implies that the rebellion is popular, limited, or is viewed as the first stage of a larger revolt to come. *African-American slave and revolutionary Nat Turner, believing himself chosen by God to lead his people to freedom, led about 60 followers in an 1831 slave insurrection in which 57 whites were slaughtered.*

[3] **bespectacled** To describe someone as *bespectacled* is to say that he's wearing eyeglasses (spectacles). *The trivia question was "Name a famous, bespectacled comedian whose last name is Allen," and I realized that either "Steve" or "Woody" could be the correct answer.*

[4] **subversive** To refer to something (speech, behavior, etc.) as *subversive* is to say that it intends to (or serves to) overthrow or undermine (weaken, impair) an established government. As a noun, a *subversive* is one who behaves in a *subversive* (rebellious) manner. *Requirements for naturalization (the process by which a foreign citizen becomes a citizen of a new country) in the United States include residency for several years, ability to communicate in English, demonstrated knowledge of American history and government, and a dedication to American values that includes no membership in subversive organizations, such as the Communist party.*

[5] **radical** A *radical* is an extremist (someone who holds strong or extreme convictions about something); in particular, one who favors or puts into effect fundamental or revolutionary economic, political, or social reform. *The Chicago Seven (which included Abbie Hoffman, Jerry Rubin, and Tom Hayden) were political radicals accused of conspiring to incite the riots that occurred during the 1968 Democratic National Convention in Chicago.*

serious trouble, interrupted the **incendiary**[2] **screed**[3] to shout, "Because Oz has never imposed an **embargo**[4] on criticism, you're really free to **rail**[5] against his policies all you like; you have every

---

[1] **foment** To *foment* something (rebellion, discord, discontent, trouble, for example) is to stir it up, to provoke it, to incite it, etc. *Seeking to foment revolutionary spirit in the colonies, political philosopher Thomas Paine in 1776 began a series of pamphlets entitled* The American Crisis *that began with the now-famous line "These are the times that try men's souls."*

[2] **incendiary** Technically, something *incendiary* causes (or is capable of causing) fire; for example, a Molotov cocktail is an incendiary bomb. But something (speech or language, for example) that inflames (stirs up, arouses, excites, stimulates, etc.) the emotions is also referred to as *incendiary*. *The mysterious 1898 explosion and sinking of the United States battleship* Maine *in Havana harbor has never been satisfactorily explained; but incendiary newspaper articles blamed the Spanish government (which then owned Cuba), and "Remember the* Maine*" became the rallying cry of the Spanish-American War.*

[3] **screed** A *screed* is a long speech or piece of writing, especially one that attacks or denounces something or someone. *French author Émile Zola is remembered for his 1898 essay "J'accuse" ("I Accuse"), a screed which strongly criticized the French government and which influenced public opinion in the Dreyfus affair (a scandal concerning a Jewish army officer accused of betraying French military secrets).*

[4] **embargo** Technically, an *embargo* is a government prohibition on trade with a foreign nation (usually for political purposes). But the word can also be used to refer to any type of prohibition or ban (on something). *In 1960, in an attempt to weaken communist leader Fidel Castro, the United Stated imposed a trade embargo against Cuba.*

[5] **rail** To *rail* against something is to angrily speak out against it; to harshly or bitterly express objections or criticisms (about it). *In September 2001 the Washington Post reported, "At a town-hall-style meeting in Falls Church [VA] to discuss the [September 11] terrorist attacks [against the World Trade Center and the Pentagon] with three Northern Virginia lawmakers, residents railed against security failings and any agency that would balk at applying the strictest measures possible."*

right to your **blasphemy**[1]. You can **decry**[2] the state of the City with your **scurrilous**[3] attacks and **demagogic**[4] appeals. You can condemn the man with your **grandiose**[5] **fulminations**[1] and

---

[1] **blasphemy** A statement or action that shows disrespect or disregard for something considered sacred (God, for example) is known as *blasphemy*. The adjective is *blasphemous*; the verb is *blaspheme*. *Indian-born British writer Salman Rushdie's 1988 novel* The Satanic Verses *was condemned by Muslims as a blasphemous attack on the Koran and the Islamic faith.*

[2] **decry** To *decry* something (a situation or condition, for example) is to openly express strong disapproval of it; to cry out against it. *In 1978, when serious rock fans were decrying disco music as mechanical and repetitious, the* London Sunday Observer *went so far as to call disco dancing "just the steady thump of a giant moron knocking in an endless nail."*

[3] **scurrilous** Something (a verbal attack, for example) described as *scurrilous* is insulting, abusive, vicious, nasty, offensive, shameless, etc. (and sometimes also coarse or vulgar in its language). *Industrialist Henry Ford was famous for producing America's first affordable car (the Model T), but he was also known for the scurrilous anti-Semitic articles he published.*

[4] **demagogue (demagogic)** A *demagogue* is a leader (often a magnetic politician) who gains power by playing upon people's emotions, passions, fears, or prejudices, and by using exaggeration, distortion, and lies. *In 1954, speaking of Republican Wisconsin senator Joseph McCarthy (a demagogue who gained power by falsely accusing hundreds of public figures of being Communists at a time when most Americans feared Communism), television commentator Edward R. Murrow said, "No one can terrorize a whole nation unless we are all his accomplices."*

[5] **grandiose** If you say that something (an idea, writing, speech, art, etc.) is *grandiose*, you mean that it's either grand (large in scope, magnificent, splendid, spectacular, awe-inspiring, etc.), as in *the grandiose operas of Richard Wagner*, or affectedly grand (showy, theatrical, ceremonious, overblown, snobby, high-and-mighty, etc.), as in *the grandiose ravings of a lunatic claiming to be Napoleon. People who suffer from a behavioral disorder known as "narcissistic personality disorder" exhibit a grandiose sense of self-importance.*

iconoclastic[2] ravings. But I really think the public **consensus**[3] of general opinion is that Oz's virtue is **unimpeachable**[4] and that nearly everyone would **vehemently**[5] defend him. So since everything's really pretty **copacetic**[6], why not give up this crazy,

---

[1] **fulminate (fulminations)** If a thing (a cannon, for example) *fulminates*, it explodes with a loud noise. If a person *fulminates*, he explodes verbally; that is, he makes a loud verbal attack or denunciation (against something or someone). As a noun, a *fulmination* is a violent or thunderous verbal attack, a shouted denunciation. *The old black-and-white newsreel showed a huge Nazi rally with a frenzied Adolf Hilter fulminating against Jews, Communists, and capitalists.*

[2] **iconoclast (iconoclastic)** Originally, an *iconoclast* was a person who destroyed or broke sacred religious images. But today people use the word to refer to someone or something that attacks traditional, popular, or cherished beliefs, ideas, or institutions. *Developed in the 20th century, modern dance resembles modern art and music in being experimental and iconoclastic.*

[3] **consensus** A general agreement (about something) or a majority opinion (about something) is known as a *consensus. The Vice President of the United States presides over the Senate, but the House of Representatives elects its presiding officer, the Speaker of the House, by consensus of the majority party.*

[4] **unimpeachable** To refer to something (a witness, a motive, etc.) as *unimpeachable* is to say that it's above suspicion, beyond doubt, impossible to discredit, unquestionable, etc. *When my son and I disagreed over whether a black leather motorcycle jacket was appropriate dress for high school, we resolved the conflict by checking with an unimpeachable authority on the subject— the school principal.*

[5] **vehement (vehemently)** To describe a verbal or written expression (a denial, defense, denunciation, protest, insistence, etc.) as *vehement* is to say that it's forceful, intense, emotional, passionate, etc. *American colonists vehemently opposed the Stamp Act of 1765 (which required the payment of a tax to Britain on a variety of papers and documents) and formed organizations to resist it.*

[6] **copacetic** This rather slangy word (whose derivation has never been agreed upon) is pronounced *koh-puh-SET-ik* and means "all right, fine, okay, completely satisfactory, etc." *Because Joe didn't want to sound like a complainer on his first day at work, when his boss asked him how everything was, instead of saying, "My office is too small and hot," he just said, "Everything's copacetic."*

THE WIZARD OF OZ VOCABULARY BUILDER

maverick[1] campaign? It really isn't fair of you to **besmirch**[2] the name of our **illustrious**[3] leader with your **disparaging**[4] remarks and **intemperate**[5] insults. Your **inculpatory**[1] claims and **seditious**[2]

---

[1] **maverick** Technically, a *maverick* is an unbranded calf (or other range animal), especially one separated from its mother. But if you call a person (an intellectual, artist, or politician, for example) a *maverick*, you mean he's a nonconformist, an individualist, someone who takes an independent stand from his colleagues (and as such is sometimes thought to be a rebel). As an adjective the word means "being independent (or exhibiting independence) in thought or action." *In the 1973 film* Serpico, *Al Pacino plays a maverick cop who fights corruption in the New York City police force.*

[2] **besmirch** To *besmirch* a physical object is to soil, tarnish, or stain it. To *besmirch* a person's reputation is to detract from the honor of it. *A July 1997 Washington* Post *editorial entitled "Tooth and Glove" said, "It's pretty hard by now to besmirch the name of prizefighting, but if anybody was capable of finding a new way of doing so it would be Mike Tyson; on [June 28] the former heavyweight champ took a bite out of each of his opponent's ears."*

[3] **illustrious** To describe a person (or a person's career) as *illustrious* is to say that he's famous, celebrated, acclaimed, distinguished, respected, etc. *Statuary Hall is a semi-circular, domed chamber in the United States Capitol that displays statues of illustrious Americans, such as Ethan Allen, Henry Clay, Sam Houston, and Daniel Webster.*

[4] **disparage (disparaging)** To *disparage* someone (or something) is to speak badly of him, to put him down. *During the 1950s, society praised mothers who stayed at home and disparaged career women.*

[5] **intemperate** To describe something (speech, behavior, etc.) as *intemperate* is to say that it's not moderate; it's unrestrained, excessive, extreme, etc. Note: The word often refers specifically to overindulgence in alcoholic beverages. *In November 1996, as ABC's election night coverage wound down, legendary TV news commentator David Brinkley created a stir with his intemperate remarks about the newly reelected President Bill Clinton (he referred to him as "a bore" and to his speeches as full of "goddamn nonsense").*

135

statements could really **undermine**[3] him."

In response to what he considered an annoyingly **sophomoric**[4] defense— especially with its **superfluous**[5] use of the word *really* and

---

[1] **inculpate (inculpatory)** To *inculpate* someone is to say that he's blameworthy (of some misdeed); to accuse or incriminate him. Something (comments, evidence, etc.) described as *inculpatory* tends to blame, accuse, or incriminate (someone). *American Revolutionary War general and traitor Benedict Arnold's 1780 plot to surrender West Point to the British was discovered when his accomplice, carrying inculpatory papers, was seized by the New York militia.*

[2] **sedition (seditious)** An act of speech or writing that promotes or encourages discontent or rebellion against a government is known as *sedition*. The adjective *seditious* refers to such speech or writing. *The United States Postal Service is empowered to ban from the mails what it considers to be seditious, fraudulent, or obscene.*

[3] **undermine** To *undermine* something (a plan, policy, or government, or a person's health, prestige, or authority, for example) is to make it ineffective or useless by (sometimes secretly or by imperceptible stages) weakening, counteracting, or impairing it. *Some historians claim that the reason the United States didn't win the Vietnam War was that antiwar protests in America undermined the will of the U.S. government to continue fighting.*

[4] **sophomoric** You probably know that a *sophomore* is a second-year student (in a high school or college). The word has an interesting derivation: From Greek, *soph* means "wise, clever" and *moros* means "foolish, silly." So literally, a *sophomore* is someone who is both wise and foolish (apparently, by their second year, students have gained some wisdom but still haven't shaken off their first-year foolishness). To describe someone as *sophomoric* is to say that he's like a *sophomore*; that is, overconfident about his knowledge, showy, immature, lacking in judgment, etc. *A 1986 New York Times article sarcastically noted that in the 1960s "[an empty, straw-covered, Italian wine bottle] with a candle stuck in its neck was an unmistakable badge of sophomoric sophistication."*

[5] **superfluous** If something is *superfluous* (pronounced with the accent on the second syllable), it's extra, extraneous, needless, unnecessary, more than necessary, etc. *In 1958, speaking of the purpose of the United Nations, the U.S. ambassador, Henry Cabot Lodge, Jr., said, "Everything it does which helps prevent World War III is good; everything which does not further that goal, either directly or indirectly, is at best superfluous."*

the **tautological**[1] **redundancy**[2] of the phrase *of general opinion*— the speaker's mouth muscles managed to produce a smile that was at the same time **sardonic**[3] and overly patient. Then, with a **petulant**[4] wave of his hand, he glared with thinly veiled **contempt**[5] at the

---

[1] **tautology (tautological)** In logic, a *tautology* is a statement that's automatically true (it can't be proven false), such as "It is either snowing or not snowing." In general usage, to refer to something as *tautological* is to say that it's needlessly repetitious, that it doesn't impart any new information or additional clarity, or that its truth is obvious and can be taken for granted. *In their* Communist Manifesto *(1848), Karl Marx and Frederick Engels point out that the proposition "there can no longer be any wage-labor when there is no longer any capital" is tautological.*

[2] **redundant (redundancy)** Speech or writing that's *redundant* is unnecessarily repetitive; for example, in the phrase "true facts," the word *true* is redundant (because facts, by definition, are true). *When I said to the waitress, "I'll have the clam chowder soup," my date laughed at me, then explained that the word* soup *was redundant because chowder means soup.*

[3] **sardonic** A facial expression or comment described as *sardonic* is snide, mocking, sneering, sarcastic, cynical, bitter, cutting, etc. *W. C. Fields, an early 20th-century American comedian famous for his top hat and raspy voice, frequently played the part of a cynical, heavy-drinking swindler who habitually aimed side-of-the-mouth-delivered, sardonic comments at his chief tormentors: women and children.*

[4] **petulant** People who are *petulant* tend to become unreasonably or unjustifiably irritable, impatient, or hot-tempered (over a trivial annoyance, for example). *Our waiter acted friendly until I asked if I could order a half portion for half price; then, instead of politely saying no, he petulantly tossed his head and said, "I should think not."*

[5] **contempt** A feeling of dislike or aversion mixed with a feeling of superiority (toward someone or something) is known as *contempt. A 1963 New York Times article described how various countries viewed the typical Englishwoman's clothing, as follows: "The French reaction is a shrug, the Italian reaction a spreading of the hands and a lifting of the eyes, and the American reaction simply one of amused contempt."*

THE WIZARD OF OZ VOCABULARY BUILDER

interlocutor[1] and **retorted**[2] **testily**[3], "My ideas may not sound so **heretical**[4] to you when I point out that while people are living in **squalor**[5], this **profligate**[1] regularly **expropriates**[2] **prodigal**[3] sums

---

[1] **interlocutor** A person who (often formally or officially) takes part in a conversation or dialogue (especially a high-level one), or a person who interjects questions into a dialogue, is known as an *interlocutor*. *In the 1200s and 1300s, Venice, strategically located at the top of the Adriatic sea, not only dominated trade between Europe and the Middle East but also served as interlocutor between the two cultures.*

[2] **retort (retorted)** To *retort* is to reply, to answer back (especially in a quick, sharp, or witty way). As a noun, a *retort* is a sharp or witty reply (especially one that counters another's remark). *When advised not to become a lawyer because the profession was already overcrowded, (American statesman and orator) Daniel Webster (1782–1852) retorted, "There is always room at the top."*

[3] **testy (testily)** People who are *testy* are touchy, grouchy, short-tempered, irritable, impatient, etc. *In his December 1998 report on the Microsoft antitrust trial, journalist Rajiv Chandrasekaran wrote, "A lawyer for the software giant and an economist hired by the government grew visibly testy yesterday as they dueled over differing views of the company's conduct."*

[4] **heretic (heretical)** A *heretic* is a person who holds opinions that are at variance with established ones (as in religion, politics, philosophy, science, etc.), especially a person who rejects the teachings of a particular church (especially the Roman Catholic Church). The maintaining of such an unconventional opinion is known as *heresy*. The adjective *heretical* means "characteristic of heretics or heresy; that is, disbelieving, freethinking, nonconforming, irreligious, rebellious, etc." *Sixteenth-century German theologian and Protestant Reformation leader Martin Luther was proclaimed a heretic for rejecting many of the beliefs of the Roman Catholic Church.*

[5] **squalor** If someone lives in *squalor*, he lives in a condition of filth, wretchedness, misery, poverty, disorder, foulness, neglect, etc. The adjective *squalid* refers to this unfortunate condition. *Jacob Riis was a Danish-American journalist and social reformer whose 1880s reports on squalid living conditions in New York City tenements led to improvements in housing.*

from the City's treasury for his personal pleasures—in spite of **stringent**[4] measures that were designed to prevent that very thing! How do you suppose this **egomaniac**[5] supports his **sybaritic**[1]

---

[1] **profligate** A *profligate* (pronounced with the accent on the first syllable) is a person who is recklessly wasteful or extravagant (especially with money); a spendthrift. As an adjective, the word means "recklessly wasteful." *Because President Franklin D. Roosevelt's New Deal social programs required vast expenditures of public funds, he developed a reputation as a profligate.* Note: In a second, unrelated meaning, a *profligate* is a lewd, immoral person (and as an adjective, *profligate* means "lewd, immoral").

[2] **expropriate (expropriates)** To *expropriate* something (money, goods, property, land, etc.) is to take it (from a person) for one's own use; to steal it. The implication is that the person doing the taking believes he has the right to do so. *In the late 1800s, German settlers in Namibia expropriated African lands and assigned Africans to reserves.*

[3] **prodigal** Depending on the context, this adjective can mean "lavish, abundant," as in *prodigal amounts,* or "wasteful, extravagant," as in *prodigal spending.* As a noun, a *prodigal* is someone who recklessly wastes money; a spendthrift. Note: Because of a famous Biblical parable known as "The Prodigal Son" (which tells the story of a son who leaves home, recklessly spends all his money, then returns home), some people (technically inaccurately, but rather commonly) use the expression "prodigal son" to refer to a person who returns home after a long absence (even though, in the parable, the word *prodigal* refers to the son's wastefulness, not to his returning home). *For his expert handling of the negotiations that ended the Arab-Israeli conflict in 1949, African-American diplomat Ralph Bunche earned prodigal praise and won the Nobel Peace Prize (1950).*

[4] **stringent** To describe laws, rules, measures, etc., as *stringent* is to say that they're restrictive, rigorous, strict, binding, severe, harsh, etc. *As a result of the 1912 Titanic disaster (in which, thanks to a shortage of lifeboats, over 1500 people drowned when the ocean liner struck an iceberg), stringent safety rules for ships were instituted.*

[5] **egomaniac** The word *egotist* denotes a conceited, self-centered, selfish person. An *egomaniac* is someone who is excessively or abnormally egotistic. *The 1941 film* Citizen Kane *traces the life of fictional publisher Charles Foster Kane (loosely based on newspaper tycoon William Randolph Hearst) as he changes from an idealistic newspaperman to a temperamental egomaniac.*

lavishness? His **superannuated**[2] ideas and **myopic**[3] **fiscal**[4] policies raise the **specter**[5] of **omnipresent**[6] poverty for us and our

---

[1] **sybaritic** Sybaris was an ancient Greek city known for its wealth and luxury. The adjective *sybaritic* means "loving or marked by (often excessive) luxury or sensuous pleasure." *The luxury accommodations offered by the new cruise ship provided a sybaritic experience that made traveling as enjoyable as arriving.*

[2] **superannuated** To refer to something (or someone) as *superannuated* is to say that it's old, obsolete, old-fashioned, outdated, outmoded, ready to be retired, etc. *While watching the parade, we wondered why, in the age of modern firearms, the soldier carried a superannuated gray sword; then we realized that, though obsolete as a weapon, the sword still plays a part in military ceremonies.*

[3] **myopic** If you're talking about someone's eyesight, *myopic* (pronounced *my-OP-ik*) means "near-sighted (able to see objects distinctly only when near the eye)." (People who have a visual defect called *myopia*, also known as near-sightedness, wear glasses to see things that are far away.) If you're talking about someone's viewpoint, thoughts, ideas, etc., *myopic* means "shortsighted; lacking judgment or perspective in long-term thinking or planning." *Some historians say that Germany lost World War II because Hitler "left his back door open"; that is, while fighting his enemies to the west (Britain, France, the United States), he was myopic about the advance of Russia's powerful Red Army from the east.*

[4] **fiscal** This word, often heard in the phrases "fiscal year" and "fiscal policy," means "pertaining to financial matters (spending, income, and debt, for example)." A *fiscal year* is a 12-month period (not necessarily January through December) for which an organization (such as a government or corporation) plans the use of its funds (money). *Dwight D. Eisenhower and Bill Clinton have been cited as Presidents who blended a belief in programs for social welfare with fiscal responsibility.*

[5] **specter** A *specter* is a ghost or ghostly figure. Figuratively, the word is used to indicate some haunting or disturbing prospect (one that's universally feared or dreaded), as in *the specter of disease* or *the specter of nuclear war*. *The article we read about 1980s Ethiopia contained the phrase "the specter of famine roamed the land."*

[6] **omnipresent** To be *omnipresent* (pronounced with the accent on the third syllable) is to exist everywhere simultaneously. *Watching the dentist examine the X-rays, the terrified child, suddenly believing God's ear to be both merciful and omnipresent, began silently praying for an absence of cavities.*

THE WIZARD OF OZ VOCABULARY BUILDER

posterity[1] for generations! Is that what you **advocate**[2]? If *you* want to foolishly embrace the **tenets**[3] and **ideology**[4] of **autocracy**[5], that's your funeral; but don't call *me* unfair. This is war! And in the **throes**[6] of battle, as they say, all is fair!"

---

[1] **posterity** The general meaning of *posterity* is "future generations; all the people of the future." But when you speak of a particular person's posterity, you're speaking of all his biological descendants (his children, grandchildren, etc.). *In 1984 the Secretary-Treasurer of the Vatican Museum said, "You can't lock up art in a vault and keep it frozen for posterity; then the artist is betrayed, history is betrayed."*

[2] **advocate** To *advocate* something (a policy, an idea, a plan, etc.) is to speak or argue in favor of it, urge it, recommend it, support it, etc. *American scientist Linus Pauling (who won Nobel Prizes for both chemistry and peace) is probably most famous for advocating the use of large doses of vitamin C to prevent sickness and to treat the common cold.* As a noun, an *advocate* is a person who speaks or argues in favor of some cause. *Tennis champ Billie Jean King was an outspoken advocate of equality for women in professional sports.*

[3] **tenet (tenets)** A *tenet* is a principle, belief, or opinion held as true by a person, or especially by an established organization or religion. *A basic tenet of Judaism is that there is but one God.*

[4] **ideology** An *ideology* is a body of ideas (beliefs, principles, theories, etc.) held by a person, or especially by a group, that form the basis of a political, social, cultural, or economic system. *Racial superiority, anti-Semitism, anti-Communism, national expansion, and state control of the economy were all part of Hitler's Nazi ideology.*

[5] **autocracy** A government in which a single person rules with unlimited power or authority is known as an *autocracy*. Such a person is known as an *autocrat, despot,* or *dictator*. *In the 1950s, Idi Amin was the heavyweight boxing champion of Uganda; in the 1970s he was its autocratic ruler, ordering the execution of thousands of people who disagreed with his policies.*

[6] **throes** This word, usually heard in the phrase "in the throes of," refers to a condition of violent or agonizing struggle, trouble, or pain. *Karen took her natural childbirth classes very seriously; but in the throes of labor, everything she'd learned about controlled breathing went right out the window.*

141

THE WIZARD OF OZ VOCABULARY BUILDER

When, in his **peroration**[1], the **malcontent**[2] **inveighed**[3] against the Wizard's **promulgation**[4] of a policy of **obscurantism**[5], then called for a **renascence**[6] of the pre-Ozian lifestyle, Dorothy's mind

---

[1] **peroration** The concluding part of a speech (which often involves a formal summary of the speech's principle points) is known as its *peroration. Our homework assignment was to find out if the line "ask not what your country can do for you; ask what you can do for your country" came from the body or the peroration of President John F. Kennedy's 1961 inaugural address.*

[2] **malcontent** The prefix *mal* means "bad" (or "wrongful" or "ill") and *content* means "satisfied" or "pleased." So, as a noun, a *malcontent* is a person who is always dissatisfied or unhappy (either in general or with an established system, such as a government). As an adjective, the word means "dissatisfied, displeased, etc." *In May 1980, journalist Kevin Klose, speaking of the deadline for participation in the Moscow Olympics, wrote, "The Soviet Union declared that American efforts to organize a massive boycott of the Games have 'completely failed.' Brushing aside the fact that more than 50 nations will not attend, including three of the top five winners at the 1976 Games, the Soviets asserted that those joining the boycott are isolated malcontents wishing only to wreck international sports."*

[3] **inveigh (inveighed)** To *inveigh* against something is to speak out against it, usually angrily, forcefully, or emotionally. *During the late 1960s, many people inveighed against U.S. involvement in the Vietnam War; among the best known were actress Jane Fonda, cultural revolutionary Abbie Hoffman, and pediatrician Benjamin Spock.*

[4] **promulgate (promulgation)** To *promulgate* something (a law or policy, for example), is to openly announce it and put it into effect. *In 1947 President Harry Truman promulgated a program that barred Communists (or people who associated with Communists) from government jobs.*

[5] **obscurantism** Opposition to the spread of knowledge or to intellectual advancement is known as *obscurantism. In 1800s America, obscurantism took the form of slave codes that made it illegal to teach blacks how to read and write (though some, by borrowing books from white owners, taught themselves).*

[6] **renascence** A *renascence* (pronounced with the accent on the second syllable) is a rebirth or reawakening (of something); a revival, a renaissance. *Hippies dressed in beads, feathers, and buckskin made the 1969 Woodstock rock music festival look more like a renascence of the race of American Indians at a tribal dance.*

became so **befuddled**[1], she rushed to the nearest exit. As she hurried out she just barely heard the **firebrand**[2] remark, "And I've never known a man with such **catholic**[3] tastes to possess so **parochial**[4] an outlook!"

Back in her room under the **bedclothes**[5], Dorothy lay **supine**[6], staring at the ceiling. With her thoughts a **farrago**[7] of hopes,

---

[1] **befuddle (befuddled)** To *befuddle* someone is to confuse him, to stupefy him, to make him fuzzy-headed or mixed up. *The intent of a practical joke known as a "phony phone call" is to befuddle, through outrageous or nonsensical talk, whoever happens to answer.* If you're *befuddled*, you are confused, baffled, bewildered, confounded, mixed-up, etc. *In their comedy act, real-life husband and wife George Burns and Gracie Allen portrayed an ever-patient man and his befuddled but imperturbable wife.*

[2] **firebrand** A person who stirs up trouble or who ignites a revolt is known as a *firebrand. As evidenced by his "Give Me Liberty or Give Me Death" speech, American Revolutionary leader Patrick Henry was a firebrand who demanded national independence.*

[3] **catholic** When this word is spelled with a capital C, it refers to a religion (Catholicism). But with a small c it means "widespread; all-inclusive." *The psychologist said that the best cure for depression was outdoor exercise and catholic interests.*

[4] **parochial** While this word often refers to a church parish (as in *parochial school*), a second meaning is "very narrow or restricted in scope," as in *parochial views* or *parochial interests. The creators of the 1970s TV series* All in the Family *intended the intolerant main character, Archie Bunker, to be a parody of parochialism in middle-class America; to their surprise, many people adopted Bunker as their hero.*

[5] **bedclothes** Coverings that are ordinarily used on a bed (sheets, blankets, etc.) are collectively known as *bedclothes. In the famous fairy tale "Little Red Riding Hood," after the wolf eats the sick grandmother, he settles himself under the bedclothes to await the little girl.*

[6] **supine** To describe someone as *supine* is to say that he's lying on his back (face upward). *In swimming, whereas the crawl and breaststroke are done facing downward, the backstroke is done in a supine position.*

[7] **farrago** A *farrago* is a confused mixture, a jumble, a hodgepodge (of various items). *The first quilt she sewed was a farrago of haphazardly arranged pieces of cloth of various shapes, colors, and sizes.*

doubts, and fears, the sleep she so needed was **elusive**[1]. Disturbing images of the long day danced **phantasmagorically**[2] across her mind's eye. With a sickening revulsion she reviewed the river crossing that had gone **awry**[3], the **virulent**[4] poppies and her near-fatal collapse, the vulgar group of laughing **demimondaines**[5], and finally the **bombastic**[6], **proselytizing**[1] **diatribe**[2] she had just heard.

---

[1] **elusive** If something is *elusive*, it's hard to capture, comprehend, or remember; it tends to escape from you or evade you. *Although some actors are highly paid, most find economic stability elusive.*

[2] **phantasmagoria (phantasmagorically)** A *phantasmagoria* is a shifting, haphazard series of fantastic images (as seen in dreams, for example), or as produced by a device such as a kaleidoscope (which causes figures to change size, pass into each other, dissolve, etc.). *The hallucinogenic effect of LSD was discovered in 1943 after a chemist accidentally swallowed some; closing his eyes, he saw a two-hour-long phantasmagoria of extraordinarily vivid, shifting colors.*

[3] **awry** If you say that something (a plan or procedure, for example) has gone *awry* (pronounced *uh-RIGH*), you mean that it's gone off course in an unexpected or undesirable fashion. *Scientists believe that viroids (infectious particles, smaller than viruses, that consist of a short strand of RNA) are parts of normal RNA that have gone awry.*

[4] **virulent** A substance (a germ or chemical, for example) described as *virulent* is toxic, poisonous, infectious, etc.; it causes disease or death. *Some cancers occur in a particularly virulent form in people with AIDS.* A *virulent* remark (such as an accusation or criticism) is hostile, bitter, spiteful, venomous, antagonistic, hateful, etc. *During his first two years with the Brooklyn Dodgers, Jackie Robinson (the first African-American to play in major league baseball) endured virulent racial insults.*

[5] **demimonde (demimondaines)** The *demimonde* (whose literal translation is "half world") refers to a class of women whose respectability and reputation is lost or doubtful (usually because of sexual looseness), or to prostitutes as a group, or to a class of people whose success is marginal. As a noun, a *demimondaine* is a member of the *demimonde*, and as an adjective, *demimondaine* means "of or pertaining to the demimonde." *The French postimpressionistic artist Toulouse-Lautrec (1864-1901) is known for his depictions of music halls, cabarets, and Paris demimonde scenes.*

[6] **bombastic** Writing or speech that is *bombastic* is overblown, self-important, puffed-up, showy, flamboyant, formal, etc. *Some scholars say that Shakespeare's early historical tragedies are somewhat bombastic and lack depth of characterization.*

THE WIZARD OF OZ VOCABULARY BUILDER

The **arrant**[3] **pandering**[4] she had witnessed— first to the whims of the City's **nabobs**[5] in the **pretentious**[6], upscale restaurant, then to

---

[1] **proselytize (proselytizing)** To *proselytize* is to urge someone to join or convert to a particular religion, or to join or embrace a particular political party or political philosophy. *All members of the religious denomination known as Jehovah's Witnesses are considered ministers and are expected to engage in door-to-door proselytizing.*

[2] **diatribe** A *diatribe* is a bitter, abusive (usually lengthy) verbal attack. *Some historians have suggested that Senator Joseph McCarthy's wild, anti-Communist diatribes of the early 1950s were the result of heavy drinking.*

[3] **arrant** This word, used to intensify a particular negative quality of a person or thing, means "absolute, complete, utter, total, out-and-out, etc.," as in *an arrant fool, an arrant coward, arrant nonsense. According to a 1965 issue of* Town & Country *magazine, real New Yorkers feel sorry for the millions of unfortunates who, "through misfortune or arrant stupidity, live anywhere else in the world."*

[4] **pander (pandering)** To *pander* is to cater to people's lower tastes, interests, and desires; to exploit them by giving them what they want even if it's of little or no value or substance. *In 1986 film director Terry Gilliam said, "People in Hollywood are not showmen; they're maintenance men, pandering to what they think their audiences want."*

[5] **nabob (nabobs)** Technically, a *nabob* is a governor in India under the Mogul Empire (1526–1857) or any person (especially a European) who becomes rich in an Eastern country (especially India). But in general use, the word *nabob* refers to any wealthy or powerful person. *In 1970 Vice President Spiro Agnew attacked prominent Vietnam protestors, calling them "nattering [chattering] nabobs of negativism."*

[6] **pretentious** People who are *pretentious* act more important, dignified, or distinguished than they really are; they're snobbish, stuck up. Places that are *pretentious* are outwardly showy. Writing or speech that's *pretentious* is overdone, flamboyant, formal. (Note the similarity of this word to the word *pretend*. In all these senses, someone or something is pretending to be better than it really is.) The noun is *pretension*. *In her 1976 autobiography, British ballerina Dame Margot Fonteyn said, "Great artists are people who find the way to be themselves in their art; any sort of pretension induces mediocrity in art and life alike."*

145

THE WIZARD OF OZ VOCABULARY BUILDER

the **prurient**[1] interests of those **dissolute**[2] **rakes**[3] and **libertines**[4] who enjoyed exchanging dirty jokes in the Palace hallways— gave her nightmares of **surreal**[5] scenes of **Dionysian**[6] **debauchery**[1].

---

[1] **prurient** This word means "arousing (especially immoral or dirty) sexual interest; pornographic," as in *prurient* literature, or "excessively interested in (especially immoral or dirty) sex," as in *prurient* thoughts. *In 1957 U.S. Supreme Court justice William Brennan said, "Sex and obscenity are not synonymous; obscene material is material which deals with sex in a manner appealing to prurient interest."*

[2] **dissolute** People who are *dissolute* are morally unrestrained; they excessively indulge in sexual pleasures. *Don Juan, a dissolute 14th-century Spanish nobleman who seduced hundreds of women and was eventually damned for his immoral ways, is the subject of Mozart's 1787 opera* Don Giovanni.

[3] **rake (rakes)** A *rake* is an immoral or lewd person, especially a man who seduces women; a womanizer, a playboy. *Of the all-time best-known rakes, two (Don Juan and Casanova) were real people and one (Lothario) was a fictional character.*

[4] **libertine (libertines)** A *libertine* is a person (male or female) who is morally or sexually unrestrained. *Charged with numerous sexual offenses, the 18th-century French libertine and author known as the Marquis de Sade spent 27 years in prisons and asylums.*

[5] **surreal** An early 20th-century art movement known as *Surrealism* aimed at expressing imagery derived from subconscious thoughts or dreams (as opposed to imagery derived from rational thought or conscious control). To describe something as *surreal* is to say that it has qualities associated with *Surrealism;* that is, it's fantastic, absurd, distorted, disproportionate, grotesque, etc. *Twentieth-century Spanish painter Salvador Dali's stark landscapes are often decorated with surreal melting clocks.*

[6] **Dionysian** In mythology, "Dionysus" is the Greek name of the Roman god Bacchus (the god of wine and fertility), so this word is synonymous with *Bacchanalian* (see *Bacchanalian*). To describe someone as *Dionysian* is to say that he's unrestrained, ecstatic, uninhibited, irrational, undisciplined, frenzied, etc. (especially in drinking and lovemaking). *In a well-known story by Robert Louis Stevenson, the virtues of Dr. Jekyll's well-intentioned medical experiments offset the Dionysian excesses of Mr. Hyde.* Note: *Dionysus* and *Dionysian* are both pronounced with the accent on the third syllable.

Chapter 13 "The Wizard"

Early the next morning, Dorothy, the Scarecrow, the Tin Woodman, and the Lion were summoned to the Throne Room. Dorothy, battling the **lethargy**[2] of sleep deprivation, gathered her dwindling forces as best she could. For a moment she considered what to wear to this important meeting, but the question became **moot**[3] when she remembered that her blue-and-white frock was all she had.

As they walked down the long passageway that led to the Wizard, the Lion, looking like a **doddering**[4] old man, tried to control the violent shaking of his knees. At the end of the hallway, they walked through a door and beheld a big, round room with a high, arched ceiling. In the middle of the room stood a large, green, marble throne. Every part of the room—walls, floor, ceiling, and

---

[1] **debauchery** Excessive indulgence in (especially immoral or depraved) sensual or sexual pleasures is known as *debauchery*. To describe a person as *debauched* is to say that he's lewd and immoral. *Nineteenth-century French poet Paul Verlaine's early life was marked by his stormy relationship with teenaged poet Arthur Rimbaud, and his later life (even though he'd returned to the Catholic faith) was marked by drunkenness and debauchery.*

[2] **lethargy** When you suffer from *lethargy*, you feel sluggish, dull, drowsy, and indifferent (as from fatigue, illness, overwork, or depression). The adjective is *lethargic*. *Chronic fatigue syndrome (known in the 1980s as "yuppie flu") begins with flu-like symptoms and is followed by months or years of lethargy and an inability to concentrate.*

[3] **moot** In general usage, to say that a question (or topic of argument) is *moot* is to say that it's no longer of any importance; it's irrelevant, it's meaningless. *The question of which nursing home to transfer him to became moot when the patient died.* Note: Ironically, the legal definition of this word means pretty much the opposite. In law, to say a question is *moot* is to say that it's arguable, subject to debate, etc.

[4] **dodder (doddering)** To *dodder* (which is something you might see an old person do when trying to walk) is to shake or tremble; to proceed feebly or unsteadily. *Veterans of each war were represented in the parade; even a few from World War I valiantly doddered by.*

throne— was **bedecked**[1] with the **ubiquitous**[2], sparkling emeralds that Dorothy by now had come to expect.

Floating above the throne, like a monstrous **apparition**[3], was a **gargantuan**[4] Head, normal in every way except that it was hairless, bigger than the head of the biggest giant, and unattached to a body to support it! Dorothy and her friends gazed at the Head with a mixture of wonder and fear. The Head's eyes moved slowly until they focused on the little group. Then the mouth began to move, and an alarmingly **stentorian**[5] voice said, "I am Oz, the Great and Terrible! Who are you, and why do you seek me?"

---

[1] **bedecked** To *deck* something is to decorate it (as with something ornamental), as in "deck the halls with boughs of holly." To say that something is *bedecked* is to say that it has been decorated or ornamented (especially in a showy fashion). *In 1867, speaking of a Cheyenne force he'd seen on the Kansas plains, General George Custer said, "Most of the Indians were mounted; all were bedecked in their brightest colors."*

[2] **ubiquitous** If you say that something is *ubiquitous*, you mean that it's found everywhere, it's extremely prevalent. *On our road trip, as we passed towns both large and small, we encountered the ubiquitous "golden arches" of MacDonald's.*

[3] **apparition** An *apparition* can be a ghost (or ghostly figure) or it can be a sudden, unusual (or startling) appearance of something. *While reflecting on my favorite albums of the sixties, I could almost see, floating above the CD player, the apparitions of grooved, 12-inch vinyl circles.*

[4] **gargantuan** To refer to something as *gargantuan* is to say that it's extremely large, enormous, gigantic, huge, etc. (*Gargantua* was the name of a giant in two satirical novels by 16th-century French writer François Rabelais.) *Easter Island, famous for its gargantuan heads carved from volcanic rock, lies about 2,300 miles west of Chili.*

[5] **stentorian** A *stentorian* voice is a very loud voice. (In Homer's epic poem the *Iliad*, Stentor was a loud-voiced proclaimer of news.) *When I told her that if she wanted to leave the party early she should give me a signal by saying "How about those Yankees," I didn't realize she'd say it in an abnormally stentorian tone during a conversation about someone's dead cat!*

THE WIZARD OF OZ VOCABULARY BUILDER

The Lion's heart beat a frantic **tattoo**[1] on his ribs. He let out a shriek and began to turn and run, but the Tin Woodman grabbed him by the tail and pulled him back. Our **plucky**[2] **protagonist**[3], with nervous determination in her voice, said, "I am Dorothy, the Small and Meek, and I have come to ask you to send me back to Kansas."

The Head thoughtfully examined the little girl for a while, as if trying to **assess**[4] her honesty. Noticing the Silver Shoes and the mark upon her forehead, he asked how she got them. Dorothy quickly explained, "The good Witch of the North gave them to me after the Wicked Witch of the East was killed by my falling house." Ordinarily, any story this fantastic would sound **apocryphal**[5], but the Head's eyes could see she was telling the truth.

Now the Head asked each of Dorothy's friends, in turn, what

---

[1] **tattoo** Technically, a *tattoo* is a drum (or bugle) signal sounded to summon soldiers (or sailors) to their quarters at night. But any kind of even or rhythmic drumming, tapping, or rapping can be called a *tattoo*. *In the 1952 film* Singin' in the Rain, *dancer Gene Kelly gracefully combined the rhythms of jazz and the tattoo of tap.*

[2] **pluck (plucky)** If you have *pluck* (or, to use the adjective, if you are *plucky*), you're brave or courageous in the face of difficulties (and you usually face those difficulties with heart, spirit, cheerfulness, determination, or spunk, too). *In the famous children's story "Jack and the Beanstalk," Jack is a poor but plucky country boy who retrieves from an unfriendly giant an enchanted goose that lays golden eggs.*

[3] **protagonist** The term for the main character of a literary or dramatic work is *protagonist*. *Our English teacher asked us if we could think of any well-known boy protagonists (discounting characters in books entitled after them, such as Peter Pan and Tom Sawyer), and we came up with Holden Caulfield from* Catcher in the Rye.

[4] **assess** When you *assess* (pronounced with the accent on the second syllable) something, you form a judgment of its value or character (based on your impressions of it). *In what is known as an Apgar test, a pediatrician assesses the general physical condition of a newborn infant (a perfect score is 10).*

[5] **apocryphal** If something is *apocryphal*, it's of doubtful or questionable authenticity; it's erroneous or fraudulent. *We thought it ironic that a story that glorified honesty (the "I cannot tell a lie" story, in which young George Washington admitted he'd chopped down his father's prized cherry tree) turned out to be apocryphal.*

they wanted, and each answered in turn. The Scarecrow explained that he wanted a brain so he could be as much a man as any other in the Wizard's kingdom. The Tin Woodman echoed the Scarecrow's **sentiments**[1], saying he wanted a heart so that he, too, could be like other men. The Lion, now slightly less fearful, said he wanted courage so he could in reality be the King of Beasts, as the **underlings**[2] of the jungle called him.

"If you expect me to use my **vaunted**[3] powers to grant your wishes," answered the Head, "then you must do something for me in return."

"What can we do?" asked Dorothy, who was ready to do just about anything.

In a **sepulchral**[4] tone the Head answered, "Kill the Wicked Witch of the West."

Dorothy protested that she was just a helpless, little girl who

---

[1] **sentiment (sentiments)** A *sentiment* (about something) is an emotional feeling (about it); an opinion, attitude (about it). *When Abraham Lincoln met author Harriet Beecher Stowe (whose 1852 novel* Uncle Tom's Cabin *helped spread antislavery sentiment), he supposedly said to her, "So you are the little woman who wrote the book that made this big war."*

[2] **underling (underlings)** An *underling* is a person of lower rank or lesser authority than another; an inferior, an assistant, a subordinate, especially one of little importance. *After the new employee gruffly contradicted our boss, I took her aside and reminded her that underlings who want to keep their jobs don't speak to the boss in the same way they might speak to coworkers.*

[3] **vaunt (vaunted)** To *vaunt* something is to boast about it, to excessively praise it. To refer to something as *vaunted* (as in *the vaunted wisdom of Solomon, the vaunted strength of Hercules, the vaunted beauty of San Francisco,* etc.) is to say that it's often boastfully or excessively praised. *According to a 1960 article in* Newsweek, *when it comes to preparing people for parenthood, "our vaunted educational system does nothing."*

[4] **sepulchral** A *sepulcher* (pronounced *SEP-ul-ker*) is a tomb (burial vault). The adjective *sepulchral* (pronounced *suh-PUL-krul*) pertains to tombs or graves. By extension, a *sepulchral* tone (or voice) is hollow and deep. *For Halloween he rigged his doorbell so that when unsuspecting trick-or-treaters rang it, instead of hearing "ding-dong," they'd hear a terrifying, sepulchral groan.*

couldn't knowingly kill anyone, but the Head **dogmatically**[1] **adduced**[2] the argument that because Dorothy was able to crush to death the Witch of the East, she could easily accomplish the same **coup**[3] with her **antipodal**[4] sister.

Smelling **sophistry**[5], the Scarecrow, having quickly **marshaled**[1]

---

[1] **dogmatic (dogmatically)** A *dogma* is a principle considered absolutely true. Someone who behaves *dogmatically* acts as if something unproven (his opinion, for example) is absolutely true; as such, he's dictatorial, arrogant, stubborn, authoritative, overbearing, etc. *In her January 1983 article entitled "In Pursuit of the Perfect Pan," journalist Linda Greider wrote, "Nothing brings out the dogmatic nature of cooks faster than a discussion of omelets; ask ten cooks how they make omelets and you'll get ten Only Ways."*

[2] **adduce (adduced)** To *adduce* something (a fact, a reason, evidence, etc.) is to bring it forward as an argument or as a means of proof in an argument. *Many people have claimed that Julius and Ethyl Rosenberg (an American couple who were executed in 1953 as spies for the Soviet Union) were convicted because of cold war hysteria and not because of the evidence adduced against them.*

[3] **coup** A *coup* (pronounced *koo*) is a highly successful action or accomplishment; a masterstroke. *Getting them to give you not only a recording contract but also a position as a record executive was quite a coup.* The word can also be used as a shortened form of *coup d'état*, which means "the sudden overthrow or seizure of a government by a small military or political group." *In 1991 hard-line communists staged a coup against Soviet president Mikhail Gorbachev.*

[4] **antipodal** On a globe, two places that are exactly or generally opposite each other (England and New Zealand, for example) are said to be *antipodal*. The word can also mean "differing; worlds apart; irreconcilable." *On (the sixties TV series) The Patty Duke Show, an American teenager and her European cousin look exactly alike but have antipodal personalities.*

[5] **sophistry** Argumentation that superficially sounds believable or logical but is nevertheless false or illogical (as might be used in order to deceive someone) is known as *sophistry*. A *sophism* is such a false argument. A *sophist* is a person who indulges in (or is skilled at) such false argumentation. *On the classic TV show I Love Lucy, Ricky always saw through Lucy's sophistry when she argued, "But honey, I actually saved you money because the dresses were on sale."*

some counter-arguments, started to **repudiate**[2] the faulty logic, but the Head, with **obstinate**[3] finality, cut him off with a **curt**[4] but bellowing "That is all!"

Back in the hallway outside the Throne Room, the Scarecrow, **disgruntled**[5] by the Head's **specious**[6] reasoning, **brooded**[1] awhile,

---

[1] **marshal (marshaled)** To *marshal* ideas (thoughts, arguments, facts, etc.) is to arrange them (in your mind) in a proper, methodical order (as in preparation for a debate, an exam, etc.). To *marshal* people (soldiers, for example) is to line them up (as for battle or for a parade). *In the Shakespeare tragedy* Hamlet, *Prince Hamlet, considering suicide as an escape from his troubles, marshals his thoughts aloud, beginning with "To be, or not to be: that is the question."*

[2] **repudiate** When you *repudiate* something (a theory, a doctrine, a statement, a claim, etc.), you reject it as (or prove it to be) invalid, unfounded, or untrue. *In 1935 the Nazis repudiated the Treaty of Versailles (the 1919 treaty that officially ended World War I and required Germany to, among other things, reduce the size of its army and navy) by introducing compulsory military service.*

[3] **obstinate** Someone who's *obstinate* stubbornly and firmly (and sometimes unreasonably) sticks to his position (opinion, attitude) or course of action; he won't yield to argument, persuasion, pleas, etc. *While busing (the transporting of schoolchildren from one neighborhood to another to achieve racial desegregation) has attained widespread support in some areas, in others it has been met with intense, obstinate resistance.*

[4] **curt** If you refer to someone's speech or manner as *curt*, you mean that it's (usually rudely) abrupt or overly concise; it's short, snappish, brusque. *Sometimes we're forced to be curt; for example, when telemarketers call, I say, "Send me the information by mail" and then hang up.*

[5] **disgruntled** When someone's *disgruntled*, he's discontented (with something); he's (often sulkily or grumpily) dissatisfied or annoyed. *In what is known as "Shays' Rebellion" (1786–1787), disgruntled Massachusetts farmers revolted against high taxes.*

[6] **specious** If an argument or reasoning is *specious* (pronounced *SPEE-shis*), it sounds true but is actually false. *We thought a certain tea company's reasoning was specious when, in their TV commercial, they said, "If you had two teabags you'd have more tea flavor; that's the idea behind our 'flow-through' teabag— not more tea, more tea flavor!"*

then **vented**[2] by hurling a string of **imprecatory**[3] **epithets**[4] in the Head's general direction. "What will we do now?" asked Dorothy after the Scarecrow's little **tirade**[5] subsided.

"There is only one thing to do," answered the Lion, greatly relieved that the Head hadn't heard the Scarecrow's **contumelious**[6]

---

[1] **brood (brooded)** To *brood* about something (something unhappy or unfortunate) is to sulkily or gloomily dwell on it (in your mind). *In 1984, after he had written 289 books, author Isaac Asimov said, "If my doctor told me I had only six minutes to live, I wouldn't brood; I'd type a little faster."*

[2] **vent (vented)** To *vent* is to unburden yourself by openly expressing your (often pent-up) feelings; to get something off your chest; to speak your mind. (Similarly, to *vent* steam is to release it through an opening to avoid an explosive buildup.) *Most people believe that if we don't vent, if we keep our feelings bottled up inside, we'll end up with an ulcer (on the other hand, Albert Einstein once gave his formula for success as* $A = X + Y + Z$, *where A is success, X is work, Y is play, and Z is keep your mouth shut!).*

[3] **imprecation (imprecatory)** An *imprecation* is a curse, either in the sense of a wish for (or a calling for) harm upon someone (an evil spell, a whammy, etc.) or in the sense of an obscene or dirty word. To describe something as *imprecatory* is to say that it pertains to or is characteristic of a curse. *In a famous fairy tale, Sleeping Beauty is a beautiful princess cast into a deep sleep through a jealous fairy's imprecation.*

[4] **epithet (epithets)** An *epithet* is a term or phrase used as a descriptive substitute for a person's actual name. While an epithet can be favorable (*The Great Emancipator* for Abraham Lincoln or *The King* for Elvis Presley, for example), people usually use the word to refer to an unfavorable, insulting substitute (a racial slur or dirty name, for example). *During the 1995 O. J. Simpson murder trial, jurors were permitted to hear only two of 41 recorded instances of former Los Angeles detective Mark Fuhrman using a racial epithet.*

[5] **tirade** A *tirade* is an (often longish) angry speech or verbal outburst (against something). *In the 1976 movie Network, we couldn't remember if the line "I'm mad as hell and I'm not going to take it anymore!" was the beginning of a long tirade or if it constituted the entirety of Peter Finch's character's outburst.*

[6] **contumelious** Remarks (or actions) described as *contumelious* (pronounced with the accent on the third syllable) are insulting, disrespectful, or rude. The noun *contumely* (usually pronounced with the accent on the first syllable) means "harsh, insulting language." *It seems that whenever a professional wrestler is interviewed on television, he does nothing but make contumelious comments about his opponent.*

yammering[1], "and that is to go to the Land of the Winkies, where the Wicked Witch lives, and destroy her. I'm too much of a coward to kill a Witch myself, but I'll go with you."

Convinced that the Wizard's decision was **irrevocable[2]**, the Scarecrow added, "I'm too stupid to know how to kill a Witch, but I'll go, too."

The Tin Woodman also thought there was no chance that the Wizard would **rescind[3]** his decision. "I don't have the heart to kill even a Wicked Witch," he said with a sigh, "but I'll go, too."

"Then we're anonymous," proclaimed the Scarecrow proudly.

"Unanimous," corrected Dorothy automatically, shooting him a look of gentle **reproof[4]**. She hoped she didn't come across like a

---

[1] **yammer (yammering)** To *yammer* is to complain or whine, or to talk loudly and persistently. *The book of Exodus in the Old Testament tells us that God guided the Israelites from Egypt to Palestine; but because of their frequent yammering and failure to trust him, He made them stay in the desert for 40 years before letting them enter the Promised Land.*

[2] **irrevocable** Something (a decision or law, for example) referred to as *irrevocable* cannot be revoked (taken back, withdrawn, repealed, recalled, annulled, voided, cancelled, reversed, etc.). *A 1980 article on sex education in* People *magazine said, "Before the child ever gets to school it will have received crucial, almost irrevocable sex education, and this will have been taught by the parents, who are not aware of what they are doing."*

[3] **rescind** To *rescind* something (a law, decision, act, etc.) is to formally put an end to it or make it void; to revoke, repeal, annul, or withdraw it. *In May 2001 journalist Craig Timberg reported that "Virginia governor James S. Gilmore III quickly rescinded a proclamation declaring [the month of] May 'European American Heritage and History Month' after learning it had been requested by a white separatist group headed by former Ku Klux Klansman David Duke."*

[4] **reprove (reproof)** When you *reprove* someone, you criticize him; but the implication is that the criticism is rather mild and has an instructive intent. As a noun, a *reproof* is a gentle, often instructive, criticism. *Perhaps the gentlest of all forms of reproof is the utterance of the expression "tut-tut," appropriate when, for example, you tell your wife you'll bring her breakfast in bed and then she tries to help you cook it!*

THE WIZARD OF OZ VOCABULARY BUILDER

captious[1] old **pedagogue**[2], but at the same time she couldn't help laughing inwardly at the **risible**[3] **malapropism**[4], and this, thankfully, **dissipated**[5] her tension a bit.

That night, they all went to bed early. Dorothy, having had very little sleep the night before, dozed off right away, but her sweet

---

[1] **captious** People who are *captious* like to (or tend to) find and point out trivial faults; they're overly critical, nitpicking, hairsplitting, etc. *We have a captious friend who corrects practically everything we say; for example, if we say that we find cockroaches' antennas disgusting, he'll say (in a rather stuffy tone), "Actually, it's antennae."*

[2] **pedagogue** A *pedagogue* is a teacher, especially a schoolteacher whose manner is stuffy, overbearing, or formal. To describe someone as *pedagogic* is to say that he's authoritative, opinionated, and overly concerned with displaying book learning (especially its trivial aspects) and formal rules. *In the classic 1951 British film* The Browning Version, *Michael Redgrave plays a stuffy pedagogue whose students both fear him (in class) and ridicule him (out of class).*

[3] **risible** If you say that something is *risible* (pronounced so that the first syllable rhymes with *fizz*), you mean that there's something about it (something funny, absurd, incongruous, etc.) that would likely cause you to laugh. *As soon as the comedian walked onstage, even before he spoke, people began laughing because of his risible appearance (he was dressed as a knight with a giant salami attached to his belt!).*

[4] **malapropism** A *malapropism* (sometimes called simply a *malaprop*) is the humorous misuse of a word (usually the unintentional substitution of an incorrect word for a similar-sounding, correct one), as in *he gave arguments to some of Sigmund Freud's tenants* [for *tenets*, which means "principles, opinions, etc."] Note: The word is coined from the name of a character (Mrs. Malaprop, who constantly mixes up words) in Richard Sheridan's 1775 satirical British play *The Rivals.* Her name, in turn, derives from the word *malapropos* ("inappropriate, out of place, etc."), which derives from the French phrase *mal à propos*, which literally means "badly to the purpose." *Not wanting to laugh at the tough-looking traffic cop's malapropism ("let me see your license and resignation"), I looked at him seriously and said "But I was only just hired today."*

[5] **dissipate (dissipated)** When something (a crowd, a mist, a feeling, for example) *dissipates*, it disappears or nearly disappears, usually by the scattering in various directions of the elements that make it up (as a crowd) or by a lessening of intensity or degree (as a feeling). *The gas that comes out of a fire extinguisher dissipates quickly and leaves no residue.*

155

THE WIZARD OF OZ VOCABULARY BUILDER

dreams of **Apollonian**[1] futures were immediately **transmogrified**[2] into grotesque nightmares of a green-**tinged**[3] **Sodom**[4], whose unearthly **luminance**[5] was surrounded by an **inscrutable**[1] **Stygian**[2]

---

[1] **Apollonian** In mythology, Apollo, a young man of great physical beauty, was the god of music, poetry, medicine, and light. As such, he represents order in civilization and in nature. To refer to something or someone as *Apollonian* (sometimes spelled with a small *a*) is to say that it's harmonious, clear, balanced, serene, disciplined, orderly, etc. *Although today American Indians can live wherever they wish, about half choose to live on reservations so they can practice and preserve the Apollonian culture of their ancestors.*

[2] **transmogrify (transmogrified)** To *transmogrify* (pronounced so that the second syllable is accented and rhymes with *fog*) something is to change it into a different shape, appearance, or form. The implication is usually that this change is in some way bizarre, grotesque, strange, fantastic, etc. *In 1984, speaking of Johann Sebastian Bach,* Newsweek *magazine said, "No composer in history has been so widely jazzed up, watered down, electrified, and otherwise transmogrified."*

[3] **tinge (tinged)** As a verb, to *tinge* something is to tint it; that is, to add a slight degree of color to it. As a noun, a *tinge* is a tint; that is, a slight degree of coloration. *We knew that a smoker once occupied the apartment because the white ceiling tiles were tinged with yellow.* Often the word refers to a slight degree of anything at all (not just color), as in *a tinge of regret, a tinge of guilt,* etc. *In 1958 author Vance Packard described rock 'n' roll as "monotony tinged with hysteria."*

[4] **Sodom** *Sodom* was one of two Biblical cities (the other was Gomorrah) destroyed by God for their wickedness and depravity. Today, if you refer to a place as *Sodom,* you mean that it's corrupt, evil, sinful, sexually immoral, etc. *After finding out that the arts-and-crafts counselors habitually took drugs and engaged in sex, Betsy's mother referred to her daughter's sleepaway camp only as "that Sodom."*

[5] **luminous (luminance)** Something *luminous* gives off light; it shines. The word is used especially to describe objects whose light is steadily glowing and is surrounded by a contrasting darkness. The noun *luminance* (also called *luminosity*) means "the state or quality of being luminous." *The New Testament tells us that the three Wise Men of the East were led to the infant Jesus by a luminous celestial object known as the Star of Bethlehem.*

darkness. The poor Scarecrow, standing awake all night, was seized by an **incipient**[3] **paranoia**[4] that eventually swirled uncontrollably through his straw-filled head. Now that he had had his first glimpse of **urbane**[5] society, he felt more than ever like a creature apart, an empty-headed **pariah**[6] sure to be **maligned**[1] and **derided**[2] by all.

---

[1] **inscrutable** To refer to something as *inscrutable* is to say that it's incapable of being *scrutinized* (carefully examined or observed); as such, it's difficult or impossible to understand; it's impenetrable, cryptic, mysterious, incomprehensible, unexplainable, etc., as in *an inscrutable smile* or *an inscrutable God. The critic said that what made the 1975 film Jaws scary wasn't so much the large, man-eating shark, but the eerie background music and the ocean's inscrutable depths.*

[2] **Stygian** Technically, this word refers to the mythological river Styx (a river of Hades across which dead souls are ferried). But when people refer to a darkness as *Stygian,* they mean that it is (or nearly is) pitch black (and is probably also rather gloomy or hellish). *When, at midnight, all the lights in the funeral home suddenly went out, the new employee was forced to descend into the Stygian darkness of the cellar to search, by sense of touch alone, for a fuse box.*

[3] **incipient** If something is *incipient,* it's just beginning to exist or appear; it's at an initial or early stage. *After World War II, the insecticide DDT reduced incipient epidemics of typhus and malaria in Europe, Asia, and Oceania.*

[4] **paranoia** A person suffering from a mental disorder known as *paranoia* falsely believes that people are secretly plotting against him, are saying bad things about him, or don't like him. The adjective is *paranoid. The comedian got his biggest laugh with the absurdly self-contradictory line "I'm not paranoid; it's just that everyone says I'm paranoid behind my back!"*

[5] **urbane** People who are *urbane* are sophisticated, worldly, refined, elegant, suave, assured, polite, gracious, etc., as from wide social experience in large cities (note the similarity to the word *urban*). *During the 1930s and 1940s, the songs of Cole Porter appealed to the general public as well as to urbane Broadway audiences.*

[6] **pariah** A *pariah* (pronounced with the accent on the second syllable) is an outcast, especially a social outcast. (But when spelled with a capital *P,* the word refers to a member of a low class in southern India.) *A 1986 New York Times article referred to AIDS patients as "social pariahs, irrationally ostracized [excluded] by their communities because of medically baseless fears of contagion."*

Chapter 14 "The Search for the Wicked Witch"

The next morning, the soldier in the green uniform led our group back through the streets of the City toward the Guardian of the Gates. Dorothy, her spirit nearly broken, gazed blindly in front of her, an **amalgam**[3] of fear and frustration in her **vapid**[4] eyes. She tried her best to **quash**[5] her doubts, but it was no use. How was she, a helpless, little girl, supposed to kill a powerful Wicked Witch?

"Which road leads to the Wicked Witch of the West?" Dorothy

---

[1] **malign (maligned)** To *malign* someone is to speak badly (sometimes even untruthfully) of him (often in order to harm him). *Although often maligned as corrupt or incompetent, big-city mayors generally work hard to handle the needs of the people.*

[2] **deride (derided)** When you *deride* someone (usually someone you feel superior to and feel an aversion toward), you treat him or speak of him as a laughingstock; you disrespectfully ridicule, mock, or insult him (often for your own amusement). *In 1992 Vice President Dan Quayle was derided by the public and the press alike for misspelling the word "potato."* The noun *derision* refers to either mocking laughter or to a state of being derided. *His newest get-rich-quick scheme was held in derision by his wife.*

[3] **amalgam** An *amalgam* is a mixture or combination of two or more diverse elements. *The population of Brazil is an amalgam of native, African, and European peoples.* Note: The word is also used to refer to the particular mixture of mercury and silver that's used in dentistry.

[4] **vapid** To describe something (an expression, a face, eyes, conversation, etc.) as *vapid* is to say that it's without life; it's empty, flat, dull, mindless, etc. *"Theater of the absurd" is the term for a form of drama (exemplified by Samuel Beckett and Eugène Ionesco's 1950s plays) that emphasizes the absurdity of human existence by employing intentionally confusing situations, illogical plots, and vapid dialogue.*

[5] **quash** To *quash* something (a rebellion, for example) is to stop it (put it down), usually forcibly and completely. *In 1976 black South African students violently protested against the use of Afrikaans (the language of the Dutch settlers) in schools; more than 600 people were killed when the army quashed the riots.*

asked the Guardian of the Gates **apathetically**[1] when they at last arrived at the edge of the City.

"There is no road," he answered, "because no one ever wishes to go that way."

The idea that she now had the **onus**[2] of somehow **divining**[3] the correct path was almost more than Dorothy could endure. She felt tears welling up behind her **smarting**[4] eyes, but she forced herself to **suppress**[5] them. "How are we supposed to find her then?" she asked, her voice shaking.

"Now, now," said the Tin Woodman soothingly, patting Dorothy's back. "We'll find her."

---

[1] **apathetic (apathetically)** When you're *apathetic* (about something) you don't care (about it); you're indifferent, unconcerned, unemotional, etc. The noun is *apathy*. *He blamed television for our young people's apathy toward reading.*

[2] **onus** An *onus* is a burden, a difficult or unpleasant responsibility. *We all agreed that we should somehow make it known to our coworker that her clothing smelled, but none of us was willing to accept the onus of actually telling her.*

[3] **divine (divining)** As a verb, to *divine* something is to figure it out or know about it by (or as if by) guesswork, intuition, or supernatural means. *In ancient Rome, special priests divined future events by studying the guts of sacrificed animals (today, thankfully, we're more civilized— we merely gaze into crystal balls or read palms).*

[4] **smart (smarting)** As a verb, if something (a part of your body) *smarts*, it (usually superficially) hurts or stings. *He doubted very much that the aspirin the doctor advised him to take would do anything to relieve the smarting insect bite.*

[5] **suppress** When you *suppress* a feeling or the physical expression of a feeling (a smile, a groan, etc.), you hold it back (you keep it hidden, you hold it in check, etc.). *Adults are generally better able than children to suppress natural feelings of selfishness.* When you *suppress* activities (of a person or group), you put an end to them. *In 1989 troops loyal to the communist regime suppressed pro-democracy demonstrations in Beijing's Tiananmen Square.* When you *suppress* an undesirable condition (a cough, turbulence, etc.) you reduce its frequency or severity. *Tape hiss (high-frequency sound picked up at random during tape-recording) can be suppressed by a Dolby system.*

THE WIZARD OF OZ VOCABULARY BUILDER

"Her **appellation**[1] indicates that she lives in the West," said the Guardian of the Gates, "so I suggest you walk toward where the sun sets."

Having now **ascertained**[2] the correct route, our curious **coterie**[3] walked west across fields of soft grass dotted here and there with daisies and buttercups. As Dorothy filled her lungs with fresh, clean air, tiny waves of optimism began to roll over her, and little by little she started to feel like her old self again. Then, when the Scarecrow shot an infectious, little smile her way, her fears melted under its warmth.

Now the Emerald City was far behind them. As they advanced, the ground became rougher and hillier, the soil less **arable**[4]. There were no trees here, so sunlight brightly illuminated their weary faces.

Now, the Wicked Witch of the West had eyes as powerful as telescopes, and they could see everywhere. As she sat in the

---

[1] **appellation** An *appellation* is a word or phrase (other than a proper name) by which a person or thing is identified or called (especially when this designation has gained acceptance through popular usage). *Today we call the wife of a President "First Lady," but until the Civil War "Mrs. President" was the common appellation.*

[2] **ascertain (ascertained)** To *ascertain* something (previously unknown) is to find out about it (learn about it, discover it, become aware of it, etc.) with certainty, usually through examination or experimentation. *An autopsy was performed to ascertain the cause of death.*

[3] **coterie** A *coterie* is a usually small, select group of people united by some common interest or activity; a clique, a gang. *F. Scott Fitzgerald, Ernest Hemmingway, and Gertrude Stein were members of a coterie of American writers living in Paris during the 1920s.*

[4] **arable** Land that is *arable* is suitable for plowing and farming; it's capable of growing crops. *Mexico is predominantly mountainous, and no more than 15 percent of the land is considered arable.*

doorway of her **imposing**[1] castle, she looked around, and her gaze fell upon Dorothy and her strange **entourage**[2]. Their presence in her kingdom, **albeit**[3] far off, immediately aroused her **wrath**[4]. Then it occurred to her that the death of her sister, the Witch of the East, had still not been **avenged**[5].

Incensed[6], the Witch went to her cupboard to get the Golden Cap. Whoever owned this magical Cap could call upon the army of Winged Monkeys, who, with **monolithic**[7] solidarity, were forced to

---

[1] **imposing** If you say that something is *imposing*, you mean that it's impressive, splendid, magnificent, majestic, grand, etc., by virtue of its size or power. *On our trip to Washington, D.C., we were able to see the imposing Washington Monument from anywhere in the city.*

[2] **entourage** An *entourage* is a group of associates or attendants (followers, companions, servants, etc.), as of an important or powerful person. *Pop artist Andy Warhol often surrounded himself with a glamorous entourage and rock group.*

[3] **albeit** This word (pronounced *all-BEE-it*) means "although," "even though," or "even if." *In 1954 the U.S. Supreme Court eliminated segregation in schools by overturning the "separate but equal" rule (a doctrine by which whites and blacks were promised equal, albeit separate, educational facilities).*

[4] **wrath** An intense anger or rage, especially one that seeks punishment or vengeance, is known as *wrath*. *Before the Age of Reason, people blamed natural disasters (hurricanes, tornadoes, earthquakes, etc.) on the wrath of God.*

[5] **avenge (avenged)** To *avenge* something (a wrongdoing) is to take vengeance (inflict pain or harm in return) on behalf of another person. *Shakespeare's* Hamlet *is a tragedy about a young Danish prince who feels he must avenge his father's murder.*

[6] **incensed** To *incense* (pronounced with the accent on the second syllable) is to cause to be extremely angry. If you're *incensed*, you're enraged, infuriated, etc. *In the fairy tale* Snow White and the Seven Dwarfs, *an evil queen becomes incensed when a magical mirror tells her that Snow White is fairer (prettier) than she is.*

[7] **monolithic** Technically, a *monolith* is a single, huge block of stone (as used in architecture or for monuments). But when people refer to something (a government, a political system, a corporation, etc.) as *monolithic*, they mean that it acts as a massive, single, solid, rigid, uniform whole. *After World War II the United States assumed that the principal threat to U.S. security and world peace was the Soviet-directed global spread of monolithic Communism.*

carry out any order they were given. She summoned them, and at once the great **horde**[1] descended, their immense wings casting a menacing shadow across the land.

The largest Monkey, who was their leader, landed close to the Witch and asked, "What is your command?"

"Fly to the revolting **vermin**[2] who have invaded my land and destroy them— especially the murderous child, the **linchpin**[3] of that **motley**[4] band," answered the Witch. "But bring the Lion to me," she added, rubbing her hands together in a show of anticipatory, **malicious**[5] glee, "for I might **yoke**[1] him like a horse so I can

---

[1] **horde** A *horde* is a large group (of something), a crowd, a multitude, etc. Sometimes the word refers specifically to a moving pack of animals, as in *a horde of mosquitoes. During the 13th century, Genghis Khan and his Mongol hordes conquered vast portions of northern China and southwestern Asia.*

[2] **vermin** Technically, the word *vermin* (thought of as plural) refers to insects or other small animals that appear in large numbers, are annoying or harmful, and are difficult to control (such as lice, termites, cockroaches, mice, etc.) But when you refer to people as *vermin*, you mean that they are obnoxious, repulsive, disgusting, revolting, etc. *According to* Grolier's Encyclopedia, *"Direct connection of sanitary [bathroom] fixtures to a sewer or private disposal system would not be possible without a means of preventing sewer gases, bacteria, or vermin from entering the building through the pipes; a water trap near the outlet of each fixture contains a short but solid column of water that isolates the incoming water from contamination."*

[3] **linchpin** Technically, a *linchpin* is a metal pin inserted crosswise at the end of an axle to keep the wheel on. Figuratively, a *linchpin* is someone or something that holds a situation together, a central unifying force. *Black Panther linchpin Huey Newton, quoting Chinese Communist party chairman Mao Tse-tung, once said, "Political power comes through the barrel of a gun."*

[4] **motley** This word is used to describe a group of people or a collection of things that's made up of a diversity or variety of elements. The word is often used as a put-down to imply that the diversity or variety is unappealing, disorderly, offensive, etc. *The 1967 war film* The Dirty Dozen *concerns a motley gang of military prisoners who are trained to fight behind enemy lines.*

[5] **malicious** A desire to harm or hurt someone, especially when based on natural meanness, is known as *malice*. The adjective is *malicious. In the late 1940s, malicious gossip columnists portrayed singer Frank Sinatra as a communist sympathizer.*

practice my **equestrian**[2] skills."

"Your command shall be obeyed," said the leader **compliantly**[3]. Then, with a low rumbling sound, the **simian**[4] **swarm**[5] flew in **echelon**[6] formation to the place where Dorothy and her friends were walking.

Swooping down, one row of soldiers seized the Tin Woodman

---

[1] **yoke** To *yoke* an animal (such as an ox or horse) is to fit its neck with a harness. Often two such animals are joined together (with their harnesses connected by a crosspiece) to pull heavy loads. *African-American author Alex Haley's 1976 book* Roots *traces his family's history to his ancestor Kunta Kinte, who was kidnapped in Africa in the 18th century, yoked, and taken as a slave to America.*

[2] **equestrian** As a noun, an *equestrian* is a person who rides (or performs) on horseback. As an adjective, the word means "relating or pertaining to horseback riders or horseback riding" or "represented on horseback," as *an equestrian statue.* *Whereas men and women compete separately in most Olympic sports, they may compete against each other in equestrian and yachting events.*

[3] **compliant (compliantly)** To *comply* with someone's requests, demands, wishes, etc., is to agree to them, to give in to them. If you're *compliant,* you tend to comply, obey, yield, etc., especially meekly or without protest. *Because her father's nature was more compliant than her mother's, Susie went to him whenever she needed money.*

[4] **simian** This adjective means "referring or pertaining to monkeys or apes." *Since 1963, simian organs have been used experimentally in human transplants.*

[5] **swarm** A *swarm* is a great number of insects (or other animals, people, or small things), especially in motion, as in *a swarm of bees. In the 1964 British film* A Hard Day's Night, *swarms of teenaged girls chase after their idols, the Beatles.*

[6] **echelon** A particular rank or level of authority in a structured organization (such as a corporation, government, or military force) is known as an *echelon.* For example, in the army, generals belong to the upper *echelon* and privates to the lower. *Civil rights activists point out that while it's not unusual for lineups of major league baseball teams to be mostly African-American, the higher echelons (managers, general managers, and owners) are mostly white.* The phrase *echelon formation* refers to a formation of troops, aircraft, etc., in which units are positioned successively in parallel lines (to the left or right of the rear unit) to form a visual impression of steps.

and carried him through the air until they were high above a **knoll**[1] covered with sharp rocks. Here they dropped the poor metal man, who, lacking any **resilience**[2], lay so dented he couldn't move.

A **phalanx**[3] of sharp-clawed Monkeys caught the Scarecrow and **eviscerated**[4] him by pulling all of the straw out of his clothes. Then they made his pants and jacket into a small bundle and flung it into the top branches of a tall tree.

A **cadre**[5] of large soldiers **pinioned**[6] the Lion's legs by winding

---

[1] **knoll** A *knoll* is a small, rounded hill. *Although the Warren Commission concluded that Lee Harvey Oswald had acted alone in the 1963 assassination of President Kennedy, some people claim that a second shot was fired at almost the same time from a grassy knoll along the motorcade.*

[2] **resilient (resilience)** If something is *resilient*, it readily returns to its original shape (it springs back) after being compressed, stretched, bent, etc. *Synthetic rubber is resilient over a wider temperature range than natural rubber.* If a person is *resilient*, he readily recovers (bounces back) from misfortune (illness, depression, disappointment, adversity, etc.). The noun is *resilience*. *After suffering numerous personal and professional setbacks during her husband's Presidency, resilient First Lady Hillary Rodham Clinton was elected to the U.S. Senate from New York in 2000.*

[3] **phalanx** A *phalanx* is a close-knit group of people united for a common purpose, especially a line of soldiers (sometimes with overlapping shields). *A phalanx of police officers stood before the stage to prevent overly eager girls from rushing the teen idol.*

[4] **eviscerate (eviscerated)** Technically, to *eviscerate* a person or animal is to remove its internal organs, especially its intestines. Figuratively, to *eviscerate* something is to remove a vital or essential part of it (the guts of it). *The elephants were transported in the eviscerated fuselage of a Boeing 747.* Note: Sometimes the word is also used figuratively to mean simply "destroy" (as if by evisceration).

[5] **cadre** A *cadre* is a select group of (especially military) personnel, one capable of assuming control or training others. *In 1960 communist cadres within South Vietnam created the National Liberation Front to challenge the U.S.-supported nationalist regime.*

[6] **pinion (pinioned)** To *pinion* someone is to restrain him; to prevent him from moving, usually by binding his arms or hands. *When the guilty verdict was announced, two guards promptly pinioned the defendant by the shoulders and led him off.*

many coils of rope around them. Then they lifted his **immobile**[1] form and flew him to the Witch's castle, where they locked him in a small yard with a high iron fence around it.

Dorothy stood, with Toto in her arms, watching the **debacle**[2] and knowing she'd be the next victim of this insane **pogrom**[3]. The leader of the Winged Monkeys, ready to complete the **rout**[4] of the queer quartet, flew up to her, his long, **hirsute**[5] arms stretched out and his ugly face grinning terribly. She gave a gasp of sheer terror, then, afraid that her fear might fan the enemy's **martial**[6] spirit, tried

---

[1] **immobile** If someone or something is *immobile*, it either can't move or it can't be moved; it's fixed, stationary, etc. *Ancient Greek astronomer Ptolemy believed that the Earth was immobile at the center of the universe with the sun, moon, planets, and stars revolving around it.*

[2] **debacle** A sudden, utter, disastrous defeat, failure, collapse, breakdown, or downfall (of something) is known as a *debacle. The United States formally entered Word War II the day after the December 1941 Pearl Harbor debacle (in which Japanese planes, without warning, attacked and destroyed a U.S. naval base in Hawaii).*

[3] **pogrom** An organized (often government-approved) massacre of a minority group (especially Jews) is known as a *pogrom* (pronounced with the accent on the second syllable). Some people use the word to refer specifically to the Holocaust (the extermination of European Jews by the Nazis during World War II). *Between 1880 and 1920, 2.5 million Jews left Europe for America to escape unemployment, discrimination, and the occasional outbreak of pogroms.*

[4] **rout** A *rout* is an overwhelming defeat (especially one in which the defeated force retreats or flees in disorder). *The November 1942 rout of General Rommel's German troops by General Montgomery's British forces at Alamein (a town on the Mediterranean coast of Egypt) was a decisive battle of World War II.*

[5] **hirsute** To describe something as *hirsute* is to say that it's hairy or covered with hair. *Bigfoot is a very large, hirsute, humanlike creature reportedly sighted hundreds of times in the Pacific Northwest and Canada (but most scientists discount its existence).*

[6] **martial** To describe something as *martial* is to say that it pertains to or is appropriate for war (fighting) or the military, as *martial law* (law administered by domestic military forces when civil authority has broken down). *In 1966 Frank Sinatra described rock 'n' roll as "the martial music of every sideburned delinquent on the face of the earth."*

her best to be still. That's when the leader saw the round mark upon Dorothy's forehead and, realizing the girl was traveling under the **aegis**[1] of the Good Witch of the North, stopped short, motioning his **lackeys**[2] not to touch her.

"We dare not harm this little girl," he said to them **circumspectly**[3], "for, as a **protégé**[4] of the Good Witch of the North, she is protected by the Power of Good, which **predominates**[5] over the Power of Evil. All we can do is carry her to the castle of the Wicked Witch and leave her there."

Carefully and gently they lifted Dorothy in their arms and carried her swiftly through the air until they came to the castle,

---

[1] **aegis** To be under the *aegis* (pronounced *EE-jis*) of someone or something is to be under its protection (as, for example, an abandoned baby whose welfare is under the *aegis* of the courts) or under its sponsorship (as, for example, a school concert held under the *aegis* of the P.T.A.). *Dr. Jonas Salk developed his polio vaccine (1957) under the aegis of the March of Dimes Foundation.*

[2] **lackey (lackeys)** A *lackey* is a flunky; a servile follower. *TV shows about comic book character Superman typically involve a scheming gangster (called "Boss") and his lackeys (named, perhaps, Lefty and Mugsy).*

[3] **circumspect (circumspectly)** If you're *circumspect*, you're careful about your conduct and you demonstrate sound judgment; you take into consideration circumstances and potential consequences; you're wary and wise. *After the 1979 Three Mile Island accident, the atomic energy industry came to a halt as circumspect consumers across America voted to close existing nuclear plants and cancel orders for new ones.*

[4] **protégé** A *protégé* (pronounced so that the first syllable is accented and rhymes with *go* and the last syllable rhymes with *bay* and has its g pronounced like the g in *mirage*) is a person whose welfare, training, or career is looked after, promoted, or supported by someone of influence. *In the 1976 remake of A Star Is Born, Barbra Streisand plays the protégé of a declining singing star (played by Kris Kristofferson), whom she eventually outshines.*

[5] **predominate (predominates)** When something *predominates* over something else, it has controlling power or influence over it; it overrules it, outweighs it, or dominates it; it prevails over it; or it exists in greater number or quantity than it. *In Taiwan, light industry is the major manufacturing sector, with electronics predominating.*

where they set her down upon the front doorstep. The leader said to the **cantankerous**[1], **craggy**[2]-faced **crone**[3], "We have obeyed you as far as we were able. The Tin Woodman and the Scarecrow are destroyed, and the Lion is tied up in your yard. The little girl we dare not harm, nor the dog she carries in her arms." Then, with a great clatter, the flying **flotilla**[4] rose into the air and were soon out of sight.

---

[1] **cantankerous** If someone is *cantankerous*, he's grouchy, irritable, quarrelsome, ill-tempered, disagreeable, stubborn, etc. *In Charles Dickens' A Christmas Carol (1843), Ebenezer Scrooge is a cantankerous old miser who eventually discovers the meaning of Christmas.*

[2] **craggy** To describe something (terrain or someone's face, for example) as *craggy* is to say that it's not smooth; it's rough, uneven, irregular, jagged, etc. *Diamonds found in nature are craggy; they must be cut and polished to bring out their true beauty.*

[3] **crone** A *crone* is a shriveled, ugly, old, frightening woman. *While witches of fairy tales ("Hansel and Gretel," for example) are depicted as evil crones, modern witches are simply women (including young, beautiful ones) popularly believed to practice sorcery.*

[4] **flotilla** A *flotilla* is a small fleet (a group of ships, planes, etc., operated as a unit). *During the Civil War, Union admiral David Farragut, famous for his battle cry "Damn the torpedoes; full speed ahead," secured control of the Mississippi River by defeating a Confederate flotilla (1862).*

Chapter 15 "The Wicked Witch of the West"

When the Wicked Witch saw the flat, round **amulet**[1] on Dorothy's forehead, she **blanched**[2], for she knew well that because the girl traveled under the **auspices**[3] of the Good Witch of the North, neither the Winged Monkeys nor she, herself, dare hurt her in any way. She looked down at Dorothy's feet and saw the magical Silver Shoes, and a tremor of fear passed over her. But then she happened to look into the child's **artless**[4] eyes and saw how simple the soul behind them was. At once she knew that the little girl was completely unaware of the wonderful power the Silver Shoes gave her. The Witch laughed insanely, her **fetid**[5] breath **obtruding**[1] itself

---

[1] **amulet** An *amulet* is something (a protective or good-luck charm, for example) worn (often around the neck) to ward off evil. *In preparation for battle, the Iroquois Indians routinely applied war paint and collected amulets.*

[2] **blanch (blanched)** To *blanch* is to turn white or become pale (as when a strong emotion causes the blood to drain from your face). *In 1984 food critic Bryan Miller, speaking of Pig Heaven, a Manhattan restaurant specializing in pork dishes, said, "The moist, flavorful meat is concealed under a thick slab of crisp fat that would make a cardiologist blanch."*

[3] **auspices** To be under the *auspices* (pronounced *AW-spih-siz*) of someone or something is to be under its sponsorship or protection. *Created in 1961 by President John F. Kennedy, the Peace Corps is a U.S. government agency under the auspices of the Department of State that sends American volunteers to developing nations to help improve living standards and provide training.*

[4] **artless** If you're *artless*, you're free of deceit or craftiness; you don't scheme or mislead; you're natural, innocent, open, forthright, trustful, etc.; you might even be naïvely unaware of the reactions of others. Note: The opposite of *artless* is *artful* (full of deceit or craftiness; sly). *In the 1971 film* Willy Wonka & the Chocolate Factory, *an artless boy named Charlie wins a tour of a candy factory and a lifetime supply of chocolate.*

[5] **fetid** Something described as *fetid* has an (often peculiarly) offensive odor; it's smelly; it's rotten; it stinks. *The thin, fetid, greenish fluid discharged from the wound sickened even the hospital workers.*

upon Dorothy's sensitive nostrils.

Then the hideous **hag**[2] threw a hard, **inimical**[3] glance at Dorothy and said, with an obvious display of **animosity**[4] in her voice, "Come with me, my **pulchritudinous**[5] little **prig**[1], and do

---

[1] **obtrude (obtruding)** When you *obtrude*, you force yourself (or your ideas) on others (sometimes simply by pushing yourself into view, and sometimes by insistently interfering). The adjective is *obtrusive*, meaning either "tending to obtrude" or "undesirably noticeable," as *an obtrusive birthmark*. *In an April 1864 letter, President Abraham Lincoln wrote to (Civil War) Union Army Commander Ulysses S. Grant, "I wish to express my entire satisfaction with what you have done up to this time, so far as I understand it. The particulars of your plans I neither know or seek to know. You are [alertly watchful] and self-reliant, and, pleased with this, I wish not to obtrude any restraints upon you."*

[2] **hag** A *hag* is a (sometimes vicious) ugly, frightening old woman; a witch. *While ninth-century Japanese poet Ono no Komachi was celebrated for her beauty, many legends have arisen about her bitter end as a wandering hag.*

[3] **inimical** This word has two meanings, depending on the context. The first is "unfriendly, hostile," as in *an inimical tone of voice*. The second is "harmful, injurious," as in *high taxes are inimical to economic growth*. Note that with the second meaning the word usually describes a situation or concept (as opposed to a person), and that in the typical construction something is said to be inimical *to* something else. *Explaining why he moved to San Francisco, Larry said, "Since extreme heat and cold are both inimical to human beings, I like to keep myself balanced between the two."*

[4] **animosity** When you feel *animosity* toward someone (or something), you feel ill will, hostility, unfriendliness, dislike, hatred, etc., toward him (or it). *Great animosity exists between Israelis and Arabs because each group claims Palestinian land as theirs by ancestral rights.* Note: A related word is *animus*, which is a feeling of ill will or hostility, especially of a personal nature, often based on one's prejudices or temperament. *Sue hated sport-utility vehicles but held no similar animus toward pickup trucks or vans (because they had a reason for being oversized).*

[5] **pulchritude (pulchritudinous)** The noun *pulchritude* (pronounced *PUL-kri-tood*) means "physical beauty." The adjective *pulchritudinous* (pronounced *pul-kri-TOOD-i-nis*) means "physically beautiful." *In Greek mythology, Helen of Troy was famous for her pulchritude; in fact, she was considered the most beautiful woman in the world.*

everything I tell you or I'll put an end to you, as I did to the Tin Woodman and the Scarecrow." Then, almost as an afterthought, she threw in, "And your little dog, too!"

An uncontrollable pounding in her chest made speech impossible, so, forgetting everything but her fear, Dorothy mutely followed her **nefarious**[2] **nemesis**[3] through a **Byzantine**[4] **labyrinth**[5] of castle hallways and **sinuous**[6] staircases. The **tortuous**[1] path at last

---

[1] **prig** A *prig* is a person who's overly concerned with being proper (polite, respectable, formal, correct, courteous, moral, righteous, etc.); a goody-goody; a prude. *In 1987 U.S. Congressman Henry Waxman, speaking of TV ads for condoms, said, "Advertising has been stopped by networks who are so priggish that they refuse to describe disease control."*

[2] **nefarious** People or deeds described as *nefarious* are extremely wicked or evil. *First-century Roman Emperor Caligula was known for his nefarious deeds (he murdered many people) and his insanity (he appointed his horse to the senate).*

[3] **nemesis** Someone's *nemesis* is anything (or anyone) that will likely cause his downfall (or undoing, ruin, doom, destruction, etc.); his constant or perpetual enemy or rival. *At the end of the play* Peter Pan, *Captain Hook is eaten whole by his nemesis, the crocodile.* Note: In Greek mythology, Nemesis is the goddess of vengeance.

[4] **Byzantine** To describe something as *Byzantine* (sometimes spelled with a small *b*) is to say that it's highly complicated, involved, intricate, intertwining, etc. *In an effort to simplify our Byzantine tax structure, many policy makers in Washington have proposed some form of flat tax or retail sales tax.*

[5] **labyrinth** A *labyrinth* is a maze or, figuratively, any bewilderingly intricate construction or problem. *In 1965 French composer and conductor Pierre Boulez said, "Music is not a vessel into which the composer distills his soul drop by drop, but a labyrinth with no beginning and no end, full of new paths to discover.* Note: In Greek mythology, the Labyrinth was the maze in which the Minotaur (a monster with a man's body and bull's head) was confined.

[6] **sinuous** Something described as *sinuous* has the form or movement of a snake; that is, it's winding, twisting, curving, etc. *The cable car was more adaptable to the wide, straight thoroughfares of American cities than to the narrow, sinuous streets of Europe.*

ended in a grimy kitchen, where the Witch handed the girl a scrub brush, towel, and broom, all of **dubious²** cleanliness, and ordered her to wash and dry all the pots and pans and to sweep the floor. When another **abominable³**, blood-curdling laugh accompanied the Witch's sudden **egress⁴**, Toto fled and hid. Now Dorothy sat in **morose⁵** solitude. Yet in reality she did have plenty of company, for right in front of her face stood the mountain of filthy

---

¹ **tortuous** Something (a road or path, for example) described as *tortuous* is marked by repeated bends or turns; it twists or winds. *The Cumberland River rises in southeast Kentucky and flows in a tortuous western course to the Ohio River.* Note: In the sense of "not straightforward," the word can also mean, by extension, "complex" or "devious."

² **dubious** To refer to something as *dubious* is to say that it arouses doubt, uncertainty, or suspicion; that it's of questionable quality; or that it has little likelihood of happening (or being accomplished). *With the 1932 serial* Singing Sandy, *actor John Wayne achieved the dubious distinction of becoming Hollywood's first singing cowboy.*

³ **abominable** Depending on the context, this word can mean either "hateful, detestable, despicable" (often with an implication of vileness or unnaturalness), as in *abominable acts of torture,* or "unpleasant, disagreeable," as in *abominable weather. The April 1995 Oklahoma City bombing (in which over 100 people were killed when a car bomb tore away the façade of the nine-story, block-long Federal building) was perhaps the most abominable act of terrorism of the 20th century.*

⁴ **egress** An act of leaving or exiting (some enclosed place) is known as *egress* (pronounced *EE-gres*). The word can also refer to the right to leave or exit, as in *refugees denied egress,* or to an exit (such as a doorway) itself. *As he paid for the 100-foot rope ladder, he explained to the salesman that his apartment building had no means of emergency egress in the event of a fire.* Note: The opposite is *ingress.*

⁵ **morose** Someone or something (such as a mood) described as *morose* is sullen, glum, gloomy, etc. *Morose* people tend to be uncommunicative and bad-tempered. *In the 1955 film* Rebel without a Cause, *James Dean plays a morose but rebellious teenager.*

crockery[1], and upon her face flowed the many little **rivulets**[2] of tears that **striated**[3] her expression of utter hopelessness.

With each dismal day, the **forlorn**[4] child became more despairing of ever seeing her aunt and uncle again. She tried to picture Uncle Henry's long, **equine**[5] face and **unkempt**[6] hair, but found her recollection of him becoming increasingly **nebulous**[7], and this made

---

[1] **crockery** Cooking pots (especially earthenware pots) are known collectively as *crockery*. *Because most people use their kitchen cupboards to store dishes, glasses, crockery, and utensils, we thought it strange when we heard that "Old Mother Hubbard went to the cupboard to fetch her poor dog a bone."*

[2] **rivulet (rivulets)** A *rivulet* is a brook or small stream. *In 1890 some 200 Native Americans were massacred by U.S. troops near a South Dakota rivulet known as Wounded Knee.*

[3] **striate (striated)** To *striate* something is to mark it with stripes or streaks. Something described as *striated* is so marked. *Zoologists say that when zebras move together in large groups, their striated coats act as camouflage.*

[4] **forlorn** People who are *forlorn* feel or express sadness, loneliness, hopelessness, despair, etc., because they have been abandoned, deserted, forgotten, forsaken, etc. *Greek mythology explains that the earth's first winter came because the goddess of the harvest (Demeter) was so forlorn over the loss of her daughter (who'd been carried off to the underworld) that she did not tend the crops.*

[5] **equine** To refer to something as *equine* is to say that it resembles a horse. *Some people say that the unicorn (a mythical, white, equine beast with a horn in the middle of its forehead) is visible only to virgins.*

[6] **unkempt** To refer to something (hair, clothing, a garden, etc.) as *unkempt* is to say that it's untidy, disorderly, messy, disheveled, straggly, etc. *By watching the 1970 film Woodstock, we could see that hippies cultivated an unkempt image in their dress and grooming.*

[7] **nebulous** In astronomy, a *nebula* is a dark, widely spread mass of gas or dust—and the word *nebulous* literally means "like a nebula." But people generally use this word figuratively to describe things (theories, ideas, arguments, images, language, etc.) that are vague, indistinct, indefinite, fuzzy, hazy, etc. *Historians claim that the wording of the 1890 Sherman Antitrust Act (which committed the American government to opposing monopolies) was nebulous because it never defined the word "trust."*

her more **disconsolate**[1] than ever. In an attempt to cheer herself, she pictured Aunt Em's glorious smile. How often she'd seen her flash it at her **reticent**[2], **laconic**[3] uncle in an attempt, usually unsuccessful, to break through his stiff barrier of **stolid**[4] **reserve**[5]. She considered writing Aunt Em a letter but immediately dismissed the idea when she realized that her **missive**[6] had no chance of ever finding a mailbox—assuming, that is, that mailboxes even existed in this crazy place. Oh, how she longed for that

---

[1] **disconsolate** People who are *disconsolate* are hopelessly sad; they're beyond being cheered up. *In the 1982 film E.T.—The Extra-Terrestrial, a young boy becomes disconsolate when his alien friend is pronounced dead.*

[2] **reticent** People who are *reticent* are quiet, shy, uncommunicative; they keep their thoughts and feelings to themselves; their behavior or manner tends to be restrained or reserved. *During the 1940s, actor Humphrey Bogart was known for playing reticent but tough characters in such films as* The Maltese Falcon *and* Casablanca.

[3] **laconic** To describe a person as *laconic* is to say that he uses few words; his language is concise, brief, short. Speech or writing described as *laconic* is similarly compact. *A famously laconic radio message sent by a U.S. Navy officer during World War II read "Sighted sub; sank same."*

[4] **stolid** If someone is *stolid*, he shows little emotion; in fact, things that might make others react emotionally probably won't provoke him at all. He tends to calmly stick to his routine. *In the TV prison movie, the new prisoner endured the strip search with stolid dignity.*

[5] **reserve** People who exhibit *reserve* are unwilling to express their feelings; they're formal, restrained, uncommunicative, distant, detached. *Psychologists describe an "anal retentive" personality as one marked by excessive orderliness, extreme fussiness, and often suspicion and reserve.*

[6] **missive** A *missive* is a letter; a written communication. *During the War of 1812, a now-famous missive was sent from Oliver Perry (naval commander in the Battle of Lake Erie) to American land armies announcing a victory for the United States; it read "We have met the enemy and they are ours."*

bastion[1] of normalcy called Kansas!

At night, in her dim, cell-like bedroom, an **anemic**[2] overhead light fixture, rather than dilute the gloom, served more to accentuate it by giving it contrast. Its **niggardly**[3] illumination seemed to mock her, to say, "Look, little girl, this is what brightness is like— when there is any."

Gradually her fear **diminished**[4], only to be **supplanted**[5] by an endless tedium that was equally horrible, pushing what little was

---

[1] **bastion** A *bastion*, literally, is a projecting portion of a fort. But people usually use this word figuratively to refer to any thing or place that historically or traditionally protects, promotes, supports, or ensures some particular (often philosophical) concept. *Our social studies teacher said that the Republican Party was a bastion of conservatism.*

[2] **anemic** Technically, people who are *anemic* suffer from a condition known as *anemia* (a deficiency of red blood cells); as such, they are pale and weak. But in general usage, anything physically weak, spiritless, feeble, ineffective, etc., can be described as *anemic*. *A recession (1990–1991) combined with an anemic economic recovery contributed to George H. Bush's defeat in the 1992 presidential election.*

[3] **niggardly** To describe someone as *niggardly* is to say that he's stingy and tightfisted and that he's grudging and petty about what little he does give. To refer to a quantity or amount (of something) as *niggardly* is to say that it's meager, scanty, meanly small, etc. *In 1974 comedian Jack Benny, famous for his fictitious niggardliness and constant age of 39, said, "Age is strictly a case of mind over matter; if you don't mind, it doesn't matter."*

[4] **diminish (diminished)** When something *diminishes* it becomes (sometimes gradually) smaller or less (in size, amount, importance, etc.). *Earthquakes usually begin with slight tremors, rapidly increase to one or more violent shocks, and diminish gradually.*

[5] **supplant (supplanted)** If someone (in an official position) or something (a method of doing something, a philosophy, a name, etc.) is *supplanted*, it's removed and replaced by something else. *In 1959 Cuban president Fulgencio Batista was supplanted by revolutionary leader Fidel Castro.*

THE WIZARD OF OZ VOCABULARY BUILDER

left of her dwindling **fortitude**[1] to its limit. Her swollen, downcast eyes, drooping mouth, and **sallow**[2] cheeks **rendered**[3] her almost unrecognizable, even to Toto.

Finding a scrap of paper one day, she imagined it to be a letter from Aunt Em. She composed it in her mind: "Dearest Dorothy, We love and miss you very much. We know where you are and are coming to rescue you. All our love, Aunt Em and Uncle Henry." Below their names she imagined she saw a string of x's and o's representing kisses and hugs. Every day the scrap of paper became another letter, each worded less **succinctly**[4] and with more x's and o's than the previous, but all of the same theme. She carefully

---

[1] **fortitude** An aspect of human character, *fortitude* (sometimes referred to as *intestinal fortitude*) is your natural ability to endure physical or mental hardship or suffering with courage; your moral strength. *In his 1962 autobiography,* My Life in Court, *attorney Louis Nizer said, "I know of no higher fortitude than stubbornness in the face of overwhelming odds."*

[2] **sallow** To describe someone's skin or complexion as *sallow* is to say that it's of a sickly, pale, yellowish color. *Doctors say that to treat frostbite (a condition caused by exposure to cold and characterized by frozen body parts and a sallow complexion), you shouldn't rub the frostbitten parts; instead, you should place them in warm water.*

[3] **render (rendered)** This verb means "cause to become; make." *In the Old Testament, Samson is rendered powerless when Delilah cuts his hair.* The word can also mean "give; provide." *The UN International Court of Justice is empowered to render judgments in international disputes brought before them.* And it can mean "show; exhibit." *An X-ray microscope is an instrument using X-rays to render a highly magnified image.*

[4] **succinct (succinctly)** To refer to speech or writing as *succinct* is to say that it's expressed in few words; it's concise, compact. *First-century B.C. Roman general and statesman Julius Caesar succinctly described one of his victories in Asia as follows: "I came; I saw; I conquered."*

stored all these imaginary **epistles**[1] in a secret drawer in her mind.

---

[1] **epistle (epistles)** An *epistle* is a letter, a written communication (especially a formal, impersonal, or instructive one). When spelled with a capital *E*, the word refers specifically to letters of the New Testament (as written by St. Paul, St. Peter, or St. John, for example). Note: A novel written in the form of a series of letters is known as an *epistolary* novel. *In 1952, in an epistle to the House Un-American Activities Committee (which was then investigating links between American leftists and the Communist party), playwright Lillian Hellman explained that she'd refuse to testify about anyone but herself with these now-famous words: "I cannot and will not cut my conscience to fit this year's fashions."*

Chapter 16 "The Escape"

Meanwhile, the Witch was becoming more and more **covetous**[1] of Dorothy's enchanted Silver Shoes. Even forgetting about their wonderful power, the mere ownership of them **conferred**[2] a certain **cachet**[3] she found irresistible.

If only she could have them, she thought, her power would reach the **acme**[4] of its supremacy, exceeding that of even the Great Oz himself! But how to get them... how to get them? The only time Dorothy took them off was when she took a bath. But water was **anathema**[5] to the Witch, so she didn't dare go near when the girl

---

[1] **covet (covetous)** To *covet* (or, to use the adjective, be *covetous* of) something (that doesn't belong to you) is to eagerly wish for it, desire it, long for it (sometimes wrongfully). *In 1973 Chinese Premier Zhou Enlai said, "China is an attractive piece of meat coveted by all, but very tough— and for years no one has been able to bite into it."*

[2] **confer (conferred)** This word has several meanings, depending on the context. We know that when people *confer* with each other, they consult with one another; they exchange ideas to reach a decision or solve a problem. And we know that when you *confer* an award or honor on someone, you graciously and courteously give it to him. But when something *confers* a quality (character, trait, or power) onto something else, it endows it with (gives to it) that quality. *A 1985* Time *magazine article on secrecy says, "From earliest childhood we feel its mystery and attraction; we know both the power it confers and the burden it imposes."*

[3] **cachet** An official or unofficial sign, mark, or expression of approval, distinction, authenticity, etc., is known as a *cachet* (pronounced *ka-SHAY*). *Ivy League schools have a certain cachet that state universities lack.*

[4] **acme** The *acme* of something is its highest level or degree (that can be attained); its utmost limit. The word generally refers to accomplishments rather than to physical objects. *In 1958, at the acme of his popular success, singer Elvis Presley was drafted into the army.*

[5] **anathema** This noun is used to refer to any person or thing that arouses extreme dislike. The implication is that this thing is so objectionable that it's always rejected out of hand or avoided. *Because cigarette smoke is anathema to my wife, she covers her nose with the top of her shirt whenever we walk past the smoking section of a restaurant.*

bathed. She considered simply asking the child for them, or, failing that, trying to **wheedle**[1] them out of her, but couldn't think of any way to **broach**[2] the subject without sounding humiliatingly **supplicatory**[3].

A savage passion now seethed within the Witch. Here was this **insipid**[4] little **upstart**[5] whose **talismanic**[1] existence threatened her

---

[1] **wheedle** To *wheedle* is to get something you want (from a person) by means of smooth talk, flattery, sweet talk, charm, coaxing, etc. *In Mark Twain's 1876 novel* The Adventures of Tom Sawyer, *the title character wheedles his friends into whitewashing a fence for him.*

[2] **broach** To *broach* a subject is to bring it up for the first time (as for discussion). *In May 1988 journalist Charles Krauthammer said, "The idea of the month— to cure the hysteria of the year— is to legalize illegal drugs. The idea has been broached by the mayors of Baltimore and Washington; it has made the front pages of the* Washington Post *and the* New York Times; *it even boasts an academic champion in a professor at Princeton University."*

[3] **supplicate (supplicatory)** To *supplicate* is to humbly (unassumingly, meekly) ask for something. The word derives from the Latin word for *kneel* (as in praying), so the implication is that the person you're asking is someone above you (sometimes God). To describe someone as *supplicatory* is to say that he's making or expressing *supplication* (the act of prayer or humble appeal). *Fifteenth-century explorer Christopher Columbus was determined to reach India by sailing west from Spain; after eight years of supplication, he finally received the backing of the Spanish monarchs (Ferdinand and Isabella).*

[4] **insipid** To describe something (or someone) as *insipid* is to say that it's bland, dull, uninteresting, unexciting, etc. *In his 1956 television appearances, singer Elvis Presley, gyrating his hips and curling his lips, shattered the world of insipid family entertainment.*

[5] **upstart** An *upstart* is a person of modest origins who has suddenly or recently become wealthy or important. The implication is that this person is objectionable because he now behaves self-importantly. As an adjective the word means "suddenly raised to a position of importance." *Among the many achievements of National Football League Commissioner Pete Rozelle was the 1970 merger of the NFL with the upstart AFL.*

very reputation! She felt herself being dragged down in **opprobrium**[2] through this pitiful thing with a blue-and-white frock and a basket! How she longed for **retribution**[3]! She thought of her old black magic handbook, with its chapter on ten effective **maledictions**[4], but exasperatedly realized they were powerless in the face of the Witch of the North's protective kiss. She yearned to **pummel**[5] the girl with her fists; then, considering it beneath her dignity to resort to **fisticuffs**[6], she instead took a **vindictive**[1] delight

---

[1] **talisman (talismanic)** A *talisman* is an object (such as a stone or ring) marked with magic signs and worn or carried for its supposed magical benefit (warding off evil, for example). The adjective is *talismanic* (of or relating to *talismans*). *To avoid the "evil eye" (the supposed power to harm someone merely by looking at him), many people wear blue beads, talismans, or other protective charms.*

[2] **opprobrium** Outrageously shameful conduct, or the public disgrace, dishonor, or condemnation that results from such conduct is known as *opprobrium*. *A March 2000 editorial in the* Washington Post *suggested to President Bill Clinton that he "should make war on guns in schools and rescue us from the opprobrium of being the only superpower that makes firearms available to children."*

[3] **retribution** Retaliation, punishment, or revenge on a person (for a wrong, an injury, etc.) is known as *retribution*. *Though military powers continue to develop new ones, the use of poison gas has been limited since World War I by fear of retribution.*

[4] **malediction (maledictions)** A *malediction* is a curse (an appeal to a supernatural force for evil to befall someone). *When trying to bring harm to an enemy, a practitioner of voodoo recites maledictions or sticks pins into a doll (made in the victim's likeness).*

[5] **pummel** To *pummel* someone is to beat him; to hit him repeatedly (as with the fists). *Finding himself in the middle of a suddenly crowded street, the purse snatcher became more afraid of being pushed and pummeled by an angry mob than of being captured by the police.*

[6] **fisticuffs** This word means "combat with the fists; fist fighting." *Professional boxers first began using padded gloves in 1892 (after bare-knuckled fisticuffs had become illegal).*

in imagining herself using her stiff, black umbrella to **bludgeon**[2] the child to a bloody pulp and then crushing whatever remained beneath the steel-rimmed heel of her hard, black boot.

Now her thoughts returned to how she might acquire the Silver Shoes. **Machiavellian**[3] **machinations**[4] aplenty whirled through the **wily**[5] Witch's evil mind, but she rejected one flawed **scenario**[1] after

---

[1] **vindictive** People who are *vindictive* want to get revenge (for some wrong); they're retaliatory. The implication is that they're naturally disposed as such (as opposed to being naturally forgiving); that they're spiteful, nasty. *Edward Albee's 1962 play* Who's Afraid of Virginia Woolf *concerns the love-hate relationship between a college professor and his vindictive but seductive wife.*

[2] **bludgeon** To *bludgeon* someone is to hit or beat him (as with a club). Note: As a noun, a *bludgeon* is a short, thick club that's thicker or weighted at one end. *During their 1781 tour of the eastern United States, Shakers (members of a religious group practicing celibacy and communal living) were whipped, bludgeoned, stoned, and dragged behind horses.*

[3] **Machiavellian** Niccolo Machiavelli (1469–1527) was an Italian political philosopher and statesman who held that in pursuing and maintaining political power, slyness, deceit, ruthlessness, and amorality are justified. Thus, to describe someone as *Machiavellian* is to say that he's sly, shrewd, deceitful, calculating, cold-hearted, amoral, wicked, etc. *After his death, Richard Nixon came to be seen as an ambitious, intelligent, if sometimes Machiavellian President (in fact, he was nicknamed "Tricky Dick"), who achieved a cease-fire in Vietnam and initiated strategic arms limitation talks with the Soviet Union.*

[4] **machinations** Tricky, underhanded dealings, plots, strategies, schemes, plans, etc., designed to achieve an evil or illegal end are known as *machinations* (pronounced *mack-ih-NAY-shinz*). *Some experts say the U.S. Tax Code needs to be complex in order to counter the machinations of not only average citizens but of clever tax attorneys (some of whom are former IRS employees!).*

[5] **wily** People who are *wily* are tricky, devious, sly, deceitful, foxy, etc.; they're disposed to deceiving, entrapping, or enticing others (to gain an end). *In one of Aesop's fables, a wily wolf disguises himself in a sheepskin, then moves undetected among a herd of sheep and kills them for food.*

the other. When at last she did find a workable **ruse**[2], the thrill of a delicious discovery ran through her, momentarily **eradicating**[3] her habitually **dour**[4] expression.

Putting her plan into action, she fetched a long metal bar, **surreptitiously**[5] placed it across the middle of the kitchen floor, then used her magical powers to raise it a few inches and to make it invisible to human eyes. Now she **skulked**[6] in the kitchen closet and waited for Dorothy to walk across the room.

But Dorothy was hard at work scrubbing a large pot. "Why

---

[1] **scenario** A *scenario* (pronounced *sih-NAR-ee-oh*) is an outline or story line of an expected or projected sequence of events. People sometimes insert the phrase "best-case" or "worst-case" before the word. *If we go on the ski trip, the best-case scenario is that we'll learn to ski, meet new people, and have a great time; the worst-case scenario is that we'll freeze, break our legs, and be miserable.*

[2] **ruse** A *ruse* (pronounced *rooz*) is a trick, ploy, false impression, etc. (employed to achieve an end). The word is often seen in the expression "clever ruse." *In Greek mythology, Odysseus helped bring about the defeat of Troy by conceiving the ruse of the Trojan horse.*

[3] **eradicate (eradicating)** To *eradicate* something is to remove it, wipe it out, erase it, etc. *In 1985 the World Health Organization began an effort to eradicate polio worldwide by 2000.*

[4] **dour** To describe something (a person's disposition or expression, for example) as *dour* is to say that it's sullen (gloomy, grave, humorless) and stern (severe, harsh, strict). *Most of the characters in Arthur Miller's 1953 play* The Crucible *(based on the Salem witch trials of 1692) are dour New England Puritans.*

[5] **surreptitious (surreptitiously)** If you're *surreptitious* about doing something, you do it secretly or sneakily, so that nobody will know (that you're doing it). *She sought therapy because she felt people didn't listen to her; then at her first appointment she noticed the doctor surreptitiously glancing at his watch.*

[6] **skulk (skulked)** To *skulk* is to lie in hiding (for some evil purpose) or to move about quietly, secretly, or sneakily (to avoid notice). *Most large cats hunt by skulking until they are close enough to their prey to catch it with a quick burst of speed.*

must you **dally**[1] so?" thought the Witch impatiently, her **ire**[2] steadily rising. Indeed, Dorothy labored over every pot and pan, for during her first few days at the Castle the Witch had **querulously**[3] **carped**[4] about substandard work— even though, to Dorothy's eyes, the pots sparkled— and the girl had **chafed**[5] at the Witch's **niggling**[6]

---

[1] **dally** To *dally* (also *dilly-dally*), is to delay, loiter, waste time, drag your feet, etc. *A 1983 article in* Esquire *magazine said that McDonald's restaurants are "for a classless culture that hasn't time to dally on its way to the next rainbow's end."*

[2] **ire** This is a somewhat literary word meaning "anger, rage." The implication is that some sort of emotional display (flushed cheeks, for example) might accompany the anger. *When New York State appointed a commission to investigate abortion, the makeup of the commission (14 men and a nun) aroused the ire of many women.*

[3] **querulous (querulously)** To describe someone as *querulous* is to say that he tends to complain a lot; he's whiny, peevish, cranky, grouchy, etc. *Sesame Street's Muppets include the endlessly hungry Cookie Monster, the naïvely innocent Big Bird, and the constantly querulous Oscar the Grouch.*

[4] **carp (carped)** To *carp* is to complain unreasonably, find fault (especially ill-naturedly), quibble, raise petty objections, etc. *In 1960, after a British critic had carped about (Pulitzer Prize–winning American author) William Saroyan's latest play, the playwright said, "One of us is obviously mistaken."*

[5] **chafe (chafed)** To *chafe* is to feel or become annoyed, irritated, discontented, etc. (at something). *Speaking of 20th-century composer Igor Stravinsky's monetary affairs, one of his biographers disclosed, "He is still chafing today because of the 26 percent service charge on his hotel bill."*

[6] **niggling** To describe a person as *niggling* is to say that he's overly concerned with trivial details; he's fussy. To describe things (details, differences, for example) as *niggling* is to say that they're annoyingly petty or trivial. As a verb, to *niggle* is to quibble, nit-pick, split hairs, etc. *First, my teacher accused me of being 15 minutes late; then, when I pointed out that I was only 14 minutes late, she accused me of niggling!*

faultfinding. Now, just so the **picayune**[1] Wicked Witch could have nothing to **cavil**[2] about, the child, **scrupulous**[3] in her efforts to please, was forced to spend twice as long scrubbing each pot!

Finally, after the last pot was cleaned and put away, the **oblivious**[4] child approached the bar, stumbled over it, and fell to the ground. In the process, one of the Silver Shoes fell off, and before Dorothy could retrieve it, the Witch, with **larcenous**[5] eyes, sprang from the closet, snatched it away, and put it on her own foot! The **malefactor**[6] was greatly pleased with her **cunning**[1]

---

[1] **picayune** Things that are *picayune* (pronounced *pick-ee-YOON*) are trivial, small, of little or negligible value or importance, etc. People who are *picayune* are overly concerned with trivialities; they're fussy, petty. *When Roger used the phrase "hollow tube," I was tempted to point out that all tubes are hollow, but I didn't want to seem picayune.*

[2] **cavil** To *cavil* is to find fault, especially unnecessarily or irritatingly; to raise petty objections; to quibble. *In 1950, in a reply to the music critic who'd caviled about his daughter Margaret's singing, President Harry Truman wrote, "Some day I hope to meet you; when that happens you'll need a new nose."*

[3] **scrupulous** Someone who is *scrupulous* is very careful and exact in performing a task or in doing what is considered morally or ethically proper; he's painstaking, precise, principled, righteous. *According to historians, U.S. Supreme Court chief justice Salmon Chase presided over the 1868 impeachment trial of President Andrew Johnson with scrupulous fairness.*

[4] **oblivious** To be *oblivious* to (or of) something is to have no conscious awareness of it (as from lack of attention or preoccupation with something else). *Lost in her crossword puzzle, Doris was completely oblivious to the fact that the train was no longer moving.*

[5] **larcenous** The legal term for theft (unlawful taking of someone's property) is *larceny*. The adjective *larcenous* can mean "having a tendency toward larceny," "guilty of larceny," or "involving or relating to larceny." *Legend has it that 12th-century English outlaw Robin Hood stole from the rich not because of a larcenous nature but because he wanted to aid the poor.*

[6] **malefactor** A *malefactor* (pronounced *MAL-ih-fak-ter*) is a person who commits a crime or does evil. *Sherlock Holmes is a fictional English detective whose incredible powers of deduction enable him to solve mysteries and identify malefactors in cases that leave all other detectives stumped.*

because now she possessed half the power of the Shoes. Her **diabolical**[2] delight **engendered**[3] another **spate**[4] of gleeful shrieks.

For Dorothy this was the final straw, and what little **forbearance**[5] she still **indulged**[6] was completely wiped away. Everything that had led up to this moment—seeing her friends

---

[1] **cunning** As a noun, this word means "clever or shrewd slyness or deception." *In Rossini's 1816 opera* The Barber of Seville, *the scheming title character, by his trickery and cunning, helps his former master win the hand of a beautiful woman.* As an adjective, the word means "cleverly or shrewdly sly or deceptive." *In the French fairy tale "Puss in Boots," a cunning cat brings great fortune to its master, a poor young man.*

[2] **diabolical** To describe something (or someone) as *diabolical* is to say that it's characteristic of a devil; that is, it's demonic, wicked, cruel, evil, fiendish, etc. *Referring to the diabolical character she portrayed in the 1962 film* Whatever Happened to Baby Jane?, *actress Bette Davis once said, "The best time I ever had with [co-star] Joan Crawford was when I pushed her down the stairs."*

[3] **engender (engendered)** When something *engenders* something else, it causes it to come into being or to happen. *President Lyndon Johnson's "War on Poverty" began in 1964 and engendered dozens of programs, including the Job Corps, VISTA, Project Head Start, Upward Bound, the Food Stamps program, and the Model Cities program.*

[4] **spate** A *spate* (of something) is a notably large number or amount (of it) appearing suddenly or within a short time; an outpouring (of it). *In 1933, shortly after taking office, President Franklin D. Roosevelt rushed through Congress a spate of economic measures aimed at ending the Great Depression.*

[5] **forbearance** If you have *forbearance*, you show restraint, patience, and tolerance when provoked (by not retaliating or expressing disapproval, for example). *The 1978 country hit "Take This Job and Shove It" tells of a man whose forbearance has reached its limit.*

[6] **indulge (indulged)** To *indulge* something is to allow it; to permit it; to humor it; to tolerate it. *When he was 16, pioneer and folk hero Daniel Boone moved with his family from Pennsylvania to North Carolina; there, on the edge of the frontier, his parents indulged his desire to hunt.*

destroyed by the Winged Monkeys, **moiling**[1] in the kitchen day after day without **respite**[2], being **coerced**[3] into performing **grueling**[4] and **stultifying**[5] **menial**[6] tasks, and finally, having her cherished Shoe **plundered**[7]— pushed her beyond all reason.

---

[1] **moil (moiling)** To *moil* is to work continually, especially with strenuous effort; to toil, slave, drudge, etc. *Between 1902 and 1905 more than 7,000 Koreans emigrated to Hawaii; most worked in agriculture, domestic service, and railroad maintenance, with a few moiling in mines.*

[2] **respite** A *respite* is a short rest period or break (as from work or duty) or a brief stop in an activity or action. *A 1986 issue of* Time *magazine quoted a college freshman's impression of spring break (a one-week respite during the spring term at school) in Fort Lauderdale, Florida, as follows: "Beaches, beer, and bikinis; sand, surf, and sex."*

[3] **coerce (coerced)** To *coerce* (pronounced *koh-URS*) someone into doing something (against his will) is to force him to do it (by means of pressure, intimidation, threats, etc.). The noun is *coercion*. *In the movie, the police tried to coerce a suspect into signing a false confession by means of the "third degree" and, when that failed, outright physical abuse.*

[4] **grueling** To refer to something (a task, a journey, a test, warfare, etc.) as *grueling* is to say that it's mentally or physically exhausting. *American Red Cross founder Clara Barton's work in nursing soldiers wounded in the Civil War was endless and grueling.*

[5] **stultify (stultifying)** To *stultify* someone's mind is to make it useless, ineffectual, sluggish, etc. (as from boring work, a boring environment, frustration, hot or humid air, etc.). *A January 2001* Washington Post *editorial referred to Muzak (soothing music that's piped into elevators and dentists' offices) as "inescapable, unending, and stultifying."*

[6] **menial** To refer to work (scrubbing floors, for example) as *menial* is to say that it requires no special skill; that's it's suitable for servants; that it involves undesirable drudgery. *During the Civil War, black soldiers were forced to serve in segregated units and to perform menial tasks.*

[7] **plunder (plundered)** To *plunder* is to rob (especially by force); to take wrongfully; to steal. As a noun, *plunder* is property that has been stolen. *From the 16th to the 19th century, the Barbary Coast (the northern coast of Africa) was used as a base by pirates who plundered ships in the Mediterranean Sea.*

THE WIZARD OF OZ VOCABULARY BUILDER

She felt her blood rise behind her temples in pulsing waves, and the **tempest**[1] in her mind made her forget everything except her deep hatred of the vicious **virago**[2] before her. Her face was drained of all color, but bright sparks flashed deep within her dark pupils. With all her puny strength she fired the words explosively, **cathartically**[3]: "GIVE ME BACK MY SHOE!!" Then, with her chest heaving and her reason returning, Dorothy watched to see how the wicked woman would respond.

But the Witch simply ignored the **brazen**[4] outburst— except that her usual **acerbic**[5] **glower**[1] was now replaced by a horrible,

---

[1] **tempest** A *tempest* is a violent storm (especially a windstorm accompanied by rain or snow) or a disturbance (commotion, uproar, etc.). The adjective *tempestuous* means "resembling a tempest; stormy." *Though highly regarded for his dramatic range, actor Richard Burton was probably better known for his tempestuous marriage to actress Elizabeth Taylor.*

[2] **virago** A *virago* is a loud, nagging, scolding, quarrelsome, ill-tempered woman. *In Shakespeare's comedy* The Taming of the Shrew, *a virago named Kate meets her match in Petruchio, a young nobleman who marries her, then systematically humiliates her to cure her of her temper.*

[3] **catharsis (cathartically)** A *catharsis* is a (sometimes sudden or violent) release or discharge of disruptive, pent-up emotions, so as to result in the permanent relief of anguish or in a cleansing of the spirit. Note: In medicine, a *catharsis* is a purging (of the digestive system, by way of the bowels). *By undergoing primal therapy (a method of psychotherapy that treats neurosis cathartically; that is, it teaches patients to express feelings through angry screaming), the substitute teacher learned to maintain her sanity in the classroom by periodically screeching "SHUT UP!!" at the top of her lungs.*

[4] **brazen** To describe someone as *brazen* is to say that he's shamelessly rude, bold, or disrespectful; he's nervy. *American showman P. T. Barnum (1810–1891) took the upper half of a dead monkey sewn onto the bottom half of a large dead fish and brazenly exhibited it as the "Feejee Mermaid."*

[5] **acerbic** To describe food as *acerbic* is to say that it has a strong, sharp taste; it's sour, bitter, tart. To describe a person's temperament or facial expression as *acerbic* is to say that it's sour or bitter (that he's a sourpuss). To describe a person's language or wit as *acerbic* is to say that it's sharp, biting, sarcastic, harsh. The noun is *acerbity*. *In Dr. Seuss's children's book* How the Grinch Stole Christmas, *an acerbic, green-skinned creature tries to prevent Christmas by stealing all the villagers' gifts.*

mocking grin. Then, as she inhaled sharply through her **scabrous**[2], **aquiline**[3] nose, Dorothy knew another fit of **loathsome**[4] laughter was **imminent**[5]. Without thinking, her body acting like a machine with a will of its own, Dorothy picked up a bucket of water that stood near and dashed it over the Witch, wetting her from head to toe. Amazingly, this **stanched**[6] the flow of nauseating laughter as soon as it had begun. In the Witch's wicked eyes, the evil black

---

[1] **glower** To *glower* (rhymes with *shower*) is to give an angry, sullen, or discontented stare or look. As a noun, a *glower* is such a look. *When I whispered in class, the professor glowered at me for a second, then went right on lecturing.*

[2] **scabrous** If a surface is *scabrous* (to the touch), it's rough (because of tiny projections, scales, etc.). *When her hands became red, itchy, and covered with scabrous patches, Betty figured she was suffering from either eczema or "dishpan hands."*

[3] **aquiline** To describe someone's nose as *aquiline* is to say that it resembles an eagle's beak; that is, it's hooked or curved. *Before the tobacco shop stood a life-sized, aquiline-nosed wooden Indian holding a cluster of cigars.*

[4] **loathsome** To describe an act, person, or thing as *loathsome* is to say that it arouses a feeling of hostility and disgust; it's hateful, detestable, repulsive, etc. *We weren't surprised to learn that that most loathsome insect— the cockroach— reproduces in dirty, damp places and has the highest tolerance to radiation of all animals.* Note: Two related words are the verb *loathe*, which means "to hate" and the noun *loathing*, which means "a feeling of hatred and disgust."

[5] **imminent** To describe an event as *imminent* is to say that it's about to occur; it's near at hand. Often the word is used when what is about to occur is bad, as in *imminent danger* or *imminent war*. *In 1945, when his defeat in World War II was imminent, German dictator Adolf Hitler committed suicide.* Note: Don't confuse this word with *immanent*, which is pronounced the same but means "naturally occurring within" as in *God is immanent in nature.*

[6] **stanch (stanched)** To *stanch* the flow of something (blood or tears, for example) is to stop it. *Doctors say that to stanch the flow of blood of a nosebleed, you should gently pinch the nostrils or apply cold compresses to the nose.*

irises[1] that had been riding a surging sea of **supercilious[2] disdain[3]** now became fixed in horror.

"No, no, no!" she shrieked in **vociferous[4]** denial, water **sluicing[5]** from her black dress. "Look what you've done! I'm melting! I'm melting!" As the Witch kept repeating the words "I'm melting," she became smaller and smaller, and her voice got softer and softer, until nothing remained but a **rancid[6], amorphous[1]** blob of **turbid[2]**

---

[1] **iris (irises)** Your *iris* is the round, colored portion of your eye. Sitting behind the cornea and surrounding the pupil, it contracts and expands to regulate the amount of light that enters your eye. *Explaining that all Christmas decorations should be red and green, Ed took out some crayons and made the cardboard Santa's eyes bloodshot with green irises.*

[2] **supercilious** People who are *supercilious* have a high opinion of themselves and look down on others (with disapproval), as if they're raising their eyebrows (in fact, *supercilium* is the Latin word for eyebrow); they're snobby, superior. *Explaining why he refused to dine at the exclusive French restaurant, Joe said, "I don't want some irritatingly self-assured, supercilious wine steward trying to intimidate me."*

[3] **disdain** When you feel *disdain* for something (or, to use the verb, when you *disdain* something), you regard it as inferior and unworthy; you look down upon it, disapprove of it, don't like it. *Some people (call them snobs, if you like) praise everything on public television and disdain everything on commercial television.*

[4] **vociferous** To describe a verbal expression (a complaint, outcry, exclamation, etc.) as *vociferous* is to say that it's loud, noisy, forceful, intense. *In 1970, over vociferous opposition, President Nixon announced the invasion of Cambodia by the United States and the need to draft 150,000 more soldiers for the Vietnam War effort.*

[5] **sluice (sluicing)** As a noun, a *sluice* is an artificial channel used to regulate a flow of water (as in irrigation or at a dam, for example). As a verb, to say that something (water, for example) *sluices* is to say that it flows or pours (as if through a *sluice*). *In the 1960 film* Psycho, *a woman driver (Janet Leigh) is nearly blinded by oncoming headlights that flash through rainwater sluicing down her windshield.*

[6] **rancid** To describe something (old food, for example) as *rancid* is to say that it's rotten, smelly, decaying, putrid, etc. *When they opened Bobby's school locker they found, in a heap at the bottom, four textbooks, a baseball glove, a jacket, and a rancid tuna sandwich.*

liquid that slowly spread over the kitchen floor.

Dorothy quickly drew another bucket of water and poured it over whatever **vestiges**[3] of the Witch remained, then swept everything out the door. She plucked the precious Silver Shoe from the **dross**[4], cleaned and dried it, and put it back on.

It took a moment for her to realize she was actually free, and as she did, Toto leaped into her arms and licked her face. At once, as if by magic, her **pallid**[5] cheeks regained their natural, rosy **hue**[6].

---

[1] **amorphous** Something described as *amorphous* has no definite or distinct shape or form. *In the 1958 science fiction film* The Blob, *an amorphous glob of goo devours people.*

[2] **turbid** To describe a liquid (water, for example) as *turbid* is to say that it's not clear because of stirred up or suspended foreign particles or sediment; it's muddy, murky, dirty, clouded, etc. *Even though we've never seen them, we thought it was a pretty good bet that Illinois' Big Muddy River was more turbid than Canada's Clearwater River.*

[3] **vestige (vestiges)** A *vestige* is a visible remaining trace (of something no longer present or in existence). *A 1986 advertisement for an upcoming CBS TV show featuring opposing archaeologists (scientists who uncover and study tools, inscriptions, and other vestiges of prehistoric cultures) read "Archaeologists dig up dirt on each other!"*

[4] **dross** Technically, *dross* is a waste product or impurity found on the surface of molten metal. But the word is generally used to denote any waste matter (garbage, junk, rubbish, debris, etc.) or to refer to anything considered worthless, trivial, or commonplace. *In December 1979 journalist Joanne Sheehy noted, "In recent years Handel's* Messiah *has been given the Great Cleansing to remove the dross added by everyone from Mozart on; tempos have been quickened, orchestras have been lightened, and overly dramatic dynamics eliminated in the effort to return to Handel's original concept."*

[5] **pallid** To describe someone's complexion as *pallid* is to say that it's pale, colorless (as from illness, strain, etc.). To describe art (writing, painting, music, etc.) as *pallid* is to say that it lacks vitality; it's dull. *Most critics agreed that the 1979 film* Rocky II *was nothing but a pallid rehash of the original.*

[6] **hue** A hue is a (particular) color, or a (particular) shade of a color. *In 1984 the* New York Times *described the first designer diaper as follows: "It is embellished with a print of Cabbage Patch Kids in muted hues of pink, blue, and green."*

Then, with her heart **tumultuously**[1] thumping with excitement, she ran to the yard where the Lion was trapped and quickly unlocked the gate. She hugged the beast **fervidly**[2] and told him how the Wicked Witch had come to an end and that they were no longer prisoners.

---

[1] **tumultuous (tumultuously)** The noun *tumult* refers to a noisy, disorderly commotion or to a turbulent emotional disturbance. To describe something as *tumultuous* is to say that it's characterized by *tumult*; that is, it's turbulent, violent, agitated, noisy, etc. *Clashes between anti–Vietnam War protesters and Chicago police made the 1968 Democratic National Convention one of the most tumultuous in history.*

[2] **fervid (fervidly)** To describe someone or something as *fervid* is to say that it shows great passion and intensity of feeling; it's enthusiastic, afire, etc. Note: The related adjective *fervent* also means impassioned; however, whereas *fervid* implies a spontaneous, fiery passion *(fervid outcries)*, *fervent* implies a steady, sincere passion *(fervent Democrats)*. *It has been said people make an effort to read better than they usually do when they are in love and reading a fervid love letter.*

Chapter 17 "The Rescue"

Dorothy and the Lion went together into the castle, where Dorothy called all the Winkies together and eagerly told them they were no longer in **thrall**[1] to the Wicked Witch of the West. There was great rejoicing among the yellow-**clad**[2] Winkies, for they had been kept in such **abject**[3] **subjugation**[4] and in such horribly **abysmal**[5] conditions for so many years, that they had long ago

---

[1] **thrall** The state of being in bondage or slavery is known as *thrall*. The word can also denote a state of being held captive emotionally, intellectually, or morally, as in *the Watergate drama held the world in thrall. In July 1992 Israeli Prime Minister Yitzhak Rabin said, "[Israel] must overcome the sense of isolation that has held us in its thrall for almost half a century; we must join the international movement toward peace, reconciliation, and cooperation that is spreading over the entire globe these days."*

[2] **clad** To be *clad* in something (a garment, an article of clothing) is to be clothed in it; to be wearing it. Note: *Clad* is the past tense and past participle of the verb *clothe. Many rock music videos feature scantily clad dancers.*

[3] **abject** To refer to a bad or unfortunate situation or condition as *abject* is to say that it's as low, degrading, miserable, wretched, and hopeless as it can possibly be. *John Steinbeck's 1939 novel* The Grapes of Wrath *is about the hardships of an American farm family who move to California in the 1930s to escape the abject poverty of the Dust Bowl (a parched region of the Great Plains plagued by drought and dust storms).*

[4] **subjugate (subjugation)** To *subjugate* someone is to make him subservient or obedient to you; to bring him under your control. *Between the 1880s and the 1960s, lynching (the unlawful hanging of a supposed criminal by a mob) was often used by whites in the South to terrorize and subjugate blacks.*

[5] **abysmal** To refer to something (a condition, ignorance, a failure, a performance) as *abysmal* is to say that it's immeasurably bad. Note: An *abyss* is an immeasurably deep cavity (chasm, pit, void, etc.). *Clifford Beers, cofounder of the National Committee for Mental Hygiene, was an early 20th-century mental-health pioneer who, as a patient, discovered abysmal conditions in asylums.*

given up hope of ever escaping the Witch's **pernicious**[1] **tyranny**[2].

"If our friends, the Scarecrow and the Tin Woodman, were only with us," said the Lion yearningly, "I would be quite happy."

"Do you suppose we could rescue them?" asked the girl.

"We can try," answered the Lion.

Dorothy asked the Winkies if they could help rescue her friends, and the Winkies replied that they would be delighted to do everything in their power for her.

They all traveled one full day and part of the next until, weary with fatigue, they at last came to the little, rocky hill where the poor, misshapen Tin Woodman lay. One of the more **sedentary**[3] Winkies, taking **umbrage**[4] at having been **dragooned**[1] into

---

[1] **pernicious** To describe a substance as *pernicious* is to say that it tends to cause serious physical harm or death; it's poisonous, toxic. To describe a condition, doctrine, or conduct as *pernicious* is to say that it tends to cause great harm or destruction; it's devastating, wicked. *In Richard Wright's 1940 novel* Native Son, *the pernicious effects of poverty and racism destroy a young black man's life.*

[2] **tyranny** A form of government or rule in which one person has absolute power (especially when dictatorial, unjust, oppressive, or abusive) is known as *tyranny*. Note: This type of ruler is known as a *tyrant*. The word can also be used figuratively to refer to the crushing or overwhelming effect of anything that seems to have absolute power over us (*the tyranny of clocks, tyrannical parents*, etc.). *In George Orwell's 1945 satirical novel* Animal Farm, *animals take over a farm to escape human tyranny.*

[3] **sedentary** To describe an occupation as *sedentary* is to say that it's characterized by much sitting. To describe a person or lifestyle as *sedentary* is to say that it's characterized by sitting or resting (as opposed to moving about or exercising). *Doctors say that osteoporosis (a disease in which the bones become fragile) is aggravated by a variety of factors, including smoking, drinking, and a sedentary lifestyle.*

[4] **umbrage** To take *umbrage* at something (a real or imagined insult or snub, for example) is to take offense (at it), to resent it. *While I understand that people generally take umbrage when called by the wrong name, I didn't think, when I accidentally called my blind date "Rosalyn," that she needed to yell, "It's Rosa-LIND!"*

participating, tried to insert a **soupçon**[2] of sarcasm into the proceedings by humming a **dirge**[3]. But when its **elegiac**[4] strains were lost in the wind, he instead panted and wiped a hand across his brow in mock exaggeration and said **wryly**[5], "Now I can skip my daily exercise routine for a week!"

When this **flippant**[6] **sally**[7] provoked nothing but icy stares of

---

[1] **dragoon (dragooned)** To *dragoon* someone into doing something is to force him (by pressure, threats, etc.) to do it; to twist his arm. *As he prepared Germany for war in the late 1930s, dictator Adolf Hitler dragooned smaller nations into giving up territory to the Nazis.*

[2] **soupçon** A *soupçon* (pronounced *soup-SAWN*) of something is a very small amount of it; a trace of it. *Our waitress said that when it comes to making smooth-tasting coffee, a soupçon of vanilla extract makes all the difference.*

[3] **dirge** A *dirge* is a funeral song or tune (or a musical composition that sounds like one; that is, one that's slow and mournful). *My cousin, a confirmed bachelor, claims that a guy can use the same slow music as both his wedding march and his funeral dirge— because he's a goner either way.*

[4] **elegiac** An *elegy* is a song or poem that mourns someone who has died. The adjective *elegiac* means "resembling or characteristic of an elegy; expressing sorrow (for something dead, lost, or past)." *In 1986 West Side Story choreographer Jerome Robbins produced an elegiac ballet* (Quiet City) *as a tribute to Joseph Duell, a New York City Ballet dancer who had committed suicide that year at age 29.*

[5] **wry (wryly)** To describe something (a remark, humor, etc.) as *wry* is to say that it's dryly (shrewdly and impersonally) cutting or sarcastic. *Early 20th-century humorist Will Rogers was known for his folksy but wry social and political commentary and for his statement "I never met a man I didn't like."*

[6] **flippant** Someone who's *flippant* is marked by disrespectful levity or a lack of appropriate seriousness; he's smart-alecky, overly casual. Note: A shortened form of the word, *flip*, means the same thing; the noun is *flippancy*. *In 1980, describing the supple, graceful coconut trees of the island of New Guinea, writer William Manchester said that they "crowd the beach like a minuet of slender elderly virgins adopting flippant poses."*

[7] **sally** A *sally* is a sudden, quick witticism; a clever, funny remark. *On leaving the White House in January 1953, President Harry Truman threw out this little sally: "If I'd known how much packing I'd have to do, I'd have run again."* Note: The word can also mean "sortie" (see *sortie*).

rebuke[1] from his comrades, he stopped short, **simpered**[2] foolishly, and vowed to himself to make his next **pithy**[3] one-liner a little more **apposite**[4]. "Hey, I was just being **facetious**[5]," he grumbled.

The other Winkies now lifted the Tin Woodman tenderly in their arms and carefully carried him back to the castle. Dorothy shed a few tears along the way, her thoughts now and then jumping back to a **lugubrious**[6] funeral **cortege**[1] she had once witnessed in

---

[1] **rebuke** As a noun, a *rebuke* is an expression of strong disapproval, a reprimand, a scolding (usually intended as a caution or to correct undesirable behavior). As a verb, to *rebuke* someone is to scold him, criticize him, etc. *In 1884 Congress rebuked President Ronald Reagan for using federal funds to place mines in Nicaraguan harbors.*

[2] **simper (simpered)** To *simper* is to smile in a silly, self-conscious way. *In* Peanuts *comic strips, perpetual loser Charlie Brown simpers whenever he sees the object of his affection, the little red-haired girl.*

[3] **pithy** To describe a verbal or written expression as *pithy* is to say that it uses few words to clearly get its point across; it's short, concise, compact, precisely meaningful. *Late 19th-century Irish writer Oscar Wilde was known for his pithy, witty sayings, such as, "I can resist everything except temptation."*

[4] **apposite** If you describe something (a reference, an image, an answer, etc.) as *apposite* (pronounced *AP-uh-zit*), you mean that it's strikingly appropriate, fitting, relevant, pertinent, applicable, etc. (to the situation). *The term* Underground Railroad *was used during the mid-1800s to describe an informal system that helped slaves escape to the North and Canada; but since the system was actually neither underground nor a railroad, a more apposite term might have been* Overground Roadway.

[5] **facetious** To be *facetious* (pronounced *fuh-SEE-shis*) is to be playfully humorous; to speak in fun; to be kidding. *In our high school year book, facetious captions appear under some of the photos; for example, under a picture of two students holding a large sheet it says "Quick! Hide the body!"*

[6] **lugubrious** To describe something (a manner, an atmosphere, a tone of voice, etc.) as *lugubrious* is to say that it's extremely, exaggeratedly, or continuously mournful, gloomy, dismal, somber, sorrowful, etc. *During the mid-1900s Emmett Kelly won fame as a circus clown ("Weary Willie") who wore tattered clothes and affected a lugubrious expression.*

THE WIZARD OF OZ VOCABULARY BUILDER

Kansas.

When they finally arrived at the castle, Dorothy said to the Winkies, "Are any of your people tinsmiths?"

"There's certainly no **dearth**[2] of tinsmiths here," one of the Winkies proudly told her. And the tinsmiths were summoned at once. They soon arrived with a gleaming **panoply**[3] of metal tools.

One older tinsmith, who seemed to be the chief, was accompanied by a large crew of helpers—some old hands, some mere **neophytes**[4]. Dorothy inquired of the chief, "Can you straighten out those dents in the Tin Woodman, bend him back into shape again, and solder him together where he's broken?"

---

[1] **cortege** A *cortege* is a ceremonial (especially funeral) procession (group of people, vehicles, etc., moving along in an orderly, formal way). *A December 1963 issue of* Newsweek *magazine, speaking of President Kennedy's funeral cortege (which had been seen on TV by more than a hundred million people in towns across America), said "[His] casket did not ride down Pennsylvania Avenue only; it rode down Main Street."*

[2] **dearth** A *dearth* (of something) is a lack (of it); a scarcity, a deficiency, a shortage, etc. *In the* Titanic *disaster of 1912, many people perished because of a dearth of lifeboats.*

[3] **panoply** Originally, a *panoply* was a suit of armor; but people use this word today to refer to any impressive or splendid array, display, or exhibition (of something). *The American Wing of New York City's Metropolitan Museum of Art contains a panoply of U.S. arts and crafts of all periods.* Note: The word can also refer to ceremonial attire (a splendid uniform, for example). *Speaking of being buried in full panoply, five-star army general Douglas MacArthur (commander of U.S forces in the Far East during World War II) once posed the question, "What greater honor could come to an American, and a soldier?"*

[4] **neophyte (neophytes)** A *neophyte* is a person who is just starting to learn or do something; a beginner, newcomer, amateur. *Early 20th-century American tennis idol "Big Bill" Tilden once gave this advice to neophytes playing mixed doubles: "Hit at the girl whenever possible."*

THE WIZARD OF OZ VOCABULARY BUILDER

The old tinsmith carefully **assayed**[1] the Tin Woodman's mangled metal skin. **Ravaged**[2] by time, wind, and rain, it now wore a sickly, green **patina**[3]. After what seemed like an eternity, the tinsmith suddenly smiled and said **elatedly**[4], "I think we can mend him so he'll be as good as ever!" Dorothy felt a sudden inward thrill.

The tinsmiths worked all day, hammering, soldering, and polishing **indefatigably**[5], but to no avail. **Redoubling**[1] their efforts,

---

[1] **assay (assayed)** To *assay* something is to test, analyze, or evaluate its quality, worth, or value. As a noun, the word denotes such a test or evaluation. *In her July 1997 article entitled "Martian Rover Makes Detailed Rock Analysis," journalist Kathy Sawyer said, "The little rover* Sojourner *planted a 10-hour equivalent of a robotic kiss on the Martian rock 'Barnacle Bill' last night, in the first chemical assay of a rock ever conducted on the Red Planet."*

[2] **ravage (ravaged)** If something (a village, countryside, a person's face, etc.) has been *ravaged*, it has suffered ruinous damage or devastation (as from war, disease, despair, etc.). *On signing the Medicare Act in 1965, President Lyndon Johnson said, "Every citizen will be able, in his productive years when he is earning, to insure himself against the ravages of illness in his old age."*

[3] **patina** Technically, a *patina* (pronounced either *PAT-ih-nuh* or *puh-TEE-nuh*) is a thin, greenish coating that appears (as a result of oxidation) on old copper, brass, or bronze. By extension, the word is often used to refer to any film, coating, or change in appearance (produced by age or use) on any substance or surface. *When the cleaning crew arrived at the house, they noticed that someone had written "Please clean and polish" in the patina of dust that covered the piano.*

[4] **elated (elatedly)** To be *elated* is to be very happy, overjoyed, ecstatic, thrilled, walking on air, flying high, etc. The noun is *elation*. *As she crossed the finish line of the marathon, a brief expression of elation passed over her tortured features.*

[5] **indefatigable (indefatigably)** If you're *indefatigable* (pronounced with the accent on the third syllable) you don't become fatigued (tired, weary, etc.); you're tireless, persevering, persistent, relentless, etc. (in some activity, effort, or cause). *Thurgood Marshall, the first black U.S. Supreme Court justice, was an indefatigable champion of civil rights.*

they worked through the night, and by morning the Tin Woodman was finally straightened out into his old form and was as good as ever.

When, at last, he saw Dorothy and had **profusely**[2] thanked her for rescuing him, he wept tears of joy. And Dorothy, smiling **beatifically**[3], had to wipe each one carefully from his face so his joints wouldn't rust. At the same time her own tears fell thick and fast at the joy of seeing her old friend again, but these tears didn't need to be wiped away.

"If we only had the Scarecrow with us again," said the Tin Woodman, when Dorothy had finished telling him everything that had happened, "I would be quite happy."

"We must try to find him," said the girl **resolutely**[4].

Once again she called on her friends the Winkies to help her, which they were only too glad to do. They walked all that day and

---

[1] **redouble (redoubling)** You might think that to *redouble* something (efforts, for example) is to double it twice (in other words, multiply it by four); but oddly enough, *redouble* means simple "double." *After the stock market crash of 1929, many members of women's voluntary associations were unable to pay club dues; on the other hand, the suffering caused by the Great Depression that followed the crash motivated other members to redouble their charitable efforts.*

[2] **profuse (profusely)** If you say that an amount (of something) is *profuse*, you mean that it's large, extravagant, plentiful, abundant, lavish, etc. *Doctors say that the symptoms of trichinosis (a disease caused by eating undercooked pork) include muscle soreness and profuse sweating.*

[3] **beatific (beatifically)** To refer to something as *beatific* (pronounced *bee-uh-TIF-ik*) is to say that is shows extreme or angelic happiness (as in *a beatific smile*) or that it causes supreme happiness or blessedness (as in *beatific peace*.) *The sunlight filtered through the church's stained-glass windows, bathing the bride and groom in beatific illumination.*

[4] **resolute (resolutely)** If you're *resolute*, you're firm and determined (about achieving some goal or supporting some cause or purpose); you're intent, unwavering, etc. *During World War II, British Prime Minister Winston Churchill resolutely refused to make peace with Germany under Aldolf Hitler.*

part of the next, **circuitously**[1] **roving**[2] fields and forests, all the while **diligently**[3] **scouring**[4] the landscape, until they at last found the tree whose top branches held the Scarecrow's clothes. It was a very tall, narrow tree, and its trunk was so smooth that no one could climb it.

Studying the scene from all angles, the same sarcastic wise guy who had earlier made an unsuccessful crack during the Tin Woodman's rescue now **quipped**[5], "We've just found the

---

[1] **circuitous (circuitously)** To refer to something (a route or an explanation, for example) as *circuitous* (pronounced *sir-KYEW-ih-tis*) is to say that it's roundabout and indirect (and often lengthy and winding). *The Snake River, which flows circuitously from Yellowstone National Park in Wyoming to the Columbia River in Washington, has spectacular deep gorges and is an important source of hydroelectric power.*

[2] **rove (roving)** To *rove* is to go from one place to another, especially over a wide area and with no definite destination; to roam, wander, etc. *The 1849 California gold rush brought thousands of prospectors to rugged wilderness regions previously known only to roving fur trappers and native Americans.*

[3] **diligent (diligently)** If you're *diligent* (about doing something) you're persevering and painstaking (about it); you're industrious, hardworking, attentive, careful, etc. *An Anglo-Norman text written around the beginning of the 15th century tells us that elephants guard their ears diligently against flies.*

[4] **scour (scouring)** To *scour* (a place, such as a countryside or a room) is to search over it (for something). *In the early 1850s British arctic explorer Sir Robert McClure, as commander of one of two ships scouring the Arctic Archipelago (a group of more than 50 large Canadian islands in the Arctic Ocean) for the lost party of explorer Sir John Franklin, proved the existence of the Northwest Passage (a water route along the northern coast of North America, connecting the Atlantic and Pacific oceans).*

[5] **quip (quipped)** As a noun, a *quip* is a quick, witty, clever, funny (sometimes sarcastic) remark (often prompted by some occasion or by some other remark). As a verb, to *quip* is to make such a remark (especially in response to something). *During a 1985 TV show, when asked what he thought of comedienne Phyllis Diller's piano playing, comedian Bob Hope quipped, "When she started to play, Steinway came down personally and rubbed his name off the piano."*

THE WIZARD OF OZ VOCABULARY BUILDER

proverbial[1] haystack in a needle!" He was so **smugly**[2] delighted with his clever **inversion**[3] of the well-known phrase that he didn't care that no one seemed to appreciate his **rapier**[4] wit. In fact, no one even heard him because they were all too busy trying to figure out how to get the Scarecrow down. Then, with a mental **acuity**[5] **redolent**[6] of the Scarecrow's, the Tin Woodman announced, "I'll

---

[1] **proverbial** To describe something as *proverbial* is to say that it's often mentioned; it's widely referred to (as if the subject of a proverb). For example, you might refer to the *proverbial* beauty of Helen of Troy or the *proverbial* wisdom of Solomon. *In 1958 radio pioneer and RCA Chairman David Sarnoff said, "I hitched my wagon to an electron rather than the proverbial star."*

[2] **smug (smugly)** To be *smug* is to be self-righteously (usually offensively) self-satisfied; to be overly pleased with yourself (with your correctness, superiority, ability, etc.). *In 1974 consumer advocate Ralph Nader said, "For almost 70 years the life insurance industry has been a smug sacred cow feeding the public a steady line of sacred bull."*

[3] **inversion** An *inversion* of something is an upside down or backwards version or rearrangement of it. *We were surprised to learn that many people who had once lived in (the New York City borough of) Brooklyn had moved to (what is now the Long Island village of) Lynbrook, and that the name "Lynbrook" was simply an inversion of "Brooklyn."*

[4] **rapier** As a noun, a *rapier* is a type of sword (a long, narrow one). As an adjective, it means "very sharp," but is used almost exclusively to describe the sharpness of someone's wit. *When asked how he became a war hero, President John F. Kennedy, who was known for his rapier wit, answered, "It was absolutely involuntary; they sank my boat."*

[5] **acuity** If you have *acuity*, you have the faculty of thinking and applying knowledge; you have keenness of perception; you're insightful, astute, discerning, intelligent, etc. The adjective is *acute*. *Actor Dustin Hoffman is known for his acute characterizations in such films as* Midnight Cowboy *(1969),* Tootsie *(1982), and* Rain Man *(1989).* Note: The word also can refer to sharpness of eyesight, as in *visual acuity of 20/20.*

[6] **redolent** This word literally means "having or emitting a fragrance or aroma of," as in *the kitchen was redolent with the aroma of coffee.* By extension, people use this word to mean "suggestive of; reminiscent of, etc."*Because football's annual Super Bowl games are numbered in Roman numerals (Super Bowl XXIX, for example), they are redolent of the grand combative amusements of ancient Rome.*

chop down the tree, and then we'll be able to get the clothes."

As soon as he had spoken, he began to chop, and in a short time the tree began to **totter**[1], then fell over with a crash. When the Scarecrow's **sodden**[2], **derelict**[3] garments fell out of the branches and onto the ground, Dorothy picked them up and had the Winkies carry them back to the castle, where they were cleaned, dried, and stuffed with nice, new straw. And suddenly, there stood our **epitome**[4] of **bedraggled**[5] inelegance, the Scarecrow, **resurrected**[1]

---

[1] **totter** To *totter* is to sway as if about to fall; to move or walk unsteadily; to stagger, falter, wobble, etc. *Early 20th-century British detective story writer Dorothy Sayers, when asked why she didn't read modern novels, answered with this poem: "As I grow older and older/And totter toward the tomb/I find that I care less and less/Who goes to bed with whom."*

[2] **sodden** To describe something as *sodden* is to say that it's thoroughly soaked (with liquid or moisture); it's sopping wet; it's saturated, waterlogged, etc. *Experts say that if you want to raise your indoor relative humidity without using a humidifier, place large pans of water around the house and put a few sodden towels inside the bathtub.*

[3] **derelict** As an adjective describing an object, *derelict* means "abandoned, forgotten, deserted, neglected, etc." *The fate of the captain and 14-man crew of the sailing ship* Mary Celeste, *found derelict but in perfect order in December 1872, has never been learned.* Note: As an adjective describing a person, the word means "negligent (in the performance of duty)." And as a noun, a *derelict* is a homeless person, a social outcast, a bum, etc.

[4] **epitome** The *epitome* (pronounced *ih-PIT-ih-mee*) of something is the highest, most perfect, or most representative example of it. *British-born American film actor Cary Grant, who during the mid-1900s was the epitome of the elegant leading man, once gave his formula for living, as follows: "I get up in the morning and I go to bed at night; in between, I occupy myself as best I can."*

[5] **bedraggled** To describe something (or someone) as *bedraggled* is to say that it's wet, limp, dirty, messy, sloppy, soiled, etc. (as if having been dragged through the mud). *Legend tells us that late 16th-century English explorer and writer Sir Walter Raleigh once spread his coat over a mud puddle so that Queen Elizabeth I could walk over it (but it doesn't tell us what became of the bedraggled coat!).*

and as good as ever, thanking them over and over for saving him!

But then Dorothy thought of Aunt Em and of Kansas and realized that their **Odyssean**[2] quest, however **peripatetic**[3], must continue. "We must go back to the Wizard and claim his promise," she **asserted**[4].

They called all the Winkies together and regretfully told them they were leaving, and the Winkies were sorry to have them go. They had grown so fond of the Tin Woodman, in fact, that they begged him to stay and rule over them and the Land of the West,

---

[1] **resurrect (resurrected)** Literally, to *resurrect* someone is to bring him back to life (to raise him from the dead). By extension, to *resurrect* something is to rouse it from a state of inactivity; to bring it back into notice or practice; to renew it, reawaken it, revitalize it, etc. *In recent years, many Plains Indians have resurrected tribal languages and religious traditions.*

[2] **odyssey (Odyssean)** An *odyssey* is a journey or long series of wanderings filled with adventures and hardships (after Homer's *Odyssey*, an epic poem that describes mythological Greek hero Odysseus's adventures during his 10-year attempt to return home to Ithaca after the Trojan War). Thus, to describe a journey as *Odyssean* is to say that it's long and filled with adventures, hardships, perils, etc. *The 1963 film* Jason and the Argonauts *tells the famous myth of Greek hero Jason, his crew of sailors, and their Odyssean search for the Golden Fleece (the golden coat of a magical flying sheep).*

[3] **peripatetic** To describe someone as *peripatetic* is to say that he walks from place to place; he wanders about, on foot. *In 1973, ten years after he won the Pulitzer Prize for portions of his biography of writer Henry James, Leon Edel said, "Any biographer must of necessity become a pilgrim— a peripatetic, obsessed literary pilgrim, a traveler with four eyes.* Note: When spelled with a capital *P*, the word means "pertaining to Aristotle" (who walked about in the Lyceum of ancient Athens while he taught philosophy).

[4] **assert (asserted)** To *assert* something (or, to use the noun, to make an *assertion* of something) is to state it or declare it in a positive, confident, or forceful way. *In 1543 Polish astronomer Nicolaus Copernicus asserted that the sun (not the earth) was at the center of the solar system and that the earth and other planets revolved around it.*

promising to **comport**[1] themselves in an appropriately **submissive**[2] manner. But finding he was determined to leave with the others, they accepted his decision **stoically**[3] and gave him a brand-new oilcan as a going-away gift. Then every one of the travelers shook hands with the Winkies until their arms ached.

Before leaving, Dorothy went to the Witch's cupboard to fill her basket with food for the journey, and there she saw the Golden Cap. **Leery**[4] of anything that belonged to one as wicked as the Witch, a fearful indecision took possession of her. But then our **doughty**[5] little heroine suddenly tried it on and found that it fit her

---

[1] **comport** To *comport* (pronounced with the accent on the second syllable) yourself (in a particular manner) is to conduct or behave yourself (in that manner). *In a 1955 address at Montgomery, Alabama, Martin Luther King, Jr., said that if black civil rights protesters can demonstrate courage and love and comport themselves with dignity, future history books will have to say, "There lived a great people— a black people— who injected new meaning and dignity into the veins of civilization."*

[2] **submissive** People who are *submissive* tend to act in accordance with other people's wishes, decisions, opinions, etc.; they're agreeable, obedient, servile. *In 1976 the Dean of the University of Southern California's College of Education said, "Human beings are full of emotion, and the teacher who knows how to use it will have dedicated learners; it means sending dominant signals instead of submissive ones with your eyes, body, and voice."*

[3] **stoic (stoically)** People who are *stoic* (or *stoical*) seem to be unmoved by pleasure or especially pain; they're unemotional, uncomplaining, stony, impassive, etc. [after the Stoic school of philosophy founded around 300 B.C. by Greek philosopher Zeno, which taught that, as a matter of principle or self-discipline, men should accept the unavoidable without complaint]. *In 1949, after having stoically endured jeers, insults, hate mail, and death threats for two years, Jackie Robinson (the first African-American to play in major league baseball) broke his silence and became an outspoken opponent of racial discrimination.*

[4] **leery** If you're *leery* of something, you're wary, suspicious, or distrustful of it. *When a stranger telephoned me to say that I had been chosen to receive a free Florida vacation, I was immediately leery.*

[5] **doughty** To describe someone as *doughty* (pronounced *DOW-tee*) is to say that he shows courage and determination. *With her doughty spirit, Helen Keller overcame overwhelming handicaps (blindness and deafness) by learning to read, write, and communicate with sign language.*

perfectly. Of course, Dorothy didn't know anything about the magic of the Cap, but she saw that it was pretty, so she decided to wear it. Then, ending their **sojourn**[1] in the West, the travelers started their journey back toward the Emerald City and the Great Wizard.

---

[1] **sojourn** As a noun, a *sojourn* is a temporary stay (brief period of residence) at a place away from home. As a verb, to *sojourn* is to temporarily reside someplace away from home. *During a sojourn in Italy, American writer Nathaniel Hawthorne wrote his last novel,* The Marble Faun *(1860).*

Chapter 18 "The Discovery"

At the suggestion of the Scarecrow, the **nomadic**[1] foursome walked toward the rising sun, and they spent three mostly uneventful days following this easterly course. The only bit of excitement occurred on the second day when they passed a large cornfield surrounded by a yellow fence. Inside the field stood what appeared to be an **antebellum**[2] Southern **belle**[3] whose **demure**[4],

---

[1] **nomadic** Technically, a *nomad* is a member of a group of people (a tribe, for example) who have no fixed home and travel from place to place (in search of food, water, etc.). By extension, if you describe someone (not necessarily a homeless person or tribe member) as *nomadic*, you simply mean that he wanders or roams from place to place. *During the 17th century the Cheyenne Indians lived in earth-lodge villages along the Cheyenne River (which flows from eastern Wyoming to central South Dakota); however, after acquiring horses (around 1760) they became nomadic buffalo hunters.*

[2] **antebellum** This word literally means "before the war." But when people describe something (an object, institution, etc.) as *antebellum*, they mean it existed or originated before the (American) Civil War. *Baton Rouge (Louisiana), Mobile (Alabama), and Tallahassee (Florida) are three Southern cities known for their beautiful antebellum houses.*

[3] **belle** A *belle* is a pretty (and often popular and charming) girl or woman, especially the prettiest of a group, as in *the belle of the ball.* The word is usually heard in the phrase "Southern belle." *British actress Vivien Leigh won the Academy Award as best actress for her roles in 1939's* Gone with the Wind *(as young Southern belle Scarlett O'Hara) and in 1951's* A Streetcar Named Desire *(as fading Southern belle Blanche DuBois).*

[4] **demure** People who are *demure* are quiet, shy, and modest (especially overly, affectedly, or slyly so). The word is used more often to describe a female than a male. *A 1956 New England Life Insurance pamphlet entitled "What Is a Girl?" observes, "A little girl can jitter around and stomp and make funny noises that frazzle your nerves, yet just when you open your mouth she stands there demure with that special look in her eyes."*

retiring[1] **demeanor**[2] approached **coyness**[3]. Her large, yellow sunbonnet did nothing to contain her **cascading**[4] golden **locks**[5]. Her long, tight-waisted yellow dress rippled tantalizingly in the soft breeze.

It took them a moment to realize that the **anachronistic**[6] image

---

[1] **retiring** To describe someone as *retiring* is to say that he's neither forceful not showy; he's withdrawn, quiet, shy, modest, etc. *Tennessee Williams' 1945 play* The Glass Menagerie *concerns a retiring young crippled woman who retreats from reality to play with glass figurines.*

[2] **demeanor** Your *demeanor* is the way you carry or present yourself to others, or the way you act or behave. From your *demeanor*, others can pretty accurately determine your attitude and even your personality. *During World War II, Marine Corps Lieutenant General Holland M. Smith's demeanor was well expressed by his nickname, "Howlin' Mad."*

[3] **coy (coyness)** To be *coy* is to pretend to be shy (especially as a form of flirtation). *When he asked to kiss her goodnight after their first date, she coyly fluttered her eyelashes and said with a smile, "I'm not that kind of girl."* Note: The word can also mean "annoyingly unwilling to make a commitment," as in (a newspaper headline that might read) *Congress coy about tax cut.*

[4] **cascade (cascading)** As a noun, a *cascade* is a waterfall. As a verb, to *cascade* is to fall, tumble, gush, flow, etc. (like water in a waterfall). *In 1950, when Yale University was looking for a new president, a member of the selection committee said that a Yale president should be, among other things, "profound with a wit that bubbles up and brims over in a cascade of brilliance."*

[5] **lock (locks)** A *lock* of hair is a piece (portion, tuft, strand, etc.) of hair. The plural, *locks*, can refer to several of these strands, or to the hair of the head in its entirety. *At the Beatles convention, someone was selling envelopes that supposedly contained locks of Paul McCartney's hair.*

[6] **anachronism (anachronistic)** Something (a person, concept, institution, custom, etc.) that exists or happens in a time (era, century, historical order, etc.) other than the one it belongs to is referred to as an *anachronism. As can be seen in the 1958 film* Witness for the Prosecution, *British trial lawyers and judges wear old-fashioned white wigs— an anachronism that signifies the continuity and dignity of the English justice system.*

was really an **inanimate**[1] female scarecrow. Just then, *our* Scarecrow experienced an exquisite yearning, and the straw that was at the center of his chest began to **smolder**[2] and smoke. Next, his **callow**[3] straw heart suddenly started to catch fire, and the Lion, using the end of his tail, had to smother the **nascent**[4] flames.

After they all calmed down and started on their way again, the Scarecrow inwardly marveled at the thrilling, new sensation he had just experienced. What he felt for his imaginary **paramour**[5] must be what people called love, he thought, and as the light in his eyes

---

[1] **inanimate** Objects described as *inanimate* don't have life; they're inert (a pencil, for example, is an inanimate object). But the word is generally used to describe what has never had life (whereas the word "dead" describes what once did). *In 2000 New York Newsday contained a photograph of mayor Rudolph Guiliani standing next to his life-size wax image at a museum— and it was impossible to tell the real one from the inanimate one!*

[2] **smolder** Literally, when a substance (coal, wood, etc.) *smolders*, it burns without flame (and with little smoke). By extension, the word can apply to emotions (such as anger, hatred, or resentment) that are repressed (held back) and seem to slowly burn. *In 1861 smoldering North-South tensions ignited, and the Civil War began.*

[3] **callow** This word describes people who are immature, young, inexperienced, etc. *During the 1960 presidential campaign, to those who saw him as callow 43-year-old, John F. Kennedy said, "To exclude from positions of trust and command all those below the age of 44 would have kept Jefferson from writing the Declaration of Independence, Washington from commanding the Continental Army, and Christopher Columbus from discovering America."*

[4] **nascent** To describe something as *nascent* is to say that it's just starting to exist, emerge, or develop. *In the 1920s Secretary of Commerce Herbert Hoover supervised regulation of the nascent radio and aviation industries.* Note: In pronouncing the word, the first syllable can rhyme with either *lace* or *lass*.

[5] **paramour** Your *paramour* is your beloved; your boyfriend or girlfriend. The word can also refer specifically to someone with whom you're having an illicit affair (a mistress or lover). *On April 29, 1945, Adolf Hitler married his longtime paramour, Eva Braun; the next day, April 30, they committed suicide.*

THE WIZARD OF OZ VOCABULARY BUILDER

became **lambent**[1] with adoration, his painted face took on a radiant, reddish glow. Then, nervously envisioning a **lethal**[2] **conflagration**[3], he fought to **attenuate**[4] his desires and to block any thoughts of **clandestine**[5] **trysts**[6] that lingered in his active little

---

[1] **lambent** To describe light as *lambent* is to say that it flickers lightly and gracefully over a surface or that it's softly radiant. To describe wit as *lambent* is to say that it deals lightly and gracefully with a subject or that it's brilliantly playful. *After the rain, the sun streamed through the budding wet trees, turning the entire forest a lambent green.*

[2] **lethal** To describe something as *lethal* is to say that it's deadly; it causes or is capable of causing death. *Of the states that impose the death penalty, not all use the same method of execution; for example, Nebraska uses electrocution, whereas its southern neighbor, Kansas, employs lethal injection.*

[3] **conflagration** A *conflagration* is a large fire (especially a destructive one spread over a considerable area). *In the great "Chicago Fire" of 1871, a conflagration destroyed 17,450 buildings and killed 250 people.*

[4] **attenuate** If a moldable object (wire, for example) has been *attenuated*, it's been thinned out, made slender or fine. And if a gas has been *attenuated*, it's been made less dense. And if a virus or bacterium has been *attenuated*, it's been made less destructive or deadly. But when you say that a feeling or condition (desire, power, love, effectiveness, etc.) has been *attenuated*, you mean that it's been reduced or weakened in force, strength, intensity, amount, value, degree, etc. *Even though ties between religion and government had become attenuated by the principle of "separation of church and state" (as required by the First Amendment), some state courts continued to use religious language; for example, in 1897 an Illinois court described a particular crime as "not fit to be named among Christians."*

[5] **clandestine** To describe something (a meeting or plot, for example) as *clandestine* is to say that it's done or kept in secret. Sometimes the implication is that there's something immoral or illegal about whatever is being kept secret. *The Iran-Contra affair was a mid-1980s clandestine U.S. government arrangement to illegally provide funds to the Nicaraguan Contras (rebels) from profits gained by selling arms (weapons) to Iran.*

[6] **tryst (trysts)** A *tryst* is a meeting (or a meeting place or an agreement to meet), especially a private and romantic one, as between lovers. *In the 1961 film* West Side Story, *star-crossed lovers Tony and Maria perform a mock wedding ceremony during their tryst in a dress shop.*

mind. In doing so, his **fatuous**[1] expression slowly turned to one of stiff, **immutable**[2] determination.

When the four travelers finally arrived at the edge of the Emerald City, the Guardian of the Gates greeted them **cordially**[3] and led them toward the door of the Great Palace. As they walked, Dorothy breathlessly told him all about their **foray**[4] in the West.

At they neared the door to the Palace, a familiar-looking man wearing green pants and a green shirt **accosted**[5] them and started

---

[1] **fatuous** Someone who is *fatuous* is not only foolish (or stupid, dull, silly, empty-headed, feeble-minded, etc.), but is at the same time smugly self-satisfied or seemingly disregardful of reality. *In 1988, when asked why he felt his parents' ties to the extreme right-wing, anti-Communist John Birch Society weren't relevant to his campaign, vice presidential candidate Dan Quayle fatuously answered, "Because I say it isn't."*

[2] **immutable** To describe something as *immutable* is to say that it's unchangeable, unalterable, changeless, etc. *In his 1986 book* The Ice: A Journey to Antarctica, *author Stephen Pyne said, "In Antarctica foreground and background were difficult to establish; on shelf and plateau the vision was of an immutable nothingness."*

[3] **cordial (cordially)** To be *cordial* (to someone) is to be courteous, gracious, friendly, warm, and kind (to him). *Although he'd once referred to the Soviet Union as an "evil empire," when President Ronald Reagan arrived there in 1988 (to negotiate a missile treaty) he was cordially welcomed by Soviet leader Mikhail Gorbachev.*

[4] **foray** Technically, a *foray* is a sudden military raid or advance (of troops). But people often use this word to refer to any type of initial venture or attempt, especially one outside one's usual area (as in *a singer's foray into acting*). *After having written ten nonfiction books (including 1979's* The Right Stuff*), journalist Tom Wolfe made a successful foray into fiction with 1987's* Bonfire of the Vanities.

[5] **accost (accosted)** To *accost* someone is to approach him and speak to him (sometimes in a bold or aggressive manner). *In 1985 mild-mannered New Yorker Bernard Goetz shot four threatening-looking youths who accosted him on a New York City subway.*

perfunctorily[1] **shunting**[2] them toward the Throne Room. As Dorothy wondered what had happened to the uniformed soldier who had escorted them before, the man suddenly covered his face with his hands and then just as quickly revealed himself in an **impromptu**[3] game of peek-a-boo. Why, this was the soldier! "I'll bet you didn't recognize me in **mufti**[4], did you?" he said **archly**[5]. Then, in a more serious tone, he explained, "My uniform's being cleaned." Dorothy couldn't think of anything to say about that, so she gave about a quarter of a smile and kept on walking.

Presently they were in the Throne Room, and there again was

---

[1] **perfunctory (perfunctorily)** To describe something as *perfunctory* is to say that it's done merely as a matter of routine or duty; that is, it's done mechanically, superficially, or hastily, without enthusiasm, interest, or care. *Whereas most public kisses between husbands and wives are rather perfunctory, Al and Tipper Gore's kiss at the 2000 Democratic Convention made news because it was long and passionate.*

[2] **shunt (shunting)** To *shunt* someone or something is to turn, move, or shove it aside or onto another course; to deflect, divert, or re-route it. *In 1815 the U.S. government began shunting Native Americans to reservations west of the Mississippi River.*

[3] **impromptu** To do something (speak, perform, etc.) *impromptu* is do it on the spur of the moment, without preparation; to do it extemporaneously. *Comedian and Tonight Show pioneer Steve Allen was known for composing songs impromptu after audience members gave him three random starting notes.*

[4] **mufti** This word means *civvies;* that is, civilian (or normal, everyday) clothes worn by someone who ordinarily wears a military (or other) uniform. *In July 1991, speaking of the Human Rights Office of the army of (the Central American country of) El Salvador, journalist Lee Hockstader reported, "Dressed in mufti, Major Roberto Molina greets a visitor with a handshake and a smile; it's a sharp departure from the usual image of gun-toting, stony-faced Salvadoran army officers, and it is meant to be— Molina is the [friendly] face that the Salvadoran military puts forward these days to meet its harshest critics: human rights organizations, religious groups, and others who come to ask about abuses attributed to the armed forces."*

[5] **arch (archly)** If you say that something (a person, a smile, a comment, a glance, etc.) is *arch* (rhymes with *march*), you mean that it's mischievously playful. *Comedian Steve Allen once began a speech with this arch opening: "Ladies, gentleman, and empty chairs... "*

THE WIZARD OF OZ VOCABULARY BUILDER

the **formidable**[1], **glabrous**[2] Head. In a solemn, **orotund**[3] voice it said, "I am Oz, the Great and Terrible. Why do you seek me?"
"We have come to claim our promise," answered Dorothy.
"Is the Wicked Witch dead?" asked the Head **haughtily**[4].
"Yes," Dorothy **averred**[5]. "I melted her with a bucket of water."
"Dear me, dear me," said the Head, **temporizing**[6]. "Well, come

---

[1] **formidable** To describe someone or something as *formidable* is to say that it (1) arouses feelings of fear or dread (in encounters or dealings) or (2) inspires feelings of awe or admiration (by virtue of superiority, size, strength, etc.) or (3) is intimidating and difficult to defeat or overcome. *Between 1949 and 1960, baseball manager Casey Stengel led the formidable New York Yankees to ten American League pennants and seven World Series championships.*

[2] **glabrous** This word is used to describe things that are hairless and smooth. *Of the glabrous-headed, bony-faced actor who so effectively portrayed the King of Siam in Rodgers and Hammerstein's* The King and I, Time *magazine said, "Yul Brynner has identified himself with a role more than any other actor since Bela Lugosi hung up his fangs."*

[3] **orotund** To describe a voice as *orotund* is to say that it has a full, rich, deep, strong, clear tone. *Known for his orotund voice, African-American actor James Earl Jones gained stardom on Broadway in 1968's* The Great White Hope, *but is perhaps best known for dubbing the dialog of villain Darth Vader in the Star Wars sequels* The Empire Strikes Back *(1980) and* Return of the Jedi *(1983).*

[4] **haughty (haughtily)** People who are *haughty* act superior and snobbish; they look down on others with disapproval or dislike. *Fed up with our haughty French waiter, we asked him, "Does your sneering come naturally, or did you take lessons?"* Note: The noun is *haughtiness* or *hauteur*.

[5] **aver (averred)** To *aver* something is to state or declare it positively and formally (as a fact). *The college sophomore was told by the housing department that if he wanted to be assigned to a private dorm room, all he had to do was aver in a letter that he required solitude for concentrated study.*

[6] **temporize (temporizing)** To *temporize* is to act evasively or draw out discussions in order to gain time (so as to postpone a decision, avoid a confrontation, etc.); to stall, delay, hedge, play for time, etc. *In July 1987 journalist David S. Broder reported that, according to the National Conference of State Legislatures (NCSL), "While Washington has temporized over taxes for the past seven months, 40 states have rewritten their revenue codes, with three-quarters of them raising taxes to meet their budget needs."*

back tomorrow, for I must have time to think it over."

"You've had plenty of time already," said the Tin Woodman, suddenly angry.

"We won't wait a day longer," said the Scarecrow, who could no longer stomach the Head's **condescending**[1] **pomposity**[2].

Now Dorothy's determination hardened. "You must keep your promises to us!" she demanded.

The Lion thought it would be a good idea to frighten the Wizard, so he gave his loudest roar. It was so fierce that Toto jumped away in alarm and knocked over a screen that stood in the corner of the room. As the screen fell with a crash they all looked that way, and the next moment they saw what the screen had been hiding. There stood a bald, **flaccid**[3]-limbed, **bulbous**[4]-nosed, little

---

[1] **condescend (condescending)** To be *condescending* is to talk down to people; to treat them in an insultingly superior manner. *Our boss was always condescending to his secretary; for example, whenever he asked her to do something, he began by saying, "Let me explain this to you very slowly."* Another meaning of the word is "to lower oneself to a level considered inferior," as in *he condescended to watch cartoons with his little brother.*

[2] **pompous (pomposity)** People who are *pompous* act overly important or dignified, and their speech is often filled with inflated, high-sounding phrases. A *pompous* person is sometimes referred to as a "stuffed shirt." *In his films actor/comedian W. C. Fields (1880–1946) often portrayed a henpecked husband with an especially low tolerance for children, dogs, his wife, policemen, and pompous officials.*

[3] **flaccid** To describe something (living tissue, for example) as *flaccid* is to say that it lacks firmness; it's limp, soft, weak, flabby, etc. By extension, anything (writing, leadership, reasoning, etc.) that's weak or ineffectual can be referred to as *flaccid*. *In 1994 TV critic Verne Gay said the* NYPD Blue *season kickoff was as "dull and flaccid as a beached flounder."* Note: Dictionaries will tell you the word is pronounced *flak-sid;* however, most people say *flas-id.*

[4] **bulbous** To describe something as *bulbous* is to say that it's shaped like a bulb; that is, it's rounded or swollen. *Early 20th-century film comedian W. C. Fields was known for his bulbous nose and his drawn-out pronunciation of vowels.*

old man, who was visibly **chagrined**[1].

"Pay no attention to that man behind the screen!" boomed the Head.

The Tin Woodman **brandished**[2] his axe and cried out, "Who are you?"

"I AM OZ—" began the Head in a loud, **hubristic**[3] tone. Then, in a feeble, apologetic tone, the old man finished, "—the Great and Terrible."

Our friends looked at him with a mixture of surprise and disgust. "I thought Oz was a great Head," said Dorothy.

The little man looked down, **abashed**[4], and said softly, "I've been making believe."

---

[1] **chagrin (chagrined)** A feeling of displeasure (sadness, disappointment, vexation, annoyance, etc.) combined with embarrassment is known as *chagrin*. As a verb, to be *chagrined* is to feel or experience this combination of displeasure and embarrassment. *Chagrined by his endorsement of Richard Nixon in 1972 (the year of the Watergate break-in), preacher and evangelist Billy Graham has since shied away from politics.*

[2] **brandish (brandished)** To *brandish* something (a stick or weapon, for example) is to wave it in a threatening or menacing manner. *In the 1975 film* Dog Day Afternoon, *Al Pacino plays a bossy bank robber who spends much more time brandishing his gun than actually using it.*

[3] **hubris (hubristic)** This word means "shamelessly rude boldness or self-assurance; nerve, gall, chutzpah." *Gentle, childlike comedian Andy Kaufman occasionally shocked his audience by appearing as his alter-ego: a swaggering, hubristic, leisure-suited, mustachioed, bewigged, third-rate lounge singer named Tony Clifton.*

[4] **abash (abashed)** If you say that someone has been *abashed*, you mean that he's been embarrassed; that his initial self-possession has been destroyed (usually by something that produces a feeling of shame or inferiority or by excessive praise). *When he learned he'd been awarded the 1958 Nobel Prize in literature, Russian writer Boris Pasternak (1890–1960) said in a telegram, "Immensely grateful, touched, proud, astonished, abashed."*

THE WIZARD OF OZ VOCABULARY BUILDER

"Making believe?" cried Dorothy, **nonplussed**[1]. She wondered for a second if this funny little man could possibly be a **dotty**[2] escapee from some nearby **geriatric**[3] center. The Scarecrow and the Tin Woodman exchanged a swift glance.

"Hush, my dear," he said. "Don't speak so loudly because if you're overheard people will know I'm just a **dissimulating**[4] little fraud, and I will surely be **vilified**[5]."

"But I don't understand," Dorothy said, looking at him **askance**[6]. "How was it that you appeared to us as a great Head?"

---

[1] **nonplussed** If you're *nonplussed* (also spelled *nonplused*) you're completely perplexed (confused, puzzled, baffled, bewildered, etc.). The implication is that your mind goes blank and that you're at a loss as to what to say, think, or do. *The prosecuting attorney became nonplussed when his chief witness suddenly insisted he hadn't seen the accident after all.*

[2] **dotty** To refer to someone as *dotty* is to say that he's senile, feeble-minded, crazy, scatterbrained, forgetful, eccentric, nuts, etc. (from or as from the mental decline associated with old age). See *dotage*. *Actress Ruth Gordon specialized in portraying dotty old ladies in such movies as 1971's* Harold and Maude.

[3] **geriatric** The branch of medicine that deals with the health and diseases of the elderly is known as *geriatrics*. The adjective *geriatric* means "relating to the elderly or to geriatrics." *When the nursing home resident began spending all her waking hours tearing newspapers into tiny pieces, the aide suggested calling in a geriatric psychiatrist.*

[4] **dissimulate (dissimulating)** To *dissimulate* is to conceal your true thoughts or motives (under a false appearance or through insincere or phony words or acts). *In 1960, when a U-2 spy plane was shot down over Russia, American officials dissimulated, claiming that the U-2 was a weather plane that had strayed off course.*

[5] **vilify (vilified)** To *vilify* someone is to speak badly of him; to make vicious statements about him; to badmouth him (usually in order to harm him). *When in 1991 she accused U.S. Supreme Court nominee Clarence Thomas of sexual harassment, law professor and former Thomas employee Anita Hill was praised by some and vilified by others.*

[6] **askance** To look at someone *askance* is to look at him with a sideways glance, as in suspicion or distrust. *I looked at the stranger askance when he pulled up alongside me and offered to repair the dent in my fender then and there for $45.*

THE WIZARD OF OZ VOCABULARY BUILDER

"Well, that was just a bit of **chicanery**[1], said Oz. "And now, for your **delectation**[2] and **edification**[3], I'll tell you how I did it. The Head you saw was just a clever **artifice**[4]— many layers of painted paper that I hung from the ceiling by a wire." He pointed to the fallen screen. "I stood behind that screen and pulled a string to make the eyes move and the mouth open. Actually, I'm capable of producing several distinct forms. With my **protean**[5] talents as a puppeteer I can also **simulate**[6] a lovely lady, a terrible beast, and a ball of fire." Then, as though speaking to himself, he added

---

[1] **chicanery** A trick or clever scheme employed for the purpose of deceiving or cheating is known as *chicanery*. *During the 2000 presidential election, some Democrats claimed that George W. Bush won the state of Florida by legal and political chicanery.*

[2] **delectation** This word (usually seen in the phrase "for your delectation") means "delight, pleasure, enjoyment, etc." *When I asked why he insisted upon reading all his poems aloud to me, he answered (with a straight face), "Strictly for you delectation."*

[3] **edification** If you say that something is done for one's *edification*, you mean that it's done for his intellectual, moral, or spiritual improvement; for his enlightenment. To use the adjective, an *edifying* experience is one that improves or enlightens (you). *Aesop's fables ("The Tortoise and the Hare," for example) often use human-acting animals to demonstrate some edifying moral lesson.*

[4] **artifice** A clever, devious means for achieving an end (a particular contrivance or trick, for example) is known as an *artifice*. But deviousness (trickery, sneakiness, slyness, etc.) in general is known as simply *artifice* (without the word *an* in front of it). *The mail order company (through misrepresentation and other artifice) convinced thousands of people to order unwanted magazine subscriptions.*

[5] **protean** In mythology Proteus was a sea god who could change his shape at will. The word *protean* now describes the ability to readily take on many different forms or to play many varied roles. *In 1974 a language professor at Dartmouth College said, "Language is a living, growing, evolving reality, and the teacher should spontaneously reflect its protean qualities."*

[6] **simulate** To *simulate* something is to (falsely) take on or assume the appearance or character of it; to imitate it. *Using a special projector, a planetarium operator can simulate on a domed ceiling a view of the night sky as seen from any latitude in the northern or southern hemisphere.*

vaingloriously[1], "My little **sham**[2] was quite **plausible**[3] and my Head did possess a certain **verisimilitude**[4]." Suddenly looking up, he added, "Oh, and I'm a ventriloquist. I threw my voice so it sounded like it was coming from the Head."

"You're more than that," said the Scarecrow. "You're a **charlatan**[5], and you should be ashamed of yourself!"

"I am ashamed," answered the little man **contritely**[6]. "But please

---

[1] **vainglory (vaingloriously)** Boastful or unwarranted pride in one's own accomplishments or abilities is known as *vainglory*. *After the school bully was given an injection in the nurse's office, he looked around at everyone and vaingloriously asked, "Did I flinch?"*

[2] **sham** A *sham* is something that is not what it claims to be; a devious scheme or fraudulent imitation. *When Irv realized that the adult education class concerning techniques for obtaining financial aid for college-bound students was in reality merely a means for the so-called teacher to recruit private clients, he turned to his wife and said, "This is a sham; let's go."*

[3] **plausible** If you say that something (a statement, for example) is *plausible*, you mean that it seems believable, reasonable, probable, convincing, valid, etc. *At 9:00 a.m. I called my boss and said in a soft, toneless voice that I couldn't come to work because I was sick; then, just to make the excuse sound more plausible, I coughed a couple of times.*

[4] **verisimilitude** The quality of appearing or seeming to be true, real, or authentic is known as *verisimilitude*. The word especially applies to what, through accurate details and other representations of reality, seems real in the arts (novels, paintings, etc.). *The play was set in the early 1970s; to give it verisimilitude the director insisted that all the young actors wear bellbottom jeans.*

[5] **charlatan** A *charlatan* is a person who is a fraud, a quack, a cheat. For example, someone at a county fair who tries to sell a (phony) miracle drug that supposedly cures all illnesses is a *charlatan*. *Because his compositions are extremely unconventional (one is nothing but silence, another consists of sounds generated by plants, and another is a series of notes and rhythms randomly selected by a computer), some music critics consider composer John Cage a charlatan.*

[6] **contrite (contritely)** To feel *contrite* about a wrong you've done (an offense or sin, for example) is to feel sorry (regretful, apologetic, remorseful) about it. The noun is *contrition*. *Although President Bill Clinton apologized to the American people for his sexual misdeeds, many felt he wasn't as contrite as he should have been.*

let me explain."

So they all listened while the old man told the following tale.

"I was born on a farm in Omaha... "

"Why, that isn't very far from Kansas!" cried Dorothy, her eyes suddenly glistening with **effervescence**[1].

"That's right! Well, as I was saying, when I was a young man in Omaha, immediately after leaving the ivy walls and **hallowed**[2] halls of my old **alma mater**[3], Nebraska Junior College, instead of joining the summer **exodus**[4] to the country resorts, I took a position with a

---

[1] **effervescent (effervescence)** To describe a liquid as *effervescent* is to say that it emits small bubbles of gas (as does ginger ale or club soda). To describe something else (art or a person's personality, for example) as *effervescent* is to say that it's bubbly, lively, sparkling, good-humored, etc. *While some of choreographer Jerome Robbins' ballets are light and effervescent (1953's Fanfare, for example), others are dark and probing (1950's Age of Anxiety, for example).*

[2] **hallowed** To refer to something as *hallowed* is to say that it's honored and respected, perhaps even holy. *An inscription on a monument located on the coast of (the French region of) Normandy, whose beaches were the focal point of Allied landings on D-day (June 6, 1944) in World War II, reads, "This embattled shore, portal [doorway] of freedom, is forever hallowed by the ideas, valor, and sacrifice of our fellow countrymen."*

[3] **alma mater** Your *alma mater* is the school (usually high school or college) you graduated from. *Felix Frankfurter (U.S. Supreme Court justice from 1939–1962) graduated from Harvard Law School in 1906; in 1914 he returned to his alma mater to join the faculty.* Note: The phrase can also refer to a school's official song.

[4] **exodus** A departure or leave-taking of a large number of people (often from one's native land to another) is known as an *exodus*. When spelled with a capital *E*, the word refers to the departure of Moses and the Israelites from Egypt (as described in the second book of the Old Testament). *In 1879, as a result of post–Civil War economic and political repression, some 20,000 African-Americans migrated from the South to Kansas; by 1880, however, because of stories of extreme poverty among the newcomers, discouragement of further immigration by native Kansans, and the difficulties of winter travel, the mass exodus had ended.*

fledgling[1] circus company. It was my job to go up in a balloon on circus day to draw a crowd so I could sell them tickets. Then— sometimes with the help of a **shill**[2]— I would **mulct**[3] them out of everything they had. Of course, I'm not proud to admit that, but the **remuneration**[4] I received for my services was so **paltry**[5] that I was forced to **cadge**[6] almost all of my meals— and if you've ever

---

[1] **fledgling** Technically, a *fledgling* is a young bird that has only recently acquired its flight feathers. But people usually use this word as an adjective to describe something very new, inexperienced, untried, etc. *Starting in the 1950s, the United States, in an effort to contain the spread of Communism, sent aid and advisers to the fledgling Republic of South Vietnam.*

[2] **shill** Technically, a *shill* is a person who assists a swindler by posing as a satisfied customer in order to drum up business (as at a gambling house, auction, county fair, etc.). But in general usage the word can denote anyone who assists in any kind of deceitful enterprise. *According to a January 2001 article in the* Washington Post, *attorney general Janet Reno was, to many Republicans, "a political shill for President Clinton— the stone wall that repeatedly [blocked] investigations of the President."*

[3] **mulct** To *mulct* someone is to take his money (or the like) by fraud; to swindle him, defraud him, con him, etc. *In the 1860s corrupt New York City politician William "Boss" Tweed and his so-called Tweed Ring (a corrupt network of New York City officials, Democratic party workers, and contractors) mulcted the city (largely through padded construction contracts) out of at least $30 million.*

[4] **remuneration** Payment (generally money) received for services or goods provided is known as *remuneration*. *A U.S. President's salary is only part of his remuneration; he also receives money for expenses and generous retirement benefits.*

[5] **paltry** To describe something as *paltry* is to say that it's lacking in quantity, extent, importance, or worth; it's meager, skimpy, scant, insubstantial, insignificant, etc. *In 1970 author John Updike said, "From infancy on, we are all spies; the shame is not this but that the secrets to be discovered are so paltry and few."*

[6] **cadge** To *cadge* something (food, money, a cigarette, etc.) is to obtain it by imposing on someone's friendship or generosity; to ask for it with no intent to repay; to bum or mooch it. *In a letter to the* Hobo Times, *recalling his adventures as a 12-year-old orphan taking off with a friend from Pennsylvania to Canada, 20th-century American novelist James Michener wrote, "We cadged stale bread and cakes from bakeries, slept in jails, and were often treated to meals by the car owners who picked us up and gave us rides."*

been in that position, you know how embarrassing it can be. And besides, the **scuttlebutt**[1] was that our company's president was experiencing **pecuniary**[2] difficulties and was about to **retrench**[3] by eliminating half the workers, including me—even though those stories about my **pilfering**[4] the elephant's peanuts and **purloining**[5] clown costumes were proven to be nothing but outrageous **canards**[6] when a **cache**[1] of various stolen items turned up in the

---

[1] **scuttlebutt** This is a rather informal word meaning "gossip; rumor." It has an interesting derivation. Technically, a *scuttlebutt* is a drinking fountain on a ship— the usual place at which sailors exchanged gossip; eventually, the gossip itself came to be referred to as *scuttlebutt. When NBC's Today show lost many of its viewers to rival morning shows, the scuttlebutt was that it was suffering from bitter, off-screen squabbles.*

[2] **pecuniary** This adjective means "of or relating to money or finance" and is used especially to refer to the monetary concerns of individuals (as opposed to those of corporations or nations). *In addition to worldwide recognition for having made an outstanding achievement in one of five fields (physics, chemistry, medicine, literature, or world peace), a Nobel Prize recipient receives a gold medal and a large pecuniary award.*

[3] **retrench** To *retrench* is to cut back (or lower) expenses (as a company might do during hard times); to economize. *In 2000, after seeing their stock prices plummet, many "dot.com" companies were forced into bankruptcy or were compelled to retrench.*

[4] **pilfer (pilfering)** To *pilfer* is to steal (especially something small or in small quantities). The noun is *pilferage. One advantage of using sealed metal containers for transporting bulk goods is that the cargo inside is less vulnerable to damage and pilferage.*

[5] **purloin (purloining)** To *purloin* something is to steal it (especially to make off with it for your own use, often in violation of a trust). *In 1797, after reorganizing northern Italy to create the Cisalpine Republic, French military leader Napoleon Bonaparte purloined priceless Italian works of art and sent them to Paris to enhance French museums.*

[6] **canard (canards)** A canard is a (sometimes deliberately misleading and usually damaging) false story, rumor, or report. *After poet and short story writer Edgar Allan Poe died (1849), his literary executor published a biographical essay that falsely represented the writer as a drunk, a negligent journalist, a fraud, and a sexual deviant; the canard was believed and Poe was condemned for faults that were never his.*

suitcase of one of the **transient**[2] laborers. Of course, I was completely **exculpated**[3] and all mention of those incidents was **expunged**[4] from my record.

"Anyway, one day I went up in the balloon and the ropes got twisted so that I couldn't come back down." Oz used his fingers to approximate the idea of twisted ropes. "It floated **vertiginously**[5] upward until it was above the clouds, and there a current of air carried it many miles away." Again he demonstrated all this with his fingers. "For a day and a night I traveled through the sky, and

---

[1] **cache** A place used for hiding or storing provisions or valuables (or the store of concealed provisions or valuables themselves) is known as a *cache* (pronounced the same as *cash*). *The eastern red squirrel stores large caches of pine and spruce cones for its winter food supply.*

[2] **transient** To refer to someone (a worker or hotel guest, for example) as *transient* is to say that he remains (in a place) for only a short time. The word can also mean "fleeting; not lasting" as in *a transient mood* or *transient grief* (that sense is also expressed by the word *transitory*). *Surveys show that drug use (including alcohol) is experimental and transient for most teenagers and occurs most often in groups.*

[3] **exculpate (exculpated)** To *exculpate* someone is to clear him of blame or guilt. Something (a particular piece of evidence, for example) described as *exculpatory* proves or tends to prove blamelessness or innocence. *In the 1957 film* Twelve Angry Men, *jurors, deliberating the fate of a boy accused of killing his father with a knife, present to each other pieces of exculpatory evidence (a look-alike knife, the near-sightedness of an eyewitness, etc.) that never came out during the trial.*

[4] **expunge (expunged)** To *expunge* something (written down or recorded, for example), is to erase it, strike it out, or destroy it. The implication is that the erasure or removal leaves no trace. *In 1833 the U.S. Senate censured (officially expressed disapproval of) President Andrew Jackson (for his removing from office two Secretaries of the Treasury who refused to withdraw government funds from the Bank of the United States and place them in state banks); however, in 1836 the Virginia legislature sought a resolution expunging censure of Jackson from the Senate record.*

[5] **vertigo (vertiginously)** A sensation of dizziness, loss of balance, or swirling (of oneself or one's surroundings) is known as *vertigo*. To describe something as *vertiginous* is to say that it spins or that it tends to cause *vertigo*, as in *vertiginous heights. Before traveling, some people take Dramamine, a drug effective in preventing both the nausea and vertigo associated with motion sickness.*

on the morning of the second day I awoke and found the balloon hovering over a strange and beautiful land.

"It came down gradually, and I wasn't hurt a bit. But I found myself in the midst of a strange people, who, seeing me come from the clouds, thought I was a great Wizard and made me their ruler! And there wasn't a single **gainsayer**[1] among them! Because they promised to do anything I wished, and because a little streak of **cupidity**[2] got the best of me, instead of admitting I was just a simple **rube**[3] who didn't even know how to handle a balloon, I allowed this **travesty**[4] to persist.

---

[1] **gainsay (gainsayer)** To *gainsay* something is to deny it, declare it's false, contradict it, oppose it, or speak out against it. One who does this (critically disagrees) is known as a *gainsayer* (or a *naysayer*). *Supporters of the U.S. government's policy of affirmative action in employment and education say that it's right to compensate blacks and other minorities for past inequalities; gainsayers, however, argue that the policy is actually reverse discrimination and as such is in conflict with the principle of equal opportunity.*

[2] **cupidity** This word means "excessive desire for money or possessions; greed." *When, in 1986, former Philippine First Lady Imelda Marcos's cupidity was revealed through an exhibition of the contents of her closet (which included thousands of pairs of shoes), U.S. Congressman Stephen Solarz said, "Compared to Imelda, Marie Antoinette was a bag lady."*

[3] **rube** A *rube* is an unsophisticated country fellow; a hick, yokel, bumpkin, hayseed. *During the Scopes "monkey" trial of 1925, journalists portrayed anti-evolutionists as uneducated rubes.*

[4] **travesty** Technically, a *travesty* is a parody (comic imitation) of a literary work. But in general usage, when people refer to something as a *travesty*, they mean that it's a distorted, unfair, dishonest, false, or degraded version or imitation of what it should be or claims to be. *In December 2000, after the U.S. Supreme Court stopped the Florida hand recount of votes cast in the presidential election, the Leon County Democratic Supervisor of Elections told a reporter, "To know that we held an election and did not count all the votes and now to be told by the Supreme Court that we cannot count them is, to me, a travesty [of justice]."*

THE WIZARD OF OZ VOCABULARY BUILDER

Then, just to amuse myself and to keep the **penurious**[1] **peons**[2] busy and off the **dole**[3], I ordered them to build this City and my Palace. After that, at my **behest**[4], they **refurbished**[5] all the outlying buildings and roads. I paid the **hirelings**[6] a small but fair wage, and

---

[1] **penurious** To describe someone as *penurious* is to say that he's poverty-stricken, penniless, bankrupt, broke, etc. *During his teens, Call of the Wild author Jack London led a difficult, penurious life as a hobo; then, after serving 30 days in jail he vowed to educate himself for a better future.* Note: The word can also mean "stingy, miserly, tightfisted, etc."

[2] **peon (peons)** Technically, a *peon* is an unskilled laborer or farm worker of Latin America or the southwest U.S. (especially one held in servitude to work off debts). But in general usage, *peons* is used (usually sarcastically) to refer collectively to insignificant, lower-class people. *The rock star said she always flew first-class because she didn't want to be seen mixing with the peons.*

[3] **dole** Technically, the *dole* was a form of paying money to the unemployed instituted by the British government in 1918. But any payment by a government to the poor can be called a *dole* (though in the U.S. it's more common to refer to such payments as *welfare* or *government assistance*). To say that someone is *on the dole* is to say that he's receiving money, as relief, from the government. As a verb, to *dole* something out is to carefully distribute it in (usually small) measured quantities. *To the surprise of their parents, the teenagers spent their Thanksgiving holiday doling out meals at a homeless shelter.*

[4] **behest** To do something at one's *behest* is to do it at his earnest (or urgent or strongly worded) request, or at his authoritative command. *In May 1998, China's President Jiang Zemin, at the behest of President Bill Clinton, wrote to the Pakistani government asking it not to test nuclear weapons.*

[5] **refurbish (refurbished)** To *refurbish* something (a theater lobby, for example) is to restore or freshen up its appearance; to renovate it, redecorate it, etc. *New York City's South Street Seaport is a complex of refurbished 19th-century buildings and newer shopping mall structures.*

[6] **hireling (hirelings)** A *hireling* is a (usually insignificant) person who does (usually tedious, boring) work only for the sake of payment. *Legend has it that some of the hirelings who built Hoover Dam (located on the Colorado River between Nevada and Arizona) were accidentally buried in the concrete.*

221

though the **ingrates**[1] never went so far as to thank me for my **innovative**[2] policies or my **largess**[3], they at least never complained. But why should they? Since I **levied**[4] only a **nominal**[5] income tax, it was I who saved their **impecunious**[6] hides from **destitution**[7]!

---

[1] **ingrate (ingrates)** An *ingrate* is an ungrateful person. The implication is that the person has reason to be grateful. *At the beginning of Shakespeare's* King Lear, *Lear considers his daughter Cordelia an ingrate because she refuses to flatter him as her two older sisters do (but he soon learns that she is the only one of them who truly cares about him).*

[2] **innovative** To describe something (an idea, plan, method, etc.) as *innovative* is to say that it introduces something new; it's original, clever, creative, imaginative, etc. *Jimi Hendrix' (1942–1970) innovative electric guitar playing greatly influenced the development of rock music.*

[3] **largess** Generosity in the giving of gifts or money (or the actual gifts or money so given) is known as *largess*. Note: The word is pronounced with the accent on the second syllable and is alternately spelled *largesse*. *During the 1960s some blacks opposed Martin Luther King, Jr., because they believed his nonviolent philosophy relied too heavily on the largess of the white establishment.*

[4] **levy (levied)** To *levy* a tax is to impose (establish and apply) a tax. *The personal income tax was first levied by the U.S. government in 1913; the rate was one percent on income above $3,000.*

[5] **nominal** Technically, this word means "existing in name only." By extension, when you refer to an amount (of money, for example) as *nominal*, you mean it's very small, tiny, inconsequential (that is, it's money in name rather than in substance). *When the photographer agreed to allow one of his pictures to be reproduced in a book for what he called "a nominal fee," the publisher automatically asked, "How nominal?"*

[6] **impecunious** To describe someone as *impecunious* is to say that he has little or no money; he's poor, penniless, poverty-stricken, etc. *Industrialist and art collector Henry Clay Frick's father was an impecunious Pennsylvania farmer; his mother, however, was the daughter of the county's wealthiest man.*

[7] **destitute (destitution)** To describe someone as *destitute* is to say that he completely lacks the means (money) for providing for the necessities of life; he's completely poverty-stricken. The noun is *destitution*. *When, at the age of 22, he was dismissed from West Point and his foster father disinherited him, writer Edgar Allan Poe found himself destitute and without a career.*

And besides, now they—not to mention all their precious **progeny**[1]—had this beautiful City and all its **amenities**[2]—a more than **munificent**[3] gift—to enjoy for generations to come.

"Because I didn't really possess any of the magical powers **imputed**[4] to me, I kept myself hidden in the Palace so no one would ever discover what I really was—a **dissembling**[5] little

---

[1] **progeny** Your descendants (that is, your children, grandchildren, great grandchildren, etc.) are collectively known as your *progeny*. *"Pennsylvania Dutch" is the name given to the progeny of German and Swiss immigrants who settled in Pennsylvania in the 17th and 18th centuries.*

[2] **amenities** Features (often unessential extras) that contribute to physical comfort or pleasure, especially when they increase the value of something (real estate, for example) are known as *amenities*. *The ad for the mountain lodge said that it overlooked a lake and offered such amenities as air conditioning and cable TV.* Note: Another meaning of the word is "social courtesies; pleasantries"; that is, little things you say ("How good to see you," for example) to be pleasant in society.

[3] **munificent** To describe a person as *munificent* is to say that he's very generous. To describe a thing (a gift, donation, bequest, etc.) as *munificent* is to say that it's characterized by great generosity; it's liberal, bountiful, etc. *Oxford University's Rhodes scholarships for foreign students were initially financed by a munificent gift from British industrialist and colonizer Cecil Rhodes (1853–1902).*

[4] **impute (imputed)** When you *impute* something (a characteristic, a quality, a result, blame, credit, etc.) to someone (or something) you attribute it to him (that is, you consider it resulting from or belonging to him). Sometimes the implication is that what is being attributed might bring discredit to the person. *Eskimos impute souls (capable of influencing human life and events) to animals and to all important aspects of the landscape and environment.*

[5] **dissemble (dissembling)** When you *dissemble*, you behave or speak falsely to hide your true motives, feelings, or character. *The fairy tale "Little Red Riding Hood" concerns a little girl in a hooded red cloak and a big, bad, dissembling wolf who'd like to devour her.*

parvenu[1]. Luckily, no one ever **impugned**[2] my motives; in fact, everyone had an **unassailable**[3] impression of me as some **venerable**[4] **patriarch**[5]— and who was I to tell them otherwise?

"But my stimulus was never **avarice**[6]; it was fear. I was terrified of the powerful, evil Wicked Witches for many years, so you can imagine how pleased I was when I heard your house had fallen on

---

[1] **parvenu** A *parvenu* is a person who has recently risen to a higher economic or social class (by suddenly acquiring wealth or position, for example), especially one who doesn't possess the dress, manner, or style appropriate to that class. *Actor Buddy Ebsen is best remembered for playing a parvenu in the 1960s TV sitcom* The Beverly Hillbillies.

[2] **impugn (impugned)** To *impugn* something (motives, statements, validity, etc.) is to call it into question, to challenge it (as false), to refuse to accept or admit its truth or value. *In 1610 Galileo's observation of four moons revolving around Jupiter forced scientists to impugn the validity of the then-popular theory that all heavenly bodies revolved around the earth.*

[3] **unassailable** If something (an argument, statement, theory, record, etc.) is *unassailable*, it's impossible to deny, dispute, disprove, attack, etc. *During the late 1930s, jazz clarinetist and bandleader Benny Goodman was regarded as the unassailable "King of Swing" (however, after Barry Bonds hit 73 home runs in 2001, some people wanted to bestow that title on him!).*

[4] **venerable** If you refer to someone (or something) as *venerable*, you mean that he commands or is worthy of respect by virtue of his great age or impressive position (or both). The verb *venerate* means "to regard or treat (someone or something old or impressive) with respect." *Since 1578, the Shroud of Turin, an ancient piece of linen believed by many people to be Jesus Christ's burial cloth, has been preserved and venerated in the cathedral of Turin, Italy.*

[5] **patriarch** The father of a large family or a father-like leader of a large group is known as a *patriarch*. *In the Old Testament, Noah was the patriarch chosen by God to build an ark (in which he, his family, and a male-female pair of each kind of animal were saved from the Flood).* Note: A *matriarch* is a woman who rules or leads a family or group.

[6] **avarice** A greedy or miserly desire to gain and hoard riches (wealth, money, possessions) is known as *avarice*. The adjective is *avaricious*. *In the classic Christmas film* It's a Wonderful Life *(1946), an avaricious, scheming banker (Lionel Barrymore) sets out to destroy an honest, ambitious competitor (James Stewart).*

the Wicked Witch of the East—the single most **stupendous**[1] episode in the entire **lexicon**[2] of Ozian events, and, I daresay, a historical **watershed**[3] sure to secure you a top position in the **pantheon**[4] of Ozian heroines!

"Now, normally I have no **proclivity**[5] for **prevarication**[6], but

---

[1] **stupendous** To describe something as *stupendous* is to say that it's amazingly large or incredible; it's marvelous, grand, astounding, etc. *In astronomy, the Big Bang theory holds that the universe began billions of years ago in a single stupendous explosion.*

[2] **lexicon** Depending on the context, a *lexicon* is an inventory or record (as of important events), or it's the particular vocabulary (the stock of words) used by a certain profession, person, language, etc. *Cuts in social welfare programs in the 1980s made the word "homelessness" part of the national lexicon.*

[3] **watershed** Technically, the word *watershed* signifies a high ridge of land that divides two drainage areas (that is, two areas drained in opposite directions by different river systems), or it designates a single area drained by a river. But in general usage, when people refer to something (an event, situation, time, etc.) as a *watershed*, they mean it's a critical turning point, change of course, line of division, etc. (as in a history, policy, philosophy, action, struggle, etc.). *In the 1950s the introduction of the electric guitar was a watershed dividing the swing and rock-and-roll eras.*

[4] **pantheon** Technically, a *pantheon* is a temple or building dedicated to the gods or to a nation's past heroes. But in general usage, a *pantheon* is a group of people most highly regarded as heroes or significant contributors to a particular field or endeavor. *We agreed that Babe Ruth should be placed at the top of the pantheon of New York Yankee greats, but we disagreed over whether Lou Gehrig, Joe DiMaggio, or Mickey Mantle should be placed second.*

[5] **proclivity** A *proclivity* (for or to something) is a natural inclination, tendency, leaning, or predisposition (toward it). *In 1984 the Chief of Neurosurgery at Harvard Medical School said, "The proclivity for extraordinary violence is not just an ailment of the mind, it is also a sickness of the body as distinct and definite as cancer or leprosy."*

[6] **prevaricate (prevarication)** To *prevaricate* is to lie, evade the truth, speak misleadingly, deliberately create an incorrect impression, etc. The noun *prevarication* is the act of *prevaricating*. *When President Bill Clinton lied about his sexual misdeeds, some people defended him, claiming that because the issues were personal (and therefore "nobody's business"), his prevarication was understandable and forgivable.*

when you came to me, I was so desperate to have that other hateful **harridan**[1] killed that I was forced to tell you anything you wanted to hear. But now that you've **liquidated**[2] her, so to speak, I'm ashamed to say I can't keep my promises." He paused, then said **repentantly**[3], "I know my **duplicity**[4] was **dastardly**[5], and I'm truly sorry." He forced a tiny, **propitiating**[6] smile, but his eyes held a desperate appeal.

---

[1] **harridan** A *harridan* is a woman who is vicious, scolding, nagging, quarrelsome, etc.; a shrew. *In its review of a 1997 TV movie, the* Washington Post *said, "Think of every rotten thing your mother ever did; now multiply by about a million and you have a rough impression of the harridan at the heart of* The Perfect Mother."

[2] **liquidate (liquidated)** This word has several meanings, depending on the context. To *liquidate* a person (an enemy, for example) is to do away with him, get rid of him, especially by killing. To *liquidate* a thing (that has been created or put into effect, such as a corporation, agency, political party, etc.) is to put an end to it, abolish it. To *liquidate* an asset (something you own that's worth money) is to convert it to cash (by selling it). *In the late 1930s Soviet leader Joseph Stalin consolidated his power by liquidating much of Russia's political and military leadership.*

[3] **repentant (repentantly)** To be *repentant* is to feel sorrow or regret for past wrongdoings, misdeeds, sins, etc. *In the Roman Catholic religion, repentant sinners can confess their sins in private to a priest and receive forgiveness.*

[4] **duplicity** Deliberate deceptiveness or dishonesty (double-dealing) in manner, action, or speech is known as *duplicity*. The adjective is *duplicitous*. *In 1982, when criticized for recycling her advice columns, Ann Landers said, "I was naïve, but I certainly was not duplicitous."*

[5] **dastardly** To describe a person (or his deeds) as *dastardly* is to say that he's sneaky, mean, and usually cowardly. *In most stories concerning (comic book character) Superman, the superhero is pitted against a dastardly villain.*

[6] **propitiate (propitiating)** To *propitiate* someone (an enemy or someone you've offended, for example) is to make him less angry or to reestablish friendship with him. *A striking aspect of Eskimo culture is that they try to propitiate the souls of animals they've hunted; for example, it's customary that when a man brings home a dead seal, his wife offers it a drink of water (as a sign of hospitality).*

Chapter 19 "The Granting of Wishes"

"I think you're a very bad man," said Dorothy, as if **upbraiding**[1] a naughty five-year-old.

The **castigatory**[2] remark seemed to hurt Oz deeply, for he flinched as if struck by an invisible arrow. "Oh no, my dear," he said **compunctiously**[3], "I'm really a very good man, just a very bad Wizard."

"Can you give me brains?" asked the Scarecrow, still naïvely hopeful that the man possessed at least a **modicum**[4] of wizardry. Oz thought for a while. He knew that these people probably considered him a **venal**[5] villain, a **mendacious**[1] **miscreant**[2]. But in

---

[1] **upbraid (upbraiding)** To *upbraid* someone is to angrily or severely scold or criticize him (for some fault or offense). *Many child psychologists urge parents to reason with their children rather than upbraid or spank them.*

[2] **castigate (castigatory)** To *castigate* someone is to punish him (for some fault or offense) or to severely criticize him (often publicly). The adjective is *castigatory* ("severely critical" or "punishing"). *Pop superstar Michael Jackson has been praised for his singing and dancing but castigated for his supposedly strange sexual behavior and constantly changing appearance.*

[3] **compunction (compunctiously)** A twinge of conscience; that is, a feeling of uneasiness caused by a sense of guilt (over wrongdoing or the prospect of wrongdoing) is known as *compunction*. The adjective *compunctious* means "feeling compunction; regretful." *Historians say that Richard Nixon was not particularly compunctious about his involvement in the Watergate affair; in fact, in 1990 he described the scandal as "one part wrongdoing, one part blundering, and one part political vendetta."*

[4] **modicum** A *modicum* of something is a small (or token) amount or quantity of it. *In Tennessee Williams' play* A Streetcar Named Desire *(1947), a sensitive, frail, aging woman struggles to retain a modicum of dignity when she moves to her sister and crude brother-in-law's shabby apartment.*

[5] **venal** To describe someone as *venal* is to say that he's apt to take a bribe or take part in some other corrupt activity; he's crooked, dishonorable, etc. *In the Teapot Dome affair of 1923, President Warren Harding's venal Secretary of the Interior (Albert B. Fall) arranged for the private development of federally owned oil fields in exchange for a $100,000 bribe.*

227

his own mind he was a pillar of **probity**[3].

Finally he said, "My dear Scarecrow, you think of yourself as nothing but a **gauche**[4] **dunderhead**[5]. But from what I can see, your natural **acumen**[6] and **sagacity**[1] surpass that of many of the Emerald

---

[1] **mendacity (mendacious)** The practice of lying (telling untruths) or the tendency to lie is known as *mendacity*. The adjective *mendacious* means "dishonest, untruthful, lying" (of a person) or "false, untrue" (of a statement). *Complaining of untruths in advertising, historian and critic Bernard De Voto once referred to the industry as a "torrent of mendacity and imbecility."*

[2] **miscreant** A *miscreant* is a person who does evil or who lacks morals or principles; a villain. *In the newspaper adventure comic strip "Terry and the Pirates," an American boy and his adult pal encountered pirates, bandits, and other miscreants.*

[3] **probity** *Probity* is absolute uprightness of character, moral excellence, honesty, integrity, goodness, righteousness, etc. *After the scandal-ridden Warren Harding administration (1921–23), Calvin Coolidge's probity helped restore public confidence.*

[4] **gauche** To describe someone (or his actions) as *gauche* (rhymes with the first part of *ocean*) is to say that he's awkward (clumsy, gawky, bumbling, etc.) or that he lacks social graces (he's tactless, unmannerly, coarse, crude, etc.). *In the 1968 film* The Party, *British comedian Peter Sellers portrays an inept Indian actor whose gauche manners and mannerisms wreak havoc at a fancy Hollywood party.*

[5] **dunderhead** A *dunderhead* is a person regarded as stupid; a dunce, blockhead, numbskull, etc. *In 1970 the Director of the Selective Service System said he'd rather recruit (into the army) an honest dunderhead than a dishonest genius, explaining, "I won't get much out of him, but with that other guy I can't keep what I've got."*

[6] **acumen** The ability or power to keenly perceive, maturely understand, and wisely judge something (such as business, law, politics, military strategy, etc.) is known as *acumen* (pronounced either *uh-KYOO-men* or *AK-yuh-men*). *During the late 19th century, Scottish-born American industrialist Andrew Carnegie, through his business acumen, made millions in the steel industry; he later gave most of the money away to educational, cultural, and peacemaking organizations, explaining that "the man who dies rich dies disgraced."*

THE WIZARD OF OZ VOCABULARY BUILDER

City's so-called **pedants**[2] and **pundits**[3]. Why, you don't need brains!
A baby in **swaddling**[4] clothes has brains, but it **prattles**[5] **inanely**[6].

---

[1] **sagacity** If you say that someone has *sagacity*, you mean that he has or shows wisdom and sound judgment. The adjective *sagacious* describes someone who is wise, discerning, and judicious; the adjective *sage* describes something (advice, for example) that is wise and judicious. A person who is famed or respected for his great wisdom is known as a *sage*. *With his limited military experience, Abraham Lincoln turned to his sagacious generals for advice in conducting the Civil War.*

[2] **pedant (pedants)** A *pedant* is a person who shows off his learning or scholarship, or a person who's overly concerned with formal rules or book learning. The adjective *pedantic* can describe someone who so behaves or something (writing, for example) characterized by a narrow, showy concern for formal rules. The manner characteristic of a *pedant* or an instance of being *pedantic* is known as *pedantry*. *Some language experts predict that one day the word* who *will assume all the functions of* whom, *and that everyone, including pedants, will give up saying "Whom do you wish to speak to?"*

[3] **pundit (pundits)** A *pundit* is a person with great knowledge (of a particular subject), especially one whose opinion is sought or respected; an expert, an authority, etc. *In 1988 political pundits predicted that the Reverend Jesse Jackson would lose the Democratic nomination for President because, as a liberal and an African-American, he was unlikely to win the general election (and they were right— the nomination went to Massachusetts governor Michael Dukakis).*

[4] **swaddling** To *swaddle* something is to bind it with strips of cloth to prevent free movement. *Swaddling* clothes are clothes consisting of long, narrow strips of cloth placed around an infant to hold its arms and legs still. *A 1975* New York *magazine article, explaining the importance of sheets, said, "Sheets are the beginning and the end: our first clothing (swaddling) and our last (the shroud)."*

[5] **prattle (prattles)** To *prattle* (also to *prate*) is to talk, usually rapidly and constantly, about unimportant things (to chatter, chit-chat, etc.) or to talk in an indistinct, unintelligible way (to blabber, babble, etc.). As a noun, *prattle* is such talk. *In 1988 journalist Warren Brown said, "I always get suspicious of auto makers who boast about the new front ends of their cars or who prattle on about the relocation of hood ornaments; I figure they've got something to hide— like cars that don't work or machines of mediocre performance."*

[6] **inane (inanely)** To describe something (an idea or comment, for example) as *inane* is to say that it's silly, foolish, meaningless, stupid, pointless, etc. *A 1979* Time *magazine article said that inane TV sitcoms are "designed to attract juveniles of all ages."*

229

THE WIZARD OF OZ VOCABULARY BUILDER

Experience is the only thing that brings knowledge, and the longer you're alive the more experience you'll get."

"That may be true," said the Scarecrow, not sure if the **rhetoric**[1] he'd just heard was **gnostic**[2] truth or **sententious**[3] **drivel**[4], "but I'll be very unhappy unless you give me brains."

The false Wizard looked at him **empathetically**[5]. "Well, I'm not much of a Wizard, as I explained, but I'll stuff your head with brains," he said, feeling like a kindly country doctor prescribing a

---

[1] **rhetoric** Originally, the word *rhetoric* denoted the art of effective speaking or writing, or the art of persuasion (as in *President Kennedy's inspiring rhetoric*). But today the word can also denote speech that's insincere or empty of meaning (as in *the candidate's promises were mere rhetoric*). *In 1985, speaking of New York City mayor Ed Koch, journalist Pete Hamill said, "He steps on stage and draws the sword of rhetoric, and when he is through, someone is lying wounded and thousands of others are either angry or consoled."*

[2] **gnostic** To refer to something (a religion, for example) as *gnostic* (pronounced *NOS-tik*), is to say that it possesses spiritual or mystical secret knowledge (revealed by God). *According to historians, the origins of witchcraft lie in ancient cults (that believed in separate powers of good and evil) and in pre-Christian gnostic sects.*

[3] **sententious** To describe a person (or his writing) as *sententious* is to say that he uses lots of stale expressions and that he tends to be self-righteous and moralizing. *Some people feel that Harry Chapin's 1974 hit "Cat's in the Cradle" (which speaks of "the man in the moon" while urging you to pay attention to your kids) is an annoyingly sententious song.*

[4] **drivel** Meaningless, idiotic, childish, or silly talk is known as *drivel*. Note: The word also denotes saliva flowing from the mouth. *If you want to see the most inconsequential drivel blown up into earthshaking events, you can find it in the tabloids (such as the* Star *and the* National Enquirer*) sold at your local supermarket.*

[5] **empathize (empathetically)** To *empathize* is to understand and be sensitive to the feelings of someone else; to sympathize with, identify with, relate to, feel compassion for, etc. The noun is *empathy*; the adjective is *empathetic*. *Psychology textbooks say that a good psychotherapist is an empathetic listener who provides an accepting environment; on the other hand, in 1980 a Yale University professor of psychiatry said, "The practicing psychotherapist is perhaps better qualified than other serious human beings to discuss boredom."*

THE WIZARD OF OZ VOCABULARY BUILDER

placebo[1] to **mollify**[2] a distraught **hypochondriac**[3]. "I can't tell you how to use them, however. You must find that out for yourself."

"Oh, thank you, thank you!" cried the Scarecrow. "I'll find a way to use them!"

"Okay, then sit down in that chair, please," replied Oz. "You must excuse me for taking your head off, but I have to in order to put your brains in their proper place."

Then the Wizard unfastened the Scarecrow's head and emptied out a small portion of straw. Next he went into the back room and got some bran cereal, which he used to fill the newly made cavity. When he had fastened the Scarecrow's head on his body again, he said to him, "You are now an intelligent Scarecrow, **cognizant**[4] of

---

[1] **placebo** A *placebo* (pronounced *pluh-SEE-boh*) is a harmless substance that looks like medicine (a pill, for example) but contains no active drug; it's given either to satisfy a patient who wants and supposes it to be a drug or as a control (a standard for comparison) in experimentally testing the effectiveness of a real drug. In what is known as the *placebo effect,* a patient improves after following a particular medicinal treatment merely because of his expectation of the treatment (not because of the treatment itself). *After dinner the doctor amused us with humorous anecdotes of complaining patients who were quieted by sugar pills, injections of sterile water, and other placebos.*

[2] **mollify** To *mollify* someone is to make him less angry or upset, especially by taking some positive action. *In 1997, to mollify critics who wanted parents to have more information about programming content, TV executives considered adding content labels (for sex, language, and violence) to ratings.*

[3] **hypochondriac** A *hypochondriac* is a physically healthy person who excessively worries about becoming ill or imagines that he is ill; he often experiences the physical symptoms (pain, for example) associated with illness. *During the 1980s people who complained of constant fatigue, weakness, and an inability to concentrate were dismissed as hypochondriacs; today these people are said to be suffering from a physical disorder known as chronic fatigue syndrome (whose cause is unknown).*

[4] **cognizant** To be *cognizant* of something is to be aware of it; to have knowledge of it; to be familiar with it. The word is used especially (instead of *aware*) in formal contexts. The noun is *cognizance. Historians say that while President Richard Nixon was not cognizant of a planned 1972 break-in at the Democratic National Committee headquarters in the Watergate apartment complex in Washington, D.C., he subsequently tried to prevent an investigation of the crime.*

even the most **arcane**[1] bits of **minutiae**[2]." The Scarecrow, believing he now **embodied**[3] the **zenith**[4] of human comprehension, was both pleased and proud at the fulfillment of his greatest wish and thanked Oz warmly.

"How about my courage?" asked the Lion.

"And you, dear Lion, think you are a **feckless**[5], **ignominious**[1]

---

[1] **arcane** To describe something (a fact, rule, word, etc.) as *arcane* is to say that it's little known, obscure, mysterious, etc. *By consulting a dictionary of football terms you can find the meaning of such arcane phrases as "zone blitz," "flea-flicker," and "nickel package."*

[2] **minutiae** The small, trivial details of a subject or event are known as (the) *minutiae* (of that subject or event). Note: The word is plural; a single trivial detail is known as a *minutia* (spelled without the final *e*). *In the 2000 film* High Fidelity, *a young record store owner and his two employees endlessly discuss the minutiae of rock music.*

[3] **embody (embodied)** When an abstract quality (goodness or evil, for example) is *embodied* (in something), it's exemplified in concrete (often human) form. *In the children's story "The Three Little Pigs," the dangers and evils of the world are embodied in the Big Bad Wolf.* When ideas (laws, principles, philosophy, etc.) are *embodied* (in something), they are collected and organized together into a united or unified whole. *The fundamental laws and principles by which the United States is governed are embodied in the Constitution.*

[4] **zenith** The *zenith* of something is its highest point. Although this high point can be a physical place (and as a technical term in astronomy the word refers to the highest point in the sky directly above an observer), the word is more often used to refer to a figurative high point, such as a time of someone's (or something's) greatest achievement, power, or development. *Baroque music, stressing strictness of form and elaborate ornamentation, reached its zenith in the works of Johann Sebastian Bach (1685–1750).*

[5] **feckless** To describe someone as *feckless* is to say that he's a good-for-nothing; he's ineffective, unproductive, weak, incompetent, unsuccessful, feeble, lazy, irresponsible, worthless, useless, etc. *In the 1985 film* Back to the Future, *a teenager watches in frustration as his feckless father allows himself to be insulted, ridiculed, and knocked on the head by a bully.*

varmed up to this vein of **sacerdotal**[1] guidance, Oz
"Dear Woodman, you think of yourself as a clanking
of tin whom no one could ever love because you have no
you are indeed lovable because you are kinder and more
than even our so-called **philanthropists**[2]. But I think
ong to want a heart because the unhappy **corollary**[3] to
is that one day someone may break it."
r all the unhappiness without a murmur if you'll only
e," promised the Tin Woodman.
ell, you will have it," answered Oz, genuinely hoping to
to the Tin Woodman's needs and thereby, in some small

Things that relate to priests or the priesthood are said to be *sacerdotal.*
high priests of ancient Judaism wore elaborate sacerdotal vestments
quare cloth "breastplate" set with 12 precious stones representing the 12
), modern rabbis generally wear simple black gowns.

pist (philanthropists) A *philanthropist* is a (usually wealthy) person
s the well-being of mankind by donating money (or other charitable
worthy causes or needy people. The noun is *philanthropy. Milton*
–1945) is most famous for manufacturing chocolate bars, but he was also
hilanthropist (in the early 1900s he established a school for orphan boys,
ed with the bulk of his fortune).

a mathematics and logic, a *corollary* is a proposition (statement) that
one already proven. In general usage, a *corollary* is any natural
result, or effect of something else. As an adjective, the word means
resultant." *An October 1979 article in the* Washington Post *notes that*
ployment (which was a problem in the 1960s and 1970s) may disappear in
laining that "the staggering national problem of teenagers seeking jobs
here— and the corollary problems of crime and social disorientation that
are rooted in the sheer numbers of these young people, and those numbers
ng into a long-term decline."

minister to someone is to tend to his wants and needs (by caring for
upon him, feeding him, giving him medical aid, etc.). *American Red*
t Clara Barton (1821–1912) began her career in 1861 as a volunteer
the wounded on Civil War battlefields.

---

coward, too **pusillanimous**[2] to deserve the **moniker**[3] "King of
Beasts." All living things— ever since the first, miserable **primeval**[4]
organisms emerged from the **primordial**[5] ooze— have been afraid
when faced with danger. True courage is in facing danger when you
are afraid, and that kind of courage you have plenty of. All you
need is confidence in yourself."

"But I'm scared just the same," said the Lion, unconvinced by the

---

[1] **ignominious** To refer to something (an action or event, for example) as
ignominious (pronounced with the accent on the third syllable) is to say that it's
marked by or deserving of disgrace or shame; it's degrading, embarrassing, etc. The
word generally implies public disapproval. Note: The noun *ignominy* (meaning
"personal dishonor or humiliation" or "disrepute, infamy, notoriety") is
pronounced with the accent on the first syllable. *In 1996, after a Russian spacecraft
aimed at Mars landed in the Pacific Ocean, the* Los Angeles Times *said, "Russia's most
ambitious space probe landed with an ignominious 6.7-ton splash in the South Pacific,
along with a chunk of the country's battered scientific prestige."*

[2] **pusillanimous** To describe someone as *pusillanimous* is to say that he lacks
courage; he's cowardly, faint-hearted, gutless, spineless, etc. *Some people claim that
both Nancy Reagan and George H. Bush's approach to dealing with drugs was
pusillanimous because they never spoke of alcohol, the drug that kills more young
Americans (in the 15–24 age bracket) than any other.*

[3] **moniker** A person's name, especially his nickname, is known as his *moniker.
Because "The Donald" is widely known as real estate developer Donald Trump's
nickname, in 1999 the U.S. Patent and Trademark Office turned down his former wife
Ivana's request to trademark the moniker (she had wanted the name for her son,
Donald Jr., to use on such products as cologne and body cream).*

[4] **primeval** To refer to something as *primeval* is to say that it belongs to or pertains
to the first or earliest age or ages (of the earth or universe); it's ancient, original,
primal. *Scientists believe that the first signs of primeval life (bacteria and blue-green
algae) appeared in oceans about three billion years ago.*

[5] **primordial** To refer to something (a chemical substance or physical event, for
example) as *primordial* is to say that it played a primary (initial) role in a (usually
large-scale) sequence of events, or simply that it has existed since the very
beginning (of something). *According to the theory of evolution, all living forms arose,
through time, from a simple, primordial mass of protoplasm.*

aphoristic[1] little speech. "I'll be very unhappy unless you give me the kind of courage that makes me forget I'm afraid."

Realizing that giving these creatures what they thought they needed would redound[2] to everyone's benefit, including his own, he said, "Very well, I'll get it for you."

He went to a cupboard and, reaching up to a high shelf, took down a square green bottle, the contents of which he poured into a beautifully carved green dish. Placing this before the Lion, who stared at it with an ambivalent[3] mixture of hope and fear, the Wizard said, "Drink it."

"What is it?" asked the Lion skeptically[4].

"Well," answered Oz, "this is unadulterated[1] liquid courage.

---

[1] aphorism (aphoristic) A concise (and often deep or stylistically distinguished) saying or verbal expression that sets forth (or intends to set forth) a bit of wisdom or truth is known as an *aphorism*. *During the mid-1770s American statesman and scientist Benjamin Franklin, in his Poor Richard's Almanac, coined such aphorisms as "Early to bed and early to rise makes a man healthy, wealthy, and wise" and "God helps those who help themselves."*

[2] redound When something (an action, decision, event, policy, etc.) *redounds* (upon someone or something), it produces an effect or consequence (as to the advantage, disadvantage, credit, discredit, etc., of that person or thing). *According to the trickle-down theory of economics, financial benefits given to large corporations will in time redound to the benefit of smaller businesses and consumers.*

[3] ambivalent When you're *ambivalent*, you're uncertain or indecisive (about what to do in a particular situation), usually as a result of a coexistence (in your mind) of two opposing feelings or attitudes. The noun is *ambivalence*. *In 1980, speaking of people who stutter, biographer Ted Morgan said, "The stammerer is ambivalent about communicating with others— he desperately wants to communicate, but is afraid of revealing himself."*

[4] skeptic (skeptically) A *skeptic* is a person who doubts (or questions or disagrees with) a particular claim or conclusion, or who habitually doubts (or questions or disagrees with) generally accepted conclusions. The adjective is *skeptical*. *In 1912 German geologist, meteorologist, and arctic explorer Alfred Wegener suggested that the earth's continents were slowly moving (at a rate of about one yard per century); many geologists were originally skeptical but eventually came to accept his theory of "continental drift."*

You know, of course, that courage is really can't be called courage until you it will behoove[2] to drink it right a

Vacillating[3] no longer, the Lion dr "I'm full of courage!" he shouted proud

The Tin Woodman had been watchi The "miracles" he had just witn tenterhooks[5], and now he could no blurted out, "What about my heart?"

---

[1] unadulterated If you say that a particular s etc.) is *unadulterated*, you mean that it's pure; t mixed with it. Figuratively, the word is u complete, total, etc.," as in *unadulterated hogw soft for many uses, it's often mixed with other met*

[2] behoove If you say that it *behooves* you to d your advantage to do it; that it would be a goo *The pickpocket told his wife that it would behoov a fellow pickpocket who'd been caught— not for t of the large crowd attracted to the execution. N subject of behoove is almost always it.*

[3] vacillate (vacillating) To *vacillate* is to b decision or course of action), especially to between two conflicting alternatives. *After vac who and whom, language expert and New Y finally said, "I favor whom's doom except after a*

[4] rapt When you're *rapt* in something, you're wrapped up in it; you're absorbed or enra spiritually transported). *We found the chess ma times we weren't sure if the lizard-like oppone concentration of if they had fallen asleep!*

[5] tenterhooks If someone is on *tenterhooks*, he anxiously waiting to see what will happen. *F U.S. presidential election (in which by a razor-th appeared to defeat Democrat Al Gore), all of A votes from the decisive state of Florida were reco*

Now answered collectio heart. Bu thoughtf you're w having or

"I'll be give me o

"Very

minister[4]

---

[1] sacerdotal *Although th (including a tribes of Isra*

[2] philanthr who increas assistance) t Hershey (185 known as a which he fun

[3] corollary follows from consequence "consequent teenage unem the 1980s; e that are not flow from it are now hea

[4] minister him, waiting Cross presid ministering

way, **redress**[1] his own mistakes. "But I'll have to cut a hole in your chest, so I can put your heart in the right place." Oz took a pair of tinsmith's shears and cut a small, square hole in the left side of the Tin Woodman's chest. Then, going to a chest of drawers, he took out a shiny, **japanned**[2] box. Opening it, he revealed a pretty, red heart, made entirely of silk and stuffed with sawdust. "Isn't it a beauty?" he asked.

"It is, indeed!" replied the Woodman, who was greatly pleased. "But is it a kind heart?"

"Oh, very!" answered Oz. He was about to say that it was a heart of gold, but since he **detested**[3] **hackneyed**[4] expressions, he said nothing as he carefully placed the sawdust-filled silk in the Tin Woodman's chest and then replaced the square of tin, soldering it neatly together where it had been cut.

"There," he said, "now you have a heart that any man might be

---

[1] **redress** To *redress* a wrong is to remedy it (set it right again) or to make amends for it (make up for it). *Affirmative action is a U.S. program that seeks to redress past discrimination by giving preferential treatment (in jobs and education) to ethnic minorities and women.*

[2] **japanned** This word is used to describe a surface (wood or metal, for example) that's coated or decorated with a hard, glossy (often black) varnish or enamel. *In the Orient, women often wear hair ornaments consisting of japanned pins and combs.*

[3] **detest (detested)** To *detest* something is to hate or despise it. *In 1964, ruling that Henry Miller's 1934 novel* The Tropic of Cancer *(banned in the U.S. until 1961 for its sexually explicit content) was not pornographic, a California Supreme Court judge said, "The creations which yesterday were the detested and the obscene become the classics of today."*

[4] **hackneyed** If you say that something (an idea, story line, verbal expression, etc.) is *hackneyed*, you mean that it has become stale, ineffective, or unappealing through overuse. *In 1959, speaking of reviews, actor Robert Mitchum said, "I never take any notice of reviews unless a critic has thought up some new way of describing me; that old one about my lizard eyes and anteater nose and the way I sleep my way through pictures is so hackneyed now."*

proud of." Then, with currents of **bliss**[1] flowing **ineffably**[2] from his metal body, the Tin Woodman, **wallowing**[3] in **bathos**[4], **mawkishly**[5] acknowledged Oz's kindness in a **treacly**[6] but heartfelt little speech.

"And now," said Dorothy, who'd been waiting patiently, "how am I going to get back to Kansas? I don't suppose you have

---

[1] **bliss** A state of extreme happiness or utter joy is known as *bliss*. *Explaining how she loves uninterrupted writing, Pulitzer Prize–winning novelist Edna Ferber (1887–1968) once said that her "idea of bliss is to wake up on a Monday morning knowing you haven't a single engagement for the entire week; you are cradled in a white paper cocoon tied up with typewriter ribbon."*

[2] **ineffable (ineffably)** If something (a feeling, for example) is *ineffable*, it's beyond words; it's indescribable, inexpressible, indefinable, etc. *In her 1962 book* Thatched with Gold, *Lady Mabell Airlie describes Queen Mary watching the (1952) funeral procession of her son King George VI as follows: "As the cortege [procession] wound slowly along, the queen whispered in a broken voice, 'Here he is,' and I knew that her dry eyes were seeing beyond the coffin a little boy in a sailor suit; she was past weeping, wrapped in the ineffable solitude of grief."*

[3] **wallow (wallowing)** Technically, to *wallow* in something (water or mud, for example) is to lie in it or roll around in it (as a pig does, for example). But when you talk about a person *wallowing* in something (sentimentality or self-pity, for example) you mean that he's unrestrainedly absorbed in it. *In his 1963 "I Have a Dream" speech, speaking of racial inequality, Martin Luther King, Jr., said, "Somehow this situation can and will be changed; let us not wallow in the valley of despair."*

[4] **bathos** The quality of being excessively sentimental or overly emotional is known as *bathos*. *Early television soap operas were notorious for their bad acting, intrusive organ music, and bathos.*

[5] **mawkish (mawkishly)** To describe something (a story, music, etc.) as *mawkish* is to say that it's overly sentimental; it's mushy. *In the mawkish 1970 movie* Love Story, *a beautiful young woman tells her husband two things: that "love means never having to say you're sorry" and that she's dying.*

[6] **treacle (treacly)** In Britain, molasses (a thick, sweet syrup) is known as *treacle* (pronounced *TREE-kl*). Figuratively, to say that something (speech, a story, music, etc.) is *treacly* (pronounced *TREE-klee*), is to say that it's overly or unrestrainedly sentimental. *Because of its sweet melody and syrupy lyrics, some people have condemned John Denver's 1974 hit "Annie's Song" as treacly.*

anything in your bag of tricks for me."

Oz, whose **facile**[1] tongue could have easily delivered another old **saw**[2], instead **pondered**[3] his success in giving the Scarecrow, the Lion, and the Tin Woodman exactly what they thought they wanted. It was easy to make them happy, he thought to himself, because they imagined I could do anything. But it will take more than a few **platitudinous**[4] pronouncements to get Dorothy back to Kansas.

"I guess I'll have to think about that for a few days," he finally answered. When Dorothy just stared at him, he added, "I know that sounds **equivocal**[5] and **dilatory**[6], but none of my **legerdemain**[1]

---

[1] **facile** If you're *facile* in doing something (working, moving, acting, speaking, etc.), you're able to do it easily, effortlessly, fluently, smoothly, etc. *During the 1960s boxer Muhammad Ali's facile rhymes— such as "Only the nose knows where the nose goes when the door close" (when asked about the relationship between sex and physical strength)— attracted the attention of the media and fans alike.*

[2] **saw** A *saw* is a familiar, often-repeated saying or expression that expresses a truth or belief; a proverb. The word is most often seen in the phrase "old saw." *Most people agree that the old saw "finders keepers, losers weepers" has absolutely no ethical merit.*

[3] **ponder (pondered)** To *ponder* something is to think about it or consider it carefully or thoroughly. *In his 1981 book* Her Side of It, *author Thomas Savage wrote, "Cosmic upheaval is not so moving as a little child pondering the death of a sparrow in the corner of a barn."*

[4] **platitude (platitudinous)** A *platitude* is a dull remark or overused expression, especially one stated as if it were fresh or significant. The adjective *platitudinous* means "in the nature of a platitude." *As the plane nose-dived toward the ground, Shirley found a bit of comfort in the platitude that "everything will turn out all right."*

[5] **equivocal** Language or speech described as *equivocal* is ambiguous, of uncertain significance, open to more than one interpretation, etc. (usually intentionally, so as to mislead or avoid commitment). To *equivocate* is to use *equivocal* language. *Not wanting to offend anyone, the candidate equivocated on the abortion issue.*

[6] **dilatory** Someone who's *dilatory* tends to delay or procrastinate; he's slow, late, etc. (sometimes intentionally, so as to avoid making a decision). *During the 1950s and 1960s Southern Democratic senators used a dilatory tactic known as a filibuster (a lengthy speech) to try to delay civil rights legislation.*

will carry you over the desert. In the meantime you can all stay in the Palace as my guests." Then he suddenly became **pensive**[2].

"Please keep my secret," he **entreated**[3], "and tell no one I'm a fake. Of course, it's not that I'm **loath**[4] to admit my mistakes, but you know how **fickle**[5] public opinion can be. If I were **debunked**[6], the press—those **purveyors**[7] of worthless **tripe**[1]— would **traduce**[2]

---

[1] **legerdemain** Another word for magic (especially sleight of hand) is *legerdemain*. The word can also be used figuratively to mean "clever deception; trickery," as in *financial legerdemain*. *While most magicians are known for their legerdemain (such as making coins disappear or pulling rabbits out of hats), the most famous of all, Harry Houdini, was known primarily as an escape artist.*

[2] **pensive** To be *pensive* is to be quietly, deeply, or dreamily (and sometimes sadly) in thought. *The pensive, seated subject of French sculptor Auguste Rodin's bronze statue* The Thinker *(1880) was originally intended to illustrate "The Inferno" (the first of three sections of Italian poet Dante's 1321 epic,* The Divine Comedy*).*

[3] **entreat (entreated)** To *entreat* (somebody) is to earnestly or urgently ask or request (something of him), especially persuasively, as to overcome resistance. *Though in the 1890s* Ladies' Home Journal *editor Edward Bok entreated women to stay at home (to fulfill their roles as wives, mothers, and homemakers), during World War I he endorsed their employment in industry.*

[4] **loath** If you're *loath* to do something, you're unwilling, reluctant, or disinclined to do it. *According to most women, men are not loath to say "I love you"; getting them to say "Will you marry me?" is another story altogether.*

[5] **fickle** Someone who is *fickle* easily or frequently changes his mind (especially about what or who he likes or dislikes). *Some people who have many ups and downs in life believe that their changes in fortune are caused by "the fickle finger of fate."*

[6] **debunk (debunked)** To *debunk* something (that falsely claims to be true or effective) is to show it to be false or ineffective. *During his later career, American magician and escape artist Harry Houdini spent much of his time debunking mediums (people who claim they have the power to communicate with the dead) by duplicating their tricks and incorporating them into his act.*

[7] **purveyor (purveyors)** A *purveyor* is someone who supplies or furnishes (sells) provisions (especially food). Figuratively, the word can refer to someone who announces or spreads something, as in *a purveyor of lies. Henry John Heinz (1844–1919), manufacturer and purveyor of ketchup, pickles, and other prepared foods, invented his company's slogan ("57 varieties").*

my character... they'd **flagellate**[3] me. Of course, any claims of serious **malfeasance**[4] on my part ultimately would be **refuted**[5], so I'm in no danger of being— to use criminal **parlance**[6]— sent up the

---

[1] **tripe** The stomach lining of a cow (or other cud-chewing animal, such as a goat or sheep) used as food (for people) is known as *tripe*. But the word is often used figuratively and informally to refer to something (speech or writing, for example) that is false or worthless. *When I told my mother that a supermarket tabloid reported that a woman's arm became a chipmunk's leg, she just said, "I don't pay attention to that tripe."*

[2] **traduce** To *traduce* someone is to make harmful, false statements about him (especially when these statements cause humiliation or disgrace). *The main difference between boys and men involved in feuds is that whereas boys punch each other, men traduce each other's character.*

[3] **flagellate** Literally, to *flagellate* someone is to whip him. Figuratively, the word means to punish (someone) or to severely scold or criticize (him). *Colorado Democratic senator Gary Hart withdrew from the 1988 presidential race after being flagellated for an extra-marital affair.*

[4] **malfeasance** The performance of a wrongdoing or illegal act, especially by a public official, is known as *malfeasance*. *In 1973 U.S. Vice President Spiro Agnew resigned amid charges of malfeasance (he was accused of taking bribes and kickbacks and failing to pay income tax) during his term of office as governor of Maryland (1966-1968).*

[5] **refute (refuted)** To *refute* something (an opinion or accusation, for example) is to show it to be in error (to disprove it) or to deny its accuracy. *Italian painter and scientist Leonardo da Vinci (1452-1519) understood the true nature of fossils (evidence in rock of the presence of a plant or animal from prehistoric times) and refuted the then-popular idea that fossils were devices Satan had put in rocks to confuse people.*

[6] **parlance** A stock of terms or manner of speaking used by people who share a particular profession, hobby, culture, etc., is known as *parlance*. *In August 1994 a Washington Post editorial said, "The floods of nostalgia over Woodstock '94 couldn't quite hide the persistence of a certain difference of opinion— known in old-fashioned parlance as a "generation gap"— in the music tastes of the audience; few doubted who in the paying crowds had come to hear Crosby, Stills & Nash and who was more interested in Nine Inch Nails."*

river. But I'd be **mired**[1] in controversy, forced to endlessly **parry**[2] any **derogatory**[3] remark thrust at me. **Obloquy**[4] would naturally **accrete**[5] around me, and my reputation would be forever **tainted**[6]."

---

[1] **mire (mired)** To be *mired* in something is to be stuck or bogged down in it, either literally (as in *mired in mud*) or figuratively (as in *mired in self-doubt*). Note: As a noun, a *mire* is an area of muddy ground; a swamp. *After the Civil War some black sharecroppers purchased farms of their own, but many who bought supplies on credit found themselves mired in debt even after their crops were sold.*

[2] **parry** In the sport of fencing, an attack is known as a *thrust*, and a defensive move that blocks or deflects a thrust is known as a *parry*. But in general usage, the verb *parry* denotes any warding off, deflecting, turning aside, evading, etc., of something (an accusation, criticism, difficult question, etc.). *The North Atlantic Treaty Organization (NATO)—a military alliance whose original members included Belgium, Canada, Denmark, France, Great Britain, Iceland, Italy, Luxembourg, the Netherlands, Norway, Portugal, and the U.S.— was established in 1949 to parry the Soviet military threat in Europe.*

[3] **derogatory** If you say that something (a remark, a term or phrase, personal information, etc.) is *derogatory*, you mean that it tends to belittle or discredit (someone); it lowers or insults (him). *While in some regions of the Southwest the term* Chicaco, *a shortened version of* Mexicano *(Mexican-American), is considered derogatory, in others it actually suggests self-determination and ethnic pride.*

[4] **obloquy** *Obloquy* (pronounced *OB-luh-kwee*) can refer either to harsh, abusive, critical language (aimed at a person, usually by a large group or by the general public) or to the disgrace, discredit, or ill repute that results from such abuse or denunciation. *Bill Clinton's Presidency was checkered with good and bad, with glory and obloquy.*

[5] **accretion (accrete)** A gradual, natural growth or increase in size (of something), as by the growing or sticking together of external parts, is known as *accretion* (for example, a coral reef grows larger through *accretion*). The verb is *accrete*. *Scientists believe that planets are formed by the accretion of gas and dust in a cosmic cloud.*

[6] **taint (tainted)** To *taint* a physical substance is to make it impure or inferior by adding a trace of something foreign. To *taint* a person's name or reputation is to tarnish or blacken it. *Sixteenth-century religious reformer John Calvin believed that all infants were born tainted by the original sin of Adam and Eve.*

THE WIZARD OF OZ VOCABULARY BUILDER

He felt a thick web of **calumny**[1] tighten around him as he realized that his story, if it were to get out, would become **fodder**[2] for the eager journalistic gristmill. "I can see it now—**yellow**[3] **rags**[4] **spewing**[5] **acrid**[1] **vitriol**[2] in **purple**[3] **prose**[4]. I'd be a laughingstock.

---

[1] **calumny** The uttering of false and harmful statements about someone (or one of those statements itself) is known as *calumny* (pronounced with the accent on the first syllable). *In 1992, facing impeachment for dishonesty in office, Brazilian president Fernando Collor de Mello denied any wrongdoing in a televised response to what he called "calumnies, defamations, and injustices" against him.*

[2] **fodder** Technically, *fodder* is food for livestock, especially coarsely chopped hay or straw. But figuratively the word is used to refer to anything that is in abundant supply and can serve as raw material for something (such as artistic creation). The phrase *cannon fodder* refers to military personnel (soldiers, sailor, etc.) considered likely to be killed or wounded in combat. *Grant Wood's 1930 painting* American Gothic *(which shows a stern-faced, pitchfork-holding Iowa farmer and his spinster daughter standing in front of a farmhouse) has been fodder for political cartoonists and advertisers since the 1950s.*

[3] **yellow** To refer to a newspaper or to journalism as *yellow* is to say that it uses sensationalism (that is, exaggeration, distortion of truth, gory details, large-type headlines, misleading photos and illustrations, etc.) to attract readers. Note: Yellow journalism began in the late 1890s when two rival New York newspapers, each covering the Spanish-American War, competed for readers. *Yellow journalism can be found in both supermarket tabloids (the* National Enquirer, *for example) and popular general newspapers (the* New York Post, *for example).*

[4] **rag (rags)** A newspaper regarded with distaste or hatred (especially one that specializes in sensationalism or gossip) is referred to as a *rag. In 1986 President Ronald Reagan referred to the Lebanese newspaper that leaked reports of U.S. arms sales to Iran as "that rag in Beirut."*

[5] **spew (spewing)** When something (a liquid, for example) is *spewed*, it's sent or forced out (usually in a stream); it's forcibly ejected in large amounts (a volcano *spews* lava, for example). The word can also refer to a discharge or gush of human anger or disgust (a person *spews* a stream of complaints or insults, for example). *The world's worst nuclear power plant accident occurred in 1986 in Chernobyl, Ukraine, when a cloud of deadly radioactive gas was spewed into the air and carried over parts of the Soviet Union, Scandinavia, and Europe (killing about 8,000 people).*

THE WIZARD OF OZ VOCABULARY BUILDER

I'd be **reviled**[5]... **lambasted**[6]... **pilloried**[1]... **ostracized**[2]!" When he

---

[1] **acrid** If something (a taste or smell, for example) is *acrid*, it's sharp, biting, bitter, irritating, etc. (to the tongue, nose, eyes, etc.). A remark or language described as *acrid* is stinging, cutting, bitter, biting, etc. *In a 1961 article in the* New York Herald Tribune *entitled "Cookout's Got to Go," journalist Donald Rogers noted, "Few things are more revolting than the spectacle of a normally reasonable father and husband gowned in one of those hot, massive aprons inscribed with disgustingly corny legends, presiding over a [barbecue grill] as he destroys huge hunks of good meat and fills the neighborhood with greasy, acrid smoke: a Boy Scout with five o'clock shadow."*

[2] **vitriol** Technically, *vitriol* is any of several chemical compounds (such as copper sulfate, iron sulfate, or zinc sulfate); these compounds are used as germicides, insecticides, preservative, dyes, etc. *Oil of vitriol* is another name for *sulfuric acid* (an extremely corrosive liquid). But the word is also used to refer to biting, stinging language (harsh criticism, for example). The adjective is *vitriolic. While Nation of Islam leader Louis Farrakhan has been praised for trying to help disadvantaged urban blacks, he has been criticized for his vitriolic anti-Semitic remarks (for example, in 1985 he was quoted as having referred to Judaism as a "gutter religion").*

[3] **purple** To refer to language or writing as *purple*, as in the expression *purple prose* (see *prose*), is to say that it's full of exaggerated literary effects; that is, it's elaborate, flowery, overblown, embellished, etc. *In his 1985* New York Times *article entitled "In Defense of Purple Prose," author Paul West (in his typically purple style), said, "Purple is not only highly colored prose, it is the world written up, intensified and made pleasurably palpable, not only to suggest the impetuous abundance of Creation, but also to add to it by showing— showing off— the expansive power of the mind itself, its unique knack for making itself at home among trees, dawns, viruses, and then turning them into something else: a word, a daub, a sonata."*

[4] **prose** *Prose* is ordinary or regular writing (as opposed to poetry). *Author Edgar Allan Poe (1809–1849) is known for both his poetry ("The Raven," for example) and his prose (horror short stories, including "The Fall of the House of Usher," for example).*

[5] **revile (reviled)** To *revile* someone is to attack him with harsh, abusive language. *Because his novel* Dr. Zhivago *(1958) was considered uncomplimentary in its portrayal of the Russian Revolution, Russian author Boris Pasternak (1890–1960) was reviled by Soviet critics and forced to refuse the 1958 Nobel Prize for literature.*

[6] **lambaste (lambasted)** To *lambaste* someone (or something) is to attack him by severely scolding or criticizing him. *In his 1965 book* Unsafe at Any Speed, *consumer advocate Ralph Nader lambasted General Motors for producing an unsafe car (the Corvair).*

paused momentarily to dwell on the consequences of **perdition**[3] and imagined himself living on the street with penniless, drunken **reprobates**[4]— or worse, dwelling in that fiery **venue**[5] far, far below the street with a red-suited, **trident**[6]-carrying **personification**[1] of

---

[1] **pillory (pilloried)** In times past (in Europe and America), wrongdoers were sometimes punished and exposed to public ridicule by being locked in a device known as a *pillory*— a piece of wood (on a post) with openings for securing the head and hands (which stick out in front). While as a verb to *pillory* (someone) can mean "to place (him) in a pillory," most often the word is used to mean "to openly condemn, denounce, or criticize (him), or to expose (him) to public ridicule." *When her greed and meanness were exposed (1989), New York "hotel queen" Leona Helmsley was pilloried by the press.*

[2] **ostracize (ostracized)** To *ostracize* someone is to exclude him (banish him, kick him out, etc.) from a group (a club, society, country, etc.). *In 1986 a spokesman for the U.S. Department of Justice said that AIDS patients are "irrationally ostracized by their communities because of medically baseless fears of contagion."*

[3] **perdition** *Perdition* is a state of eternal damnation; a state of being in hell (or in a hell-like situation). *When news correspondent Lucky Severson was sent to Nome, Alaska, in 1986, he felt like he'd been cast into perdition, saying, "If you don't believe hell freezes over, you haven't been to Nome."*

[4] **reprobate (reprobates)** A *reprobate* is a person who is morally unprincipled, wicked, depraved, etc.; a scoundrel, wretch, degenerate, etc. Note: In theology a *reprobate* is a person rejected by God and condemned to eternal damnation. *In Charles Dickens' 1838 novel* Oliver Twist, *a miserly reprobate named Fagin teaches orphaned boys to pick pockets and steal for him.*

[5] **venue** The setting (scene, locale, auditorium, etc.) where something (an event, action, etc.) takes place is known as a *venue*. *Large New York–area rock concerts are generally presented in one of three venues: Manhattan's Madison Square Garden, New Jersey's Meadowlands, or Long Island's Nassau Coliseum.*

[6] **trident** A *trident* is a three-pronged spear, fork, or weapon. *In Greek mythology the sea god Poseidon always carried a long trident, which he used to raise or quiet storms and earthquakes.*

evil— his eyelids began to quiver. In a pleading voice he continued, "I **implore**[2] you. After all, I'm only human and therefore **intrinsically**[3] not perfect. We all have our **foibles**[4], our little **peccadilloes**[5]. And I assure you that I've already been sufficiently

---

[1] **personify (personification)** To *personify* something (an object or abstract idea, for example) is to attribute human characteristics to it (as in speech or writing) or to represent it in human form (as in painting). To say that someone *personifies* a particular quality or idea (goodness or evil, for example) is to say that he embodies or typifies that quality or is a perfect example of it. *In 1982, after fighting broke out in the Falkland Islands (a group of islands off the coast of Argentina controlled since the 1830s by Great Britain and claimed by both countries) the Secretary-General of Peru personified the faltering peace negotiations by summarizing them thusly: "The patient is in intensive care but still alive."*

[2] **implore** To *implore* is to urgently or anxiously ask or request; to beg. *In 1986, in an address to the nation with President Reagan, First Lady Nancy Reagan said, "For the sake of our children, I implore each of you to be unyielding and inflexible in your opposition to drugs."*

[3] **intrinsic (intrinsically)** Things that exist as part of the essential nature of something are said to be *intrinsic* (to it); that is, they are "built in," naturally occurring, etc. For example, you might speak of the intrinsic brightness of a star or of the intrinsic value of a gemstone. *According to* Grolier's Encyclopedia, *"As demonstrated by the Woodstock Festival in August 1969, rock music was by [that] time an intrinsic element in the life of American youth and a powerful articulation of their moods, hopes, and fears."* Note: The opposite is *extrinsic*, meaning "not forming an essential part (of something); originating or existing outside (of something)."

[4] **foible (foibles)** A *foible* is a minor weakness or fault in a person's character; in fact, it may be so minor that it might be overlooked or even considered endearing. *For 50 years in his comic strip "Peanuts," cartoonist Charles Schulz (1922–2000) used children and animals to make us smile at our own foibles, follies, and frustrations.*

[5] **peccadillo (peccadilloes)** A trivial or petty sin or fault (such as saying or doing something inappropriate) is known as a *peccadillo. In 1987 the* New York Times, *reporting that the* London Times *began including "descriptions of human peccadilloes in its obituaries," said, "[They are] uninhibitedly publishing articles on the passing of a [cheated upon] poet, a rock promoter strangely addicted to collecting orangutans, and an Italian writer striving 'to avoid becoming a bore.'"*

chastened[1] and that I've learned my lesson."

They felt sorry for the **beleaguered**[2] old man, and they all accepted the proposed **covenant**[3] **amenably**[4]. Dorothy, thinking that Oz showed a few outward signs of genuine **penitence**[5], decided that if he could find some way to send her back to Kansas, she'd be willing to **condone**[6] everything he had done.

---

[1] **chasten (chastened)** To *chasten* someone is to scold or punish him in order to correct, strengthen, or improve him. The implication is that he will be left humbled (brought down a notch) or subdued. *Seemingly chastened by the frightening possibility of nuclear war— over the tension-filled Cuban Missile Crisis (1962), in which the U.S. sought to prevent the USSR from constructing launching sites for nuclear missiles in Cuba— the Americans and Soviets signed a treaty (1963) barring atmospheric testing of nuclear weapons.*

[2] **beleaguered** If someone (or something) is *beleaguered*, he's filled with (or plagued or harassed by) troubles, worries, problems, annoyances, etc. *In 1974, amid accusations that he'd obstructed justice (in the Watergate cover-up), abused presidential powers, illegally bombed Cambodia (in 1969), and used public funds to improve his private property, a beleaguered President Richard Nixon resigned from office.*

[3] **covenant** A *covenant* is an agreement, especially a formal or binding one; a promise, pact, contract. *According to the Bible, God made a covenant with the ancient Israelites in which he promised to protect them if they were faithful to him and kept his law.*

[4] **amenable (amenably)** If you're *amenable* you tend to respond to things favorably or you're ready and willing to do what is required; you're agreeable, yielding, open-minded, receptive, responsive, dutiful, obedient, etc. *After World War II President Truman adopted measures designed to block Soviet expansion; his European policies were highly successful, but Asia was less amenable to U.S. intervention.*

[5] **penitent (penitence)** If you're *penitent* about something (a wrongdoing or sin, for example), you feel or express sorrow or regret for it. *In his resignation speech (August 1974), a penitent President Richard Nixon said, "I regret deeply any injuries that may have been done in the course of the events that led to this decision; I would say only that if some of my judgments were wrong— and some were wrong— they were made in what I believed at the time to be in the best interest of the nation."*

[6] **condone** To condone something (a wrongdoing, sin, offense, etc.) is to pardon, forgive, or disregard it. *Though the practice is universally outlawed today, in many societies since ancient times (especially among peoples with insufficient food), the killing of a newborn by a parent was socially condoned.*

Chapter 20 *"The Confession"*

For three days Dorothy heard nothing from Oz. These were sad days for the little girl, although her friends were all quite contented. The Scarecrow, thankfully noticing that his constant fear of publicly embarrassing himself—by committing some **grievous**[1] social **faux pas**[2] or grammatical **solecism**[3]—had at last subsided, told everyone that he was **contemplating**[4] **abstruse**[5] theories and

---

[1] **grievous** To refer to an offense (wrongdoing, misdeed, mistake, etc.) as *grievous* is to say that it's atrocious, outrageous, flagrant, dreadful, shameful, etc. Note: The word can also mean "causing or bringing grief or anguish," as in *grievous news,* or "serious, grave, dire," as in *grievous consequences. In his May 1940 "Victory at All Costs" speech (his first address as British Prime Minister), Winston Churchill referred to war with Germany as "an ordeal of the most grievous kind," then went on to say that "without victory there is no survival."*

[2] **faux pas** This phrase (which derives from the French and literally means "false step") describes any (usually social) blunder, error, or mistake (as in manners, conduct, or etiquette). Note: The singular is pronounced *foh-PAH,* and the plural, which is spelled the same, is pronounced *foh-PAHZ. To make sure he didn't commit a faux pas at the fancy tennis club, he yelled "sorry" every time he hit the ball badly, but also yelled "sorry" every time he hit one too well.*

[3] **solecism** An error in grammar or a violation in etiquette is known as a *solecism. Since the late 1800s grammar books have warned students against a solecism known as the dangling modifier, in which (sometimes humorously, but not intentionally so) a phrase that has no subject of its own seems to modify the subject of a following main clause, as in "Flying low, a herd of cattle could be seen."*

[4] **contemplate (contemplating)** To *contemplate* something is to think about it or consider it carefully and at length. *In the classic Christmas film* It's a Wonderful Life *(1946), a failing banker contemplating suicide is saved by a guardian angel.*

[5] **abstruse** If you say that something (a theory, idea, explanation, etc.) is *abstruse,* you mean either that it's difficult to understand or comprehend (it's complex, deep, etc.), or that it can be understood only by a select few (by members of a particular profession, for example). *In college I found calculus so difficult that not only did I not understand the abstruse expressions written on the blackboard [ff(x)dx=g(b)-g(a), for example], but I didn't even know (in general terms) what calculus was—even after the teacher patiently explained that it dealt with "the differentiation and integration of functions of variables."*

248

recondite[1] facts, but that he couldn't say what they were because they were far too **esoteric**[2] for anyone but himself to comprehend. When the Tin Woodman walked about he felt his new heart moving around in his chest, and he told Dorothy he had discovered it to be a kind and **clement**[3] one. The Lion declared he was afraid of nothing on earth and would gladly face a dozen bloodthirsty Kalidahs.

On the fourth day, to Dorothy's great joy, Oz sent for her, and when she entered the Throne Room he greeted her pleasantly. "Sit down, my dear," he said. "The reason I haven't summoned you for the past few days is not because I've been **remiss**[4]; it's just that it

---

[1] **recondite** To describe a fact or other piece of information as *recondite* (usually pronounced with the accent on the first syllable) is to say that it's little known, obscure, hidden. To describe a theory or idea as *recondite* is to say that it's complex and difficult to understand. *In nuclear physics the name "quark" (a hypothetical subatomic particle that supposedly forms the basis of all matter) originated from a recondite line in Irish writer James Joyce's 1939 novel* Finnegan's Wake: *"Three quarks for Muster Mark."*

[2] **esoteric** This word describes things (subjects, references, forms or works of art, philosophies, etc.) that are aimed at or understood by only the members of a select group (who have special knowledge of or special interest in the particular subject in question). *Although Jacob Grimm (with his brother Wilhelm) is best remembered as the author/compiler of the popular Grimm's Fairy Tales (1812-1815), he also wrote treatises on such esoteric subjects as ancient German law and consonants in Indo-European languages.*

[3] **clement** To describe a person (especially one in authority—a judge, for example) as *clement* is to say that he's lenient, compassionate, merciful, humane, forgiving, etc. To describe weather as *clement* is to say that it's mild, pleasant, etc. Note: The noun *clemency* means "an act or instance of being compassionate, merciful, or forgiving." *Although President Gerald Ford denied amnesty (exemption from criminal prosecution) to Vietnam War draft evaders, he did offer clemency to those who were willing to do public service work.*

[4] **remiss** To be *remiss* (in attending to some duty) is to be neglectful, negligent, forgetful, careless, or slow (in carrying it out). *After city police shot and killed an unarmed man, the mayor's critics called him remiss for not immediately phoning the victim's family to express apologies and condolences.*

would have been pointless for me to make meaningless **prognostications**[1]. But now I think I've found a way to get you back to Kansas."

Dorothy felt her heart skip, and she watched him intently. "You see," he continued, "when I came to this country it was in a balloon. You also came through the air, being carried by a cyclone. So I believe the best way to get you back home is through the air. Now, it's quite beyond my **ken**[2] to make a cyclone, but it's certainly within my **bailiwick**[3] to make a balloon."

Starting to feel slightly less like some pathetic **also-ran**[4], Dorothy asked, "How?"

"A balloon," said Oz, envisioning his old circus balloon

---

[1] **prognosticate (prognostications)** To *prognosticate* is to make predictions about the future. *The more than 900 prognostications of French physician and astrologer Nostradamus (which some interpreters claim foretold the Great Fire of London, details of the French Revolution, the rise of Napoleon and Hitler, and World War II) were written in vague language in four-lined rhymed verses in a book entitled* Centuries *(1555).*

[2] **ken** Your *ken* is your range of knowledge, understanding, or perception. *In the song "Sixteen Going on Seventeen" (from Rodgers and Hammerstein's* The Sound of Music*), an inexperienced girl admits, "Totally unprepared am I to face a world of men; timid and shy and scared am I of things beyond my ken."*

[3] **bailiwick** Your *bailiwick* is your specific area of skill, knowledge, training, or study; your field, specialty, etc. *American zoologist Dian Fossey (1932-1985), whose bailiwick was gorillas, urges the preservation of this endangered species in her 1983 book* Gorillas in the Mist.

[4] **also-ran** Technically, an *also-ran* is a horse who doesn't finish among the first three in a race. But the word can be used to refer to anyone who loses any type of competition (a contest, election, race, etc.) or to someone who is generally unsuccessful or untalented. *In 1987 Pulitzer Prize–winning commentator George Will said, "In the 1940s a survey listed the top seven discipline problems in public schools [as] talking, chewing gum, making noise, running in the halls, getting out of turn in line, wearing improper clothes, [and] not putting paper in wastebaskets; a 1980s survey lists these top seven: drug abuse, alcohol abuse, pregnancy, suicide, rape, robbery, [and] assault— arson, gang warfare, and venereal disease are also-rans."*

archetypally[1], "is made of silk, which is coated with a **veneer**[2] of glue to keep the hot air in. I have plenty of silk in the Palace, so it will be no trouble to make the balloon. The only danger is that if the air gets cold the balloon will start to drop and we'll have to **jettison**[3] our supplies. At worst, we'll drop back to the ground and be lost in the desert— a **sobering**[4] thought."

"We?" exclaimed the girl. "Are you going with me?"

---

[1] **archetype (archetypally)** An original pattern or form upon which imitations or variations are modeled is known as an *archetype* (pronounced *ARE-kih-type*). *The New York Times once said that the novels* Frankenstein *(1818) and* Dracula *(1897) were "the archetypes that have influenced all subsequent horror stories."*

[2] **veneer** A *veneer* is a thin outer covering (of a certain material applied to another); a facing, surface treatment, etc. But when the word refers to human behavior it means "an insincere, superficial, or deceptive show (of something)," as in *a veneer of concern. In William Golding's 1954 novel* Lord of the Flies, *English schoolboys stranded on an island revert to savagery, showing, perhaps, that civilization is merely a veneer hiding our natural animal instincts.*

[3] **jettison** To *jettison* something (goods, supplies, provisions, fuel, etc.) is to cast or throw it overboard or off (as from a ship or plane that needs to be lightened or stabilized in an emergency). Informally, the word can be used to denote the throwing away or discarding of anything (a burden, obstacle, difficulty, etc.), as in *they jettisoned the plan.* (By the way, cargo or equipment that has been jettisoned from a ship is known as *jetsam;* however, wreckage that remains afloat after a ship has sunk is known as *flotsam.* The phrase *flotsam and jetsam*— or either of those words alone— can be used informally to mean "discarded odds and ends; junk." The word *flotsam* alone also can be used informally to refer to undesirable people— vagrants, derelicts, bums, lowlifes, etc.) *During the Watergate hearings (1973), in an effort to preserve his Presidency, Richard Nixon jettisoned his top assistants and fired Special Prosecutor Archibald Cox.*

[4] **sober (sobering)** Technically, to describe someone as *sober* is to say that he's not under the influence of alcohol. But the word can also be used to describe someone whose manner is serious, quiet, subdued, composed, reasonable, calm, restrained, controlled, etc. To describe something (an idea, thought, prospect, etc.) as *sobering* is to say that (usually because it's frightening or dangerous) it causes one to become suddenly serious, subdued, quiet, etc. *The investment company's TV commercial made the sobering claim that by the time a newborn reaches college age tuition will cost $200,000 (or some such incredible amount).*

THE WIZARD OF OZ VOCABULARY BUILDER

"Yes, of course," replied Oz. "I'm sick of this ridiculous **mummery**[1] and I'm tired of being a **hypocrite**[2]. And sitting **entrenched**[3], or shall I say **immured**[4], in my Palace day after day is **tantamount**[5] to **languishing**[1] in prison! It gets unbearably boring,

---

[1] **mummery** Technically, a *mummer* is a person who wears a mask or elaborate disguise (as at festive holidays), and *mummery* is a performance (pantomime, for example) by a *mummer*. But any kind of display, performance, or ceremony regarded as false, insincere, or ineffective can be referred to as *mummery*. *After pointing out that most top-level business executives were white men, the congressman referred to the existing laws that prohibit discrimination in employment as "the mummery of equal opportunity."*

[2] **hypocrite** A *hypocrite* (pronounced *HIP-uh-krit*) is a person who claims or pretends to have certain (usually desirable) qualities or beliefs he doesn't actually possess or a person whose actions contradict his statements; a deceiver; a phony. The noun *hypocrisy* refers to the practice of (or an instance of) such falseness. *To people who accused him of being conceited and domineering, architect Frank Lloyd Wright (1869-1959) once explained, "Early in life I had to choose between honest arrogance and hypocritical humility [modesty]; I chose honest arrogance and have seen no occasion to change."*

[3] **entrench (entrenched)** Technically, to *entrench* yourself is to dig a ditch or trench around yourself (for protective purposes, as in a war). But when people say someone (or something) is *entrenched* (in something), they mean he's in a position of strength or firm protection, as in *entrenched in his castle*, or *entrenched behind the arm of the law*. *Though Northern states began abolishing slavery as early as 1774 (in Rhode Island), in the South, where the institution was more deeply entrenched, slaveholding continued until the passage of the 13th Amendment (1865).*

[4] **immure (immured)** To *immure* someone (or something) is to enclose him within (or as if within) walls, to confine or imprison him, or to entomb him in a wall. *After a tremor in his hand prevented him from writing, Nobel Prize–winning playwright Eugene O'Neill's (1888-1953) health deteriorated and he spent the last two years of his life in isolation, immured in a Boston hotel.*

[5] **tantamount** If you say that something is *tantamount* to something else, you mean that the two things are equal or equivalent to such an extent that they are practically identical (in value, impact, effect, significance, force, etc.). *Some U.S. states have declared that if a man and woman live together for a certain period of time, their union can be treated as tantamount to a marriage for legal purposes.*

and the **ennui**[2] makes me **restive**[3]."

He paused for a while with his eyes closed, then continued **candidly**[4], "Do you know how I really spend my time? I try to **luxuriate**[5] in my leisure, but it's a **farce**[1]. Mostly I sit alone,

---

[1] **languish (languishing)** To *languish* is to lose strength or vitality (as from living in miserable or depressing conditions, or from remaining neglected or unattended); to weaken, decline, deteriorate, fade, droop, waste away, etc. *According to news correspondent Shana Alexander's 1985 book* Nutcracker, *"Until quite recently dance in America was the ragged Cinderella of the arts; [Greek goddess of dancing] Terpsichore was condemned to the chimney corner, and there she languished until the early 1930s."*

[2] **ennui** *Ennui* (pronounced *ahn-WEE*) is boredom, or a feeling of weariness or dissatisfaction (sometimes depression) resulting from boredom or overindulgence (in something). *Short story writer O. Henry (whose works include the still-popular "The Gift of the Magi" and "The Ransom of Red Chief") first began writing to escape the ennui of prison life (in 1898 he was jailed for embezzling funds from a bank).*

[3] **restive** This is a difficult word because it looks as if it may mean the opposite of what it really does. If you're *restive*, it doesn't mean that you're restful; rather, you're restless, impatient, anxious, uneasy, fidgety, skittish, antsy, etc. (when confined or restricted). *After being appointed (1771) concertmaster to the archbishop of Salzburg, teenaged Austrian composer/performer Wolfgang Amadeus Mozart grew restive and left to seek his fortune in Vienna.*

[4] **candid (candidly)** To describe a statement or opinion as *candid* is to say that it's frank, forthright, blunt, honest, sincere, direct, up front, free-spoken, etc. (it's free of pretense or disguise). A photo described as *candid* is one in which the subject is unposed, unrehearsed, unaware, etc. (and as such is also honest and free of pretense). *In his August 1973 address to the nation, explaining why he refused to surrender his oval office "Watergate" tapes, President Richard Nixon said, "If I were to make public these tapes, containing blunt and candid remarks on many different subjects, the confidentiality of the office of the President would always be suspect."*

[5] **luxuriate** To *luxuriate* is to unrestrainedly indulge yourself or take pleasure or delight (in something enjoyable or luxurious). *While some celebrities hide from the public (*Catcher in the Rye *author J. D. Salinger, for example), others luxuriate in the admiration of their fans (former President Bill Clinton, for example).*

jumping back and forth between painting watercolor landscapes—with as much dash and **verve**[2] as I can muster, which, in spite of my best efforts to **juxtapose**[3] light and shade, isn't really very much—and clumsily playing popular melodies on my flute. When I tire of one, I try the other. Back and forth, back and forth, like an **infernal**[4] Ping-Pong ball. I'm really just a hopeless **dilettante**[5], and I

---

[1] **farce** Technically, a *farce* is a humorous play (or other dramatic work) whose comic appeal depends upon exaggerated situations and characters (TV comedies such as *I Love Lucy* and *The Honeymooners* are examples of *farce*). But usually when people refer to something (other than a play) as a *farce*, they mean it's a ridiculous, false, empty, or inferior version (of something). *After his horse came in last he said, "The race was a farce; it was fixed from the beginning."*

[2] **verve** If something (an artistic work or a person, for example) has *verve*, it has vitality, energy, spirit, liveliness, etc. *The large-nosed hero of (Edmond Rostand's 1897 French play)* Cyrano de Bergerac *uses his wit and verve to rise above his facial defect.*

[3] **juxtapose** To *juxtapose* two or more things is to set them close together or side by side for the purpose of comparing them, contrasting them, showing how they enhance each other, showing how they form a strange combination, etc. *In the 1970 film* M*A*S*H, *scenes of bloodshed and death are juxtaposed with scenes of sarcasm and high jinks.*

[4] **infernal** Technically, to describe something as *infernal* is to say that it's hellish or that it pertains to hell. But informally, the word can be used to describe anything dreadful, sinister, horrible, outrageous, etc. *In his opening statement at the Nazi war crimes trials (at Nuremberg, Germany, December 1946), prosecutor Telford Taylor said, "These defendants and others turned Germany into an infernal combination of a lunatic asylum and a charnel house [building where bones or bodies of the dead are placed]."*

[5] **dilettante** A *dilettante* is a person who takes up a subject or activity in an amateurish, superficial way; a dabbler (as distinguished from an expert or professional). *Many sensational news videotapes (the 1991 beating of black motorist Rodney King by four white Los Angeles policemen, for example) were actually shot by amateur videographers— dilettantes who just happened to be near the scene with camera in hand.*

sometimes embarrass myself with my **tyronic**[1] blunders. It's **ironic**[2], actually, because when I played the flute as a boy, my mother, who was something of a **connoisseur**[3] of music, and my teacher, the old **dowager**[4] who lived in the large but **dowdy**[5] house next-door, each referred to me, **patronizingly**[6], I now realize, as

---

[1] **tyro (tyronic)** To refer to someone as a *tyro* is to say that he's a beginner or newcomer (in learning something). *The FCC (Federal Communications Commission) issues six classes of licenses to ham radio operators; the one most favored by tyros is the Technician license (the only one that doesn't require knowledge of Morse code).*

[2] **ironic** If you refer to an outcome of events as *ironic*, you mean that it's (sometimes humorously) contradictory to the expected or anticipated outcome (especially when it involves a twist of fate or improbable coincidence). *In O. Henry's short story "The Gift of the Magi" (1906), at Christmastime a poor young man sells his pocket watch to buy a set of combs for his wife's beautiful long hair; ironically, at the same time she cuts off her hair and sells it to buy him a chain for his watch.*

[3] **connoisseur** A person with expert knowledge or discriminating taste, especially in the fine arts or in food and drink, is known as a *connoisseur*. *In 1963 Lord Champion of Pontypridd, speaking of fish and chips wrapped in newspapers, sarcastically said, "I am such a great connoisseur that I can tell the difference between the tang of the Beaverbrook Daily Express and the mellow flavor of the Times."*

[4] **dowager** Technically, a *dowager* is a widow with money or property derived from her deceased husband. But the word can be used to refer to any rich or important (especially widowed) older woman. *In 1963 journalist Tom Wolfe, speaking of New York City women meeting for lunch, said, "On their way into the Edwardian Room of the Plaza Hotel they all had that sort of dutiful, forward-tilted gait [manner of walking] that East Side dowagers get after 20 years of walking small dogs up and down Park Avenue."*

[5] **dowdy** If something (a room, a person's clothing, etc.) is *dowdy*, it's not stylish; it's frumpy, old-fashioned, tasteless, shabby, etc. *In 1987, speaking of her heavy makeup and of being the wife of TV evangelist Jim Bakker, Tammy Faye Bakker said, "You don't have to be dowdy to be a Christian."*

[6] **patronize (patronizingly)** To *patronize* someone is to offensively talk down to him, treat him younger that he is, treat him as a child, etc. *I felt my dentist was patronizing me by referring to that thing that sucks up your saliva as "Mr. Thirsty"; but I couldn't protest because Mr. Thirsty was in my mouth.* Note: To *patronize* a business is to economically support it (see *patron*).

'my **precocious**[1] little **prodigy**[2]'! For a long time I didn't know how badly I played, and I actually considered music my **métier**[3]! I even considered taking up a second instrument, the cello, because I loved its **sonorous**[4] tone, but it just seemed too heavy to carry around.

"Other than that, I usually sit alone in my library, which is **contiguous**[5] to the Throne Room." He gestured in its general direction. "I'm an **avid**[6] reader, you know. Even as a boy, whenever I wasn't **tooling**[7] around the neighborhood on my shiny, green bicycle, I spent most of my time reading— especially the many fairy

---

[1] **precocious** To refer to a child as *precocious* is to say that he's mature, mentally developed, or talented at a very early age. *A precocious child, actress Shirley Temple displayed a talent for singing and dancing by the age of six.*

[2] **prodigy** A young person, especially a child, with extraordinary talent or ability is known as a *prodigy*. *A child prodigy, Wolfgang Amadeus Mozart (1756–1791) began composing music before the age of five.*

[3] **métier** Your *métier* is your field of work or expertise; your specialty or profession; your forte; your "thing." *Some say that Harry Houdini's métier wasn't magic, but showmanship.*

[4] **sonorous** This word describes tones or sounds that are full, deep, and rich. *A "gong" is a round, metallic percussion instrument that, when struck with a padded mallet, produces a sonorous, reverberating tone.*

[5] **contiguous** When places share a border or are next to each other (that is, they are adjacent, neighboring, adjoining, touching, etc.), they are said to be *contiguous* (as in *Kansas and Nebraska are contiguous*). *People in Alaska often refer to the 48 contiguous U.S. states as "the Lower 48."*

[6] **avid** If you're *avid* about something (an activity, for example), you're keenly interested in it or enthusiastic about it; you (sometimes greedily) crave it. *The author of some 60 western adventure stories (including 1912's* Riders of the Purple Sage*), former dentist Zane Grey (1872–1939) was an avid outdoorsman who also wrote nonfiction works on hunting and fishing.*

[7] **tool (tooling)** To *tool* a car (or other vehicle) is to drive (or ride in) it. *In the 1973 film* American Graffiti, *teenagers tool around the streets of a 1962 northern California town the night before they're scheduled to leave for college.*

THE WIZARD OF OZ VOCABULARY BUILDER

tales by those **prolific**[1] **Teutonic**[2] masters, the brothers Grimm, even though they gave me disturbing nightmares of **wispy**[3] **wraiths**[4] and wicked witches." He reflected a moment, then said, "Maybe that's why even today—" He stopped in mid-sentence with a slightly frightened look in his eyes. He paused again and, having composed himself, continued, "Today my tastes in reading are **eclectic**[5], and my library is a **mélange**[1] of every type of book

---

[1] **prolific** One who is *prolific* is productive; he produces large quantities (of something), as in *prolific author, prolific composer,* etc. *In May 1998 the* Washington Post *reported, "The police department's most prolific ticket writer was ordered to pay $5,000 to a heart surgeon who said he was put in a headlock and suffered a broken hand after being stopped for speeding; a jury ruled that [the officer], a 24-year veteran who writes 3,000 tickets a year, had gone too far after ticketing [the driver] for going 53 mph in a 40-mph zone."*

[2] **Teutonic** To refer to a person as *Teutonic* is to say that he's German (or northern European); to refer to a thing (language, art, etc.) as *Teutonic* is to say that it's characteristic of Germany or Germans; it's Germanic. *Johannes Brahms' (1833–1897) love of German folk song gave his music a Teutonic character.*

[3] **wispy** This word is used to describe things that are made up of faint or thin fragments or streaks (clouds or smoke, for example), or that are light, delicate, flimsy, airy, gauzy, lacy, threadlike, fragile, etc. *In science class we learned that "mare's tale" is the name for both a long, narrow, wispy cirrus cloud and a certain aquatic plant that rises about two feet above the water (each of which resembles a horse's tail).*

[4] **wraith (wraiths)** A *wraith* is a ghost (or anything shadowy and insubstantial). *Legend has it that the snowy wraiths that swirl across the dunes of New Mexico's White Sands National Monument are Spanish maidens searching for their lost lovers (but scientists know that they're really wind-carried crystals of water and gypsum).*

[5] **eclectic** If something (a collection or someone's taste or style, for example) is *eclectic,* it's made up of elements from a variety of sources; it's not uniform. *Canadian singer/songwriter Joni Mitchell, whose music is an eclectic mix of folk, jazz, rock, pop, and pre–rock era ballads, was inducted into the Rock and Roll Hall of Fame in 1997.*

imaginable. I try to give equal consideration to **genres**[2] as **disparate**[3] as **Gothic**[4] romance and science fiction—though I usually find the **former**[5] too **florid**[6] and **melodramatic**[1] and the

---

[1] **mélange** A *mélange* is a mixture, especially a confused collection of various items; a hodgepodge, mixed bag, etc. *Nobel Prize-winning German writer Thomas Mann's complex fiction (which includes 1924's* The Magic Mountain*) is a mélange of elements: psychology, philosophy, mythology, and politics.*

[2] **genre (genres)** A particular category (or class, type, style, etc.) of artistic endeavor (music, literature, film, etc.) is known as a *genre*. *Writer/director Mel Brooks' movies are often parodies of popular film genres, such as the western (1974's* Blazing Saddles*), horror (1975's* Young Frankenstein*), suspense (1977's* High Anxiety*), and space fantasy (1987's* Spaceballs*).*

[3] **disparate** If you say that two or more things are *disparate*, you mean that they're fundamentally different (in kind) and distinct; they are unalike, dissimilar, separate, etc. *New Orleans' Creole cuisine (cooking) is a unique blend of disparate influences: French, Spanish, African, and Native American.*

[4] **Gothic** A *Gothic* (or *gothic*) novel—Charlotte Brontë's *Jane Eyre* (1847), for example—is one set among a decaying setting (a ruined castle, for example) and characterized by an atmosphere of gloominess, mystery, and evil. Note: The word also refers to a style of European architecture prevalent during the Middle Ages, characterized by slender towers, pointed arches, and high ceilings (as Paris's Cathedral of Notre Dame). *In 1980 Pulitzer Prize-winning author/commentator Anna Quindlen, speaking of Belvedere Castle (in New York City's Central Park), said, "It looms above the landscape like the cover drawing on a Gothic novel—a true castle in the air."*

[5] **former** When two people or things have been mentioned, the first-mentioned is referred to as the *former* (and the second-mentioned is the *latter*). *In the 1950s singer Frank Sinatra starred in the films* From Here to Eternity *and* Guys and Dolls; *he won an Academy Award for his performance in the former.*

[6] **florid** To describe something (language, music, architecture, etc.) as *florid* is to say that it's flowery, showy, ornamental, fancy, intricate, etc. *While in the 1970s Linda Ronstadt specialized in singing simple country/rock songs, in 1981 she made her debut on Broadway singing the florid melodies of Gilbert and Sullivan's* Pirates of Penzance.

THE WIZARD OF OZ VOCABULARY BUILDER

latter[2] too **dry**[3] and **didactically**[4] **allegorical**[5]. But I confess I have a real **predilection**[6] for murder mysteries, and I've devoured entire **oeuvres**[7] of mystery writers both **renowned**[1] and obscure. I like

---

[1] **melodrama (melodramatic)** A *melodrama* is an intense, overly dramatic story; that is, it's characterized by exaggerated emotions and conflicts (as a TV soap opera, for example). To refer to something (a situation, for example) as *melodramatic* is to say that it has the emotional intensity and appeal of *melodrama*, or that its emotions are exaggerated or false. *In 1962 Abigail Van Buren ("Dear Abby") referred to the mother-in-law as the "queen of the melodrama when her acts of self-sacrifice go unnoticed, [whose] banner is the tear-stained hanky."*

[2] **latter** When two people or things have been mentioned, the second-mentioned is referred to as the *latter* (and the first-mentioned is the *former*). *Of Oliver Wendell Holmes (1809–1894) and Oliver Wendell Holmes, Jr. (1841–1935), the latter was the Supreme Court justice (the former, his father, was the essayist and poet who wrote "Old Ironsides").*

[3] **dry** To refer to an artistic endeavor (writing, for example) as *dry* is to say that it lacks emotion (tenderness, warmth, etc.); it's severe, minimal, sterile, cold, unadorned, stark, etc. *Because we found Ernest Hemingway's writing kind of dry (with his short sentences and limited use of adjectives and adverbs), we were surprised to learn he'd won the Nobel Prize for literature in 1954.*

[4] **didactic (didactically)** If a person (or his writing) is *didactic*, he tends to (sometimes excessively) teach, lecture, or moralize. *Greek storyteller Aesop (sixth century B.C.) is known for his didactic animal fables (including "The Tortoise and the Hare," which teaches that steady effort leads to success).*

[5] **allegory (allegorical)** An *allegory* is a story in which the literal characters and events presented actually symbolize or represent some deeper abstract idea or principle. *George Orwell's 1945 novel* Animal Farm, *which on the surface is about animals who take over a farm, is an allegory attacking Stalinism.*

[6] **predilection** A *predilection* is a predisposition to favor a particular thing; a partiality, leaning, or inclination (toward something). *Composer Johann Strauss, Jr., (1825–1899) had a predilection for Viennese waltzes; he composed several hundred of them, including "The Blue Danube."*

[7] **oeuvre (oeuvres)** The complete works of a painter, writer, or composer, considered as a whole, is known as his *oeuvre* (after the French word for *work*). *Only 10 of Emily Dickinson's (1830–1886) poems were published during her lifetime— it wasn't until 1955 that her entire oeuvre of 1,775 poems appeared.*

them because I can't resist a good plot and because they're so superficial and obvious—they're never **tendentious**[2], nor do they try to **posit**[3] any complex moral **dilemmas**[4] or other **profundities**[5] under hazy layers of meaning. By the way, I don't know why, but I especially prefer stories that feature an **eccentric**[6], upper-class, male

---

[1] **renown (renowned)** Widespread fame, glory, celebrity, etc., is known as *renown*. As an adjective, *renowned* means "widely known, famous, celebrated, etc." Note: Be careful to spell the word without a *k* (*renown*, not *reknown*). *During his lifetime playwright and short story writer Anton Chekhov (1860–1904) was widely known in his native Russia; it wasn't until the 1920s, when his stories were translated into other languages, that he gained international renown.*

[2] **tendentious** To refer to something (a novel or newspaper article, for example) as *tendentious* is to say that it has a slanted point of view; that is, it shows a definite tendency or leaning. *Because political cartoons are tendentious by nature, they generally appear on the editorial pages of newspapers.*

[3] **posit** To *posit* something (an idea, for example) is to put it forth (state it) as a principle to be taken for granted without proof or as a theory to be considered or studied. *The Declaration of Independence posits that "all men are created equal."*

[4] **dilemma (dilemmas)** Technically, a *dilemma* is a situation or problem that requires making a difficult choice between two (sometimes undesirable) alternatives; but the word often is used informally to refer to any type of problematic situation. *In 1979 Wisconsin seminary professor Robert Cooper said, "There is no dilemma compared with that of the deep-sea diver who hears the message from the ship above, 'Come up at once; we are sinking.'"*

[5] **profundity (profundities)** The quality or an instance of (a person) being *profound* (penetrating, intellectual, wise, deep) is known as *profundity*. And matters that are considered *profound* (significant, far-reaching, intense, important, deep, etc.) are known as *profundities*. *A 1986 Newsweek magazine article suggested that the stark, rural scenes in the paintings of (20th-century realistic American artist) Andrew Wyeth contain "a mood of gloom or longing that people mistake for profundity."*

[6] **eccentric** To describe a person (or his behavior) as *eccentric* is to say that he's peculiar, odd, strange, bizarre, weird, offbeat, wacky, nutty, etc. To describe an object as *eccentric* is to say that it deviates from a recognized standard or pattern; it's unconventional, irregular, unorthodox, etc. *In 1984 Smithsonian magazine said, "A toe shoe is as eccentric as the ballerina who wears it; their marriage is a commitment."*

detective. But the truth is that the **ephemeral**[1] pleasures I get from reading these **trifles**[2] really don't add up to much—unless you count the guilt I sometimes feel for having **squandered**[3] my time." He paused and looked at Dorothy, then continued, "In a fit of ambition, I once tried to write a murder mystery myself, but soon discovered that— well, let's just say that I posed no immediate threat to the literary **elite**[4]. I stopped after only a few pages when I realized that the slangy **vernacular**[5] I tried to use sounded forced

---

[1] **ephemeral** If you say that something is *ephemeral*, you mean that it lasts or exists for only a very short time; it's fleeting, short-lived, momentary, brief, temporary, etc. *In 1961 Pulitzer Prize–winning playwright and novelist Thornton Wilder (1897–1975) said, "I am not interested in the ephemeral— such subjects as the adulteries [extramarital affairs] of dentists; I am interested in those things that repeat and repeat and repeat in the lives of the millions."*

[2] **trifle (trifles)** Anything considered unimportant, trivial, or cheap, or any work (literary, musical, or artistic) perceived as having no merit or lasting value can be referred to as a *trifle*. *A 1984* Time *magazine article, speaking of writers across America typing away at kitchen tables in the hope of becoming hugely successful, said, "Who cares if the roast burns or the dog sheds on the couch— such trifles must wait their turn behind dreams of hitting it big."*

[3] **squander (squandered)** To *squander* something (money, time, etc.) is to waste or misuse it. *In 1979 Frederick Akuffo, ousted chief of state of (the African country of) Ghana, was charged with squandering public funds and executed.*

[4] **elite** As a noun, the *elite* (of a group or class of people) are those at the highest level of skill in a certain category (as in *basketball's elite*), or at the highest social level (as in *Manhattan's elite*). As an adjective the word means "indicative of the best or most select" (as in *an elite private school*). *At the 1958 Interzonal tournament in (the Balkan country of) Slovenia, 15-year-old Bobby Fischer secured a permanent place among the world's chess elite as the all-time youngest world championship candidate.*

[5] **vernacular** As a noun, *vernacular* is the ordinary, everyday language of a people or place (as opposed to literary or scholarly language), or the specialized language of a profession or group. As an adjective, the word means "using or expressed in everyday language." *In the 1960s the Roman Catholic church substituted the use of vernacular languages for Latin in the Mass.*

and that I didn't have my own style— only an **ungainly**[1] **pastiche**[2] of other writers' styles. And true artistry, as you know, **transcends**[3] mere imitation; true artistry is that rare **confluence**[4] of originality, style, and technique. Anyway, I keep my mystery collection stored behind the lovely leather-bound **tomes**[5] on the top shelf of my bookcase— all, that is, except my prized possession, the only

---

[1] **ungainly** To refer to something as *ungainly* is to say that it's noticeably ungraceful, awkward, clumsy, etc. *In Hans Christian Andersen's fairy tale "The Ugly Duckling," an ugly, ungainly young bird in a family of ducks grows into a beautiful, graceful swan.*

[2] **pastiche** A literary, musical, or artistic work comprised of (often unrelated) elements or fragments borrowed from various sources is known as a *pastiche*. *Whereas most 20th-century musicals begin with an overture (an instrumental pastiche of the work's principle songs), Rodgers and Hammerstein's Carousel (1945) opens with an independent instrumental theme entitled "The Carousel Waltz."*

[3] **transcend (transcends)** To *transcend* something (an aspect of human experience, for example) is to greatly go beyond or rise above the ordinary limits of it; to exceed or surpass it. *In 1959 an advertisement for the British Travel Association read, "A cathedral transcends the noblest single work of art— it is a pinnacle [high point] of faith and [an] act of centuries; it is an offering of human hands as close to Abraham as it is to Bach."*

[4] **confluence** A flowing or meeting together of two or more things (especially rivers) is known as a *confluence*. Note: When speaking of rivers, the word also denotes the place of junction or the new body of water so formed. *The historic town of Harpers Ferry (where in 1859 abolitionist John Brown raided the federal arsenal in an unsuccessful attempt to liberate Southern slaves), is located in the northeast corner of West Virginia, at the confluence of the Potomac and Shenandoah rivers.*

[5] **tome (tomes)** A *tome* is a book, especially a thick, large, heavy, or scholarly one. *In 1986 the New York Times said that the books most often stolen from the New York Public Library were J. D. Salinger's 1951 novel The Catcher in the Rye, Truman Capote's 1958 novella Breakfast at Tiffany's, and tomes detailing the lives of (20th-century Spanish painter) Joan Miró and (16th-centruy Italian painter and sculptor) Michelangelo.*

THE WIZARD OF OZ VOCABULARY BUILDER

extant[1] copy of *Munchkin Murder Omnibus*[2], which I keep locked in my safe. Did you know that practically every **seminal**[3] figure is represented in the **voluminous**[4] writings of that anthology?" Dorothy wasn't sure if he expected her to answer, but before she could, he continued, "You know, people believe I'm a man of great **erudition**[5], a **consummate**[1] scholar— and I probably could've been,

---

[1] **extant** If you say that something (an old book or painting, for example) is *extant* (usually pronounced with the accent on the first syllable), you mean that it still exists; that is, it hasn't been destroyed, lost, etc. Note: If you say that a particular animal species is *extant*, you mean that it exists; it's not extinct. *The Gutenberg Bible (1455), of which fewer that 50 copies are extant, was the first book printed from movable type.*

[2] **omnibus** As a noun, an *omnibus* is a printed collection of various works of a single author (or single theme); an anthology. As an adjective, *omnibus* means "containing or dealing with numerous items or objects at the same time." *In 1854 reformer and feminist Elizabeth Cady Stanton addressed the New York legislature on an omnibus women's rights bill.*

[3] **seminal** This word is used to describe people or things (artistic or scientific works, for example) that are highly original or creative and that serve as a starting point for further development by others. *T. R. Reid's 1985 book* The Chip *says of the development of the microchip, "It was a seminal event of postwar science— one of those rare demonstrations that changes everything."*

[4] **voluminous** When speaking of writing, *voluminous* means "lengthy; sufficient to fill a large volume." When speaking of objects, the word means "very large (in size, number, fullness, extent, etc.)," as in *a voluminous basket. American artist and naturalist John J. Audubon's realistic bird drawings and paintings were printed in his* Birds of America *between 1827 and 1838; his voluminous field notes, however, were published in a separate, five-volume set entitled* Ornithological Biography *(1831– 1839).*

[5] **erudite (erudition)** To refer to a person (a professor, for example) as *erudite* is to say that he has great learning; that is, he's well-trained, scholarly, educated, well-read, well-informed, etc. The noun is *erudition. In the 1991 film* Silence of the Lambs, *Welsh actor Anthony Hopkins plays Hannibal Lecter, an erudite but psychopathic psychiatrist.*

if only I'd been more selective in my reading... if only I'd **winnowed**[2] out the trash. After all, for years my library, the largest **repository**[3] of information and knowledge in all of Oz, has been the **virtual**[4] **hub**[5] of my existence.

"Oh, and let's not forget about all the time I spend eating... or

---

[1] **consummate** As an adjective, this word means "complete, perfect," as in *consummate beauty*, or "supremely skilled or accomplished (in some area)," as in *a consummate actor. After seeing John F. Kennedy's first televised press conference (January 1961),* New York Times *columnist Russell Baker wrote that the President was "a new star with a tremendous national appeal" and had "the skill of a consummate showman."*

[2] **winnow (winnowed)** To *winnow* something is to selectively separate out (get rid of) the bad parts (impurities, worthless items, etc.) from the good. *When pretty, petite, 39-year-old Carol (who likes romantic dinners and long walks on the beach) received over a hundred written responses to her personal ad, she began sorting them by winnowing out any envelopes addressed in crayon or that had a federal penitentiary as a return address.*

[3] **repository** A place (warehouse, vault, storeroom, bank, lost-and-found, reservoir, library, museum, etc.) where things are kept for safekeeping or storage is called a *repository. Established in 1934 by an act of Congress, the National Archives (Washington, D.C.) is the official repository for U.S. federal government records (including the Declaration of Independence, the Constitution, and the Bill of Rights).*

[4] **virtual** To refer to something as *virtual* is to say that in actuality it's not existent or true, but that in effect or in essence it is (that is, it might as well exist or be true because it's so close to existing or being true), as in *the race ended in a virtual tie.* The word is also used to mean "figurative" (as opposed to "literal") as in *a virtual witch-hunt,* a *virtual explosion of diet books,* etc. *In the 1990s (computer software giant) Microsoft achieved a virtual monopoly within the computer operating system industry, raising the question of antitrust law violation.*

[5] **hub** The physical center of something (a wheel or fan, for example) or the figurative center of something (an area of activity or interest, for example) is known as a *hub. Second-century Egyptian astronomer Ptolemy believed that the stars and planets revolved in circular orbits around a motionless, central Earth, whereas 16th-century Polish astronomer Copernicus believed that they revolved around the Sun (but today many New Yorkers insist that Times Square is the actual hub of the universe).*

shall I say **gormandizing**[1]. Now, there's one **endeavor**[2] in which I'm no **novice**[3]!" He winked at her, then continued, "If I want to, I can **gorge**[4] myself with nothing but **epicurean**[5] delicacies— one of the **perks**[6] of this **cushy**[1] **sinecure**[2]. I tried that for a while but

---

[1] **gormandize (gormandizing)** To *gormandize* is to eat excessively or greedily; to binge, feast, "pig out," etc. Note: A *glutton* is a person who *gormandizes*, and a *gourmand* is either a glutton or a gourmet (someone with refined taste in food), or both. *In 1979 an article in the* New York Times *said, "The mere fact of an undiscovered restaurant, in a city where gourmands travel in [hungry] packs, creates an excitement unrelated to the quality of the [food]."*

[2] **endeavor** An *endeavor* is an earnest, conscientious attempt or effort at something (as in *artistic endeavors, political endeavors,* etc.); an undertaking, a venture, etc. *Physicist Albert Einstein (1879–1955) once philosophically said, "Concern for man and his fate must always form the chief interest of all technical endeavors; never forget this in the midst of your diagrams and equations."* Note: As a verb, the word is a rather formal-sounding synonym for *try* or *attempt*, as when President Franklin D. Roosevelt, in his first inaugural address (1933) said, "We must endeavor to provide a better use of the land."

[3] **novice** A *novice* is a person who is new to a particular field or activity; a beginner, learner, amateur, etc. *In 1967 a computer language called BASIC (Beginners All-purpose Symbolic Instruction Code) was developed to give computer novices an easy-to-understand programming tool.*

[4] **gorge** To *gorge* yourself is to stuff yourself (with food); to overeat. *In 1986, speaking of former first lady of the Philippines Imelda Marcos,* Newsweek *magazine said, "Enriched beyond the dreams of any normal person's [greed], she accumulated possessions with a single-minded lust that calls to mind those ancient Romans who gorged themselves, then vomited so they could gorge again."*

[5] **epicure (epicurean)** An *epicure* is a person with refined or cultivated taste (especially in food and drink). To describe something (a food, for example) as *epicurean* is to say that it's fit or suitable for an epicure. *Because of the epicurean appeal of European sole, American flounder is often marketed as sole.*

[6] **perk (perks)** Benefits given to an employee in addition to his normal salary (such as free or discounted merchandise, use of a company car, paid vacations, etc.) are known as *perquisites*— or, to use the more common, shortened version, *perks. Established in 1900 in New York City, the International Ladies' Garment Workers' Union was one of the first U.S. unions to include such perks as health insurance and pensions in its contracts with employers.*

quickly became **jaded**[3]. The truth is, my tastes are much more **provincial**[4] than they are **patrician**[5]. What I really long for—if I had my **druthers**[6]—is a nice stuffed cabbage like my mother used

---

[1] **cushy** To refer to a job as *cushy* is to say that it's easy, pleasant, comfortable, makes few demands, etc. Note: The word is rather informal, even slangy. *So that they could earn some pocket money, the members of the college football team were given cushy part-time jobs—such as watering the athletic field (which had automatic sprinklers!).*

[2] **sinecure** A *sinecure* is a job or position that requires little or no work but that provides a salary. *In 1985 the U.S. Congress created the post of U.S. poet laureate; the holder of this sinecure is not required to write any poems, but he's asked to deliver a lecture in the fall and a poetry reading in the spring.*

[3] **jaded** If you've become *jaded* with something, then (as a result of overuse of it, overexposure to it, or overindulgence in it) you've become dulled to it; that is, you're no longer moved by it, enthusiastic about it, or interested in it. *Jaded with sitcoms and crime dramas, TV audiences in 2000 turned to the reality series* Survivor, *in which contestants competed for a million dollars by living in the wild.*

[4] **provincial** If you say that someone's tastes or views are *provincial,* you mean that they're simple, unsophisticated, unpolished, unfashionable, etc., or that they're narrow, limited, etc. To describe a place as *provincial* is to say that it's rural, rustic, etc., or that its people have unsophisticated tastes or narrow viewpoints. *In 1956 poet Phyllis McGinley said, "The East is a montage—it is old and it is young; very green in summer, very white in winter; gregarious [sociable], withdrawn; and at once both sophisticated and provincial."*

[5] **patrician** As a noun, a *patrician* is a person of high social rank with refined manners and taste; an aristocrat. As an adjective, the word describes anything befitting or characteristic of such a person. *Before she became Princess of Monaco (1956), actress Grace Kelly's beauty and patrician bearing were successfully exploited by director Alfred Hitchcock in such thrillers as* Dial M for Murder *(1954) and* Rear Window *(1954).*

[6] **druthers** This word is usually heard in the phrase "if I had my druthers," which means "if I had my way (choice, preference, etc.)." *Aviator Charles Lindbergh (who in 1927 made the first solo transatlantic flight) once said that if he had his druthers, he'd "rather have birds than airplanes."*

to make— with a little **dollop**[1] of **piquant**[2] horseradish. She served it at Thanksgiving, and, with its aroma **permeating**[3] the entire house, it was a **perennial**[4] source of joy." He sniffed as if trying to detect the aroma. "Can you smell it? Just telling you about this miracle of **culinary**[5] art lets me experience it **vicariously**[6]." He

---

[1] **dollop** A *dollop* of something (a semi-liquid food, for example) is a small portion or quantity of it; a lump or blob of it, as in *a baked potato with a dollop of sour cream. According to the* Los Angeles Times, *Tammy Faye Bakker's eyelashes are permanent, but they're "augmented by generous dollops of L'Oreal mascara."*

[2] **piquant** When this word describes food, it means "pleasantly tart or spicy"; when it refers to people (their writing, speech, wit, smiles, etc.) it means "appealingly or agreeably provocative, stimulating, interesting, etc." *In 1997 the* Los Angeles Times *said that "Louisiana politics is a lot like a bowl of gumbo, or a pot of jambalaya, or a bottle of Tabasco— piquant and pungent and simmering with Cajun intrigue."*

[3] **permeate (permeating)** When one thing (a smell, color, emotion, etc.) *permeates* another (a place, fabric, work of art, etc.), the first flows or spreads throughout the second, completely saturating or penetrating it. *The Blue Grotto (a cavern on the island of Capri, Italy) is so named because of the unusual blue light that permeates it.*

[4] **perennial** To refer to something as *perennial* is to say that it recurs (or seems to recur) each year, as in *the perennial performance of Handel's Messiah,* or simply that it endures or continues year after year, as in *a perennial favorite. In 1985* Time *magazine said that "tooth decay was a perennial national problem that meant a mouthful of silver for patients, and for dentists a pocketful of gold."*

[5] **culinary** This word means "pertaining to cooking or the kitchen," as in *culinary* delights, *culinary* techniques, *culinary* wares, etc. *Culinary expert and TV personality Julia Child once said, "I was 32 when I started cooking; up until then, I just ate."*

[6] **vicarious (vicariously)** To experience something (an emotion, a thrill, etc.) *vicariously* is to experience it through another person (by sharing that person's emotions or by imagining what it would feel like if you were that person). For example, if you feel excited because your daughter is going to her high school prom, your excitement is *vicarious* (felt or experienced through your daughter). *From comic books to TV series to feature films, readers and viewers (perhaps fantasizing about ultimate power for themselves) participate vicariously in the adventures of Superman as he uses his flying ability, super strength, and X-ray vision to keep America safe.*

winked again, then continued, "I know you're thinking that roast turkey with stuffing is the **quintessential**[1] holiday fare, and of course you're right—but to each his own." Dorothy realized that she *was* thinking that, but didn't say anything. "And for dessert," he continued, "we always had lots of chocolate—my one **vice**[2]. Even now I eat way too much of it. I try to give it up **sporadically**[3], but I'm too much of a **recidivist**[4]. I think it must contain some **subliminal**[5] pleasure-producing ingredient! Anyway, then five

---

[1] **quintessential** To refer to something as *quintessential* is to say that it represents the most typical or perfect example of something. *Although other actors have successfully played the role, most film critics agree that Sean Connery was the quintessential (fictional British secret service agent) James Bond.*

[2] **vice** A bad (often immoral, degrading, illegal, or evil) habit or practice (such as gambling, drinking, womanizing, etc.) is known as a *vice*. The word is also used somewhat sarcastically to refer to a minor fault (habitually eating candy or reading over people's shoulders, for example). *In 1980 actor Peter Ustinov, speaking of legendary Hollywood columnist Hedda Hopper, said, "Her virtue was that she said what she thought; her vice that what she thought didn't amount to much."*

[3] **sporadic (sporadically)** If something happens or occurs *sporadically*, it happens only occasionally, at irregular intervals. *Whereas some of Yellowstone National Park's geysers (Old Faithful, for example) eject water regularly, others (Steamboat Geyser, for example) erupt sporadically.*

[4] **recidivism (recidivist)** A return or lapse back to some former undesirable habit (criminal activity, antisocial behavior, smoking, etc.) is known as *recidivism*. *Although Sweden has been praised for its humanitarian prison system (which offers inmates psychiatric treatment and a university release program), rates of recidivism remain high.*

[5] **subliminal** If you say that something (a stimulus) is *subliminal*, you mean that it operates below the threshold of your conscious awareness but that it nevertheless exerts an influence on your mental state or behavior. (Subliminal techniques are often used in TV advertising, as when messages are briefly flashed on the screen.) *In 1963 orchestra leader Meyer Davis said, "What we provide is an atmosphere of orchestrated pulse which works on people in a subliminal way—under its influence I've seen shy [debutantes] and severe [old ladies] kick off their shoes and raise some wholesome hell."*

months later came the **decadent**[1] **utopia**[2] of that **vernal**[3] delight, Easter morning. As an only child, the entire **trove**[4]—dozens of little chocolate eggs in shiny, gold foil—was all mine to find and devour!"

He thought for a while, then said, "Don't repeat this to anyone, but I think if my **plebeian**[5] tastes became public knowledge, the

---

[1] **decadent** Technically, this word means "decaying, declining, deteriorating," as in *a decadent Southern setting* or (to use the noun) *moral decadence.* But to say that someone's behavior is *decadent* is to say that it's marked by a tendency or need to obtain gratification by indulging in unwholesome or unhealthful activities (such as having too much candy, too much alcohol, too much sleep, too much sex, etc.). *In 1972 actress/singer Liza Minnelli won an Academy Award for her performance in* Cabaret, *a film concerning a Pre–World War II Berlin nightclub and the decadent behavior of its employees.*

[2] **utopia** An ideal place (or perfect state, heaven on earth, paradise, etc.) in known as a *utopia* (after an imaginary island society free of poverty and suffering described in English statesman Sir Thomas More's 1516 political essay *Utopia*). *Hellen Keller once said of reading, "Literature is my utopia; no barrier of the senses shuts me out from the sweet, gracious discourse of my book friends."*

[3] **vernal** To refer to something as *vernal* is to say that it pertains to, appears or occurs in, or is suggestive of, springtime. *Whereas a violet's summer flowers are green, its vernal petals are purple, blue, pink, yellow, white, or multicolored.*

[4] **trove** A collection of valuable items (money, antiques, jewelry, etc.) found hidden is known as a *trove* (or *treasure-trove*). *In 1922 two British archaeologists uncovered the tomb of (14th-century B.C. Egyptian pharaoh) King Tutankhamen, which was filled with a rich trove of artifacts, including a solid gold coffin, a gold mask, and jewelry.*

[5] **plebeian** In ancient Rome the common people (as opposed to the nobility or aristocracy) were known as *plebs.* Today, to refer to something (a joke, entertainment, someone's taste, someone's origins, etc.) as *plebeian* (pronounced *pluh-BEE-in*) is to say that it's commonplace, unrefined, coarse, uncultivated, lowbrow, low-class, or vulgar. *The paintings of German expressionist Otto Dix (1891–1969) often depict the plebeian life of alcoholics, prostitutes, and thieves.*

THE WIZARD OF OZ VOCABULARY BUILDER

Brahmins[1] would condemn me as a **philistine**[2]." Then he startled Dorothy by suddenly laughing very loudly. "But I **digress**[3]," he continued. "I know all these **tangential**[4] **musings**[5] aren't really

---

[1] **Brahmin (Brahmins)** In Hinduism (the major religion of India) a *Brahmin* is a member of the highest class. But in informal usage, when people refer to someone as a *Brahmin*, they mean he's a cultured, intelligent, highborn, upper-class person, especially a member of New England's upper-crust society (as in *Boston Brahmins*). *As niece of President Theodore Roosevelt, Eleanor Roosevelt began life as a sheltered Brahmin; as wife of President Franklin D. Roosevelt she became an outspoken champion of social justice.*

[2] **philistine** In the Old Testament, the *Philistines* were enemies of the Israelites. (Note: In the famous Biblical story of David and Goliath, David was an Israelite and Goliath a Philistine). Today, if you refer to someone as a *philistine*, you mean that he's looked down upon as lacking in (or being opposed to) culture and art; he's ignorant, uncultured, narrow-minded, usually middle-class; he has commonplace tastes and ideas. *A year before her death, British experimental poet Dame Edith Sitwell (1887–1964), who usually referred to critics of her work as "philistines," said, "I am an unpopular electric eel in a pool of catfish."*

[3] **digress** In speaking or writing, to *digress* is to stray from the main topic or purpose; to go off the subject, go off on a tangent, etc. The noun is *digression*. *The exciting wilderness novels of James Fenimore Cooper (1826's* The Last of the Mohicans, *for example) contain frequent social and political digressions.*

[4] **tangential** If something (a remark, a discussion, etc.) is *tangential*, it's only superficially or indirectly related (to the topic at hand). Note: In mathematics a *tangent* is a line that touches a curve at only a single point. *His paper on the philosophical concept of materialism (the theory that only matter exists; that is, the soul, spirit, and mind do not) included a short, tangential discussion of the ethical concept of materialism (the theory that the possession of material objects constitutes the greatest good).*

[5] **musings** To *muse* is to (usually silently) meditate or reflect (on some subject); to think (about something). *Musings* are these reflections or thoughts. *In James Thurber's 1939 short story "The Secret Life of Walter Mitty," a man finds relief from his nagging wife by daydreaming; in his musings he becomes a heroic pilot, a famous surgeon, and a fearless soldier.*

THE WIZARD OF OZ VOCABULARY BUILDER

germane[1] to our balloon discussion, but I really needed to talk to someone— especially to a fellow Midwesterner!— and this little **tête-à-tête**[2] was just what the doctor ordered. You see, because I'm alone all the time, I crave conversation— any kind of conversation, from **frivolous**[3] **persiflage**[4] to **earnest**[5] and intelligent **discourse**[6]. I hope

---

[1] **germane** If something (a remark, question, fact, etc.) is *germane*, it's pertinent, relevant, applicable, etc. (to the matter at hand). *In July 1960 John F. Kennedy, contending that his Roman Catholicism was not germane to his ability to serve as President, said, "I hope that no American will throw away his vote by voting either for me or against me solely on account of my religious affiliation."*

[2] **tête-à-tête** A private or intimate conversation or meeting between two people is known as a *tête-à-tête* (which in French literally means "head to head"). *During TV journalist Barbara Walter's 1986 tête-à-tête with President Ronald Reagan, the former movie star said, "I've often wondered how some people in positions of this kind manage without having had any acting experience."*

[3] **frivolous** If you refer to something (a remark or action, for example) as *frivolous*, you mean either that it's of little or no importance (it's trivial, worthless, senseless), or that it's inappropriately silly (it's foolish, childish, flighty). The noun is *frivolity*. *To those who believe playing trivia games is a frivolous pastime, the makers of the Trivial Pursuit board game say, "Every American is entitled to Life, Liberty and the Pursuit of Trivia."*

[4] **persiflage** Light, good-humored, playful (sometimes teasing) talk or conversation is known as *persiflage*. *What made the 1934 murder mystery* The Thin Man *so popular with critics and filmgoers was the witty persiflage between husband-and-wife detectives Nick and Nora (William Powell and Myrna Loy).*

[5] **earnest** To be *earnest* (about something) is to be serious and sincere (about it), as when you have a purpose or goal and are steadily eager in pursuing it. *In 1901, after assuming the Presidency of the assassinated William McKinley, Theodore Roosevelt said of his predecessor, "No President— not even Lincoln himself— was ever more earnestly anxious to represent the well-thought-out wishes of the people."*

[6] **discourse** A (usually formal or lengthy) communication of thoughts (such as a speech, essay, or conversation) is known as a *discourse*. The word also denotes conversation in general. *In 1985 journalist Lucy Howard said of President Ronald Reagan, "In the heat of a political lifetime, [he] innocently squirrels away tidbits of misinformation and then, sometimes years later, casually drops them into his public discourse, like gumballs in a quiche."*

you can forgive me." He peered at her face from beneath lowered eyelids. "Anyway, enough of these **peripheral**[1] matters. The point is, I'd much rather go back to good old **pedestrian**[2] Omaha and work with a circus again— maybe even become an **impresario**[3], like P. T. Barnum! Now, if you'll help me sew the silk together, we'll begin work on our balloon."

---

[1] **peripheral** The outermost part or edge of an area or region is known as its *periphery*. Thus, your *peripheral* vision is what your eyes see off to the sides (as opposed to straight ahead). Figuratively, to refer to a subject as *peripheral* is to say that it's concerned with only a superficial or unessential aspect of the matter at hand. *Japan's surprise attack on Pearl Harbor (December 7, 1941) abruptly changed the United States' role in World War II from one of merely peripheral involvement to one of center-stage responsibility.*

[2] **pedestrian** As a noun, a *pedestrian* is a person traveling on foot (as opposed to, say, a motorist). But as an adjective the word means "commonplace, ordinary, undistinguished, uninspired, dull, etc." *Gustave Flaubert's classic French novel* Madame Bovary *(1857) concerns a bored, young, small-town housewife who tries to escape the drabness of her pedestrian existence by committing adultery.*

[3] **impresario** The organizer, manager, sponsor, or producer of a large-scale public entertainment (such as an opera, ballet, Broadway show, or concert) is known as an *impresario*. *Impresarios* often scout out, work with, and introduce entertainers to the public. *Television's rock 'n' roll impresario Dick Clark (whose dance program* American Bandstand *aired for 30 years and helped launch or promote the careers of such early performers as Fabian, Bobby Rydell, and Frankie Avalon) was inducted into the Rock and Roll Hall of Fame in 1993.*

Chapter 21 "The Balloon"

Forcing herself to overcome the **inertia**[1] of quietly sitting and listening to Oz's strange but **poignant**[2] confessions, Dorothy now stood and, without responding, accepted the needle and thread he held out to her. Then, as he carefully cut strips of green silk into the proper shape, she **punctiliously**[3] sewed them together. It took three long days to bring their efforts to **fruition**[4], but when they were finally finished they had a bag of silk more than fifty feet long. Then Oz painted it with a thin coat of glue to make it airtight.

Realizing they'd need a basket to ride in, Oz sent the soldier in the green uniform to fetch a large clothesbasket. When the **aide-de-**

---

[1] **inertia** As you learned in eight grade science, *inertia* is the technical term that describes the tendency of a body at rest to stay at rest or of a body in motion to stay in motion (in the same direction and at the same speed). But people often use the word figuratively to refer to a state of sluggish inactivity; a resistance or disinclination to act, move, or change. *He suggested that people often remained in doomed marriages merely because of inertia; in other words, that people are basically lazy and that hiring a lawyer and filing for divorce would take too much effort.*

[2] **poignant** If something (a story, a painting, etc.) is *poignant*, it affects the emotions; it's moving, touching, etc. The noun is *poignancy*. *In his 1949 memoir* Death Be Not Proud, *journalist John Gunther tells the poignant story of his teenaged son's valiant bout with brain cancer.*

[3] **punctilious (punctiliously)** To be *punctilious* (about performing a task or behaving in a particular manner) is to be carefully attentive to small details; to be exacting, demanding, precise, conscientious, etc. *In 1984 an article in* Harper's *magazine said that what makes London hotels elegant is "the punctilious attention to detail in a time when nobody even bothers to get the spelling of your name right."*

[4] **fruition** When something worked for over time has been completed (or realized, attained, achieved, fulfilled, etc.) it's said to have been brought to *fruition*. *U.S. efforts to develop an atomic bomb during World War II came to fruition when one was successfully tested in New Mexico on July 16, 1945.*

273

camp[1] returned, Oz used strong ropes to tie the basket to the bottom of the balloon. Next Oz sent word to his people that he was going up into the clouds to attend a conference of the world's most **eminent**[2] Wizards. The news **propagated**[3] rapidly throughout the City, and all of Oz's **adherents**[4], as well as many of his **detractors**[5], came to see their **reclusive**[6], **enigmatic**[1] Wizard and

---

[1] **aide-de-camp** An *aide-de-camp* is a military officer who serves as confidential assistant to a superior (usually a general or admiral). Sometimes the word is used informally to refer to someone whose function is similar to that of an aide-de-camp. *U.S. soldier and statesman Alexander Hamilton (who served as General George Washington's aide-de-camp during the Revolutionary War and later as America's first secretary of the treasury) was shot and killed (1804) in a duel with Vice President Aaron Burr.*

[2] **eminent** To describe someone as *eminent* (as in *an eminent historian*) is to say that he's of high rank; he's distinguished, noted, celebrated, prominent, famous, etc. *The Scopes "monkey" trial was held in 1925, with eminent lawyers on both sides— William Jennings Bryan for the prosecution and Clarence Darrow for the defense.*

[3] **propagate (propagated)** When an organism (plant or animal) *propagates*, it multiplies (through natural reproduction). When a thing (a rumor, idea, etc.) *propagates*, it spreads, expands, etc. *In April 1999 Pulitzer Prize–winning commentator William Raspberry said, "It can be fascinating to watch young people create and propagate their special codes— slang— to keep us older ones from understanding what they're talking about; sooner or later, though, we catch on and the kids coin new formulations."*

[4] **adherent (adherents)** Someone who supports, upholds, or follows a leader or a cause is known as an *adherent*. *Although in the early 1920s the Ku Klux Klan had more than two million adherents, by the 1930s it had lost nearly all its power.*

[5] **detractor (detractors)** A *detractor* is a person who criticizes or tears down another person (usually a public figure), an institution, or a cause; an attacker, antagonist, faultfinder, etc. *Whereas fans of hip-hop admire the music's inventiveness, detractors criticize it for promoting violence.*

[6] **recluse (reclusive)** A *recluse* is a person who (usually for religious or social reasons) lives alone, apart from others; a hermit. The adjective is *reclusive*. *Swedish-born American film sensation Greta Garbo retired in 1941 and lived as a recluse until her death in 1990; interestingly, her famous declaration, "I want to be alone," was uttered not by the actress herself, but by her screen character (a weary ballerina) in 1932's* Grand Hotel.

THE WIZARD OF OZ VOCABULARY BUILDER

the wonderful balloon.

Oz ordered a few **functionaries**[2] to take the balloon outside, in front of the Palace, and, overcoming their natural **indolence**[3], the **sluggards**[4] managed to **lackadaisically**[5] carry out his request. The

---

[1] **enigma (enigmatic)** An *enigma* is something (speech or behavior, for example) that's difficult to interpret, figure out, understand, comprehend, etc.; a mystery, a puzzle. The adjective is *enigmatic* (as in *the* Mona Lisa's *enigmatic smile*). *Whereas fifties rock groups usually had simple, descriptive names (the Crew-cuts, the Platters, the Monotones), sixties bands often had non-descriptive, enigmatic ones (Strawberry Alarm Clock, Jefferson Airplane, Buffalo Springfield).*

[2] **functionary (functionaries)** A *functionary* is a person (often a non-elected government official) who functions in a particular (often low-level) capacity; a bureaucrat, civil servant, pen-pusher, etc. (as in *the UN has a staff of about 13,000 functionaries*). *By inserted a few of his own jazz compositions between "Feelings" and "My Way," the cocktail pianist was able to assert himself as a creative artist, not just a dining room functionary.*

[3] **indolent (indolence)** People who are *indolent* avoid exertion; they're lazy, sluggish, etc. The noun is *indolence*. *In Greek mythology the Lotus-Eaters were a people of northern Africa who, because they subsisted on the intoxicating fruit of the lotus tree, led a life of indolent ease and contented forgetfulness.*

[4] **sluggard (sluggards)** A *sluggard* is a person who is habitually lazy or inactive; a lazybones, loafer, etc. The adjective is *sluggardly*. *In 1984 Secretary of State George Shultz implied that government workers were more sluggardly than their private sector counterparts when he sarcastically said, "I learned in business that you had to be very careful when you told somebody that's working for you to do something, because the chances were very high he'd do it; in government you don't have to worry about that."*

[5] **lackadaisical (lackadaisically)** To describe an effort as *lackadaisical* is to say that it lacks vigor or determination; it's halfhearted, unenthusiastic, etc. To describe a person as *lackadaisical* is to say that he's lazy, sluggish, indifferent, etc. *In August 1998, speaking of that season's major league home run race, journalist Linton Weeks said, "What happened to August? Didn't the eighth month used to be laid-back and lackadaisical? No longer. This August has been a gust of activity, manic as Mark McGwire, slamming as Sammy Sosa."*

assembled **proletariat**[1] gazed upon the large, sun-drenched green balloon in awe from behind a **cordon**[2] of green-uniformed police officers. A group of young girls struggled with the breeze to display a flimsy sign with the words *Good-bye, Oz* **blazoned**[3] across it. A **passel**[4] of the City's business **magnates**[5] and political **luminaries**[6] stood beside the basket.

---

[1] **proletariat** The working class of a society (that is, the class of people who depend for their support on daily employment) is known as the *proletariat*. *According to 19th-century German economist and philosopher Karl Marx, because business owners take advantage of workers, the proletariat will become increasingly poor and eventually revolt.*

[2] **cordon** A line of soldiers (or police, warships, etc.) guarding or enclosing an area is known as a *cordon*. As a verb, to *cordon* (or *cordon off*) an area is to block movement into it by means of such a line. *At the 1969 Rolling Stones concert in Altamont, California, access to the stage area was blocked by a cordon of (members of the motorcycle gang) Hell's Angels; violence broke out and four people were killed.*

[3] **blazon (blazoned)** To *blazon* something (letters, a sign, etc.) is to make it conspicuously visible; to publicly display it, broadcast it, publicize it, etc. *The day we left for summer camp, the walls of Grand Central Terminal were draped with colored banners, across each of which was blazoned the word* Camp, *followed by the colorful name of an American Indian tribe (Chippewa, Onondaga, Kickapoo, and so on).*

[4] **passel** A group or quantity (of people or things) that is largish but of indeterminate number is known as a *passel*, as in *a passel of diplomats*. *According to the* Christian Science Monitor, *a U.S. President "faces a passel of domestic issues."*

[5] **magnate (magnates)** A *magnate* is a person of great influence, standing, or importance in a particular field, especially business (as in *shipping magnate*); a tycoon. *Orson Welles' landmark film* Citizen Kane *(1941) is a character study loosely based on the life of publishing magnate William Randolph Hearst.*

[6] **luminary (luminaries)** Technically, a *luminary* is something that gives light (the sun, for example). But when you refer to a person as a *luminary* you mean that he's attained top standing in his field; he's famous; he's a celebrity, an inspiration, a leading light, a star. *Sun Records producer Sam Phillips, the first to record such early rock luminaries as Elvis Presley, Jerry Lee Lewis, and Roy Orbison, was inducted into the Rock and Roll Hall of Fame in 1986.*

THE WIZARD OF OZ VOCABULARY BUILDER

The Tin Woodman, having **sedulously**[1] chopped a large pile of wood into small, neat pieces, now made a fire of them. Oz held the bottom of the balloon over the flames so that the rising hot air would be caught inside the silken bag. Gradually the balloon swelled out and rose into the air until finally the basket barely touched the ground.

Then Oz climbed into the basket and said to all the spectators in a **resonant**[2], official voice, "The Great Wizards of the World conference— which, as you know, is a yearly gathering of the world's most **preeminent**[3] wizards— will be starting shortly. Because I fit that **rubric**[4], my attendance is **mandatory**[5]. But don't

---

[1] **sedulous (sedulously)** To be *sedulous* (about performing some task) is to be constant, persevering, persistent, untiring, etc., and at the same time careful, painstaking, thoroughgoing, etc. *Time magazine once said of a certain specialty store that it was an "oasis of elegant gadgets" that would appeal "to the sedulous and casual collector alike."*

[2] **resonant** A voice or sound described as *resonant* has a strong, deep, resounding (ringing out, echoing) tone. The noun is *resonance*. *Nonfiction writer John McPhee once said that the resonance of actor Richard Burton's voice was "so rich and overpowering that it could [make a recipe for rabbit stew sound like poetry]."*

[3] **preeminent** To describe someone (or something) as *preeminent* is to say that he's superior to or more notable than others (as in a particular field or activity); he's dominant, distinguished, outstanding, excellent, etc. *In 1995 journalist Curt Suplee reported, "The garden spider, nature's preeminent acrobat-architect, is also a distinguished physicist; a new study of webs shows that the structures employ a sophisticated and unexpected system of aerodynamic damping (that is, they take advantage of air drag on the silk threads to buffer the shock of capturing even large prey without catastrophic damage to the web)."*

[4] **rubric** A heading, category, class, or title is known as a *rubric*. For example, judo and karate fall under the *rubric* "martial arts." *We weren't too impressed when the TV commercial said that the electric razor used "space age" technology; after all, everything invented since 1957 fits that rubric.*

[5] **mandatory** If you refer to something (an activity ordered by an authority, for example) as *mandatory*, you mean that it's required, compulsory, obligatory, etc. (and that failure to carry it out will result in punishment). Note: The opposite is *voluntary*. *In the United States, mandatory service in the armed forces was first introduced during the Civil War.*

think of this as my **swan song**[1], for I shall return," he lied. "During my **junket**[2], the Scarecrow, by virtue of his **inimitable**[3] brain, will rule over you. I hereby **enjoin**[4] you to **abide**[5] by his orders as you would mine."

---

[1] **swan song** A *swan song* is a final appearance or effort of a celebrity, creative artist, organization, historical period, etc., before dying, retiring, disbanding, etc. (from the legend that a swan sings as it dies). *Actress Marilyn Monroe's swan song, the 1961 film* The Misfits, *was actor Clark Gable's last hurrah as well.*

[2] **junket** A (usually short) trip or tour, especially one made by a government official at public expense (or by a businessman at company expense), is known as a *junket*. Because during these trips the working (fact-finding, for example) traveler often stays at a fancy resort in an exotic location and enjoys himself (by playing golf, feasting, etc.), the word generally carries a somewhat negative connotation. Note: The word can also be used informally to refer to any short pleasure trip or outing (as in *a gambling junket to Atlantic City*). *In a November 1989 article entitled "Shopping Junkets for Hill Spouses," the* Washington Post *reported, "Don't expect all of your elected representatives to be home for the holidays; some will give themselves and their spouses Christmas presents from you in the form of first-class junkets to warm climates for 'official business.'"*

[3] **inimitable** To refer to someone or something as *inimitable* is to say that it's beyond imitation; that is, it's unparalleled, matchless, unequaled, peerless, unique, etc. *In the 1930s Louis Armstrong's inimitable singing style became as well known as his trumpet tone.*

[4] **enjoin** To *enjoin* (someone to do something) is to, with authority, command or order (him to do it). *The Act of Supremacy (1534) enjoined subjects to recognize King Henry VIII (as opposed to the pope) as head of the Church of England.* In another sense, the word means "to prohibit or forbid." *In 1971 television and radio stations were enjoined from broadcasting cigarette ads.*

[5] **abide** To *abide* by something (an order, rule, etc.) is to go along with it without question or complaint; to accept it, support it, obey it, comply with it, etc. *On March 3, 1991, when Allied and Iraqi military leaders meet on the battlefield to discuss terms for a formal cease-fire to end the Persian Gulf War, Iraq agreed to abide by all of the UN's terms, including the destruction of Iraq's unconventional weapons (but later sought to frustrate the carrying out of UN inspections).*

THE WIZARD OF OZ VOCABULARY BUILDER

This announcement came as a surprise to the **aggrandized**[1] Scarecrow, who was about to **demur**[2] on the grounds of **obtuseness**[3]. But then, remembering his new brain, he kept quiet.

The balloon was by this time tugging hard at the ropes that held it to the ground, for the air within it was hot, and this made it so much lighter than the air outside it that it pulled hard to rise into the sky.

"Come, Dorothy!" urged Oz. "Hurry, or the balloon will fly away!"

"I can't find Toto anywhere!" yelled the girl, who refused to leave her little dog behind. Toto had run into the crowd to chase a kitten, causing a **frenetic**[4] **melee**[1]. Dorothy tried to follow after

---

[1] **aggrandize (aggrandized)** If a person has become *aggrandized,* he's become greater in power, rank, importance, influence, reputation, etc.; he's been magnified, glorified, etc. If a thing (land, for example) has been *aggrandized,* it's become greater in size; it's been enlarged, increased, extended, etc. *Historians say that one of the main causes of World War II was territorial aggrandizement (by Japan in China, by Italy in Ethiopia, and by Germany in central and eastern Europe).*

[2] **demur** To *demur* is to voice an objection or hesitate (when someone suggests that you do something). *When it was suggested to Italian opera composer Giuseppe Verdi that his Aida be premiered in Egypt to coincide with the opening of the Suez Canal (1869), he demurred, believing the new work would not be ready in time.*

[3] **obtuse (obtuseness)** To describe a person as *obtuse* is to say that he's not quick in perception or intellect; he's stupid, dull-witted, etc. To describe an object as *obtuse* is to say that it's not pointed or sharp; it's blunt, rounded, etc. Note: In geometry, an *obtuse* angle is one that measures more than 90 degrees but less than 180 degrees. *In 1986 Pulitzer Prize-winning novelist John Updike said, "Writers take words seriously, and they struggle to steer their own through the crosswinds of [interfering] editors, careless typesetters, and obtuse reviewers into the lap of the ideal reader."*

[4] **frenetic** To describe something (action or behavior, for example) as *frenetic* is to say that it's (often wildly) frantic, frenzied, hectic, agitated, etc. *The jitterbug, a dance performed to swing music, can range anywhere from easygoing two-step patterns to frenetic improvisation using swings, lifts, turns, and acrobatics.*

them, but they were too quick. As the **pursuer**[2] and his **spry**[3] little **quarry**[4] darted here and there, the onlookers, trying to be helpful, kept screaming out Toto's location to her, but their words were lost in the confused **babel**[5] of everyone talking at the same time. Then,

---

[1] **melee** A *melee* (pronounced *MAY-lay*) is a noisy, disorderly fight or scuffle; a brawl, a free-for-all. Note: Sometimes the word refers to any noisy, disorderly mingling of a crowd (without fighting). *In 1964 in Lima, more than 300 soccer fans were killed in a melee and panic that occurred after a goal was disallowed in a Peru vs. Argentina Olympic qualifying match.*

[2] **pursue (pursuer)** To *pursue* someone running away or fleeing is to follow or chase him in an effort to overtake and capture him. One who does this is called a *pursuer*. Note: The word has two other related meanings: To *pursue* a goal (or purpose, end, reward, etc.) is to strive to attain it (aspire to it, aim for it, etc.), and to *pursue* a thought or argument is to continue with it (carry on with it, proceed with it, etc.). The noun is *pursuit*, as in *the pursuit of happiness*. *At the end of the children's story "Jack and the Beanstalk," Jack chops down the beanstalk, and the giant, who is pursuing him, falls to his death.*

[3] **spry** If someone is *spry*, his movements are (sometimes unexpectedly) quick (lively, brisk, active) and limber (springy, flexible). *Thickset comedian/actor Jackie Gleason (1916–1987), best remembered for his portrayal of fictional Brooklyn bus driver Ralph Kramden, often surprised and delighted audiences with his spry dance moves.*

[4] **quarry** An animal hunted or chased is known as *quarry*. Sometimes the word is used to refer to any object (other than an animal) being hunted or searched for. *Bred to hunt foxes, foxhounds are medium-sized dogs used in packs to run down their quarry while hunters follow on horseback.* Note: Another meaning of this word is "an open pit from which rock or stone is obtained," as in *limestone quarry*.

[5] **babel** A confused mixture of voices, sounds, or noises is known as *babel* (from the Biblical story of the Tower of Babel, in which when descendants of Noah tried to unite all people by building a tower to Heaven, God stopped them by making them all speak in different languages so that their speech was incomprehensible to one another). *While some music critics call composer John Cage's* Imaginary Landscape No. 4 *(a 1951 experimental piece scored for 12 radios tuned at random) a work of art, others call it babel.*

THE WIZARD OF OZ VOCABULARY BUILDER

when Toto, in his **feisty**[1] chase, **fortuitously**[2] passed right before her, Dorothy ended the **fracas**[3] by scooping him into her arms. Now, while simultaneously **chiding**[4] the dog for acting like a naughty little **scamp**[5] and **dotingly**[6] petting him, she worked her way as **expeditiously**[7] as possible through the throng, toward the

---

[1] **feisty** If a person or animal is *feisty,* he's quarrelsome or touchy, but in a lively, spirited way; he's spunky. *Singer/actor Frank Sinatra won an Academy Award for his portrayal of a feisty army private in the 1953 film* From Here to Eternity.

[2] **fortuitous (fortuitously)** Something (often lucky or fortunate) that happens by chance or accident is said to be *fortuitous. In 1928 British bacteriologist Sir Alexander Fleming discovered the antibiotic drug penicillin when a bit of mold that had fortuitously fallen from a culture plate in his laboratory destroyed bacteria around it.*

[3] **fracas** A *fracas* is a noisy, disorderly fight or disturbance; an uproar, a brawl. *Sioux leader Sitting Bull was killed (1890) in a fracas with police after he refused to stop the people of South Dakota's Grand River Valley from joining the Ghost Dance (a tribal religion based on the belief that all whites would disappear and dead Indians and buffalo would return).*

[4] **chide (chiding)** To *chide* someone is to scold or criticize him mildly or gently, usually to correct a fault. *After my English teacher chided me for ending a sentence with a preposition, he winked and said, "Then again, sometimes it's a good word to end a sentence with."*

[5] **scamp** A *scamp* is a (sometimes amusingly) mischievous (often young and worthless) person (or animal); a rascal, a devil, etc. *Child film star Jackie Coogan specialized in playing troublemaking scamps in such films as* Peck's Bad Boy (1921) *and* Tom Sawyer (1930).

[6] **dote (dotingly)** To *dote* on someone is to (often on a regular basis and often foolishly) bestow excessive amounts of fondness, love, care, attention, etc., on him; to pamper him, baby him, etc. *In the 1980 film* Ordinary People, *Mary Tyler Moore plays a wealthy but stiff suburban housewife who dotes on her emotionally troubled teenaged son.*

[7] **expeditious (expeditiously)** To do something *expeditiously* (or, to use the adjective, in an *expeditious* manner) is to do it promptly, quickly, and efficiently. Note: To *expedite* something is to speed it up; make it happen faster. *With the introduction of Zip codes (1963), the U.S. Post Office was able to sort and deliver mail more expeditiously.*

balloon. She was within a few steps of it, and Oz was holding out his hands to help her into the basket, when her passage was unexpectedly blocked by a passing woman with a green **parasol**[1]. Just then the ropes cracked and the **tumescent**[2] balloon started rising into the air without her.

"Come back!" she screamed, **appalled**[3]. "I want to go, too!"

"I can't come back, my dear," called Oz helplessly from the basket. "I don't know how."

Now the **ersatz**[4] Wizard, the **cynosure**[1] of all eyes, rose swiftly

---

[1] **parasol** A *parasol* is a small, light (often colorful) umbrella used (generally by women) for providing shade (from the sun). *In French neoimpressionist painter Georges Seurat's 1886 nearly mural-sized masterpiece,* Sunday Afternoon on the Island of La Grande Jatte, *parasol-carrying middle-class Parisian women, along with husbands, children, and pets, lounge on a tree-dotted, grassy shore.*

[2] **tumescent** To describe something as *tumescent* is to say that it's inflated, bloated, swollen, etc. (as from internal pressure). *When a blowfish senses danger, it defensively doubles its size and becomes balloon-shaped (by inflating its stomach with air); the tumescent form suggests to a predator that the blowfish is too big to swallow.*

[3] **appalling (appalled)** If you say that something (an action or behavior, for example) is *appalling*, you mean that it causes horror, shock, dismay, outrage, alarm, etc. *In 1986, recalling a temper tantrum of British Shakespearean actress Dame Edith Evans (1888–1976), British actor Alec Guinness said, "She flung herself full-length on the stage, drummed with her feet and, taking the corner of a small Persian rug in her teeth, [shook] it, while I sat rigid and appalled on the sofa, pressed back against the cushions."*

[4] **ersatz** This word is used to describe things (commercial products, for example) that are made of a (usually inferior) artificial, synthetic, or substitute substance (to replace something genuine or natural), as in *ersatz chocolate made of carob.* The word can also be used to describe anything fake, phony, artificial, counterfeit, etc. *The Kentucky coffee tree (which doesn't produce coffee beans) got its name from the practice of 18th-century Kentucky settlers using its seeds (contained in pods) to make ersatz coffee.*

into the sky. With every passing moment he grew smaller and smaller. As they watched him vanish into nothingness, the Tin Woodman's metal hand, as if of its own **volition**[2], gently placed itself upon Dorothy's shoulder in a kind of mute consolation.

---

[1] **cynosure** Something that (by virtue of its brilliance, interest, etc.) is a center of attention (such as Elvis Presley when he walked onstage) is known as a *cynosure*. Note: The word has an interesting derivation. *Cynosura* was the Roman name for the constellation Ursa Minor, which contains the North Star (Polaris). Because this star remains in a nearly fixed position in the sky, mariners have long used it as a navigational focal point (a center of attention). *When the Beatles arrived in the U.S. in the mid-1960s, not only was the English rock group the cynosure of all eyes, they were the objects of mass worship; in fact, in 1966 band member John Lennon contended, "We're more popular than Jesus Christ now."*

[2] **volition** To do something of your own *volition* is to willfully do it; to consciously choose or decide to do it. *You operate some of your muscles (your biceps, for example) of your own volition; others (your diaphragm, for example) operate automatically.*

Chapter 22 "The Letter"

Feeling she had reached the **nadir**[1] of her hopes, a **mantle**[2] of profound hopelessness enveloped Dorothy. And her companions grieved over losing their kindly **mentor**[3].

The next morning the four travelers met in the Throne Room to discuss matters. The Scarecrow sat on the Throne with his **lanky**[4] limbs **splayed**[5] awkwardly over its edges.

"Well then, what can be done about getting Dorothy home?" the Tin Woodman said to no one in particular.

Eager to demonstrate that with his new brain he was neither

---

[1] **nadir** The *nadir* of something is its lowest point. Although technically this is an astronomical term that refers to a point opposite the *zenith* (see *zenith*), the word is generally used to refer to a low point in someone's (or something's) life or development. *National unemployment, which first became a problem in the U.S. after the Civil War, reached its nadir during the Great Depression of the 1930s (when roughly 25 percent of the labor force was out of work).*

[2] **mantle** Anything (darkness, a substance, a particular mood, etc.) that covers, surrounds, envelopes, or conceals (something) is known as a *mantle*. *In the early morning a mantle of fog hung over the dew-covered meadow.*

[3] **mentor** A *mentor* is a wise and trusted person who advises or guides another (sometimes officially or professionally); a counselor, coach, teacher, guru, etc. (from Homer's *Odyssey*, wherein Mentor is Odysseus's trusted friend and advisor). *Russian-born conductor Serge Koussevitzky (1874–1951) achieved fame in the U.S. as leader of the Boston Symphony Orchestra and as musical director of Massachusetts' summer Berkshire Music Festival, where he became Leonard Bernstein's conducting teacher and mentor.*

[4] **lanky** To describe someone (or his arms or legs) as *lanky* is to say that he's thin (especially ungracefully so), gaunt, gangly, bony, etc. *In appearance, President Abraham Lincoln (1809–1865) was very tall and lanky, and often wore a tall, black, silk hat.*

[5] **splayed** If you say that something (someone's arm or leg, for example) is *splayed* out, you mean that it's (sometimes clumsily) spread out or extended. *The body of a tarantula (a large, hairy spider) may measure 3 inches long and, with legs splayed out, up to 10 inches across.*

THE WIZARD OF OZ VOCABULARY BUILDER

addled[1] nor **irresolute**[2], the Scarecrow immediately suggested a plan. "Let's ask the soldier in the green uniform," he said. Now, even though, as far as plans go, this wasn't much of one, no one **scoffed**[3] at it. When the would-be **oracle**[4] was summoned, he entered the Throne Room timidly, for while Oz was at the **helm**[5]

---

[1] **addled** If someone is *addled* (or *addlebrained* or *addlepated*), his mind is confused or muddled; he's illogical, harebrained, foolish, etc. *Nobel Prize-winning playwright Eugene O'Neill (1888–1953) once remarked, "My brain is a bit addled by whiskey."*

[2] **irresolute** If you're *irresolute* (about something), you're uncertain or undecided (about it); you can't make up your mind (about how to act or proceed). *Historians say that after taking office in January 1993, President Bill Clinton acted decisively on such issues as gays in the military and the appointment of women and minorities to high federal posts, but that he appeared inexperienced and irresolute in dealing with foreign crises (as in Bosnia, Somalia, Rwanda, Cuba, and Haiti).*

[3] **scoff (scoffed)** To *scoff* at something (an idea, a suggestion, etc.) is to openly (and often emphatically) express doubt about it and disapproval of it; to put it down, poke fun at it, mock it, etc. *In 1866, when Secretary of State William H. Seward recommended buying Alaska from Russia for $7.2 million in gold, many scoffed at the idea, referring to it as "Seward's folly."*

[4] **oracle** A highly regarded person who delivers wise, authoritative pronouncements or opinions (on a particular subject) is known as an *oracle*. Note: In ancient Greece an *oracle* was a priest or priestess through which a god's (often ambiguous) response to a question was delivered— or it was the response itself, or the shrine (such as the one at Delphi) where the priest or priestess spoke. *In 1985, speaking of the 40th-anniversary edition of his book* Child and Baby Care, *child-rearing oracle Dr. Benjamin Spock modestly said, "I really learned it all from mothers."*

[5] **helm** In nautical terminology, the *helm* of a ship is its steering wheel or steering apparatus. But if you say that someone is "at the *helm*" (of something other than a ship), you mean that he's in a position of leadership; he's in charge, in command, etc. *At the beginning of his term at the helm of the New York Mets (1962–1965), (former Yankees manager) Casey Stengel disappointedly asked, "Can't anybody here play this game?"*

he never was allowed inside the **sacrosanct**[1] inner chamber.

"This little girl," said the Scarecrow to the soldier, "wishes to go back to Kansas. How can she do so?"

"She can't," answered the soldier **tersely**[2]. Suddenly aware that his answer may have sounded **glib**[3] or possibly **cavalier**[4] to his new ruler, he quickly clapped his hand over his mouth and made a **protracted**[5] show of **sycophantic**[1] bowing. Then, standing at

---

[1] **sacrosanct** If something (a philosophy or physical place, for example) is *sacrosanct*, it's secure from violation, trespass, assault, attack, etc., because it's regarded as sacred. While the word can apply to places where people worship (churches, temples, altars, etc.), it's most frequently used to refer to non-religious places or concepts. *What sets criminals apart from the rest of us is that they don't seem to understand that life is sacred and that personal property is sacrosanct.*

[2] **terse (tersely)** To describe speech or language as *terse* is to say that it's effectively (or sometimes rudely) brief, concise, short, etc. *When we told Jim his answering machine greeting ("Leave a message") was rudely terse, he explained that he was merely saving the caller the inconvenience of having to wait a long time for the beep.*

[3] **glib** If you refer to a remark as *glib*, you mean that it's said easily and offhandedly, but with little or no thought, concern, or sincerity. *In 2001 a former drug addict who felt that former First Lady Nancy Reagan's 1980s anti-drug motto, "Just say no," was glib, posted this note on the Internet: "I remember sitting in front of the TV hearing Nancy Reagan say 'Just say no' and thinking to myself, 'Just say how, Nancy'; if it were a matter of just saying no, there would be few, if any, addicts."*

[4] **cavalier** To be *cavalier* is to show offhand disregard (for something); to be (sometimes inappropriately) unceremonious, carefree, nonchalant, casual, etc. (about it). *In his autobiography, Confessions (1781), French philosopher Jean Jacques Rousseau tells of a great princess who, on being informed that the country people had no bread, cavalierly replied, "Then let them eat cake" (a statement often falsely attributed to French queen Marie Antoinette).*

[5] **protracted** If an action or activity is *protracted*, it lasts (or continues for) a long time, or it lasts (or continues) longer than it should; it's prolonged, drawn out, extended, etc. *In 1957, after protracted financial negotiations with temperamental opera star Maria Callas, Metropolitan Opera manager Rudolf Bing wrote to the Greek-American diva's Italian representative: "If that is not enough [money], will you please politely indicate that she can go to hell."*

THE WIZARD OF OZ VOCABULARY BUILDER

attention with serious **mien**[2], he continued in a tone **imbued**[3] with **piety**[4], "Perhaps Glinda, the Good Witch of the South, might help you." As he spoke he inwardly feared that his silly **toadyism**[5] might in some way **denigrate**[6] the memory of his former ruler, but he

---

[1] **sycophant (sycophantic)** A *sycophant* (pronounced with the accent on the first syllable) is a person who tries to win (someone's) favor by being overly kind, attentive, complimentary, or servile; a bootlicker, hanger-on, yes-man, flatterer, etc. *Historians say that Civil War Confederacy President Jefferson Davis kept incompetent friends in office and discouraged disagreement; as a result, many of his advisors were merely sycophants.*

[2] **mien** Your outward appearance (facial expression, posture, etc.), especially as it reveals your state of mind or personality, is known as your *mien* (pronounced the same as *mean*). *In the* Incredible Hulk *TV series, actor Bill Bixby maintained a mild mien until something angered him (at which point he turned into an enraged green creature).*

[3] **imbue (imbued)** If a person's mind or spirit has become *imbued* with something (a philosophy, teachings, etc.), it's been filled with it or inspired by it. If a thing (a fabric, a painting, food, for example) has been *imbued* by something (liquid, color, aroma, etc.), it's been penetrated by it or saturated with it. *Few cities in the United States are more imbued with early U.S. history than Philadelphia (home to such historical monuments as Independence Hall, the Liberty Bell, and the Betsy Ross House).*

[4] **piety** Respect and devotion (for God, parents, family, etc.) is known as *piety*. The adjective is *pious*, which can mean either "respectful; devoted" or "falsely or insincerely respectful or devoted." *Chivalry was the code of conduct by which knights of medieval Europe were guided; it combined military virtues (bravery, strength, daring) with those of Christianity (piety, generosity, courtesy).*

[5] **toady (toadyism)** A *toady* is someone who self-servingly or submissively flatters, attends to, or yields to another; a bootlicker, parasite, hanger-on, etc. The practice or an act of this behavior is known as *toadyism*. *In the 1980 film* Superman II, *actors Gene Hackman and Ned Beatty play a criminal mastermind (Lex Luthor) and his comically bungling toady (Otis).*

[6] **denigrate** To *denigrate* someone (or his name, reputation, memory, etc.) is to speak badly or damagingly of him; to badmouth, criticize, ridicule, or belittle him. *In 1987, when (rap group) the Beastie Boys were accused of denigrating women (in their song lyrics), a band member responded, "It's not as if we just insult women; our insults go across the board."*

couldn't help himself. He finished in the same respectful, **staid**[1] manner, "She's the most powerful of all the Witches and she rules over the Quadlings."

"How can we get to her castle?" asked the Scarecrow.

"The road is straight to the South," he answered **complaisantly**[2], with a **gratuitous**[3] smile. Being unaccustomed to his new ruler's personality, the soldier wasn't sure exactly how much **groveling**[4]—

---

[1] **staid** To behave in a *staid* manner is to be (sometimes overly) serious and correct; to be stiff, proper, straight-laced, etc. To describe artistic works (writing, painting, music, etc.) as *staid* is to say that they're (sometimes overly) conservative, colorless, stiff, formal, serious, etc. *In 1981 the* London Times, *speaking of the capital of Scotland, said, "After the annual festival [the International Festival of Music and Drama], Edinburgh reverts to its staid character— a stern old lady counting the cash from her annual fling."*

[2] **complaisant (complaisantly)** If you're *complaisant* you have or show a desire to please (others); you're agreeable, obliging, gracious, accommodating, friendly, etc. The noun is *complaisance*. *In the early 20th-century comedy team of Laurel and Hardy, Stan Laurel played a complaisant but dimwitted Englishman, and Oliver Hardy a fat, irritable American.* Note: Don't confuse this word with *complacent* (which is pronounced the same); see *complacent.*

[3] **gratuitous** Another word for *tip* (extra money given to a waitress or cab driver, for example) is *gratuity*. So in one sense, to say that something is *gratuitous* is to say that it's not obligatory (it's voluntary). But when people refer to something (a remark, an insult, a shock element, etc.) as being *gratuitous*, they usually mean that it's unnecessary; that there's no reason for it; it's unwarranted, unjustified, groundless, etc. *Because the director believed his new horror film might sell more tickets with an R rating, at the last minute he added a gratuitous scene of the female lead showering.*

[4] **grovel (groveling)** Technically, to *grovel* is to (with head downward) lie on or creep along the floor before someone of power (in subservience, humility, fear, etc.)— something you'll probably never see, except in cartoons. But in general usage, when people say that someone *grovels*, they mean that he degradingly (and often exaggeratedly) humbles or lowers himself before another while insincerely flattering him (to win favor) or desperately begging (for something). *In 1984 Frank Louchheim (head of an employment agency for executives), speaking of the phrase "You're fired!" said, "No other words can so easily and [concisely] reduce a confident, self-assured executive to an insecure, groveling shred of his former self."*

or of what sort— was appropriate. Then as he walked toward the door, it suddenly occurred to him that, though he still secretly worshiped the Wizard, it probably would be **politic**[1] to congratulate his new boss. Whether he was a phony, traitor, or **apostate**[2], he supposed, depended on one's point of view. As he reached the doorway, he turned, bowed, and, feeling more **perfidious**[3] than ever, said in a **stilted**[4] manner, "My **felicitations**[5]

---

[1] **politic** If you refer to a behavior or action as *politic* (pronounced with the accent on the first syllable), you mean that it's shrewd, savvy, wise, practical, diplomatic, or tactful. Behaving in a *politic* manner will generally keep you out of trouble. *In 1980 Pulitzer Prize–winning sports columnist Red Smith said, "A punch in the nose is about as direct a statement as you can make, but it is not always politic."*

[2] **apostate** A person who abandons his political party, religion, cause, etc. (often to join another), is known as an *apostate*. The act of such abandonment is known as *apostasy*. Note: As an adjective, *apostate* means "at variance with or disrespectful of established beliefs or values," as in *an apostate scientist*. *In 1983 U.S. District Court judge John H. Pratt, in ruling that Howard University had violated federal civil rights laws by dismissing a white faculty member and then arguing that as a mostly black institution it can "take race in consideration" in choosing its professors, said that the university had become "an apostate to the cause of racial equality."*

[3] **perfidious** To describe someone as *perfidious* is to say that he has betrayed (or has a tendency to betray) someone's (expected) trust or confidence; that is, he's disloyal, unfaithful, untrustworthy, traitorous, etc. The noun is *perfidy*. *In 1987, after talks in Moscow with U.S. Secretary of State George Shultz, Soviet Premier Mikhail Gorbachev said, "It is better to discuss things, to argue and engage in [debate], than make perfidious plans of mutual destruction."*

[4] **stilted** If someone's writing, speech, or manner is *stilted*, it's unnaturally stiff or overly formal. *At her interview for a job as a lawyer's assistant, Mary tried to sound intelligent by never ending a sentence with a preposition and by using phrases she'd seen in legal documents; but by doing so her speech ended up sounding (to the interviewer's ear) comically stilted (as when she said, "Paid vacations and/or medical benefits, or cash equivalent of same, is that for which I wish").*

[5] **felicitate (felicitations)** To *felicitate* someone is to congratulate him; to wish him well upon a happy event. Expressions of such good wishes are known as *felicitations*. *In 1968 Los Angeles Dodger Don Drysdale pitched a record-breaking 58 consecutive scoreless innings; when this record was broken in 1988 by fellow Dodger Oren Hershiser, Drysdale was among the first on the field to offer his felicitations.*

on your new position." He closed the door behind him.

Now everyone looked to the Scarecrow, who, trying hard to sound **omniscient**[1], proclaimed, "The best thing we can do is travel to the Land of the South and ask Glinda to help Dorothy."

They started leaving the room in single file, with Dorothy at the rear. Just as she was about to exit, her attention was drawn to an envelope lying on a nearby table. As her curiosity became more and more **piqued**[2], her pace became correspondingly **laggard**[3]. Staying behind to have a look, she **furtively**[4] picked up the envelop and examined it. Though it and the paper inside had been turned yellow

---

[1] **omniscient** If you say that a person (or God) is *omniscient* (pronounced *om-NISH-int*), you mean that he's all-knowing (that is, he knows everything; he has total or infinite awareness or understanding). *In the 1977 film* Oh, God! *a series of impossibly difficult questions is posed to test the omniscience of an ordinary-looking old man in tennis shoes and a golf hat (actor/comedian George Burns) who claims to be God.*

[2] **pique (piqued)** To *pique* (pronounced *peek*) someone's interest or curiosity is to arouse, stimulate, or excite it. *In Greek mythology, when Zeus gave Pandora (the first woman on earth) a closed box with instructions never to open it, her curiosity became piqued; unable to control herself, she lifted the lid, allowing all the world's evils to escape.* Note: In another sense the word means "to irritate," as in *she was piqued by my discovery of her secret hiding place.* And when used as a noun in that sense, as in the phrase "in a pique," it means "a feeling of anger or annoyance, as from a slight, insult, invasion of privacy, etc."

[3] **laggard** If someone is *laggard* (or moves in a *laggard* manner), he's slow (to act), falls behind, lags, etc.; he's sluggish, unhurried, slow-footed, etc. As a noun, a *laggard* is one who moves in this manner or fails to keep up (with others); a straggler. *In 1975 drama critic Walter Kerr said, "Reviewers must normally function as huff-and-puff artists blowing laggard theatergoers stageward."*

[4] **furtive (furtively)** When you do something *furtively*, you do it quietly and secretly (and often slyly), so that no one will know you're doing it. *I found myself on the commuter train with nothing to read; but by furtively looking over shoulders, I was able to enjoy a newspaper and an entire chapter of a book!*

and brittle by the normal **depredations**[1] of time, the writing on them was perfectly **legible**[2]. As soon as she started reading, she realized that this was a letter the Wizard had written long ago but had never mailed. Unable to stop herself, she read the whole thing, as follows:

Dear Mom,

I have to tell you about one of the strangest places I've encountered here in Oz. It's a land whose floor is as smooth and shiny as the bottom of a big platter.

One day when I was out for my daily **constitutional**[3]—the totality of my feeble exercise **regimen**[4]—I came upon a large wall. Climbing over it, I was amazed to see many houses made entirely of china. And they were so small that the biggest of them reached only as high as a Munchkin's waist! But the strangest things were the people and animals who lived in this queer country. They were all

---

[1] **depredation (depredations)** Damage, loss, or ravage (as from natural decay or unlawful attack) is known as *depredation*. Note: The word is often used in the plural. *In 1965 President Lyndon Johnson signed the Medicare Act to protect citizens from the depredations of illness in their old age.* Note: In a related sense, the word means "unlawful taking of property by force (a raid, attack, robbery, ransacking, etc.)."

[2] **legible** If you refer to something (handwriting, lettering, etc.) as *legible,* you mean that it's readable, understandable, clear, etc. (If it's *illegible,* it's not readable). The noun is *legibility. After vetoing hundreds of possible wedding invitation typefaces for being either too common-looking or too hard to read, the bride finally found one that she felt perfectly balanced beauty with legibility (and the groom, when asked, said he liked it, too).*

[3] **constitutional** A walk taken on a regular basis for the benefit of one's health is known as a *constitutional. When Bill confessed to his friend Steve that he was too lazy to engage in any exercise other than his 15-minute daily constitutional, Steve replied, "I don't even do that; in fact, the only thing I exercise is caution!"*

[4] **regimen** A particular, regulated system or course (as of diet, exercise, therapy, etc.) intended to promote health or attain some result is known as a *regimen. At summer camp, after a bunkmate told him that the treatment for rabies involves a regimen of painful injections to the stomach over a period of many weeks, Bobby refused to ever hike in the woods again (in case he got bitten by a chipmunk).*

made of china, too, including their clothes, and were so small that the tallest of them was no higher than a Munchkin's knee!

I began walking through this country of tiny china people, and the first thing I came to was a china milkmaid milking a **piebald**[1] china cow. As I came near, the cow, startled by the sound of my **footfalls**[2], suddenly kicked and knocked over the stool, the pail, and even the milkmaid herself. All fell to the china ground with a great clatter. I was shocked to see that the cow had broken her leg off, that the pail was shattered, and that the poor milkmaid had nicked her left elbow. She stood up, **bridled**[3], and said to me with **asperity**[4], "See what you've done? What do you mean by coming here and frightening my cow?"

She picked up the leg sulkily and led her cow away, the poor

---

[1] **piebald** To describe something (an animal or landscape, for example) as *piebald* is to say that it has patches of dark and light colors (especially black and white). *The pinto (a piebald horse) wasn't recognized in the United States as a breed until 1963.* Note: A related word is *pied* (as in *the Pied Piper of Hamelin*), meaning "having patches or splotches of two or more colors" or "wearing pied clothes."

[2] **footfall (footfalls)** A footstep or the sound of a footstep is known as a *footfall*. *From the bedroom it was always easy to tell which family member was on the way up the stairs— each one's footfalls had a distinctive rhythm and intensity (but it was impossible to distinguish between our two cats).*

[3] **bridle (bridled)** Technically, to *bridle* is to lift the head and draw in the chin as an expression of anger, annoyance, resentment, disapproval, etc. But the word is also used to mean simply "to become angry, annoyed, etc." (without actually lifting the head or drawing in the chin). *American colonists bridled (1765) when the British government passed the Stamp Act (which required the payment of a tax to Britain on newspapers and legal documents).*

[4] **asperity** If someone is angry, upset, or irritable, his manner or tone of voice is likely to be sharp or bitter. This sharpness or bitterness of expression is known as *asperity. In June 1982, speaking of President Ronald Reagan's "pilgrimage [journey] of peace" to the Vatican, journalist Mary McGrory said, "[Pope John Paul II]— judging from the austerity [severity], and even asperity, of his remarks— thinks that Reagan must try harder [to be a peacemaker]."*

animal limping on three legs. As she walked away the **irascible**[1] woman kept casting **aspersions**[2] at me, but at the same time she **incessantly**[3] stared at her nicked elbow as if obsessed with her **infirmity**[4]. I must say, in view of my **culpable**[5] disregard of her cow's potential reaction to my sudden **propinquity**[6], the

---

[1] **irascible** Someone who's *irascible* (pronounced with a silent *c*) is easily angered; he's irritable, cranky, short-tempered, testy, etc. *In 1981 irascible tennis star John McEnroe shouted to the umpires, spectators, and reporters at Wimbledon, "You are the pits of the world! Vultures! Trash!"*

[2] **aspersion (aspersions)** An *aspersion* (as in the phrase "cast aspersions") is an unfavorable, damaging, or accusatory remark (directed at someone); a criticism, put-down, slur, etc. *On a TV show in 1979, writer Mary McCarthy cast aspersions on playwright Lillian Hellman's honesty, saying, "Every word she writes is a lie, including 'and' and 'the.'"*

[3] **incessant (incessantly)** This word describes things (actions, activities, etc.) that continue or repeat without interruption; they're continuous, constant, never-ending, etc. *After watching some ants mill about in our backyard, we wondered if they all walk incessantly or if they sometimes (though we've never seen it) stop to rest.*

[4] **infirmity** An *infirmity* is a physical ailment or weakness; a disease, disorder, sickness, condition, injury, etc. The adjective *infirm* means "weak in body; sick, sickly, feeble, etc.," as in *infirm nursing home residents. The first generations of settlers in the Virginia colonies were so plagued by life-threatening infirmities that historian Edmund Morgan entitled one of his essays about the region "Living with Death."*

[5] **culpable** If you're *culpable* (in regard to something bad that happened), you're blameworthy, guilty, etc. The noun is *culpability. In his 1995 book* Oswald's Tale, *writer Norman Mailer discusses the possible culpability of (accused Kennedy assassin) Lee Harvey Oswald.*

[6] **propinquity** The state of being in proximity to (physically close to or near) a particular thing or place is known as *propinquity. In 1979, in a Supreme Court ruling that a search warrant does not automatically authorize police to search anyone who happens to be at the site, Justice Potter Stewart said, "A person's mere propinquity to others independently suspected of criminal activity does not give rise to probable cause to search that person."*

milkmaid's **censure**[1] of me was probably **tenable**[2]. I felt quite guilty about this little **contretemps**[3], and I decided I'd have to be very careful here or I might hurt these pretty little people so badly they would never mend. I imagine this society has a very high rate of **attrition**[4] from breakage alone!

A little farther on I met a beautifully dressed, perfectly **coifed**[5],

---

[1] **censure** As a noun, a *censure* (pronounced *SEN-sher*) is a strong expression of disapproval. Note: In politics the word refers to an official expression of disapproval (as by a legislature or one of its members). As a verb, to *censure* (someone) is to strongly or harshly scold or criticize (him). To refer to something (language, for example) as *censorious* (pronounced *sen-SOR-ee-us*) is to say that it's severely critical. *In the late 1990s, some members of Congress suggested that President Bill Clinton be censured (rather than impeached) for his sexual misdeeds.*

[2] **tenable** If you refer to a statement or idea as *tenable*, you mean that it can be maintained, defended, or supported in argument; that is, it's reasonable, rational, acceptable, sound, etc. If you say that a place (a fort or city, for example) is *tenable*, you mean that it can be held or defended against military attack. *An ancient theory of astronomy, no longer tenable, held that the sun revolves around the earth.*

[3] **contretemps** A usually minor, embarrassing, unforeseen, disruptive event or occurrence (as between countries or individuals) is known as a *contretemps* (pronounced *KON-truh-tahn*, with the final syllable nasalized, as in French). Note: The same spelling is used for both the singular and plural. *The late-1970s and early-1980s TV sitcom* Three's Company *specialized in creating and then resolving embarrassing contretemps between the characters (a young single man and two young single women who share an apartment rented from an older married couple).*

[4] **attrition** A decrease in number or size— especially a gradual, natural reduction in the size of a company's work force or a group's membership (as through retirement, resignation, or death)— is known as *attrition*. *In 1985, explaining West Point's high rate of attrition (33 percent) compared to that of private colleges, the military academy's Director of Admissions said, "Harvard doesn't consider anyone a loss until he dies without a diploma— because they say he can always come back and finish."*

[5] **coif (coifed)** A *coif* (or *coiffure*) is a particular style of arranging or wearing the hair; a hairstyle or hairdo. As a verb, to *coif* the hair is to arrange it (in a particular style). *On the animated TV series* The Simpsons, *mother Marge sports a blue beehive coif.* Note: A *coiffeur* is a hairdresser.

young Princess, who stopped short as she saw me, then started to run away. I wanted to see more of her, so I ran after her. Then the china girl suddenly turned around and cried out, "Don't chase me! Don't chase me! If I run I may fall down and break myself."

I stopped and, admiring her clear, **comely**[1] face, asked, "But couldn't you be mended?"

"Yes, but no one's ever as pretty after being mended," she replied. "For example, take our oldest clown. He's broken himself so many times that he's been mended in a hundred different places and doesn't look at all pretty—and that's made him **curmudgeonly**[2]. Here he comes now, so you can see for yourself." Indeed, an ancient clown came slowly walking toward us, and even a **cursory**[3] glance—I didn't want to be so impolite as to stare—revealed that he was completely covered with cracks, showing plainly that he had been mended in many places.

He gave me a **surly**[4] look, which seemed highly **incongruous**[1]

---

[1] **comely** A person (or face) described as *comely* (pronounced *KUM-lee*) is pleasing in appearance (especially wholesomely so); she's (or he's) attractive, good-looking, pretty, handsome, etc. *President John F. Kennedy first met (1952) his comely wife, Jacqueline (Jackie), when she was working as a reporter for the* Washington Times-Herald.

[2] **curmudgeon (curmudgeonly)** A *curmudgeon* is an ill-tempered, cranky, grouchy person. *Actor Walter Matthau specialized in humorously portraying curmudgeons in such films as* The Odd Couple *(1968),* The Sunshine Boys *(1975), and* Grumpy Old Men *(1993).*

[3] **cursory** If you describe something (an inspection, an analysis, a look, etc.) as *cursory*, you mean that it's performed in a hasty, superficial manner, with little attention to detail. *After a cursory inspection of New Orleans' Mardi Gras celebration, we asked the logical question, Why did we purchase Louisiana in the first place?*

[4] **surly** People who are *surly* are both irritable and rude; they're abrupt and discourteous in their manner or speech. *We agreed that our surly New York waiter was better suited to some other field— like debt collecting or slum demolition!*

with his big red nose and brightly painted smile. Then he puffed out his cheeks and stood on his head! "Don't mind him," the Princess said to me. "He's cracked in the head, and that makes him **churlish²**." With her index finger she made little circles in the air next to her ear. As the clown walked off, he barked a string of **profanities³** that hung in the air awhile, then evaporated.

"Oh, I don't mind him," I said, ignoring the Princess's **droll⁴** wit and the clown's **Parthian⁵ volley⁶** of **expletives¹**. I realized the

---

¹ **incongruous** If you say that something is *incongruous* (to or with something else), you mean that it's inharmonious or incompatible; it's out of place or out of keeping; it's unfitting. *In 1984 the president of the American Medical Association, calling for a ban on professional boxing, said, "It seems to us extraordinarily incongruous [to the promotion of public health] that we have a sport in which two people are paid to get into a ring and try to beat one another to death."*

² **churlish** People described as *churlish* are ill-natured, rude, uncouth, coarse, and ungracious. *When Sesame Street's Oscar the Grouch worked in a diner, the churlish green trashcan dweller tossed a salad (across the room) and replied to a waitress's request for a glass by asking her whether she wanted it dirty or broken.*

³ **profanity (profanities)** A *profanity* is a dirty word, a vulgarism. *In 1991 (department stores) K-Mart and Wal-Mart boycotted (hard rock band) Guns N' Roses' profanity-filled albums.*

⁴ **droll** To describe something (a person's humor or wit, for example) as *droll* (rhymes with *bowl*) is to say that it's amusing, but in an odd way. *Ogden Nash (1902–1971) was an American poet known for his droll rhymes ("A bit of talcum is always walcum," for example).*

⁵ **Parthian** In the ancient country of Parthia (located where Iran is today), soldiers customarily shot arrows rearward while fleeing on horseback. Today, to refer to something (the utterance of a last word or sharp remark, for example) as *Parthian* is to say that it's delivered in departing. *When his bullying big brother finally released him from the hammerlock and stopped calling him a sissy, little Bobby's Parthian shot ("You mean you are!"), demonstrated that, while he was no logician, he had a natural grasp of the art of argumentation.*

⁶ **volley** A *volley* is a simultaneous or concentrated discharge of something (missiles, words, or blows, for example); a barrage, bombardment, burst, etc. *At a 1970 anti–Vietnam War demonstration at Ohio's Kent State University, National Guardsmen let loose a volley of shots, killing four students.*

choleric² little creature was in his **dotage³** and didn't know any better. "But you're such a pretty little knickknack," I continued, "that I'd like to carry you home and stand you on my mantelpiece— if you'd **deign⁴** to permit it."

"I'm afraid I can't **accede⁵** to your request," answered the china Princess. "You see, here in our country we can talk and move about as we wish. But whenever any of us is taken away, our joints

---

¹ **expletive (expletives)** An *expletive* is an obscene or vulgar word or phrase; a dirty word, four-letter word, curse, etc. *When President Richard Nixon's Oval Office tapes (which contained blunt conversations concerning the Watergate cover-up) were transcribed to paper, all expletives were replaced by the now-famous phrase "expletive deleted."*

² **choleric** People described as *choleric* (pronounced either *KOL-uh-rik* or *kuh-LER-ik*) are bad-tempered or easily angered; they're crabby, grouchy, irritable, touchy, etc. *After seeing the 1938 animated film* Snow White and the Seven Dwarfs, *we couldn't remember Doc's personality type; on the other hand, the names of the other six dwarfs defined their natures (for example, there was the shy Bashful, the choleric Grumpy, and so on).*

³ **dotage** If someone is in his *dotage,* his mental facilities have deteriorated as a result of old age; he's become senile, feeble-minded, etc. A person in his *dotage* is known as a *dotard,* and his behavior is described as *dotty* (see *dotty*). *The nursing home comedian's opening joke ("What's a dotard's number-one pickup line? 'Do I come here often?'") was received with blank stares.*

⁴ **deign** To *deign* (to do something) is to agree to lower yourself from your level of dignity or importance (to do it). *In 1985, speaking of parents who deign to take their kids to fast-food restaurants that serve meals rich in unsaturated fats, cardiologist Dr. Tazewell Banks said, "It would be better if they told their children, 'Go out and play in traffic.'"*

⁵ **accede** When you *accede* to something (especially something insisted upon or urged by another), you agree to it (or comply with it or permit it). *At the Munich Conference (1938), Britain and France, in an effort to maintain peace, acceded to Hitler's demand that Germany immediately annex the Sudetenland (western Czechoslovakia).* Note: Another meaning of this word is "assume (or attain, arrive at, or succeed to) an office, title, or position," as in *Spanish king Juan Carlos acceded to the throne upon the death of Francisco Franco (1975).*

ossify[1], and we can only stand straight and look pretty. That would make me very unhappy. You know, many **expatriate**[2] china people are standing miserably on mantelpieces right now, **pining**[3] for their homeland, but with no hope of **repatriation**[4]."

She was so tiny, I could have taken her in spite of her unwillingness and she would have been forced to **capitulate**[5]— but,

---

[1] **ossify** Technically, when something (a tendon or cartilage, for example) *ossifies*, it turns to bone or becomes bone-like. But in general usage, to say that something (a behavior or philosophy, for example) *ossifies* is to say that it becomes rigidly set, hardened, stiff, etc. *When President John F. Kennedy talked with his adversary (Soviet leader) Nikita Khrushchev in Vienna (1961), the meeting served only to ossify Soviet-American hostility.*

[2] **expatriate** As an adjective, *expatriate* means "residing in another country." As a noun, an *expatriate* is a person who has been banished from or withdrew himself from his native country. *In the 1942 film* Casablanca, *Humphrey Bogart plays an American expatriate who owns a Moroccan nightclub during World War II.*

[3] **pine (pining)** To *pine* for something is to deeply yearn for it; to painfully long for it. The implication is that a wasting away might occur from this longing or grief. *In Greek mythology, Echo was a mountain nymph who fell in love with Narcissus (a beautiful young man); when her love went unreturned, she pined away until only her voice remained.*

[4] **repatriation** The sending back of someone (a refugee or prisoner of war, for example) to his native country is known as *repatriation. In January 1973, the United States and North Vietnam signed the Paris Peace Agreement, which provided for the withdrawal of U.S. troops from South Vietnam, the repatriation of U.S. prisoners of war, the recognition of the right of the South Vietnamese people to determine their own future, and the establishment of an international peace-keeping force.*

[5] **capitulate** To *capitulate* is to surrender (give up, yield, succumb, etc.) or to act in accordance with another's wishes (agree, submit, obey, etc.). *V-E Day and V-J Day are historic dates marking the end of World War II; V-E (Victory in Europe) Day was celebrated following the surrender of Germany (May 8, 1945), and V-J (Victory over Japan) Day designates the date (September 2, 1945) Japan officially capitulated.*

of course, my **innate**[1] sense of right and wrong and my **inviolable**[2] conscience force me to **temper**[3] all my decisions with compassion. So let's just say we made a **bilateral**[4] agreement to part.

I walked very carefully through the rest of the china country. All the little people and animals scampered out of my way, fearing, understandably, that I might knock them over and break them.

After an hour or so I reached the other side of the country and came to another wall, in front of which stood a row of about six

---

[1] **innate** If something (talent, curiosity, common sense, honesty, etc.) is *innate*, it exists or occurs naturally, since birth; it's inborn (as opposed to being acquired through study or experience). *In his 1973 book* The Seduction of the Spirit, *Harvard University divinity professor Harvey Cox said, "All human beings have an innate need to hear and tell stories and to have a story to live by; religion, whatever else it has done, has provided one of the main ways of meeting this need."*

[2] **inviolable** Things that are *inviolable* are incapable of being violated; that is, they're untouchable, sacred, unassailable, well-protected, invulnerable, impregnable, etc. *The English Bill of Rights (1689) stated that no Roman Catholic would rule England; in addition, it gave inviolable civil and political rights to the people and political supremacy to Parliament.*

[3] **temper** As a verb, to *temper* something (justice or punishment, for example) is to make it less severe or extreme; to moderate it, tone it down, mellow it. Note: When speaking of physical materials or ideas, to *temper* something is to modify it by blending it with something else. *Pool great Minnesota Fats' (1900–1996) loudness and boastfulness were tempered by his sense of humor and good-naturedness.*

[4] **bilateral** In Latin, "bi" means *two* and "lateral" means *side*. So something *bilateral* (a decision, for example) is two-sided (that is, both parties agree to it). Note: In Latin, "uni" means *one*; so something *unilateral* (a cease-fire, for example) is one-sided. *Because there is no international law governing extradition (the sending back of a fleeing criminal or suspected criminal to his own country for trial), the delivery of such persons occurs under the authority of specific bilateral treaties between nations.*

simple, **utilitarian**[1] buildings. In climbing the wall I accidentally upset the **penultimate**[2] little **edifice**[3]— a china church— with my foot and smashed it to pieces. Three winged angels— really just an artist's stained-glass portrayal of them as **corporeal**[4] beings— actually flew a few feet into the air before shattering loudly among the **detritus**[5] below! With one stroke I may have transformed the

---

[1] **utilitarian** To describe something (a building, appliance, tool, etc.) as *utilitarian* is to say that it exhibits or stresses usefulness (practicality, workability, functionality, etc.) over beauty, aesthetics, ornamentation, etc. Things that are *utilitarian* generally work efficiently but are not especially pretty. *During the Bronze Age— a period of human culture between the Stone Age and Iron Age (roughly 4000 B.C.–2000 B.C.)— people used bronze (an alloy of copper and tin) to make both utilitarian utensils and art objects.*

[2] **penultimate** This word is a fancy way of saying "next to last." In a series of objects or things, the next to last one is known as the *penultimate* one (and the last is the *ultimate* one). *While some people pronounce the word* microcomputer *with the accent at the beginning* (MI-cro-com-put-er), *others stress the penultimate syllable* (mi-cro-com-PUT-er).

[3] **edifice** An *edifice* is a building or structure, especially a large or impressive one. *On a tour of a Washington, D.C., museum that was once Ford's Theatre (where President Abraham Lincoln was fatally shot in 1865), we learned that 28 years after the assassination, part of the edifice collapsed, killing 28 people.*

[4] **corporeal** Saying that something is *corporeal* (pronounced *kor-POR-ee-ul*) is the opposite of saying that it's spiritual. In other words, it relates to the physical body or to some actual, physical thing; it's concrete, material, tangible, real, etc. *Seventeenth-century British philosopher and scientist Thomas Hobbes suggested that human feelings are merely corporeal motions within the brain.*

[5] **detritus** Technically, *detritus* is small, disintegrated particles of rock or other material, worn away from a mass (as by erosion). But in general usage, people use this word to refer to any kind of debris, junk, garbage, waste, castoffs, etc. *Swiss-born motion-art sculptor Jean Tinguely (1935–1991) was known for salvaging the discarded detritus of the machine age and recycling it into huge, motor-powered sculptures.*

cleric[1] and all his parishioners into **infidels**[2]! It was unfortunate, and I wished there were something I could have done to **redeem**[3] myself for the damage I caused, but I think I was lucky in not doing these **frangible**[4] people more harm than breaking a cow's leg and a church.

That's all for now, Mom. I hope all is well with you. I love and miss you very much.

Love, Sonny

Marveling at how strange it all was, but touched by the **filial**[5] devotion evident in the final paragraph, Dorothy carefully put the letter back exactly as she had found it and hurried out.

---

[1] **cleric** A *cleric* (or *clergyman*) is a person ordained for religious service; for example, a minister, priest, reverend, pastor, chaplain, rabbi, etc. *In 1968, comparing clerics St. Paul (ancient Christian preacher and teacher) and Norman Vincent Peale (Protestant minister and author of the 1952 self-help book* The Power of Positive Thinking*), former presidential candidate Adlai Stevenson said, "I find Paul appealing and Peale appalling."*

[2] **infidel (infidels)** A person with no religious beliefs, or a person who rejects or doubts a particular religion, is known as an *infidel*. (Infidels are sometimes looked down upon.) *The Crusades (1096–1291) were military expeditions in which European Christians sought to recapture the Holy Land (where Jesus had lived) from Muslim infidels.*

[3] **redeem** To *redeem* yourself for some fault or shortcoming is to make amends for it, make up for it, offset it, etc. *In the U.S. Civil War, Union general Philip Sheridan was unable to maintain his lines at Chickamauga, Georgia (September 1863), but was able to redeem himself two months later by successfully storming Missionary Ridge (a range of hills) at Chattanooga, Tennessee.*

[4] **frangible** If something is *frangible*, it's capable of being broken (but it's not necessarily weak— earthenware pottery, for example, is strong but *frangible*). *The magazine ad's "before" and "after" pictures of a pretty vase looked oddly identical— then we realized the advertiser was a moving company that promised to deliver all frangible items completely intact and unscratched.*

[5] **filial** This adjective means "pertaining to a son or daughter" or "having the relationship of child to parent." *Billionaire oil executive and art collector Jean Paul Getty (1892-1976), father of five sons, changed his will 21 times, using it as a weapon to punish what he perceived as filial disloyalty.*

Chapter 23 "The Fighting Trees"

The next morning our friends shook hands with the soldier in the green uniform, who, with **impeccably**[1] **decorous**[2] **deportment**[3], had walked with them as far as the gate. When the Guardian of the Gates saw them again he wondered why they would leave the beautiful City to get into new trouble, but he kept his thoughts to himself and merely wished them luck. Then, suddenly remembering that it was the Scarecrow to whom Oz had **bequeathed**[4] his throne, he yelled to him, "You're our ruler now, so you must come back to us as soon as possible."

"I certainly will if I am able," replied the Scarecrow, "but first I must help Dorothy get back to Kansas."

---

[1] **impeccable (impeccably)** If something (one's behavior or clothing, for example) is *impeccable*, it's faultless, perfectly correct, flawless, etc., as in *impeccably clean clothes* or *he speaks French impeccably*. *In 1927 satirical writer Dorothy Parker said, "Those who have mastered ettiquette, who are entirely, impeccably right, would seem to arrive at a point of exquisite dullness."*

[2] **decorous** This word is used to describe people whose conduct, manner, appearance, etc., are characterized by properness and social correctness; they're well-behaved, polite, respectful, gentlemanly (or ladylike), etc. The noun *decorum* refers to either the well-mannered behavior of an individual toward others or to the overall observance (by a group) of the rules of polite society. *In the 1989 based-on-fact film* Lean on Me, *actor Morgan Freeman plays the new principle of a gang- and drug-infested New Jersey high school; in an effort to restore decorum and to provide an effective place of learning, he calls all troublemakers to the stage of the auditorium and then abruptly expels them.*

[3] **deportment** Your *deportment* is the way you conduct or behave yourself (especially as measured against some prevailing code of social behavior). *As the head servant in a household, the butler, in addition to being in charge of food service and the care of silverware, is responsible for the deportment of the other servants.*

[4] **bequeath (bequeathed)** To *bequeath* something to someone is to hand it down or pass it on to him (often upon death, as indicated in a will). *Alfred Nobel was a 19th-century Swedish chemist and engineer who invented dynamite (1866) and bequeathed his fortune to institute the Nobel Prizes.*

THE WIZARD OF OZ VOCABULARY BUILDER

The sun shone brightly as our **itinerant**[1] friends turned their faces toward the Land of the South. Throughout the morning they walked through green fields **peppered**[2] with bright flowers, but in the afternoon they came to a **portentously**[3] thick forest that seemed to extend to the right and left as far as they could see.

They didn't dare change the direction of their journey for fear of getting lost. So, in spite of the unknown, **sylvan**[4] dangers that lurked within, they decided to walk through the woods. Now they

---

[1] **itinerant** An *itinerant* person is one who travels from place to place (especially to perform work or duty); he has no fixed home. *At about the age of 20, African-American ragtime composer Scott Joplin (1868–1917) became an itinerant pianist, traveling throughout the Midwest.*

[2] **pepper (peppered)** If you say that something (an otherwise uniform surface, material, idea, speech, etc.) is *peppered* with something, you mean that it's dotted, studded, sprinkled, or speckled with it (often intentionally to make it more lively or vivid). *As broadcaster of New York Yankees baseball games, (former Yankee shortstop) Phil "The Scooter" Rizzuto often peppered his commentary with personal anecdotes.*

[3] **portentous (portentously)** If you refer to something as *portentous,* you mean that it tends to signal or indicate in advance that something (usually something significant or bad) will happen. The word can also describe something that is frighteningly large or impressive, but not actually dangerous. Note: As a verb, to *portend* (pronounced with the accent on the second syllable) is to foretell, foreshadow, etc.; and as a noun, a *portent* (pronounced with the accent on the first syllable) is an indication of something (usually significant or bad). *In the 1963 film* The Birds, *hundreds of black crows silently but portentously gather on a school playground's monkey bars.*

[4] **sylvan** In Roman mythology, *Sylvanus* was the god of the woods. Today, to refer to something as *sylvan* is to say that it pertains to or is characteristic of the woods or forest, or that it's located in or inhabits the woods or forest. Walden *is a book by (American writer and naturalist) Henry David Thoreau (1817–1862) describing his two years of life living alone in a cabin he had built near the shore of a sylvan Massachusetts pond (Walden Pond).*

looked for a gap in the thick **foliage**[1] where they could enter.

The Scarecrow, who was in the lead, discovered a big tree with such wide-spreading branches that there was room for the party to pass underneath. Now, this tree was one of an enchanted species, **endemic**[2] to this region, that didn't take kindly to strangers **encroaching**[3] on their land. So when the Scarecrow walked under the tree's branches, they bent down and twined around him. The next minute he was raised from the ground and flung headlong among his fellow travelers.

"And that's what we do with people who **flout**[4] the rules of **propriety**[5]!" shouted the tree.

"Let me try," said the Tin Woodman. Shouldering his axe, he

---

[1] **foliage** The leaves of a plant (especially a tree), collectively, are known as *foliage*. The word can also refer to leaves in general (or to a cluster of leaves) or to any ornamental display of leaves, stems, and flowers (as in painting). *In Massachusetts autumn travelers can view spectacularly colored foliage from marked highway trails.*

[2] **endemic** This word is used to describe things (customs, diseases, food shortages, etc.) that are peculiar to (or prevalent in) a particular locality or people. *One might think that Rocky Mountain spotted fever (an infectious disease caused by a microorganism transmitted by ticks) is endemic to the Rocky Mountains, but it actually occurs throughout North America.*

[3] **encroach (encroaching)** To *encroach* is to (sometimes illegally, sometimes gradually or sneakily) advance beyond proper limits; to trespass, infringe, overstep, etc. *Crazy Horse was a 19th-century Sioux chief who resisting the encroachment of whites in the Black Hills of South Dakota.*

[4] **flout** To *flout* something (a rule or code of conduct, for example) is to disregard it and scoff at it. *In November 1995 President Bill Clinton repealed the federal 55-mile-per-hour speed limit law, which had been in place since 1974 but widely flouted (especially in Western states).* Note: Don't confuse this word with *flaunt*, which means "to show off or conspicuously display," as in *she flaunted her diamonds.*

[5] **propriety** Conformity to established standards of proper behavior, social correctness, or good manners is known as *propriety*. *French-born American clergyman and writer Thomas Merton (1915–1968) once described the city of London as follows: "Men in [derby hats] and dark suits with their rolled-up umbrellas; men full of propriety, calm and proud, neat and noble."*

marched up to the tree. This second **sortie**[1] only **exacerbated**[2] the tree's anger. A big branch flung itself furiously at the Tin Woodman, who chopped at it like a **dynamo**[3] until it was cut it in two. At once the tree began shaking all its branches as if in **excruciating**[4] pain, and the Tin Woodman passed safely under it.

"Come on! Be quick!" he shouted to the others, desperate to end this queer **imbroglio**[5] once and for all. They all ran forward and passed under the tree without injury. The thought of these

---

[1] **sortie** Technically, a *sortie* (pronounced *sor-TEE*) is a military attack or raid (especially from a place surrounded by enemy forces). But the word can also be used figuratively to refer to non-military attacks or raids, or to any sort of journeying forth (as in *the lunar astronauts made two exploratory sorties on foot*). *In August 1995, after more than three years of hesitation, NATO planes flew more than 200 sorties to pound Bosnian Serb targets with air strikes.*

[2] **exacerbate (exacerbated)** To *exacerbate* something is to make it even worse (more severe, violent, etc.) than it already is; to heighten, deepen, or intensify it. *Population growth, industrial expansion, and automobile exhaust led to an increase in pollution in the 1960s; exacerbating the problem was the appearance of synthetic substances (plastics and fibers, for example) that degrade extremely slowly or not at all.*

[3] **dynamo** Technically, a *dynamo* is an electric generator. But people use the word informally to refer to a person who is energetic, tireless, forceful, hard-working, powerful, etc. *Basketball player "Pistol" Pete Maravich (1948–1988) was a dynamo on the court, dazzling fans with his quick, deceptive ball-handling.*

[4] **excruciating** To describe something (pain, for example) as *excruciating* is to say that it's unbearably severe or intense; it's torturous, agonizing, etc. *When the patient complained of excruciating nighttime spasms in his calf muscles, the doctor told him that the next time it happens, he should try bending his toes back (toward his head).*

[5] **imbroglio** Depending on the context, this word (pronounced *im-BROHL-yoh*), can mean either "a messy confused situation; a mix-up, scandal, to-do, etc.," or "a bitter misunderstanding or disagreement; a dispute, conflict, set-to, etc. (as between people or countries)." *After the Watergate scandal (1972–1974), it became easy to nickname any Washington imbroglio; all one had to do was add the suffix "gate" to the topic at hand, as in 1993's "Nannygate" (in which President Clinton's first two choices for Attorney General, Zoe Baird and Kimba Wood, were accused of employing illegal aliens as household workers).*

presumptuous[1] trespassers entering the forest make the tree **livid**[2]. It quickly threw out a **serpentine**[3], **prehensile**[4] branch that tightly and painfully encircled Toto's body, and the terrified, **ululating**[5] dog was shaken mercilessly until the Tin Woodman set him free by

---

[1] **presumptuous** If you're *presumptuous*, you're overly or unwarrantedly bold or forward; you go beyond what is proper or right; you're overconfident, uppity, brash, arrogant, rude, etc. *In the Bible, when Noah's descendants (who spoke one language) tried to build a tower (the Tower of Babel) reaching to Heaven, God, thinking this presumptuous, stopped them by making them speak in different languages (so they couldn't communicate intelligently with each other).*

[2] **livid** Technically, someone described as *livid* has skin that has become a dull grayish or purplish blue, as from bruising, strangulation, etc. But in general usage, when people refer to someone as *livid*, they mean simply that he's extremely angry, enraged, furious, etc. (And you can imagine that if someone is angry enough, his skin might appear or threaten to become purplish blue, as from emotional strangulation.) *In a famous fairy tale, an old dwarf named Rumpelstiltskin tells a woman who has promised him her first-born child that he will not hold her to her promise if she can guess his name; when she finds it out, he becomes livid, then destroys himself.*

[3] **serpentine** Anything described as *serpentine* is snakelike (in shape, form, or movement); that is, it's winding, bending, crooked, etc. *In the winter sport known as bobsledding, two or four people race a long, steel-bodied sled down a serpentine ice track.*

[4] **prehensile** To describe something (a possum's tail or an elephant's trunk, for example) as *prehensile*, is to say that it's adapted for grasping, seizing, or taking hold of something, especially by wrapping around it. *The seahorse (a small upright-swimming fish whose head resembles that of a horse) anchors itself by curling its thin, prehensile tail around seaweed or other plants.*

[5] **ululate (ululating)** To *ululate* (pronounced *YULE-yuh-late*) is to utter or emit wailing, howling, or yowling sounds (like those of a wolf). The noun is *ululation*. *The hyena's well-known calls include the strange "laugh" during the mating season and the evening ululation for food.*

chopping off the **flailing**[1] limb with one mighty swing of his axe.

The other trees of the forest did nothing to keep them back, so they made up their minds that it was only that crazed **zealot**[2] in the first row who had the powers of a magical **sentinel**[3]. The four travelers now walked with ease until they came to the other edge of the woods. Before them they saw a disagreeable country, full of **morasses**[4] and covered with wildly **proliferating**[5] weeds.

---

[1] **flail (flailing)** If something (someone's arm for example) is *flailing*, it's vigorously (and usually continuously) moving to and fro, waving about, etc.; it's thrashing, flapping, swinging, etc. *In the animated film, we enjoyed watching the mermaid propel herself through the water by gracefully waving her tail back and forth (but we didn't like it when she was captured by fishermen and her tail flailed helplessly in the net).*

[2] **zealot** Enthusiastic, passionate devotion to a cause, person, object, goal, ideal, etc., is know as *zeal* (rhymes with *deal*). If you're *zealous* (pronounced ZELL-us), you show or feel *zeal* (passion or enthusiasm for something). The noun *zealot* (pronounced ZELL-it) can indicate a person who simply shows or feels *zeal* (a fan, enthusiast, devotee), but more often it indicates one who shows excessive zeal or holds extreme views (a fanatic, addict, maniac, radical, etc.). *In 1979 Egyptian president Anwar Sadat signed a peace treaty with Israel; two years later he was assassinated by a group of Muslim zealots who opposed his policies.*

[3] **sentinel** A *sentinel* is a person assigned to stand guard, keep watch, provide protection, etc.; a lookout, watchman, etc. *The New York Public Library (the largest city public library in the U.S.) is easily recognizable by the two large marble lions on its front steps— silent sentinels who stand guard day and night.*

[4] **morass (morasses)** A *morass* is an area of low, soft, wet ground; a swamp, marsh, bog, etc. But the word is also used figuratively to refer to any sort of difficult situation or predicament. *In his 1978 memoirs, former President Richard Nixon complained, "If I talked about Watergate, I was described as struggling to free myself from the morass; if I did not talk about Watergate, I was accused of being out of touch with reality."*

[5] **proliferate (proliferating)** When something *proliferates,* it reproduces or multiplies rapidly or excessively (as vegetation, viruses, etc.), or it increases or spreads rapidly or excessively (as video games, self-help groups, nuclear arms buildups, etc.). The noun is *proliferation. Leukemia is a disease characterized by the abnormal proliferation of white blood cells and the consequent crowding out of other blood elements.*

Chapter 24 "The Giant Spider"

It was difficult to walk through the **quagmire**[1] without falling into muddy holes, for here the weeds were so thick that they hid the holes from sight. Normally, Dorothy wasn't **averse**[2] to hiking, but now, terrified of the possibility of stepping into deadly quicksand, she silently cursed their **antediluvian**[3] mode of travel. But by carefully picking their way, they got safely along until they reached solid ground.

Now the country grew wilder with every step they took. The

---

[1] **quagmire** A *quagmire* is land with a soft, muddy surface that yields as one steps on it; a swamp, marsh, bog, etc. Figuratively, the word indicates a difficult, dangerous, or worrisome situation, especially one that is hard to escape; a predicament, mess, jam, quandary, etc. *In 1961, speaking to President John F. Kennedy about Vietnam, French president Charles de Gaulle said, "I predict you will sink step by step into a bottomless quagmire, however much you spend in men and money."*

[2] **averse** If you're *averse* to something (a plan, idea, activity, etc.), you're opposed to it, you're disinclined toward it, or you strongly dislike it. *In his personal memoirs (1885–1886), former Civil War general Ulysses S. Grant said of President Abraham Lincoln, "[The Secretary of War and the Chief of Staff] both cautioned me against giving the President my plans of campaign, saying that he was so kindhearted, so averse to refusing anything asked of him, that some friend would be sure to get from him all he knew."* Note: Don't confuse this word with *adverse*, which means "contrary to one's welfare or interests; harmful, unfavorable, etc.," as in *the patient had an adverse reaction to the drug.*

[3] **antediluvian** Technically, *antediluvian* pertains to the period of time before the Flood (the one concerning Noah and the ark written about in the Bible). But figuratively, the word can be used to refer to anything considered extremely old, antiquated, or old-fashioned. *In 1980, in a ruling that wives have the right to sue their husbands, the Massachusetts Supreme Judicial Court said, "[It is time to end] antediluvian assumptions concerning the role and status of women in marriage."*

THE WIZARD OF OZ VOCABULARY BUILDER

downward **devolution**[1] seemed to cast a **pall**[2] over the proceedings, and their expressions grew increasingly **saturnine**[3] as they continued onward. Dorothy had an uneasy **presentiment**[4] that more **adversity**[5] lay just ahead. Then suddenly they entered another forest, where the trees were bigger and older than any they had ever

---

[1] **devolution** A *devolution* is a stage-by-stage passage or evolution, usually to a lower or worse condition. *In 1841, years before he became involved with circus management, P. T. Barnum opened a New York City museum featuring fossils, historical relics, and what he called "freaks of nature"; his exaggerated publicity techniques did not lesson the educational value of his exhibits, but they did represent a devolution from earlier ideals.* The verb is *devolve.* When something (a responsibility or duty, for example) *devolves,* it's passed on or down (from one person to another). *The U.S. Constitution tells us that "in case of the removal of the President from office, or of his death, resignation, or inability to discharge the powers and duties of the said office, the same shall devolve on the Vice President."*

[2] **pall** A *pall* (rhymes with *ball*) is something that covers, surrounds, or envelops, especially with gloom or darkness; a gloomy atmosphere or effect. *The 1992 Los Angeles riots, sparked by the acquittal of four white policemen accused of beating African-American motorist Rodney King, cast a pall over future American race relations.* Note: The word can also denote a cover (often black velvet) for a coffin.

[3] **saturnine** To describe someone as *saturnine* is to say that his mood or temperament is gloomy, sluggish, sullen, cheerless, etc., and that he has a tendency to be uncommunicative and bitter. *The circus we visited featured two clowns— the first was a happy, white-faced, red-nosed one with baggy clothes and enormous shoes; the second (who looked more like a saturnine hobo) had a sad, dirty, unshaven face and wore tattered clothes.*

[4] **presentiment** A *presentiment* is a feeling or sense that something (often, but not always, something bad) is about to happen. *In the Bible, the Queen of Sheba (the ruler of an ancient Arabian country) tells (ancient Israel's) King Solomon that she has a presentiment that Jesus will be nailed to the True Cross (sacred wood that was originally a branch of the Tree of Knowledge).*

[5] **adversity** A condition or state of hardship, misfortune, trouble, difficulty, etc., is known as *adversity.* The word is often used in the plural *(adversities)* to refer to particular unfortunate events or circumstances of one's life (such as poverty, hunger, illness, accidents, etc.). *Helen Keller (1880–1968), who overcame personal adversity (blindness and deafness) to become a famous author, lecturer, and humanitarian, once gave this advice to a five-year-old: "Never bend your head; always hold it high; look the world straight in the eye."*

seen.

"This forest is perfectly delightful!" **emoted**[1] the Lion, obviously overcome by the majesty of the **august**[2] trees. "Never have I seen a more beautiful place. I'd like to live here all my life."

They started walking through it, and before they had gone very far, they heard a loud rumbling sound. When they came to a clearing, they saw hundreds of beasts of every kind. There were tigers, bears, wolves, foxes, and all the others of the animal kingdom, and for a moment Dorothy was afraid. But the Lion explained that the animals were holding a meeting. He judged by their snarling and growling that they were in the midst of some kind of **internecine**[3] feud.

The beasts suddenly caught sight of him and were at once hushed

---

[1] **emote (emoted)** To *emote* is to express emotion, especially excessively or theatrically. *In 1970, speaking of Christianity's traditional attraction for blacks, evangelist Calvin Marshall said, "Our religion had to mean more to us. We had to emote; we had to lose ourselves in it. We had to sing and shout, and after it was all over we had to have a big meal and have something going on Sunday afternoon. Because when Monday came, it was back out into the fields, or back to the janitor's job, or back to Miss Ann's kitchen scrubbing the floor."*

[2] **august** To describe a person or thing as *august* (pronounced *aw-GUST*) is to say that it inspires respect, admiration, or awe by virtue of its high rank, age, importance, dignity, grandeur, stateliness, majesty, etc. *In 1987, referring to the time he tested a live microphone before a broadcast by saying into it, "I've signed legislation that will outlaw Russia forever; we begin bombing in five minutes" and the time he fell asleep in the august presence of the pope, President Ronald Reagan joked, "Those were the good old days!"*

[3] **internecine** If you say that a conflict or struggle is *internecine*, you mean that it occurs within a group, organization, or nation (as opposed to between different groups). Note: In pronunciation, the third syllable, which gets the accent, can rhyme with either *geese* or *guess*, and the last syllable can rhyme with either *dean* or *dine*. *Although the Arab League (an association or over 20 Arab countries, including Egypt, Saudi Arabia, Syria, Lebanon, Iraq, and Jordan) was formed (1945) to coordinate the political interests of its members, it has really become more a forum for internecine squabbles (as when members clashed over Egypt's 1979 peace treaty with Israel and Iraq's 1990 invasion of Kuwait).*

by his **puissant**[1] presence. The largest of the tigers approached the Lion and bowed, saying, "Welcome, O King of Beasts! You have **opportunely**[2] arrived to bring peace to our **strife**[3]-ridden forest once more."

"What's the trouble?" asked the Lion with genuine concern.

"We're all threatened," answered the tiger, "by an enemy who is the **blight**[4] of our existence. It's a most tremendous monster, like a gigantic spider, with a body as big as an elephant's and eight legs as

---

[1] **puissant** To describe something as *puissant* (pronounced *PWISS-int, PYEW-ih-sint,* or *pyew-ISS-int*) is to say that it's powerful, mighty, strong, etc. (often in the sense of being influential, significant, effectual, important, prominent, etc.). *After founding the League of Women Voters in 1920 (the year women won the right to vote under the 19th Amendment) Carrie Chapman Catt sought to make women voters a puissant force in national politics.*

[2] **opportune (opportunely)** To describe an event (especially a chance event) as *opportune* is to say that it occurs at an advantageous or suitable time; it's fortunate, favorable, etc. Note: To describe something else (a remark, for example) as *opportune* is to say that it's fitting or appropriate (for a particular occasion, circumstance, or purpose); it's suitable, right, apt, etc. *The settlers of Jamestown (the first permanent English settlement in North America, founded in 1607 in Virginia) were nearly wiped out by disease and famine; only the opportune arrival (1610) of colonial administrator Baron De La Warr with supplies and more men convinced the survivors to remain.*

[3] **strife** Depending on the context, this word can denote bitter disagreement, actual fighting, or an ongoing state of competition or rivalry (as between people, countries, organizations, etc.). The implication is that the friction results more from a struggle for superiority than from fundamental philosophical differences. *Since the 19th century, the city of Belfast (the capital of Northern Ireland) has been scarred by (often violent) strife between the majority Protestants and the minority Catholics.*

[4] **blight** Any cause of destruction, ruin, or impairment (illness, poverty, severe weather, pollution, etc.) is known as a *blight*. Note: The word also refers specifically to any sudden, severe plant disease. *With its noise, ugliness, and gloom, the elevated railroad was the blight of the neighborhood.*

long as tree trunks. As this **behemoth**[1] crawls through the forest, it seizes its **prey**[2] with a leg and drags it to its mouth, where it slowly and mercilessly **masticates**[3] it. Like most spiders, it's **omnivorous**[4], so both **flora**[5] and **fauna**[6] are at risk. We don't know where this

---

[1] **behemoth** Technically, a *behemoth* is a huge animal described in the Old Testament (perhaps an elephant or hippopotamus, according to Biblical scholars). But in informal usage, the word can refer to anyone or anything enormous (in size or power). The word can also be used as an adjective, meaning "enormous." *Among the works of Russian-born artist Marc Chagall (1887–1985) are two huge murals designed for New York City's behemoth (4,000-seat) Metropolitan Opera House (at Lincoln Center for the Performing Arts).*

[2] **prey** An animal hunted or captured for food is know as *prey*. The word can also refer to a person (especially a helpless or defenseless one) who is the victim of a swindler, mugger, etc. Note: The word is also used as a verb (followed by *upon* or *on*), meaning "to hunt, capture, or eat" (as in *foxes prey upon rabbits*) or "to victimize or profit from" (as in *loan sharks prey on the poor*). *The rattlesnake has specialized heat receptors that enable it to not only sense the presence of warm-blooded prey in the dark, but also to strike at it accurately up to a distance of about 20 inches.*

[3] **masticate (masticates)** To *masticate* food is to chew it (especially to reduce it to a pulp by grinding the teeth). *Wasps begin a colony by making small cells of masticated plant material mixed with saliva.*

[4] **omnivorous** An *omnivorous* animal is one that eats both animal and plant foods. Note: A *carnivorous* animal (a wolf, for example) is one that eats meat, and a *herbivorous* animal (a sheep, for example) is one that eats plants. *The omnivorous daddy longlegs (an animal related to a spider but having fewer eyes) feeds not only on plant fluids and animal tissue but on other daddy longlegs!*

[5] **flora** Plants considered as a whole (especially the plants of a particular region or plants as distinguished from animals) are known as *flora*. Note: In Roman mythology, Flora was the goddess of flowers. *Botany Bay, a small Australian inlet just south of Sydney, was visited in 1770 by British explorer James Cook ("Captain Cook") and named by the botanist in his crew for the exotic flora on its shores.*

[6] **fauna** Animals considered as a whole (especially the animals of a particular region or animals as distinguished from plants) are known as *fauna*. *The Galápagos Islands, a group of 13 volcanic islands in the Pacific Ocean about 600 miles west of Ecuador, are famous for their rare species of fauna, including the giant land tortoises for which they are named ("galápagos" is the Spanish word for "tortoises").*

beast comes from, but it's certainly not **indigenous**[1] to this or any other nearby areas. Not one of us is safe while the creature is alive. Our normally **cohesive**[2] group seems to have become **polarized**[3], and I fear our **partisan**[4] conflicts will **vitiate**[5] our ability to defend

---

[1] **indigenous** If something (a plant, animal, race of people, cookery, folk music, etc.) is *indigenous* to a certain region or country, it originated there; it's native to it. *In his 1979 book* The Americans, *British-born American TV journalist Alistair Cooke said, "Texas does not, like any other region, simply have indigenous dishes; it proclaims them; it congratulates you, on your arrival, at having escaped from the slop pails of the other 49 states."*

[2] **cohesive** To refer to something (a social group, a chemical mixture, etc.) as *cohesive* is to say that the parts that make it up are unified; that is, they hold together firmly or exist together without conflict. *One of the earliest musicals to fully integrate plot and music into a cohesive whole was Rodgers and Hammerstein's* Oklahoma! *(1943).*

[3] **polarize (polarized)** A group that has become *polarized* possesses or shows two opposing points of view; that is, it's split, in conflict, in disagreement, etc. (Think back to eighth grade science and you'll remember that, similarly, negatively and positively charged iron filings cluster around the opposite *poles* of a magnet.) The noun is *polarity* or *polarization. In 1983, speaking to the UN General Assembly following the Soviet downing of a Korean passenger plane, President Ronald Reagan said, "The founders of the United Nations expected that member nations would behave and vote as individuals after they had weighed the merits of an issue— rather like a great, global town meeting; the emergence of blocs and the polarization of the United Nations [threaten] all that this organization initially valued."*

[4] **partisan** As an adjective, *partisan* means "being partial to (showing favoritism toward) a particular person, political party, cause, etc." As a noun, a *partisan* is a supporter of a particular person, political party, cause, etc. *The League of Women Voters prides itself on placing the public interest over partisan politics.*

[5] **vitiate** To *vitiate* something is to lower, ruin, impair, or destroy the quality, character, validity, purity, or effectiveness of it (as by the introduction of a fault or defect, for example). Note: The word can also mean "to morally corrupt" or "to legally invalidate." *In the unanimous 1974 Supreme Court decision ordering President Richard Nixon to turn over to special prosecutor Leon Jaworski his secret Watergate tapes, Chief Justice Warren Burger said, "A President's acknowledged need for confidentiality in the communications of his office is general in nature; [it] will not be vitiated by disclosure of a limited number of conversations preliminarily shown to have some bearing on pending criminal cases."*

ourselves. We were at **loggerheads**[1] and just debating what to do, rather loudly, I'm afraid, when you most **propitiously**[2] came along."

The Lion thought for a moment while he studied the assemblage. He noticed **ursine**[3], **lupine**[4], and **vulpine**[5] **factions**[6], but he didn't notice any other lions. When he inquired about this, the tiger answered, "There were some lions, but even they were helpless to stop the **carnage**[7]. The **leviathan**[1] has eaten them all. But none of

---

[1] **loggerheads** To be "at *loggerheads*" is to be engaged in dispute; to be quarreling. *In 1985, when New York City hotel labor and management came to loggerheads, Mayor Ed Koch said to them, "If you seek violence, we will seek to put you in jail."*

[2] **propitious (propitiously)** To refer to something as *propitious* is to say that it's likely to result in or produce a successful outcome; it's favorable, promising, lucky. *Some people, hoping to determine the most propitious time to undertake a particular important activity (starting a business, traveling by plane, etc.), consult an astrologer.*

[3] **ursine** This word means "pertaining to or characteristic of bears; bearlike." *Although it's sometimes called a "koala bear" (because of its ursine appearance), the koala is actually a small, Australian marsupial (pouched mammal).*

[4] **lupine** This word means "pertaining to or characteristic of wolves; wolflike." *In a famous fairy tale, when Little Red Riding Hood notices her bedridden "grandmother's" lupine fangs, she exclaims, "Grandma, what big teeth you have!"*

[5] **vulpine** This word means "pertaining to or characteristic of foxes; foxlike." *The flying fox (so named because of its vulpine head) is actually a large, fruit-eating, tropical bat.*

[6] **faction (factions)** A *faction* is a group (bloc, camp, clique) within a larger group (such as a political party, company, or government). It's usually formed to pursue a goal or express an opinion contrary to that of the majority or other factions. *In the 1850s the state of Kansas came to be known as "Bleeding Kansas" because of the violence between anti- and pro-slavery factions.*

[7] **carnage** The slaughter of many people (as in a war or massacre) is known as *carnage*. The word can also refer to corpses (as of men killed in battle). *In 1963 a lawyer/spokesman for the World Conference on World Peace through Law said, "What we lawyers want to do is to substitute courts for carnage."*

them was as large or brave as you."

"Take good care of these friends of mine," said the Lion with **aplomb**[2], "and I'll go at once to fight the monster." He said good-bye to his comrades and, determined to either return a hero or die a **martyr**[3], he **steeled**[4] himself to do battle and proudly marched away.

---

[1] **leviathan** The word *leviathan* can designate something that's extremely large and powerful (a monster, a giant, a corporation, etc.), something that's unusually large of its kind (especially a ship), or a sea monster (as mentioned in the Biblical story of Job) or large sea animal (especially a whale). *Herman Melville's 1851 novel* Moby Dick *tells the tale of a whaling captain's obsessive search for the leviathan that had ripped off his leg.*

[2] **aplomb** A feeling of self-confident assurance (poise, composure, steadiness, calmness, imperturbability, etc.), especially in difficult or challenging situations, is known as *aplomb* (pronounced *uh-PLUM*). *American tennis player Chris Evert (nicknamed the Ice Maiden for her cool aplomb on the court) was ranked number one in the world seven times (1974–78, 1980–81).*

[3] **martyr** Originally this word referred to a person who chose to die rather than give up his religion. Today, anybody who (sometimes willingly) dies or undergoes constant hardship or suffering on behalf of any cause, belief, principle, etc., is known as a *martyr* . Also, someone who pretends to suffer or makes a great show of suffering, as to arouse sympathy or "win points," can be called a *martyr*. The state of being a *martyr* (constant suffering, for example) is known as *martyrdom*. *In 1962 advice columnist Abigail Van Buren (Dear Abby) said that a mother-in-law is the "queen of the melodrama [exaggerated emotional display] when her acts of self-sacrifice and martyrdom go unnoticed and unrewarded."*

[4] **steel (steeled)** As a verb, to *steel* yourself (to face or endure a difficult situation) is to make yourself become strong or tough (as by calling upon your inner resources). When you become steeled *by* something (a painful experience, for example) you become strengthened or hardened by it. *In 1850 Mexican soldiers ambushed and killed (Apache war leader) Geronimo's wife, mother, and three young children; perhaps more than anything else, this tragic event steeled the young man for his long life of frequent conflict.*

THE WIZARD OF OZ VOCABULARY BUILDER

A **nocturnal**[1] hunter, the **repugnant**[2] beast was deep in his **diurnal**[3] slumber when the Lion found him. Nearby, a **host**[4] of **maggots**[5] feasted on the **sinewy**[1] **carrion**[2] of the monster's latest

---

[1] **nocturnal** To refer to something as *nocturnal* is to say that it pertains to or occurs during the night (as opposed to during the day). If you refer to animals (raccoons or hyenas, for example) as *nocturnal*, you mean that they become active or hunt at night. *At the Bronx Zoo's "World of Darkness" exhibit, the day-night cycle has been reversed so that visitors can see nocturnal animals in action.*

[2] **repugnant** Anything (or anyone) *repugnant* arouses a feeling of disgust, hate, etc.; it's offensive, distasteful, objectionable, repulsive, detestable, etc. *The cockroach, perhaps the most repugnant of all insects, reproduces in dirty places, eats garbage, and spreads germs; moreover, it's scary looking and runs alarmingly fast.*

[3] **diurnal** To refer to something as *diurnal* is to say that it pertains to or occurs during the day (as opposed to during the night), or that it pertains to or occurs in a 24-hour period (that is, it occurs once a day). If you refer to animals (eagles or kangaroos, for example) as *diurnal*, you mean that they are active during the day (as opposed to during the night). *(Dutch painter) Rembrandt's largest and most famous group portrait,* The Night Watch *(1642), was renamed* The Shooting Company of Capt. Frans Banning Cocq *after a cleaning (1946–47) revealed it to be a diurnal scene.*

[4] **host** A *host* is a multitude or indeterminately large number (of things or people); a slew, pack, mass, drove, army, legion, etc. *In 1983 an article in* Esquire *magazine noted, "Television has changed how we choose our leaders; it elected a host of Kennedy-look-alike congressmen with blow-dried hair and gleaming teeth."*

[5] **maggot (maggots)** Technically, a *maggot* is a larval (newly hatched) fly. It's soft-bodied, legless, wingless, wormlike, and usually white; it consumes plant or animal tissue. But the word is sometimes used informally to refer to any kind of tiny insect (especially one that infests or exists in multitudes) or to any person considered despicable, detestable, etc. *The belief in spontaneous generation (the theory that life develops spontaneously from nonliving matter) arose in ancient times as a way of explaining why certain living creatures are commonly found in association with certain inanimate materials (maggots on decaying meat, for example).*

victim. The **malodorous**[3] meal sickened the Lion, but, doing his best to ignore the **noisome**[4] **offal**[5], he approached the **dormant**[6] enemy.

Its legs were as long as the tiger had said, and its body was covered with coarse, black hair. It had a huge mouth with a row of

---

[1] **sinew (sinewy)** A *sinew* (pronounced *SIN-yoo*) is a tendon; that is, it's a tough band of tissue that connects muscle to bone. To describe a person as *sinewy* is to say that he has strong *sinews;* he's lean and muscular. To describe meat (beef, for example) as *sinewy* is to say that it contains many *sinews;* it's stringy and tough. *Henry Wadsworth Longfellow's poem "Under the Spreading Chestnut Tree" (1841) begins with the words "Under the spreading chestnut tree the village smithy stands. The smith, a mighty man is he, with large and sinewy hands."*

[2] **carrion** The decaying flesh (meat, muscle, fat, etc.) of a dead animal is known as *carrion. The vulture (a large bird with dark feathers and a small, featherless head) is nature's great scavenger; instead of hunting and killing prey, it feeds on carrion.*

[3] **malodorous** To describe something as *malodorous* is to say that it has or gives off a bad or foul smell. Note: The prefix *mal* means *bad. When fresh, ambergris (a substance formed in the intestines of sperm whales) is black, greasy, and malodorous; but after exposure to the air it hardens, turns gray, and develops a pleasant aroma (and is used in perfumes!).*

[4] **noisome** This is a tricky word because it looks as if it might pertain to noise; but in fact, the first syllable derives from *noy* (a variant of *annoy*). To describe something as *noisome* is to say either that it's offensive, disgusting, putrid, foul, rotten, stinking, etc. (as in *a noisome odor*) or that it's harmful, noxious, injurious, destructive, deadly, hurtful, etc. (as in *noisome fumes*). *Deposited material must be regularly flushed out of sewer systems; otherwise, bacterial action can produce noisome, explosive gases (hydrogen sulfide, for example).*

[5] **offal** The inedible waste parts of a butchered animal are known as *offal.* But the word is also used as a synonym for *carrion* (see *carrion*) or to denote refuse (trash, garbage, rubbish) in general. *The meat packing industry uses offal (an animal's feet, hide, and intestines, for example) to produce such non-meat products as pharmaceuticals, cosmetics, glues, and gelatins.*

[6] **dormant** When something is *dormant*, it's lying asleep or at rest, or it's currently inactive but capable of becoming active (as in *dormant volcano* or *dormant bank account*). *According to medical experts, 15 million Americans carry the dormant tuberculosis bacteria.*

foot-long, triangular teeth, each of which, while rather blunt at the base, was razor sharp at the **apex**[1]. But the spider's head was joined to its pudgy body by a **gossamer**[2] neck, and this gave the Lion a hint of the best way to attack the creature.

As he knew it was easier to fight it asleep than awake, he gave a great spring and landed directly upon the monster's back. Then, with one blow of his heavy, sharp-clawed paw, he sliced the spider's head clear off its body. Jumping down, he watched for a long time as the **moribund**[3] beast's long legs wiggled disgustingly. When they finally stopped, he knew the monster's heart no longer beat. That's when he became conscious of the hammering of his own heart.

The Lion went back to the clearing where the beasts of the forest were waiting for him and, with his **leonine**[4] pride bursting, said, "You needn't fear your enemy any longer." An explosion of

---

[1] **apex** Depending on the context, this word can refer to something's highest physical point (as in *the mountain's apex*), its point of culmination (as in *the apex of Greek drama*), or its pointed end or tip (as in *the leaf's apex*). *In the food pyramid (a diagram used in nutrition education that fits various food groups into a triangle), oils and sweets appear at the apex, with a recommendation that they be used sparingly.*

[2] **gossamer** As a noun, *gossamer* is something delicate, light, or flimsy (especially the thread of a spider's web or any thin, light fabric). As an adjective, the word means "thin and light; delicate, sheer, airy, gauzy, flimsy, threadlike, wispy, etc." *In her book* I Leap over the Wall *(1950), Monica Baldwin, speaking of first encountering modern lingerie after spending 27 years as a cloistered nun, said "[It looked like] a wisp of gossamer, about the size and substance of a spider's web."*

[3] **moribund** Technically, this word means "dying; in a dying state; approaching death" (as of a terminal hospital patient, for example). But the word more often refers to things (groups, ideas, activities, industries, customs, etc.) that are dying out, becoming outmoded or obsolete, collapsing, etc. *French king Louis XIII (1601–1643) wore a wig of long curls to hide his baldness, and the style became widespread in England during the reign of Charles II (1660–1685); but smaller wigs gradually replaced elaborate ones, and by the end of the next century the fashion was moribund.*

[4] **leonine** This word means "pertaining to or characteristic of lions; lionlike." *The sphinx, a mythical creature with a leonine body and a human head, was frequently the subject of ancient Egyptian sculpture.*

THE WIZARD OF OZ VOCABULARY BUILDER

approbation[1] filled the air as the great gathering burst into a triumphant **paean**[2]. With **adulation**[3] pouring from their eyes, they bestowed a **deluge**[4] of **accolades**[5] and **kudos**[1] upon their new King.

---

[1] **approbation** An expression of warm or enthusiastic praise or approval (kind words, cheers, applause, etc.) is known as *approbation*. *In 1964 singer Barbra Streisand admitted that she didn't know how to acknowledge the approbation of an admiring audience, saying, "What does it mean when people applaud? Should I give 'em money? Say thank you? Lift my dress? The lack of applause— that I can respond to."*

[2] **paean** A *paean* (pronounced *PEE-in*) is a song of joyful praise (as to God, for example); a hymn. But people usually use the word to denote any expression (a song, poem, speech, essay, painting, etc.) of praise or admiration (toward anyone or anything). *In 1999 the Los Angeles Times referred to the role of hosting the Academy Awards as "three hours of patter, paeans, and paying attention."*

[3] **adulate (adulation)** To *adulate* someone is to show excessive devotion to him or to excessively admire or praise him; to adore, idolize, or cherish him. *In 1984, when interviewed on the occasion of her 50th birthday, French film star and sex symbol Brigitte Bardot said, "I have been very happy, very rich, very beautiful, much adulated, very famous, and very unhappy."*

[4] **deluge** Technically, a *deluge* (pronounced *DELL-yooj*) is a great flood (of water) or a heavy downpour (of rain). (In the Bible, the Deluge is the great flood that covered the earth at the time of Noah.) But people often use the word to denote an abundant or overwhelming flow or flood of anything. As a verb, to be *deluged* by something (requests, orders, applications, mail, etc.) is to be flooded or overwhelmed by it. *When birth control clinics offering contraceptive information and services first opened (1914–1918) in major cities across the U.S., they were deluged with clients.*

[5] **accolade (accolades)** An expression of approval or praise (or a special acknowledgment or award) is known as an *accolade*. The word is usually used in the plural. *No poet won more Pulitzer Prizes or received more accolades from universities and foundations than did New Englander Robert Frost (1874–1963).*

THE WIZARD OF OZ VOCABULARY BUILDER

Following the **plaudits**[2], the largest tiger delivered a formal but spirited **encomium**[3], and the Lion, overwhelmed by the **laudatory**[4] remarks— especially the **commendation**[5] on his "**meritorious**[1]

---

[1] **kudos** Praise, approval, or acclaim for outstanding achievement is known as *kudos*. Note: Even though the word looks like a plural, it's actually singular (there is no such thing as a single *kudo*). In pronunciation, many people, believing the word to be plural (in the same way that *accolades* is the plural of *accolade*), pronounce the final consonant as a z *(KOO-dohz)*; however, if you want to emphasize the word's singularity, pronounce the final consonant as an s *(KOO-dohs)*. *In his debut as a director, actor Robert Redford won kudos (and an Oscar) for the 1980 film* Ordinary People.

[2] **plaudits** Enthusiastic expressions of praise, approval, or admiration are known as *plaudits*. *In 1991 U.S. General Norman Schwarzkopf won plaudits for his role in the quick and decisive defeat of Iraqi forces in the Gulf War.*

[3] **encomium** An *encomium* is a (usually formal and usually spoken) expression of high (or warm, enthusiastic, glowing, etc.) praise (or admiration, approval, etc.); a tribute, salute, homage, etc. *Typically, the recipient of a special Academy Award for lifetime achievement doesn't appear onstage until after the presenter delivers a 15-minute encomium.*

[4] **laudatory** To refer to something (remarks, a speech, writing) as *laudatory* is to say that it expresses praise; it's complimentary, flattering, approving, etc. *George Washington's role as a symbol of American virtue was enhanced after his death by (clergyman) Mason Weems' laudatory, fictionalized 1800 biography (a later edition of which first contained the "I cannot tell a lie" legend).*

[5] **commend (commendation)** To *commend* someone is to (sometimes officially) award him with praise; to say he did a good job (on something). The implication is that the praise is usually emotionally restrained or awarded by a superior. The noun is *commendation;* the adjective is *commendable. In 1971, in a ruling that upheld the press's right to publish the Pentagon Papers (a secret Defense Department study of the Vietnam War that revealed deception by U.S. policymakers), Supreme Court justice Hugo Black said, "Far from deserving condemnation for their courageous reporting, the New York Times, the Washington Post, and other newspapers should be commended for serving the purpose that the Founding Fathers saw so clearly."*

conduct" and the descriptions of him as "a **paragon**[2] of bravery" and "the **apotheosis**[3] of courage"—felt his heart expand till it nearly burst. When the round of **panegyrics**[4] was finally over, the Lion promised everyone he would return to rule over them as soon as Dorothy was safely on her way back to Kansas.

---

[1] **meritorious** To refer to something (an act, deed, conduct, performance, etc.) as *meritorious* is to say that it's worthy of praise or reward. The implication is sometimes (but not always) that the praiseworthy conduct involves bravery. *The Bronze Star is a U.S. military decoration awarded for meritorious achievement in ground combat.*

[2] **paragon** A *paragon* is a person or thing that has no match or equal; a model of excellence or perfection; an ideal; a standard of comparison. *Italian painter, sculptor, architect, musician, engineer, and scientist Leonardo da Vinci is considered the paragon of Renaissance thinkers.*

[3] **apotheosis** Technically, an *apotheosis* (pronounced *uh-poth-ee-OH-sis*) is the elevation of someone to the level of a god or the transformation of someone into a god (for example, in Greek mythology Hercules was *apotheosized*). But the word is usually used to refer to a person or deed as a glorified ideal or highest level (of something) or to any supreme or perfect example of something. *Mel Brooks' 1968 film comedy and 2001 Broadway musical* The Producers *concerns a sleazy Broadway producer and his accountant who plan to mount the world's worst play (an apotheosis of bad taste entitled* Springtime for Hitler*) so that they can keep their investors' money after it flops.*

[4] **panegyric (panegyrics)** A *panegyric* is a formal or elaborate speech or piece of writing giving high praise to someone or something. *Abraham Lincoln's Gettysburg Address (1863) was a panegyric to both the brave Civil War soldiers who died on the battlefield and to American democratic ideals.*

Chapter 25 "The Hammer-Heads"

While the four travelers passed safely through the rest of the woods, the Lion proudly **regaled**[1] the others with a narrative, **replete**[2] with gory, **macabre**[3] details, explaining how he **annihilated**[4] the monster. The gruesome images disturbed Dorothy, but at the same time she was thrilled to see the Lion in such fine **fettle**[5]. Just when her stomach could take no more, they came out into the light and saw before them a long, steep hill,

---

[1] **regale (regaled)** To *regale* someone is to entertain or delight him, as by telling him a stream of interesting stories, performing for him, or serving him choice food and drink. *At the end of the 19th century, millions of readers were regaled by the more than 100 novels of Horatio Alger (which concerned poor boys who, through hard work, honesty, and perseverance, attained great wealth).*

[2] **replete** If you say that something is *replete* (with something), you mean that it's filled or abundantly supplied (with it). *T. S. Eliot's most famous poem,* The Waste Land *(1922), is replete with obscure literary, historical, and mythical references.*

[3] **macabre** This word (pronounced either *muh-KAHB* or *Muh-KAHB-ruh*) describes things (stories or descriptions, for example) that pertains to death (especially the grimness or ugliness of death) or that arouse feelings of horror or dread; they're gruesome, ghastly, grisly, nightmarish, morbid, horrible, weird, etc. *Twentieth-century American cartoonist Charles Addams' macabre cartoons (in which humanoid monsters were shown in everyday situations) were the basis for the 1960s TV sitcom* The Addams Family.

[4] **annihilate (annihilated)** To *annihilate* something is to completely destroy it; to wipe it out; to kill, exterminate, eradicate, demolish, or slaughter it. The noun is *annihilation. In his 1963 radio and television speech on the Nuclear Test Ban Treaty (an agreement by Britain, the Soviet Union, and the United States not to test nuclear weapons in the air, in outer space, or under the sea), President John F. Kennedy, after describing the horrors of nuclear war, said, "So let us try to turn the world away from war; let us check the world's slide toward final annihilation."*

[5] **fettle** This word, usually seen in the phrase "in fine fettle," refers to your condition (especially your readiness for action or soundness) or to your emotional state or spirits. *Popeye, in fine fettle after eating his spinach, effortlessly hoisted his ship's anchor.*

covered from top to bottom with large rocks. "That will be a hard climb," said the Scarecrow, "but we must get over the hill, nevertheless."

He started up the **arduous**[1] path and the others followed. They had nearly reached the first rock when they heard a **belligerent**[2]-sounding voice **elliptically**[3] cry out, "Back!" Then a head showed itself over the rock and the same voice said, "This hill belongs to us, and we don't allow anyone to cross it."

"But we must cross it," said the Scarecrow. "We're going to the country of the Quadlings."

"You shall not!" replied the voice **contentiously**[4], and there

---

[1] **arduous** If something (a task, activity, etc.) is *arduous*, it demands or requires great (and usually sustained) effort or exertion; it's laborious, difficult, wearisome, burdensome, toilsome, exhausting, etc. To say that a hill or path is *arduous* is to say that it's difficult to climb or cross. *The Oregon Trail (a 2,000-mile overland route through prairies, deserts, and mountains from Missouri to the Pacific Northwest) was opened in 1842; attracted by fertile land, thousands of pioneers made the arduous journey during the next few years.*

[2] **belligerent** To describe someone (or his attitude, voice, tone, behavior, words, etc.) as *belligerent* is to say that he's eager or inclined to fight; he's combative, warlike, hostile, aggressive, militant, etc. Note: The word also describes countries actively engraved in war (as in *the belligerent nations of World War II*). *In 1990 Iraq began making belligerent threats against Kuwait (whom it accused of breaking agreements limiting oil production, thereby drastically lowering world oil prices and costing Iraq billions of dollars in annual revenue).*

[3] **elliptical (elliptically)** This word describes a phrase or statement that's expressed with extreme brevity or conciseness. Note: The word can also mean (of speech or writing) "ambiguous, obscure." *When we saw a vacant chair at the dinner table and threw our host a questioning look, he half-grinned and murmured elliptically, "Bashful"; then he got up, went to the doorway, and screamed (to his daughter, we supposed), "Christine, get down here!"*

[4] **contentious (contentiously)** To describe someone as *contentious* is to say that he has a tendency to argue; he's quarrelsome, disputatious, antagonistic, etc. To describe a thing (a situation, an issue, a book, etc.) as *contentious* is to say that it causes or involves controversy or argument. *Baseball manager Leo Durocher (1906–1991) had a reputation for being outspoken and contentious; in fact, he was nicknamed "The Lip" and was suspended (1947) for "cumulated unpleasant incidents."*

stepped from behind the rock the strangest man the travelers had ever seen.

He was quite short and **rotund**[1] and had a big head, which was flat at the top and supported by a thick neck full of wrinkles. But he had no arms at all, and the Scarecrow didn't see how their climb up the hill could possibly be **thwarted**[2] by a creature who looked so helpless. "I'm sorry not to do as you wish, but we must pass over your hill whether you like it or not," he said with **temerity**[3] as he continued walking through the **proscribed**[4] area.

---

[1] **rotund** If an object (fruit, for example) is *rotund,* it's round or rounded (in shape). If a person is *rotund,* he's round in figure, he's plump, fat, etc. The noun is *rotundity. In Lewis Carroll's* Through the Looking-Glass *(1872)— the sequel to* Alice's Adventures in Wonderland *(1865)— Alice meets the White Knight, Humpty Dumpty, and the rotund twins Tweedledum and Tweedledee.*

[2] **thwart (thwarted)** To *thwart* something (someone's plan, effort, ambition, etc.) is to block it or prevent it; to successfully oppose it. Note: As a noun, a *thwart* is a seat across a boat (a rowboat or canoe, for example) upon which a rower sits. Also note: The word *athwart* as an adverb means "crosswise; from side to side," as in *the rowboat's oars lay athwart,* and as a preposition means "across; from one side to the other of," as in *he lay the paddles athwart the canoe.* Interestingly, the link between all these meanings lies in the word's derivation— it comes from the Old Norse word *thvert,* meaning "cross." *In 1970, in a unanimous opinion that a disorderly defendant may forfeit his constitutional right to be present in court, Supreme Court justice Hugo Black said, "It would degrade our country and our judicial system to permit our courts to be bullied, insulted, and humiliated and the orderly progress thwarted and obstructed by defendants brought before them charged with crimes."*

[3] **temerity** Reckless boldness or foolhardy disregard for danger is known as *temerity.* People who display *temerity* are rash, impulsive, overconfident, nervy, etc. They tend to ignore or underestimate the consequences of their brash behavior. *In its review of Diana Trilling's 1981 true-crime book* Mrs. Harris: The Death of the Scarsdale Diet Doctor *(concerning the fatal shooting of cardiologist Herman Tarnower by boarding school headmistress Jean Harris), the* London Observer *wrote, "Facts have long since upstaged fiction, and the novelistic imagination now contents itself with documenting incidents it wouldn't have the temerity to invent."*

[4] **proscribe (proscribed)** To proscribe something is to refuse to allow it; to prohibit, forbid, ban, or outlaw it. *By the late 1950s significant numbers of Americans began to call for repeal of the regulations that proscribed abortion.*

THE WIZARD OF OZ VOCABULARY BUILDER

The Scarecrow soon found that the strange creature's **injunction**[1] was not mere **bluster**[2] when, as quick as lightning, the man's head shot forward and his neck stretched out until the top of his head, where it was flat, struck the Scarecrow in the middle and sent him tumbling, over and over, down the hill. Almost as quickly as it came, the head recoiled back to the body, and the man said **pugnaciously**[3], "You won't try that again if you know what's good for you!"

A chorus of **boisterous**[4] laughter came from the other rocks, and Dorothy saw that the hillside was **teeming**[5] with the armless

---

[1] **injunction** An *injunction* is an order (often a formal court order) that requires a person or organization to either not perform a particular act (as in *the injunction prevented the workers from going on strike*) or to perform a particular act (as in *the injunction forced the strikers to return to work*). *In a majority (7-2) opinion in the 1973 Roe v. Wade case (which established the constitutional legality of abortion), Supreme Court justice Harry Blackmun explained, "Jane Roe, a single woman who was residing in Dallas County, Texas, instituted this federal action in March 1970 against the District Attorney of the county; she sought a judgment that the Texas criminal abortion statutes were unconstitutional and an injunction restraining the defendant from enforcing the statutes."*

[2] **bluster** Loud, overbearing (or bullying or arrogant) talk filled with empty threats is known as *bluster*. *In a 1965 news conference, discussing the U.S. government's attitude toward the escalating Vietnam War, President Lyndon Johnson said, "We do not want an expanding struggle with consequences that no one can perceive, nor will we bluster or bully or flaunt our power; but we will not surrender and we will not retreat."*

[3] **pugnacious (pugnaciously)** Someone who's *pugnacious* is likely to argue or fight; he's combative, aggressive, quarrelsome, antagonistic, hostile, etc. *The bulldog is well known for its stocky body, large head, and pugnacious expression.*

[4] **boisterous** To describe someone or something (a party or celebration, for example) as *boisterous* is to say that it's noisy, rowdy, unrestrained, etc. *At a political party's national convention, a flowery nominating speech is generally followed by boisterous demonstrations staged by the nominee's supporters.*

[5] **teem (teeming)** When things (animals, people, etc.) *teem*, they exist or move in great numbers; they abound, swarm, throng, mob, gush, bustle, etc. *Cape Cod (a sandy, hook-shaped resort area of southeast Massachusetts) was named by its discoverer (English navigator Bartholomew Gosnold) for the codfish that teemed off its shores.*

THE WIZARD OF OZ VOCABULARY BUILDER

Hammer-Heads. The Lion, **roiled**[1] by the laughter at the Scarecrow's expense, gave a loud roar and dashed up the hill.

Again a head shot swiftly out, and this sudden **salvo**[2] sent the Lion rolling down the hill as if he had been struck by a cannonball. Dorothy, followed by the Tin Woodman, ran down the hill to help her battered friends to their feet. Like a miniature **triage**[3] nurse, she tried to weigh their relative needs, but was momentarily paralyzed because those needs seemed to her in **equipoise**[4]. Then, when she saw the Tim Woodman move toward the Lion, she automatically turned to help the Scarecrow. Both were shaken up, but otherwise

---

[1] **roil (roiled)** Technically, to *roil* a liquid (water or wine, for example) is to make it muddy or murky by stirring up sediment. But when you speak of a person becoming *roiled*, you mean that he has become disturbed or irritated (or annoyed, provoked, bothered, aggravated, displeased, riled, etc.). *In 1984, to critics roiled by a delay in installing security devices in the U.S. embassy in Beirut (after a bombing there claimed many lives), President Ronald Reagan explained, "Anyone that's ever had their kitchen done over knows that it never gets done as soon as you wish it would."*

[2] **salvo** Technically, a *salvo* is a concentrated discharge of firearms or artillery (that is, a barrage of bullets from a gun, cannonballs from a cannon, bombs from an airplane, etc.). But people also use the word to refer to anything resembling this (for example, any physical, verbal, or written assault or attack). *The April 1861 Confederate bombardment of Charleston (South Carolina) harbor's Fort Sumter was the opening salvo of the U.S. Civil War.*

[3] **triage** When medical resources are limited (as at a battlefield, disaster site, or hospital emergency room) the injured or sick are prioritized according to how urgently they require immediate treatment; this process is known as *triage*. *In September 2001 journalist Andrew DeMillo, describing the heroism of Navy medical crews after a hijacked plane crashed into the Pentagon, wrote, "Chief Petty Officer Warren Terrell sprinted into action as soon as he heard the fire alarms, setting up a makeshift triage unit in a nearby gymnasium; as they tended to the wounded, Captain Steve Frost and Captain John Feerick didn't raise their heads from their work [even] when they heard security guards warning of another plane headed toward the building."*

[4] **equipoise** A state of equality (equilibrium, balance) of weight or force is known as *equipoise*. For example, when two sides of a scale are perfectly balanced, they are said to be in *equipoise*. *In his review of a June 1983 chamber music concert, critic Lon Tuck said that the performers perfectly "captured the sublime equipoise of the Mozart Clarinet Quintet."*

THE WIZARD OF OZ VOCABULARY BUILDER

intact[1]. "It's useless to fight people with shooting heads," said the Lion, getting to his feet. "No one can withstand them."

"What can we do?" Dorothy fretted. But no answer came because no one could think of a way to pass the **insuperable**[2] barrier or even to **ameliorate**[3] the **knotty**[4] situation. Suddenly losing her **equanimity**[5], the child angrily paced back and forth. Such **arrogance**[6]!... Such **impertinence**[1]!... Such **gall**[2]! It stuck in

---

[1] **intact** If you say that something is *intact*, you mean that it remains whole, complete, or sound; that is, it's unbroken, unimpaired, etc. *Though heavy Allied bombing in World War II destroyed much of Tokyo, the city's Imperial Palace remained intact.*

[2] **insuperable** To describe something (a hardship, an obstacle, etc.) as *insuperable* is to say that it's impossible to overcome; it's insurmountable. *In the 1976 film* Rocky, *an unknown boxer overcomes seemingly insuperable odds to "go the distance" with the world heavyweight champ.*

[3] **ameliorate** To *ameliorate* something (a bad condition that demands change, for example) is to make it less bad; improve it; bring it to a better state. *The New Deal (a group of government programs and policies established under President Franklin D. Roosevelt in the 1930s) was designed to ameliorate the devastating economic effects of the Great Depression.*

[4] **knotty** To describe something (a situation, for example) as *knotty* is to say that it's difficult to resolve; it's tangled, intricate, involved, complex, etc. *Although in 1973 the U.S. Supreme Court ruled that abortion is legal, for many political candidates this knotty, "litmus test" issue remains a trying one.*

[5] **equanimity** A state of emotional calmness, coolness, composure, etc. (especially under stress or strain), is known as *equanimity*. *In his July 1963 speech on nuclear testing, President John F. Kennedy said, "If only one thermonuclear bomb were to be dropped, [it] could release more destructive power than all the bombs dropped in the Second World War; neither the United States nor the Soviet Union can look forward to that day with equanimity."*

[6] **arrogant (arrogance)** People who are *arrogant* are conceited (big-headed, superior, self-important, cocky, boastful, etc.) and domineering (pushy, bossy, overbearing, high-handed, dictatorial, etc.). The noun is *arrogance*. *In his last major public address (the October 1963 dedication of the Robert Frost Library at Massachusetts' Amherst College), President John F. Kennedy said, "When power leads man toward arrogance, poetry reminds him of his limitations."*

her **craw**[3]. She paced faster and faster until it looked as if she were doing some kind of strange dance.

"Look! A **gamboling**[4] **gamine**[5]!" shouted one of the Hammer-Heads **epigrammatically**[6]. Then, with an exaggerated **litheness**[1] of

---

[1] **impertinent (impertinence)** People who are *impertinent* are disrespectfully or intrusively rude; they go beyond the limits of proper manners. The noun is *impertinence. In his 1845 autobiography, escaped slave and abolitionist Frederick Douglass said, "I have no accurate knowledge of my age [and] I was not allowed to make any inquiries of my master concerning it— he [considered] all such inquiries on the part of a slave improper and impertinent."*

[2] **gall** Shameless, outrageous rudeness or aggressiveness (utter nerve, chutzpah, etc.) is known as *gall. I asked my lawyer if he wanted to hear a funny lawyer joke, and he said yes; then he had the gall to bill me for the time it took to tell it!*

[3] **craw** Technically, your *craw* is your stomach. But if you say that something (a situation, action, behavior, etc.) "sticks in your craw," you mean that it causes you feelings of resentment, anger, discontent, irritation, annoyance, etc.; that it's not easily tolerated. *When Brian first learned that the U.S. Government (the Agricultural Adjustment Administration) paid farmers not to grow corn (in an attempt to raise prices by lowering supply), it stuck in his craw and he complained, "Hey, I don't grow corn— where's my money?"*

[4] **gambol (gamboling)** To *gambol* is to lightly skip, frolic, or leap about (as when dancing or playing). *British-born American poet W. H. Auden (1907-1973) once said, "We all have these places where shy humiliations gambol on sunny afternoons."*

[5] **gamine** A *gamine* is a petite (small and slender), often appealingly and playfully mischievous, girl or young woman. *The star of such films as* Breakfast at Tiffany's *(1961) and* My Fair Lady *(1964), the beautiful and gamine-like Audrey Hepburn (1929-1993) devoted most of her later years to charitable causes, especially to UNICEF.*

[6] **epigram (epigrammatically)** An *epigram* is a clever or witty, briefly expressed, often brilliantly worded, often satirical, saying or phrase. *American author and humorist Mark Twain (1835-1910) was known for his epigrammatic remarks; for example, the text of a cablegram he sent from London to the press in the U.S. after his obituary had been mistakenly published read "The reports of my death are greatly exaggerated."* Note: Don't confuse this word with *epigraph*, which is an inscription (as on a building or statue) or a quotation (as at the beginning of a book).

THE WIZARD OF OZ VOCABULARY BUILDER

limb and a womanly **lissomeness**[2], he **minced**[3] back and forth with great **élan**[4] in a cruel, mocking imitation of the girl. His **cohorts**[5] behind the adjacent rocks laughed uncontrollably as if this queer **posturing**[6] were the funniest thing they had ever seen.

---

[1] **lithe (litheness)** To describe a thing (a tree branch, for example) as *lithe* (or *lithesome*) is to say that it's easily bent; it's flexible, etc. To describe a person (a dancer, for example) as *lithe* (or *lithesome*) is to say that she's limber and effortlessly graceful. *In Greek mythology a giant named Sinis (the "Pine-Bender") killed his victims by tying their arms and legs to two different bent pine trees and then releasing the strong but lithe trunks to tear their bodies apart.*

[2] **lissome (lissomeness)** If you're *lissome* (or *lithesome*), you're flexible, limber, and graceful. *At the 1976 Olympics at Montreal, Nadia Comaneci, a lissome 14-year-old, 86-pound Romanian gymnast, won six medals, twice scoring an unprecedented perfect 10.*

[3] **mince (minced)** To *mince* is to walk with short, exaggeratedly dainty steps. *In the 1959 film Some Like It Hot, two nightclub musicians who accidentally witness Chicago's St. Valentine's Day Massacre deceive the gangsters intent on killing them by mincing in women's clothes and joining an all-girl band.*

[4] **élan** Enthusiastic liveliness (spirit, dash, verve, spunkiness, zip, gusto, etc.) is known as *élan* (pronounced *ay-LAHN*). *American pianist Liberace (1919–1987) is best remembered for his outlandish costumes, his virtuosity, and his élan.*

[5] **cohort (cohorts)** Your *cohorts* are the people you hang out with; your companions, associates, buddies, friends, etc. Sometimes the word has a negative connotation; that is, if you refer to so-and-so and his *cohorts*, you may be implying that they're up to no good. *In 1975 Richard Nixon's cohorts John Mitchell, H. R. Haldeman, and John Ehrlichman were found guilty of the Watergate cover-up and sentenced to prison.*

[6] **posture (posturing)** To *posture* is to adopt a particular mental attitude, or to (through bending or contorting the body, for example) assume an affected, exaggerated, or unnatural physical pose. As a noun, *posturing* is the assuming of such a pose or attitude. *In the 1980s, Grammy-winning pop singer Rickie Lee Jones was criticized for her onstage cursing, liquor drinking, and sexual posturing.*

THE WIZARD OF OZ VOCABULARY BUILDER

Dorothy heard the **invidious**[1], **pointed**[2] **barb**[3] and was reminded of a time in Kansas when, on her way home from school, passing by a **cul-de-sac**[4], a couple of **wayward**[5] **urchins**[1] had **waylaid**[2] her

---

[1] **invidious** If something is *invidious*, it arouses (or tends to arouse) feelings of ill will, resentment, aversion, anger, envy, etc. (as in *an invidious comparison*), or it contains or implies a slight or insult (as in *an invidious accusation*). *In 1986, in a ruling that compulsory drug testing of government employees was unconstitutional, U.S. District Court judge H. Lee Sarokin said, "The invidious effect of such mass, roundup urinalysis is that it casually sweeps up the innocent with the guilty."*

[2] **pointed** If you say that a comment is *pointed*, you mean either that it's sharp, piercing, cutting, etc. (as in *pointed wit*), or that it's obviously directed at or making reference to a particular person or group (as in *pointed criticism*). If you say that an aspect or quality of something is *pointed*, you mean that it's clearly evident, conspicuous, obvious, etc. (as in *pointed simplicity*). If you say that a particular venture or endeavor is *pointed*, you mean that it's marked (clearly defined and noticeable), emphasized, concentrated, etc. (as in *a pointed effort*). *During the 1980 presidential campaign (at the dedication of the Carter Presidential Center in Atlanta), Ronald Reagan, speaking of the economy, pointedly explained, "Recession is when your neighbor loses his job; depression is when you lose yours; and recovery is when Jimmy Carter loses his."*

[3] **barb** A *barb* is a critical, cutting, or sarcastic remark; a wisecrack, dig, put-down, etc. *In 1984 Queen Elizabeth II apparently better tolerated the public's barbs about her "awful hats" than did her milliner (hat maker), who responded, "She is not a fashion plate, she is a monarch; you can't have both."*

[4] **cul-de-sac** A *cul-de-sac* is a dead end; that is, it's a dead-end street (or something that resembles a dead-end street in that it's closed at one end) or a dead-end situation (one in which further progress is impossible; a deadlock, impasse, stalemate, etc.). *Your appendix is a small, hollow, worm-shaped cul-de-sac projecting from your large intestine into your lower right abdominal cavity.* Note: The word sounds foreign because it comes from the French, meaning, literally, "bottom of the sack."

[5] **wayward** To describe someone (or his actions or behavior) as *wayward* is to say that he (usually willfully, perversely, or unpredictably) deviates from what is expected or desired (especially in order to satisfy his own inclinations); he's disobedient, unruly, contrary, irregular, flighty, etc. *During the pre–Civil War secession crisis (in which 11 Southern states proclaimed their desire to withdraw from the Union), New York City newspaper editor Horace Greeley (1811–1872) urged that the government let the "wayward sisters depart in peace," but only after a popular vote.*

THE WIZARD OF OZ VOCABULARY BUILDER

to make fun of her freckles. By comparison, that was good-natured **raillery**[3], **innocuous**[4] **badinage**[5]. But these **outré**[6] antics were

---

[1] **urchin (urchins)** An *urchin* is a mischievous young boy. Note: Sometimes the word is used to refer to any youngster (boy or girl, mischievous or not). *Speaking of the return (April 1919) to New York City of his heroic World War I Rainbow Division (the famed 42nd Division of Allied Expeditionary Force in France), commander Douglas MacArthur complained, "Where was that howling mob to proclaim us monarchs of all we surveyed? One little urchin asked us who we were and when we said, 'we are the famous 42nd,' he asked if we had been to France."*

[2] **waylay (waylaid)** To *waylay* someone is either to ambush him (lie in wait and attack him) or to accost him (suddenly approach and detain him by speaking to him). *In Greek mythology, the Sphinx of Thebes (a winged monster with the head of a woman and the body of a lion) waylaid travelers and killed any of them who could not solve her riddle.*

[3] **raillery** Good-humored ridicule (teasing, ribbing, etc.) is known as *raillery. The Dean Martin celebrity roast (at which the guest of honor's show-biz friends and acquaintances, seated at a banquet table, made short speeches that ran the gamut from sincere praise to playful raillery to out-and-out insult) evolved from a segment of the singer's 1970s TV variety show into its own weekly series (1975-1984).*

[4] **innocuous** If a physical substance (a drug, chemical, or fume, for example) is *innocuous*, it has no injurious effect; it's harmless, non-toxic, safe, etc. *During the 1880s doctors believed that cocaine was innocuous, and there were no restrictions on its sale or distribution.* If a remark or situation is *innocuous*, it's not likely to offend, annoy, or irritate (anyone); it's unobjectionable, innocent, gentle, etc. *When Charlie was called into his boss's office, he worried that he was about to be fired— but it turned out to be an innocuous meeting about the office copy machine.*

[5] **badinage** Light, playful, good-humored conversation or teasing is known as *badinage* (pronounced *bad-ih-NAH*J). Note: A synonym is *banter. Legendary talk show host Steve Allen (1921-2000) was known for exchanging hilarious badinage with members of his studio audience; for example, a women once asked, "Can I have your autograph?" and Allen, from the stage, answered, "Only if you have a very long pen."*

[6] **outré** To refer to something (behavior, for example) as *outré* (pronounced oo-*TRAY*) is to say that it goes beyond what is considered proper or conventional; it's extreme, bizarre, eccentric, etc. *During the 1960s, (British Rock group) the Who were known as much for their outré stage performance (they smashed their instruments) as for their music.*

331

beyond the **pale**[1]. The **overt**[2] hostility of these **bumptious**[3] **misanthropes**[4] produced in her a raging, **inundating**[5] **enmity**[6], and

---

[1] **pale** In the phrase "beyond the pale," the word *pale* means "limits, bounds, etc."
To refer to something as "beyond the pale" is to say that it goes beyond the limits or boundaries of what is considered proper, acceptable, courteous, etc. *In 1986 U.S. Ambassador to the USSR Arthur Hartman felt that the use of "spy dust" (a powdery chemical used to track the movements of U.S. diplomats) went beyond the pale, explaining, "It is unacceptable to subject Americans in Moscow to any substance that is not present in the general environment."*

[2] **overt** To refer to something (anger, symptoms, behavior, etc.) as *overt* is to say that it's open (to view or knowledge); that is, it's not hidden or secret; it's observable, apparent, obvious, etc. *In 1972 an appeals court overturned the 1970 convictions of the Chicago Seven (political radicals, including Abbie Hoffman and Jerry Rubin, accused of causing the riots that occurred during the 1968 Democratic National Convention in Chicago), citing the original judge's procedural errors and his overt hostility to the defendants.*

[3] **bumptious** To describe someone as *bumptious* is to say that he's overly (or offensively, loudly, crudely, etc.) self-assertive or cocky. *Whereas (1980s hard rock band) Guns N' Roses' (lead singer) Axl Rose has been widely criticized for his bumptious attitude (on stage and off), Rolling Stone magazine once praised him for his "manly scream."*

[4] **misanthrope (misanthropes)** A *misanthrope* is a person who hates or mistrusts people; one who expects the worst from everybody; a cynic, pessimist, skeptic, scoffer, etc. *In the 1940 film comedy classic The Bank Dick, W. C. Fields plays Egbert Souse, a drunken misanthrope who is made a bank guard as a reward for accidentally capturing a bank robber.*

[5] **inundate (inundating)** Technically, to *inundate* something is to cover it with water; to saturate it with liquid; to flood it. But people generally use this word to refer to anything that resembles a flooding; that is, to any overspreading or overwhelming (of something) by anything. *After the 2001 Tony Awards presentation, the theatre showing (the Mel Brooks musical) The Producers was inundated with requests for tickets.*

[6] **enmity** A feeling of (often mutual) deep hostility or hatred (such as might be felt between enemies during a war) is known as *enmity*. *The United Provinces of Central America, a political confederation that included Costa Rica, El Salvador, Guatemala, Honduras, and Nicaragua, existed from 1823–1838; since that time, numerous attempts to restore the union have been frustrated by ongoing enmity between the countries.*

THE WIZARD OF OZ VOCABULARY BUILDER

swift waves of **rancor**[1] rose chokingly in her throat till she nearly gagged. But she decided she had already **surmounted**[2] too many obstacles to give up now. With her **inveterate**[3] **hardihood**[4]— and despite a sudden, nearly paralyzing **xenophobia**[5]— she tightened her will and vowed to get past these **bellicose**[6] bullies one way or

---

[1] **rancor** A feeling of bitterness, resentment, ill will, or hatred (especially when produced by past grievances that have led to a desire for revenge) is known as *rancor*. *The modern Olympic Games salute the athletic talents of citizens of all nations and, perhaps more importantly, strive to replace the rancor of international conflict with friendly competition.*

[2] **surmount (surmounted)** To *surmount* something (an obstacle, barrier, hardship, etc.) is to overcome it; that is, to successfully or safely pass over or across it. *Surmounting racial barriers and health obstacles, singer/dancer/actor Sammy Davis, Jr. (1925-1990), conquered Broadway and film, and became a top recording artist.*

[3] **inveterate** If you describe something (a particular behavior, for example) as *inveterate*, you mean that it's firmly established (hardened, fixed, set) through long continuance; it's habitual, confirmed, chronic (as in *an inveterate gambler, an inveterate liar, an inveterate schemer*, etc.). *An inveterate art collector, American oil tycoon Jean Paul Getty (1892-1976) established (1954) a museum in Malibu, California, to publicly display his vast collection.*

[4] **hardihood** *Hardihood* is the capability of enduring fatigue and hardship; the determination to survive; sturdiness, boldness, daring, fitness, soundness, etc. *As a people, Eskimos have been able to survive in cold, severe environments not only because they learned to make clothing, tools, and weapons from sea mammals, but because they strongly emphasized courage and hardihood in the training of their young males.*

[5] **xenophobia** A *phobia* is an irrational, abnormal, or excessive fear or dread (of something). In particular, *xenophobia* (the x is pronounced as a z) denotes an unreasonable or undue fear, hatred, or distrust of foreigners or strangers. *In 1917, as World War I hysteria heightened American xenophobia, Congress, in an effort to sharply reduce the number of immigrants from southern and eastern European countries, enacted a literacy bill (which required immigrants to demonstrate literacy in some language).*

[6] **bellicose** To describe someone (or something) as *bellicose* is to say that he's inclined or eager to fight; he's warlike, combative, hostile, etc. *On February 22, 1991, President George H. Bush gave (Gulf War enemy) Iraq a bellicose ultimatum to withdraw its troops from neighboring Kuwait by noon of the following day.*

another.

The Scarecrow, now deep in a **brown study**[1], scratched his head. Dorothy, thinking that scratching her own head might help her think of a way to ease the situation's mounting **volatility**[2], took off her Golden Cap and held it in her hand. But the ugly **altercation**[3] had **rankled**[4] her too much for her to concentrate. As her annoyance at the **contumacious**[5] **cabal**[1] **festered**[2] in her mind, she

---

[1] **brown study** To be in a *brown study* is to be deeply absorbed in thought; to be lost in thought. *If you visit the museum's Picasso exhibit, skip the 15-minute guided tour by headphones; instead, simply enjoy the fuzzy brown study that comes from gazing into the silent masterpieces.*

[2] **volatile (volatility)** To describe something (a situation, atmosphere, era, etc.) as *volatile* is to say that it will or threatens to break out into violence; it's explosive. The noun is *volatility*. *Pitcher Roger Clemens, who in 1986 struck out 20 batters in a single game, is known for his volatile temper.*

[3] **altercation** An *altercation* is a heated verbal (or sometimes physical) conflict; a fight, clash, dispute, quarrel, argument, etc. *A race riot, such as Los Angeles's Watts riot (1965) or "Rodney King" riot (1992), is typically sparked by small altercations between individuals, usually in public places.*

[4] **rankle (rankled)** To *rankle* someone is to cause him irritation, annoyance, resentment, etc. *At the beginning of his Presidency (1977), Jimmy Carter rankled leaders of the USSR with his concerns for international human rights.*

[5] **contumacious** To describe someone as *contumacious* is to say that he's stubbornly or willfully rebellious or disobedient; he's defiant, peg-headed, headstrong, unyielding, inflexible, contrary, etc. *In a 1970 ruling that a disorderly defendant may forfeit his constitutional right to be present in court, Supreme Court justice Hugo Black said, "We believe trial judges confronted with disruptive, contumacious, stubbornly defiant defendants must be given sufficient discretion to meet the circumstances in each case."*

THE WIZARD OF OZ VOCABULARY BUILDER

kept mumbling to herself, "The **insolence**[3]!... The **audacity**[4]!... The **impudence**[5]!... The **effrontery**[6]!"

---

[1] **cabal** Technically, a *cabal* (pronounced with the accent on the second syllable) is an (often secret) group of plotters (that is, people who conspire to work against or overthrow a government or authority). But the word is also used informally to refer to any small group (a clique, circle, company, etc.) who share characteristics; for example, they might all pursue the same artistic endeavor (as in *a cabal of poets*), or they might all be devoted to or trail after a particular celebrity. *In 1991, after Soviet president Mikhail Gorbachev sought to revive his country's ailing economy by introducing elements of capitalism and democracy, a cabal of hard-line Communists tried (unsuccessfully) to overthrow him.*

[2] **fester (festered)** When a sore (or wound, cut, etc.) *festers*, it forms pus, decays, rots, etc. When a feeling (bitterness or resentment, for example) festers (in one's mind), it increasingly causes irritation, annoyance, anger, etc. *In 1983, speaking of a plan to improve the image of the Bronx by covering the windows of abandoned city-owned buildings with decals depicting pleasant interiors, (New York City) mayor Ed Koch explained, "In a neighborhood, as in life, a clean bandage is much, much better than a raw or festering wound."*

[3] **insolence** Disrespectful rudeness (as in speech or manner) is known as *insolence*. The adjective is *insolent*. *In 1963 British author Aldous Huxley (1894–1963) observed, "No man ever dared to [show] his boredom so insolently as does a Siamese tomcat when he yawns in the face of his [passionately persistent] wife."*

[4] **audacity** Depending on the context, this word can mean either "bold, reckless daring; derring-do" or "disrespectful rudeness; nerve." The adjective is *audacious*. *U.S. army general George Patton (1885–1945) once noted, "In war nothing is impossible, provided you use audacity."*

[5] **impudence** Disrespectful rudeness (freshness) or offensive boldness (shameless immodesty) is known as *impudence*. The adjective is *impudent*. *In 1969 Vice President Spiro Agnew referred to opponents of the involvement of the U.S. in the Vietnam War as "impudent snobs who characterize themselves as intellectuals."*

[6] **effrontery** Shamelessly arrogant rudeness or boldness (nerve, brashness, etc.) is known as *effrontery*. *In August 1999 New York Newsday printed the following letter to the editor from an eight-year-old: "[That] Hillary Clinton [should] formally proclaim her candidacy for senator from New York [is the height of] effrontery. Who is this woman that she should presume to represent our state? She comes from Arkansas!"*

THE WIZARD OF OZ VOCABULARY BUILDER

Her little **litany**[1] of **pejoratives**[2] was interrupted when an **effulgent**[3] flash of sunlight suddenly struck the inside of the shiny brim of the Golden Cap and was **providentially**[4] reflected directly into the Tin Woodman's eye. "Look, Dorothy!" he said. "There's something written inside the brim of your Cap!"

---

[1] **litany** Technically, a *litany* is a form of prayer (as in the Christian religion) in which a priest (or other clergyman) speaks or sings a series of requests to God, to which the congregation as a whole repeats a fixed response ("Lord, have mercy," for example). But people use this word informally to refer to any repetitive (non-religious) recitation or recital that resembles a litany—especially an (often prolonged, monotonous, or dreary) list, enumeration, or account of something (as in *her mother-in-law's usual litany of complaints*). *In July 1984, referring to speakers at the Democratic National Convention in San Francisco,* Time *magazine noted, "One after another recited a litany of races and classes and minorities and interests and occupations; some, in fact, made the nation sound like an immense gathering of victims— terrorized senior citizens, forsaken minorities, [and] Dickensian children."*

[2] **pejorative (pejoratives)** As a noun, a *pejorative* is any word or term that carries a negative connotation; its very usage belittles or discredits someone or something. For example, if you refer to an attractive but empty-headed woman as a "bimbo," you're using a *pejorative*. As an adjective, the word means "tending to insult or belittle," as in *"redneck" is a pejorative term (for a rural white Southerner). In 1998 a group of Native Americans, intent on eliminating from football what they say is a racial slur, urged a federal agency to cancel the trademark protection of the Washington Redskins, explaining, "There is no context in which the term 'Redskins' is not offensive; there is no context in which it is not insulting, pejorative, or racist."*

[3] **effulgent** To describe something (light, beauty, wit, etc.) as *effulgent* is to say that it shines brilliantly; it's splendidly radiant. The noun is *effulgence*. *The nickname "Sun King" for France's Louis XIV (1643–1715) captures the magnificence of his court and the effulgence of his Palace of Versailles (which boasted silver furniture and a glittering Hall of Mirrors).*

[4] **providential (providentially)** To describe an event or occurrence as *providential* is to say that it happens (or seems to happen) as the result of the care and guardianship of God; it's heaven-sent, fortunate, lucky, etc. *The Rosetta Stone (a large slab of rock inscribed with both Greek and ancient Egyptian writing that provided scholars with the key to translating hieroglyphics) was providentially discovered in northern Egypt (1799) by a group of soldiers in Napoleon's army.*

THE WIZARD OF OZ VOCABULARY BUILDER

They all stared intently at the Cap. **Etched**[1] into the metal, in tiny letters, were the words *Whosoever possesses this Golden Cap shall command the Flying Monkeys.* After that, in even smaller letters, were what appeared to be a string of magic words: *Ep-pe, pep-pe, kak-ke! Hil-lo, hol-lo, hel-lo! Ziz-zy, zuz-zy, zik!*

Remembering that it was the Monkeys who had **abetted**[2] the Wicked Witch in her **execrable**[3] acts, the Scarecrow and the Tin Woodman were rather afraid to have anything to do with them. But then, realizing the Monkeys were merely acting according to

---

[1] **etch (etched)** If something (a design or inscription, for example) is *etched* onto the surface of a hard material (metal or glass, for example), it's cut into it (by the action of a sharp tool, acid, etc.). If something (an image or conversation, for example) is *etched* in your mind or memory, it's deeply or permanently implanted or imprinted there (you can't forget it). *In 1985, speaking of the Vietnam Veterans Memorial in Washington, D.C. (a nearly 500-foot, V-shaped black granite wall inscribed with names of the more than 58,000 Americans killed or missing during the Vietnam War),* the New York Times said, *"In each sharply etched name one reads the price paid by yet another family; in the sweeping pattern of names, chronological by day of death, 1959 to 1975, one reads the price paid by the nation."*

[2] **abet (abetted)** To *abet* someone is to assist or aid him (especially in something wrongful or evil). *In 1968, after his indictment on charges of aiding and abetting resistance to Selective Service laws, pediatrician, author, and political activist Benjamin Spock explained, "I'm not a pacifist; I was very much for the war against Hitler and I also supported the intervention in Korea— but in this war we went in there to steal Vietnam."*

[3] **execrable** To describe a certain behavior or action (theft, assault, rape, murder, etc.) as *execrable* is to say that it's deserving of hate; it's utterly offensive, detestable, reprehensible, etc. To describe the quality of something (a performance, food, etc.) as *execrable* is to say that it's very bad, inferior, shabby, etc. *Whereas some people support vivisection (the cutting into of a healthy living animal for the purpose of scientific research), others view it as an execrable act of cruelty.*

THE WIZARD OF OZ VOCABULARY BUILDER

protocol[1], the Scarecrow pushed aside his **jaundiced**[2] point of view and pointed out that their seemingly **iniquitous**[3] behavior was understandable because, whether they liked it or not, the Monkeys' only **fealty**[4] was to the owner of the Cap.

---

[1] **protocol** An accepted standard of (social or professional) conduct in a particular situation, or an accepted or expected manner of doing something (that involves others) is known as *protocol*. For example, one might say, "I can't go over my boss's head because it goes against protocol," or "When I vacation in Venice, how much am I supposed to tip the gondolier?— I don't know the protocol." *While U.S. ambassador to the UN (1961–1965), former Democratic presidential candidate Adlai Stevenson observed, "A diplomat's life is made up of three ingredients: protocol, Geritol, and alcohol."*

[2] **jaundiced** Medically speaking, to say that someone is *jaundiced* is to say that his skin has taken on a yellowish cast (as from yellow fever, hepatitis, malaria, or cirrhosis). But in general usage, to say that someone's viewpoint or attitude is *jaundiced* (toward something) is to say that it's prejudiced, hostile, slanted, colored, etc. (often as the result of a particular bad experience). *In 1986 Wole Soyinka (a Nobel Prize–winning writer from the war-torn African country of Nigeria) said of his 1962 play* A Dance of the Forests, *"[It] takes a jaundiced view of the [much-praised] glorious past of Africa."*

[3] **iniquitous** To describe something (an act, decision, etc.) as *iniquitous* is to say that it's grossly unjust; it's wicked, sinful, unprincipled, evil, perverse, immoral, wrong, unfair, etc. The noun is *iniquity*. *In 1962, referring to laws against the iniquitous practice of white mobs hanging black men without due process of law, civil rights leader Martin Luther King, Jr. (1929–1968), said, "It may be true that the law cannot make a man love me, but it can keep him from lynching me, and I think that's pretty important."*

[4] **fealty** Under feudalism (a political and economic system of Europe during the Middle Ages) *fealty* was the fidelity (loyalty, allegiance, faithfulness, devotedness, etc.) a serf (peasant) owed his lord (in return for land). But today the word refers to any compelling fidelity; that is, any fidelity one has pledged or vowed to uphold (as in *a judge's fealty to the laws of the land, a witness's fealty to the truth, a husband's fealty to his wife,* etc.). *In 1861 General Robert E. Lee, believing he owed fealty to his home state, turned down an offer to command the Federal army; he resigned his commission (in the U.S. Army) and offered his services to Virginia (when it seceded).*

THE WIZARD OF OZ VOCABULARY BUILDER

The Tin Woodman, still afraid, at first **dissented**[1]. But then, because he didn't want to **usurp**[2] the Scarecrow's authority, and because he realized a **surcease**[3] of hostilities was unattainable because any attempt to verbally **conciliate**[4] the **intransigent**[5] enemy would prove **futile**[6], he finally agreed that using the charm

---

[1] **dissent (dissented)** To *dissent* is to hold a differing opinion (from someone else or from the majority), or to withhold assent (agreement) or approval (as in a meeting); to disagree, oppose, contradict, vote "no," refuse, etc. *In December 1941, when President Franklin D. Roosevelt asked Congress to declare war on Japan (the day after Japan attacked the U.S. naval base at Pearl Harbor) only one member of Congress dissented.*

[2] **usurp** To *usurp* someone's position, title, power, or authority is to, usually unwarrantedly or unlawfully (and sometimes forcibly), take it (as one's own). *In the 1994 animated film* The Lion King, *the evil Scar usurps the throne by killing his brother, the king.* Sometimes the word refers to the natural or inevitable displacement of some long-standing but outmoded custom, practice, idea, device, etc. *In the 1970s the role of the slide rule (in making rapid mathematical calculations) was usurped by the pocket calculator.*

[3] **surcease** A *surcease* (pronounced with the accent on the second syllable) is a bringing or coming to an end (of something); a stop, halt, discontinuance, etc. *The July 1953 armistice (truce) that ended the Korean War resulted in a surcease of hostilities and a prisoner exchange, but left the peninsula divided.*

[4] **conciliate** To *conciliate* is to try to win peace or favor (as from an enemy or opponent), especially by demonstrating a willingness to be fair or accommodating. The adjective is *conciliatory* ("tending to conciliate"). *In 1977 Egyptian president Anwar Sadat angered his Arab allies by traveling to Jerusalem as a conciliatory gesture to Israel.*

[5] **intransigent** To describe someone as *intransigent* is to say that he inflexibly maintains a position (as in politics, for example), or that he firmly sticks to an intention or purpose; he's uncompromising, unyielding, stubborn, etc. *In May 1856 Massachusetts senator Charles Sumner, an outspoken and intransigent opponent of slavery, was physically assaulted by a congressman at odds with his views.*

[6] **futile** If something (an attempt, action, plan, etc.) is *futile*, it won't or can't produce the desired result; it's useless, pointless, ineffective, etc. The noun is *futility*. *From 1876 to 1886 Apache chief Geronimo led strong but futile efforts to stop white expansion into the Southwest.*

of the Cap was their only **feasible**[1] alternative. "You possess the Golden Cap, Dorothy," he said at last. "Summon the Winged Monkeys."

Knowing that even one misplaced syllable would probably **nullify**[2] the charm, Dorothy carefully **perused**[3] what was printed inside the Cap. Only then did she begin to **intone**[4] the **incantation**[5]. Gliding her index finger back and forth over the

---

[1] **feasible** If you describe something (an idea, plan, etc.) as *feasible*, you mean that it's capable of being carried out or accomplished; it's workable, doable, suitable, reasonable, practical, possible, attainable, etc. The noun is *feasibility*. *In June 1942, after a year of study, the OSRD (Office of Scientific Research and Development) informed President Franklin D. Roosevelt that the creation of an atomic bomb (capable of affecting the course of World War II) appeared to be feasible.*

[2] **nullify** To *nullify* the power or strength of something is to counteract or neutralize the effectiveness or force of it. To *nullify* a contract, warrantee, or the like is to (often legally) make or declare it invalid, void, inoperative, canceled, etc. *In his political philosophy, Southern politician and slavery supporter John C. Calhoun (1782-1850) maintained that individual states had the right to nullify any federal laws they considered unconstitutional.*

[3] **peruse (perused)** To *peruse* something (a report, for example) is to read it; the implication is often that the reading is thorough or careful. Note: Many people misuse the word to imply just the opposite— that the reading is superficial or quick. *During his 1988 presidential campaign, George H. Bush pledged, "Read my lips; no new taxes"; then after he was in office, I was perusing the newspaper one day and saw that he and Congress had agreed to raise taxes!*

[4] **intone** To *intone* something (a set of instructions or rules, minutes to a meeting, etc.) is to recite it (say it out loud), especially in a monotonous or chant-like way. *In her 1980 book* Hearts, *Hilma Wolitzer says: "The waitress intoned the specialties of the day, 'Chicken Cordon Bleu, Sole Amandine, Veal Marsala'; she might have been a train conductor in a foreign country, calling out the strange names of the stations."*

[5] **incantation** A formula (or string) of supposedly magic words (as used in a spell or charm) is known as an *incantation*. Note: The word also refers to the recitation (of magic words) itself, or to any non-magical utterance recited or repeated mechanically or thoughtlessly. *In the 1973 film* The Exorcist, *a Jesuit priest uses holy water and incantation to drive the devil from a young girl.*

letters as she spoke produced a pleasant **tactile**[1] sensation that helped soothe her. In a few moments the entire band of Monkeys stood before her.

"What is your command?" inquired the King of the Monkeys, bowing low.

"Please carry us over the hill to the country of the Quadlings," answered the girl.

"It shall be done," said the King, and at once the Monkeys took the travelers in their arms and flew away with them. As they passed over the hill, the **irate**[2] Hammer-Heads repeatedly shot **fusillades**[3] of flying heads in the air, which, even at their **apogee**[4], couldn't reach the high-flying Monkeys.

---

[1] **tactile** This word means "pertaining to the sense of touch." *Blind and deaf since early childhood, Helen Keller used her tactile sense to learn hand signals and Braille so that she could communicate with the world around her.*

[2] **irate** If someone is *irate*, he's very angry (enraged, irritated, etc.) The implications are that his anger is apparent rather than hidden and that he's likely to take some action as a result of his anger. *At the age of 32, Bill Clinton was elected (1979) as the nation's youngest governor (of Arkansas)— but he was defeated for re-election by voters irate at a rise in the state's automobile license fees!*

[3] **fusillade (fusillades)** A *fusillade* is a concentrated outburst or continuous discharge of firearms (or, in an extended sense, of anything, as in *a fusillade of protests*). *(Maryland lawyer and poet) Francis Scott Key's (1779–1843) "Star-Spangled Banner" words— "the rockets' red glare, the bombs bursting in air"— describe fusillades fired by British frigates against Baltimore's Fort McHenry during the War of 1812.*

[4] **apogee** The *apogee* of something is its highest point (physically or figuratively). Note: As a technical term in astronomy, the *apogee* of something (the moon or a man-made satellite, for example) is the point in its orbit at which it's furthest from earth (and its opposite, the *perigee*, is the point at which it's closest). *Although they've had numerous hits before and after, the British-Australian rock group the Bee Gees reached their apogee in 1977 when their disco songs were featured in the film* Saturday Night Fever.

Chapter 26 "The Flying Monkeys"

Dorothy found herself being carried easily by the King, and after a time her curiosity **impelled**[1] her to ask, "Why is it that you have to follow the command of whoever owns the Golden Cap?"

"It's a long story," he answered, "but since we have some time before we reach the country of the Quadlings, I'll tell you. I just hope it won't bore you too much."

"Of course not," replied the girl, wondering if asking may have been a mistake.

"Very well. You see, once we were a free people, living **capriciously**[2] in a great forest, flying from tree to tree, eating nuts and fruit, and doing just as we pleased without having to answer to anyone. Some of us were a little too **puckish**[3] at times, flying down

---

[1] **impel (impelled)** To be *impelled* to do something is to be forced (or driven, motivated, propelled, etc.) to do it (usually by your own moral sense, but sometimes by the urging of others). *In 1962, when accepting his Nobel Prize for literature, novelist John Steinbeck (1902–1968) said, "I am impelled not to squeak like a grateful and apologetic mouse, but to roar like a lion out of pride in my profession."*

[2] **capricious (capriciously)** To describe someone or something as *capricious* is to say that it's liable to change, especially without warning; it's whimsical, fickle, flighty, etc. *In his 1867 book* The English Constitution, *British economist and social scientist Walter Bagehot said, "Our law very often reminds one of those outskirts of cities where you cannot for a long time tell how the streets come to wind about in so capricious and serpent-like a manner."*

[3] **puckish** *Puck* is the name of a mischievous fairy in Shakespeare's *A Midsummer Night's Dream* (1595). To describe someone as *puckish* is to say that he's impishly mischievous, playfully prankish, etc. *When you play "This Little Piggy Went to Market" with a small child, try not to spoil the surprise by wearing too puckish a grin just before saying "And this little piggy cried 'Wee! Wee! Wee!' all the way home."*

to pull animals' tails, or chasing birds, or **bedeviling**[1] people who walked in the forest by throwing nuts at their heads. You could say our **hallmark**[2] was a refusal to behave in an civil manner, but we were happy and carefree and we enjoyed every minute of our **untrammeled**[3] freedom.

"There was living here then, too, a wise and beautiful Princess hailed by all as the very **avatar**[4] of goodness. Though everyone loved her, she couldn't find anyone to love in return because all the men here were too ugly or stupid. At last, however, she found a young boy, the **scion**[5] of a **genealogically**[1] respectable family, who

---

[1] **bedevil (bedeviling)** To *bedevil* someone is to (especially continuously) torment or annoy him (with something); to cause him worry, frustration, etc. *In her 1988 book* The Worst Years of Our Lives, *columnist and feminist Barbara Ehrenreich said, "Consider the Vice President, George [H.] Bush, a man so bedeviled by bladder problems that he managed, for the last eight years, to be in the men's room whenever an important illegal decision was made."*

[2] **hallmark** Technically, a *hallmark* is an official stamp used in marking gold that meets established standards of purity. But in general usage, the word refers to any conspicuous or distinguishing feature (of something), as in *violent slapstick was the hallmark of the Three Stooges. The use of tools, once thought to be the hallmark of humans, is now known to be common in chimpanzees.*

[3] **untrammeled** To describe something as *untrammeled* is to say that it's unrestricted, unrestrained, unlimited. *In 1962 former Democratic presidential candidate Adlai Stevenson said, "The first principle of a free society is an untrammeled flow of words in an open forum."*

[4] **avatar** Technically, an *avatar* is the human embodiment (personification) of a god; for example, in Hinduism, Buddha is an *avatar* of Vishnu. But in popular usage, an *avatar* is an embodiment or manifestation of a principle, attitude, quality, or concept. *After the Civil War, Confederate forces commander Robert E. Lee was seen as a symbol of courage in defeat and an avatar of the finest elements of Southern heritage.*

[5] **scion** A *scion* (pronounced with a silent *c*) is someone descended from parents or ancestors; an offspring, child, heir, etc. *Distant cousins Franklin Delano Roosevelt (the scion of an old, wealthy New York family) and Anna Eleanor Roosevelt (a niece of President Theodore Roosevelt) were married in 1905 and had six children (one of whom died in infancy).*

was both handsome and smart and who, she was convinced, possessed many **latent**[2] abilities. The Princess made up her mind that when he grew up she would make him her husband. She **discreetly**[3] took him to her palace and molded his **malleable**[4] young mind into one as wise and good as hers, for she knew that having these fine attributes in common **augured**[5] well for **conjugal**[1]

---

[1] **genealogy (genealogically)** A record or study of family ancestry or lineage is known as *genealogy. In his 1976 book* Roots, *author Alex Haley traces his genealogy back seven generations to his ancestor Kunta Kinte, who was abducted in Africa and taken as a slave to America.*

[2] **latent** If something (a trait, ability, tendency, etc.) is *latent,* it's present or in existence, but not visible, evident, or active. The implication is that it has the potential to become visible or active. *In 1962 Richard Nixon said, "Only in losing himself in a cause bigger that himself does [a man] discover all the latent strengths he never knew he had and which otherwise would have remained dormant."*

[3] **discreet (discreetly)** To be *discreet* (about something) is to wisely use self-restraint in conduct or speech (as when you keep quiet about a delicate situation, for example). The noun is *discretion. While he was married to Anne Boleyn, England's King Henry VIII (1509–1547) pursued his wife's lady in waiting (attendant), Jane Seymour, with gifts— but she discreetly rejected his advances.*

[4] **malleable** If something (a physical material or a person's mind, for example) is *malleable,* it's moldable or shapeable; it's not fixed or rigid. *In constructing the Statue of Liberty, metalworkers placed thin sheets of copper in wooden forms (that followed the shape of the plaster model of the statue); then they bent and hammered the malleable metal into the shape of the forms.*

[5] **augur (augured)** When this verb takes an object, it means "predict, foretell, foreshadow, etc.," as *in bad weather augurs low voter turnout.* When it doesn't take an object, it means "to be a sign or omen (of)," and is usually followed by the word *well* (if what is to follow if good) or *ill* (if what is to follow is bad), as in *a bad appetizer augurs ill for the rest of the meal.* Note: As a noun, an *augur* is a person who predicts future events, and an *augury* is an omen or sign (of things to come). *The 1964 Free Speech Movement at the University of California at Berkeley (in which 800 students were arrested for protesting against the school's restrictions on on-campus political activities) augured the nationwide college campus anti–Vietnam War protests of the late '60s.*

felicity[2].

"When the boy at last reached adulthood, he was said to be the wisest and handsomest man in all the land. The Princess was greatly **enamored[3]** of him and **hastened[4]** to make everything ready for the **impending[5] nuptials[6].**

"At that time the King of the Winged Monkeys was my

---

[1] **conjugal** To describe something as *conjugal* is to say that it refers to marriage or to the relationship between a husband and wife. *The films of Woody Allen (1986's* Hannah and Her Sisters, *for example) often explore the bonds of conjugal and adulterous relationships.*

[2] **felicity** The state of being greatly happy is known as *felicity. In his Farewell Address to the House of Representatives (1796), President George Washington said, "[Concern] for your welfare and the apprehension of danger urge me to offer some sentiments, which appear to me all important to the permanency of your felicity as a people."*

[3] **enamored** To be *enamored* of someone or something is to love it or be in love with it. *In the 1991 animated film* Beauty and the Beast, *the Beast becomes enamored of his prisoner, the beautiful Belle.*

[4] **hasten (hastened)** To *hasten* is to hurry (or cause to hurry); to move (or cause to move) with speed. *Jazz singer Billie Holiday's (1915-1959) death was hastened by her drug addiction.* The noun is *haste* ("swiftness of motion; speed"). *Cinderella leaves the ball just as midnight is striking, and in her haste she drops a slipper.*

[5] **impending** If a particular event is *impending,* it's about to happen or it threatens to happen. *In 1936, responding to rumors of the impending war (World War II), British science fiction writer H. G. Wells said, "If we don't end war, war will end us."*

[6] **nuptials** As an adjective, *nuptial* (pronounced *NUP-shil*) means "pertaining to marriage or the wedding ceremony." But the word is most often seen as a plural noun *(nuptials)* meaning "a wedding ceremony or marriage." *In the final sequence of the 1967 Academy Award–winning film* The Graduate, *Benjamin (Dustin Hoffman) disrupts Mrs. Robinson's daughter's nuptials and carries her off.*

grandfather—on the **distaff**[1] side—and the old guy loved to play practical jokes. Interestingly, whereas my parents were always very serious, I'm also rather mischievous, and I accept this **atavistic**[2] trait as my grandfather's **legacy**[3]." To prove his point he smiled **roguishly**[4] and pretended he was about to drop his passenger, producing in Dorothy a flash of panic. Then, holding her securely, he continued, "Anyway, one day, just before the wedding, my grandfather was flying out with his band of Monkeys when he saw

---

[1] **distaff** When speaking of marriage and family, the *distaff* side is the female (or mother's) side of the family as opposed to the male (or father's) side. Note: The male side is known as the *spear* side. *In 1973 broadcaster and author Barbara Howar (who had had an adulterous affair with a U.S. senator) noted, "By and large, wife-changing and high office are not compatible; this accounts for the many dull women in Washington and is the cause of much smug [self-satisfaction] on the distaff side of political marriages."*

[2] **atavistic** This word is used to describe a trait or characteristic (in an individual) that has been inherited not from parents, but from previous ancestors; that is, the trait or characteristic has reappeared after having skipped one or more generations. Note: Sometimes the word is used informally to refer to characteristics of remote ancestors or primitive people in general. *In 1957 Swiss author and critic Max Frisch (1911-1991) said, "Today we have means of communication that bring the world into our homes; to travel from one place to another is atavistic."*

[3] **legacy** Something (a work of art, principle, philosophy, improvement, tradition, monetary gift, trait, etc.) handed down or passed on (to succeeding or future generations) is known as a *legacy*. *In his August 1974 resignation speech, President Richard Nixon said, "As a result of [my] efforts, I am confident that the world is a safer place today and that all of our children have a better chance than before of living in peace rather than dying in war; this, more than anything, is what I hope will be my legacy to you, to our country."*

[4] **rogue (roguishly)** Depending on the context, a *rogue* can be either a playfully mischievous person or a dishonest scoundrel. *In the 1975 cult film* Rocky Horror Picture Show, *actor Tim Curry wears black leather and a lipstick-covered, roguish sneer as he sings his opening number, "Sweet Transvestite."*

the Princess's **betrothed**[1] walking beside the river. This **touchstone**[2] of wisdom and **virility**[3] was dressed in a rich costume of **sequined**[4] purple velvet and **diaphanous**[5] pink silk—a bit **meretricious**[6] and **effete**[1] for my taste, I must say, and probably for

---

[1] **betrothed** As an adjective, *betrothed* means "engaged (to be married)." As a noun, your *betrothed* is the person you're engaged to. *In the 1934 film classic* It Happened One Night, *an out-of-work reporter (Clark Gable) agrees to help a runaway heiress (Claudette Colbert) get from Florida to her betrothed in New York in return for her story, which will land him a job.*

[2] **touchstone** Technically, a *touchstone* is a hard, black stone formerly used to test the purity of gold or silver (by the color of the streak produced on it by rubbing it with either metal). But in general usage, the word refers to anything used as a standard (a model, a perfect example, etc.) by which other similar things can be measured. *When actor Cary Grant died (1986), the* New York Times *wrote, "[He] was not supposed to die; [he] was supposed to stick around, our perpetual touchstone of charm and elegance and romance and youth."*

[3] **virile (virility)** If you say that someone is *virile*, you mean that he's manly or masculine (that is, he's strong and vigorous), or that he's capable of performing sexually as a male. The noun is *virility*. *According to* Grolier's Encyclopedia, *British novelist Ian Fleming (1908–1964) "wrote 13 James Bond novels, establishing the hero's stylish trademarks, including his taste for dry vodka martinis and his invincible virility."*

[4] **sequin (sequined)** A *sequin* is a small, round, shiny (usually metallic) ornament sewn onto clothing. The adjective is *sequined* ("having sequins"). *American pianist and entertainer Liberace's clothing (white mink, pink feathers, sequins, and rhinestones) was as ornamental as his musical style.*

[5] **diaphanous** To describe something (clothing, for example) as *diaphanous* is to say that it's very sheer and light; it's transparent, flimsy, gauzy, airy, wispy, etc. *In 1890s Paris, American dancer Loie Fuller created a sensation with her swirling, diaphanous skirts under continually changing colored lights.*

[6] **meretricious** This word is used to describe things (clothing, ornamentation, decor, etc.) that attracts attention, but in a cheap, tasteless, gaudy, showy, or vulgar way. *Pop artist Andy Warhol, whose repetitious silk-screens of movie stars celebrated both the impersonal and the meretricious, once said, "When I got my first television set, I stopped caring so much about having close relationships."*

my grandfather's, too, for he **whimsically**[2] decided, as was his **wont**[3], to see what kind of trouble he could cause.

"At his suggestion, the band of Monkeys **connivingly**[4] flew down, seized the **foppishly**[5] dressed young man, and carried him until they were over the middle of the river. Then, sarcastically asking him whether it was an elf, pixie, or **fey**[6] aunt who had lent

---

[1] **effete** To describe someone as *effete* (pronounced *ih-FEET*) is to say that he's physically or spiritually weak, over-refined, or effeminate. *In his 1945 book* A Texan in England, *historian James Dobie said, "It is part of American folklore as respects Englishmen to suppose that they are effete."*

[2] **whimsical (whimsically)** If you refer to something (an idea, a notion) as *whimsical*, you mean that it's playfully odd or fanciful. *In 1974 in Ethiopia, anthropologists uncovered the skeleton of a three-million-year-old female human ancestor who walked fully upright; they whimsically named her "Lucy."*

[3] **wont** Your *wont* is your customary practice or habitual way of behaving (concerning a particular thing). *Airline companies, as is their wont, oversell seats to compensate for no-shows.*

[4] **connive (connivingly)** To *connive* is to secretly cooperate with others (usually to do something illegal or immoral); to conspire. The noun is *connivance*. *In 1963, with the connivance of the United States, military leaders in South Vietnam overthrew their president, Ngo Dinh Diem.*

[5] **fop (foppishly)** A *fop* is a man whose clothing and manner are overly elegant; a dandy. *When Yankee Doodle stuck a feather in his cap and called it "macaroni," he didn't mean that the feather was pasta; he meant that the feather was suggestive of a "macaroni" (an English fop of the 18th century whose fancy clothing, powdered wig, rouge, and red lips strove to imitate Italian fashion).*

[6] **fey** People described as *fey* have an otherworldly, unreal, or magical aspect about them. Sometimes they appear a bit crazy, as if under a spell; other times they are in unnaturally high spirits. *In the 1971 cult classic* Harold and Maude, *actress Ruth Gordon plays a fey 79-year-old who falls in love with a 20-year-old man who devises elaborate fake suicides (to shock his mother).*

him the outfit he'd been **flaunting**[1], they dropped him into the water. Realizing it was all in fun, he laughed good-naturedly and **unflappably**[2] swam to shore. But when the Princess came running out to him and found his silks and velvet ruined by the water, she was outraged by the **puerile**[3] prank.

"She knew, of course, who did it, so she had all the Monkeys brought before her and, in an attempt to **inculcate**[4] them with a love of virtue, she began delivering a moralizing **homily**[5]. She pointed out that each Monkey's life, both **temporal**[6] and eternal, is

---

[1] **flaunt (flaunting)** To *flaunt* something (that you're proud of) is to conspicuously display it; to show it off, parade it, etc. *Two peafowl may be brought together at the proper moment for mating by the peacock flaunting his brilliant blue or green tail feathers before the drabber peahen.*

[2] **unflappable (unflappably)** To describe someone as *unflappable* is to say that he's always calm (during times of both trouble and success); he's not easily upset or excited. *The English novelist and humorist P. G. Wodehouse is famous for his comic stories featuring an unflappable valet named Jeeves.*

[3] **puerile** To describe something (an action or behavior, for example) as *puerile* is to say that it's childish, immature, juvenile, babyish, etc. *In 1918 journalist and critic H. L. Mencken (1880–1956) said, "The average schoolmaster, on all the lower levels, is essentially an idiot, for how can one imagine an intelligent man engaging in so puerile an [occupation]?"*

[4] **inculcate** To *inculcate* someone is to fix or impress an idea in his mind by frequent instruction or repetition. *Most elementary and secondary school social studies curriculums in the U.S. don't consist merely of the study of history, geography, and government; teachers also try to inculcate their students with a sense of patriotism, democracy, and morality.*

[5] **homily** A *homily* is a formal lecture or speech (or written essay) that gives moral advice or warning; a sermon. *English poet and preacher John Donne (1572–1631) is famous for his spellbinding homilies and the well-known phrases they contained ("for whom the bell tolls," and "No man is an island," for example).*

[6] **temporal** To describe something as *temporal* is to say that it pertains to life in the present and the material world (as opposed to the afterlife or the spiritual world). *In 1831 French writer Honoré de Balzac (1799–1850) said, "Science is the language of the temporal world; love is that of the spiritual world."*

affected by his behavior. Then, while encouraging them to **sublimate**[1] their **impish**[2] urges by participating in relay races, one of the younger Monkeys, hidden among the **serried**[3] ranks, **grimaced**[4] and groaned. Suddenly unable to stomach the sight of any of them, she **callously**[5] declared that all their wings should be tied and they should be treated as they had treated her fiancé and

---

[1] **sublimate** To *sublimate* an undesirable behavior or biological impulse (a sexual or aggressive urge, for example) is to redirect the energy you would have expended (on it) to some other, socially acceptable (or even beneficial) activity. *In 1952 Spanish surrealist painter Salvador Dali (1904–1989) said, "Never try to correct [mistakes]; on the contrary, rationalize them, understand them thoroughly— after that, it will be possible for you to sublimate them."*

[2] **imp (impish)** An *imp* can be a small evil spirit (devil, demon, etc.) or a mischievous child. To describe someone's behavior as *impish* is to say that it's (sometimes amusingly) mischievous. *The 1993 film* Dennis the Menace *(based on Hank Ketcham's famous comic strip) concerns the relationship between an impish six-year-old and his grouchy neighbor, Mr. Wilson.*

[3] **serried** The obsolete verb *serry* meant "to close ranks (as troops)." But today, to describe something with the adjective *serried* is to say that it's crowded or pressed closely together (especially in rows). *As we entered the ancient church, a serried line of candle flames all leaned to one side, then righted themselves again.*

[4] **grimace (grimaced)** As a noun, a *grimace* is a (sometimes ugly or contorted) facial expression that conveys displeasure, disapproval, pain, etc. As a verb, to *grimace* is to make such an expression. *In his 1886 book* Beyond Good and Evil, *German philosopher Frediedrich Nietzsche (1844–1900) said of telling lies, "One may indeed lie with the mouth— but with the accompanying grimace one nevertheless tells the truth."*

[5] **callous (callously)** People described as *callous* are emotionally hardened; they're unsympathetic, uncaring, hardhearted, unfeeling, insensitive, indifferent, etc. *At the Nuremberg (Nazi war crimes) trials of 1946, the prosecution said, "The defendants in this case are charged with murders, tortures, and other atrocities committed in the name of medical science"; he then continued, "German militarists, callous to the sufferings of people whom they regarded as inferior, were willing to gather whatever scientific fruit these [medical] experiments might yield."*

dropped into the river. But my grandfather **expostulated**[1] with her because he knew the Monkeys would drown if their wings were tied. At first, because she **deemed**[2] them **egregious**[3] troublemakers, the Princess was **impervious**[4] to the potential suffering— and probable **dissolution**[5]— of the Monkeys.

---

[1] **expostulate (expostulated)** To *expostulate* with someone is to express objection (especially in the form of earnest reasoning) to something he intends to do or has done (in an effort to dissuade or correct him). *Social reformer Carry Nation (1846–1911) not only expostulated with the American public about the evils of alcohol, she also used a hatchet to destroy barroom liquor and property!*

[2] **deem (deemed)** To *deem* is to hold a certain opinion about something; to regard it, consider it, judge it, look upon it, or think of it in a particular way, as in *the book was removed from the school library because its language was deemed inappropriate for children. In 1948 the White House was deemed structurally unsound; over the next four years it was gutted and its interior structure was replaced with steel framing.*

[3] **egregious** To describe something (an error or violation, for example) as *egregious* is to say that it's outrageously, glaringly, or conspicuously bad or offensive. *In the late 1970s, a white man named Allan Bakke was denied admission to a California medical school that had admitted black candidates with lower test scores (as a result of the school's affirmative action policy that set aside 16 percent of openings for racial minorities); Bakke, who saw this as an egregious violation of the equal protection clause of the 14th Amendment, sued, and in 1978 the U.S. Supreme Court ordered that he be admitted.*

[4] **impervious** To describe a physical material as *impervious* is to say that it can't be penetrated (by something else, such as moisture, heat, etc.). To describe a person as *impervious* is to say that he can't be emotionally affected (that is, he's uninfluenced by pity, fear, etc.). *Because philosophers seek wisdom through meditation and moral self-restraint, people sometimes think of them as being impervious to the ups and downs of everyday life.*

[5] **dissolution** The *dissolution* of something (a marriage, corporation, organization, etc.) is the (often legal or official) breaking up and ending of it. *After the dissolution of the Soviet Union (1991), Russia and ten other Soviet republics joined in a Commonwealth of Independent States.*

THE WIZARD OF OZ VOCABULARY BUILDER

"Finally, however, perhaps because of my grandfather's **ardent**[1] **remonstrations**[2], her **obdurate**[3] heart softened and she became **dispassionate**[4]. She decided, while not **exonerating**[5] them, to at least spare them on the condition that they should forever after be forced to obey the wishes of the owner of the Golden Cap. This Cap had been bought as a wedding present for her husband— after the Princess, with tremendous difficulty, finally succeeded in persuading the previous owner to sell it. But that turned out to be a

---

[1] **ardent** If you're *ardent* about something, you show great intensity of feeling or emotion about it; you're enthusiastic, passionate, devoted, etc. The noun is *ardor*. *An ardent opponent of fascism, Spanish cellist and conductor Pablo Casals (1876–1973) exiled himself from Spain (and for a time stopped performing) in protest against the regime (1939–1975) of (Spanish dictator) Francisco Franco.*

[2] **remonstrate (remonstrations)** To *remonstrate* (pronounced with the accent on the second syllable) is to express opposition by argument (by presenting objections) or to plead in protest. As a noun, a *remonstration* (or *remonstrance*) is a particular statement of strong disapproval or the act of remonstrating in general. *In his "Give Me Liberty or Give Me Death" speech (1775), American Revolutionary leader Patrick Henry said, "We have done everything that could be done to [avoid] the storm [that] is now coming on: We have petitioned; we have remonstrated— our petitions have been slighted [and] our remonstrances have produced additional violence and insult."*

[3] **obdurate** To describe someone as *obdurate* (pronounced with the accent on the first syllable) is to say that he's stubborn and inflexible, especially cold-heartedly so. *In the 1968 British movie musical* Oliver!, *a poor orphan's innocent mealtime request ("Please, sir, I want some more") is met not only with an obdurate refusal but with severe punishment.*

[4] **dispassionate** If someone is *dispassionate* (about a particular issue), he's fair, impartial, unbiased, unprejudiced, etc. (that is, he's not influenced by personal emotions). *In the Introduction to his* Origin of Species *(1859), British naturalist Charles Darwin (1809–1882) wrote: "I can entertain no doubt, after the most deliberate study and dispassionate judgment of which I am capable, that the view which most naturalists until recently entertained, and which I formerly entertained— namely, that each species has been independently created— is erroneous."*

[5] **exonerate (exonerating)** To *exonerate* someone is to (often officially) clear him of blame or guilt. *In 1995 a court-martial exonerated Air Force captain Jim Wang of causing 26 deaths in the accidental shooting (1994) of two Army helicopters over Iraq.*

352

THE WIZARD OF OZ VOCABULARY BUILDER

Pyrrhic[1] victory, so the story goes, because the Cap's **extortionate**[2] price was more than the Princess could afford. She ended up borrowing the money from a **usurer**[3], and the excessive interest forced her to survive on **frugal**[4] meals for months! But today few

---

[1] **Pyrrhic** To refer to a victory as *Pyrrhic* is to say that it's been gained at too great a cost (that is, what has been lost is as much or more than what has been gained). Note: Pyrrhus (319–272 B.C.) was the king of Epirus (an ancient country of western Greece); in 280 B.C. he defeated the Romans, but with such heavy losses that he said, "One more such victory and I am lost." *At World War II's Battle of the Coral Sea (a May 1942 naval battle in the waters located between Australia and New Guinea), Americans lost more ships and planes than did the Japanese; however, the battle was at best a Pyrrhic victory for Japan because it forced them to abandon their plans to capture the chief Allied base on New Guinea (thereby ending their threat to Australia) and because their losses helped tip the scales in favor of the Americans at the Battle of Midway a month later.*

[2] **extortion (extortionate)** The criminal offense of obtaining money from someone by force or intimidation is known as *extortion*. To describe something (a cost, price, interest rate, etc.) as *extortionate* is to say that it's excessive, exorbitant, unreasonable, etc. *During the first decade of the 1900s, the mayors of Detroit, Toledo, and Cleveland accused streetcar companies of charging extortionate fares and providing poor service.*

[3] **usury (usurer)** The practice of lending money at an unlawfully high rate of interest is known as *usury* (pronounced *YOOJ-uh-ree*). One who does so is a *usurer*. The adjective is *usurious* (pronounced *youj-OR-ee-us*). *Egyptian ruler Ismail Pasha (1830–1895) sought to modernize Egypt by borrowing huge sums of money at usurious rates of interest to carry through vast public works (the completion of the Suez Canal and the construction of irrigation facilities, for example).*

[4] **frugal** To refer to a person as *frugal* is to say that he exercises care or restraint in spending money; he's not wasteful; he's thrifty, economical, etc. To refer to a thing as *frugal* is to say that it entails little expense. *In his first inaugural address (1801), President Thomas Jefferson stressed the necessity of "a frugal Government, which shall not take from the mouth of labor the bread it has earned."*

give much **credence**[1] to that story. Of course, my grandfather and all the other Monkeys at once agreed to the condition, and that's how it happens that the Monkeys are the slaves of whoever owns the Cap.

"The new Prince, being the first owner of the Cap, was the first to impose a wish upon the Monkeys. As his bride had a natural **antipathy**[2] toward them, he called all of them together and ordered them always to keep where his wife wouldn't set eyes on them, which they were glad to do, for they were all afraid of her and had no desire of any **rapprochement**[3].

"And this was all they ever had to do until the Golden Cap fell into the hands of the Wicked Witch of the West, who forced them

---

[1] **credence** To give *credence* to something (a statement, story, report, etc.) is either to accept its truthfulness (as in *he didn't give any credence to the rumor*) or to cause it to become more believable (as in *new evidence gave credence to the allegations*). *In June 1998 about 90 lawmakers and community activists, in an informal but symbolic test of water quality, removed their shoes and socks, linked hands, and strolled into a tributary river of Chesapeake Bay (an inlet of the Atlantic Ocean that separates Maryland and Virginia); that they were still able to see their feet more than 100 feet from shore gave credence to scientific reports suggesting that the Chesapeake was becoming less polluted.*

[2] **antipathy** A (sometimes natural or instinctive) feeling of dislike, hatred, ill will, hostility, opposition, etc. (toward something or someone), is known as *antipathy* (pronounced with the accent on the second syllable). *ROTC (Reserve Officers Training Corps) enrollments dropped during the late 1960s and 1970s, when the Vietnam War provoked student antipathy toward the military.*

[3] **rapprochement** The reestablishment of friendship or harmony (as between nations) is known as *rapprochement* (pronounced with the accent on the last syllable, which is nasalized, as in French). *When the USSR broke up into a loose confederation of independent states (1991), President George H. Bush quickly recognized them and sought a rapprochement with the new Russian president, Boris Yeltsin.*

to **wantonly**[1] **pillage**[2] all the nearby villages. The Monkeys, of course, having no desire of **rapine**[3], were horrified and guilt-ridden by the **reprehensible**[4] acts they were forced to commit."

Just when the King finished his story by saying, "... and everyone hated them and referred to them as 'the **scourge**[5] of the land,'" the Monkeys carefully set the travelers down in the beautiful country

---

[1] **wanton (wantonly)** To describe an action (an attack, for example) as *wanton* (pronounced *WAHN-tin*) is to say that it's done without justification, motive, provocation, or regard for what's right; it's groundless, heedless, uncalled for, immoral, etc. *In his 1917 speech asking Congress for a declaration of war against Germany, President Woodrow Wilson referred to Germany's submarine attacks against American passenger and commercial ships as "the wanton and wholesale destruction of the lives of men, women, and children engaged in innocent and legitimate pursuits."*

[2] **pillage** To *pillage* something (a town or countryside, for example) is to rob it (of goods) by force or destroy it (especially in time of war). *During the 17th century, English buccaneers (pirates) pillaged the Spanish Main (a section of the Caribbean Sea crossed by Spanish ships carrying gold back to Spain).*

[3] **rapine** The forcible or violent seizure (and carrying off) of another's property is known as *rapine* (pronounced *RAP-in*). *In his 1903 book* The Souls of Black Folk, *African-American civil rights leader and NAACP cofounder W. E. B. Du Bois (1868–1963) said that the end of the Civil War (1865) "inaugurated the crusade of the New England schoolmarm, [who, with her dress waving] behind the [war's] mists of ruin and rapine [sought] a life work in planting New England schoolhouses among the white and black of the South."*

[4] **reprehensible** To describe something (action or behavior, for example) as *reprehensible* is to say that it's deserving of blame or criticism; it's objectionable, wicked, etc. *In 1977 Supreme Court Justice Byron White said, "[Rape] is highly reprehensible, both in a moral sense and in its almost total contempt for the personal integrity of the female victim."*

[5] **scourge** Any source or cause (disease, famine, natural catastrophe, etc.) of widespread suffering, devastation, hardship, distress, misfortune, misery, etc., is known as a *scourge* (rhymes with *urge*). *The Preamble of the Charter of the United Nations (adopted 1945) says, "We the peoples of the United Nations [are] determined to save succeeding generations from the scourge of war, which twice in our lifetime has brought untold sorrow to mankind."*

of the Quadlings. "How interesting," Dorothy said. Then, waving to the Monkeys as they rose into the air and flew away, she yelled, "Thank you!"

Chapter 27 "The Land of the South"

Now Dorothy surveyed the surrounding area. The country of the Quadlings appeared **affluent**[1] and happy. There was field upon field of ripening grain—the **mainstay**[2] of their economy—with well-paved roads running between, and pretty rippling brooks with strong bridges across them. The fences and houses were all painted red, and the **amicable**[3]-looking Quadlings themselves, who were short but **portly**[4], were all dressed in red—except a lone teenaged

---

[1] **affluent** A person (or town, neighborhood, etc.) described as *affluent* is rich, wealthy, prosperous, well-off, etc. *In 1966 New York governor Nelson Rockefeller (1908–1979), urging Syracuse University graduates to enter public service, said, "There are many other possibilities more enlightening than the struggle to become the local doctor's most affluent ulcer case."*

[2] **mainstay** As a nautical term, the *mainstay* of a sailing vessel is the *stay* (heavy rope or wire cable) that steadies and supports the *mainmast* (large forward mast). But in general usage, a *mainstay* is someone or something that acts as a chief support or part of something, as in *tourism is the mainstay of Bermuda's economy. For 30 years comedian Johnny Carson was a mainstay of late-night television as host of* The Tonight Show *(1962–1992).*

[3] **amicable** To describe someone as *amicable* is to say that he's pleasant and easy to get along with; he's friendly, agreeable, peaceable, good-natured, personable, etc. To describe a relationship (as between people or countries) as *amicable* is to say that it's friendly, peaceable, etc., with the implication that the parties involved have a desire not to quarrel. *In his first inaugural address (1861), President Abraham Lincoln said, "One section of our country believes slavery is right, while the other believes it is wrong; physically speaking, we cannot remove [them] from each other—they cannot but remain face to face, and [communication], either amicable or hostile, must continue between them."*

[4] **portly** Although this word means "fat, stout, overweight, etc.," it's usually used either as a polite substitute for the word "fat" or to describe a person who's heavy but also stately or dignified (actor Raymond Burr in his TV portrayal of fictional defense attorney Perry Mason, for example). *British Prime Minister Winston Churchill (1874–1965) was easily recognized by his portly frame, balding head, bowler hat, and cigar.*

boy. This **renegade**[1], convinced that the Emerald City was the **bellwether**[2] of the fashion industry, sported an outfit of bright, **bilious**[3] green.

"How far is it to Glinda's Castle?" Dorothy asked a passerby, a **porcine**[4] little man with a **cherubic**[1], **rubicund**[2] face.

---

[1] **renegade** Technically, a *renegade* is a person who rejects or deserts a particular cause, party, group, religion, etc. (usually for another). But the word is often used to describe anyone who takes his own path: a rebel, traitor, outlaw, runaway, etc. *In May 1996, reporting on the trial of a pathologist who helped 28 sick, anguished people commit suicide, the* Washington Post *said, "A jury has begun to debate whether Jack Kevorkian is a dangerous social renegade who has put himself above the law or a heroic champion of freedom of choice."* As an adjective, the word means "resembling a renegade"; that is, rebellious, traitorous, self-styled, nonconforming, etc. *White House special assistant and Watergate plotter G. Gordon Liddy held a renegade theory that the Watergate burglars were actually looking for pictures of call girls kept in the desk of a secretary.*

[2] **bellwether** Originally, a *bellwether* was a male sheep, wearing a bell, that led a flock. But today a *bellwether* is anyone or anything (a group, company, city, etc.) that assumes a leadership role and acts as an indicator of future trends. *The Dow Jones industrial average (the average of 30 blue-chip stocks) is a bellwether for the health of the entire stock market.*

[3] **bilious** Your liver secretes a yellow or greenish bitter liquid, known as *bile*, which aids in the digestion of fats. People described as *bilious* suffer from excessive secretion of bile (they have indigestion) or they act *as if* they have excessive bile (they're cranky, irritable, etc.). To describe a thing (a work of art or article of clothing, for example) as *bilious* is to say that it's distasteful or unpleasant, or that its color resembles that of bile. *In July 1989 the* Washington Post *explained that the Library of Congress, "famous for its priceless collection of books and manuscripts," is also the secret storehouse for all short-lived products of pop culture, such as "a grinning Richard Nixon clown doll or a [3-D picture] of the Last Supper in bilious brown plastic."*

[4] **porcine** This word means "pertaining to or characteristic of pigs; piggish, hoggish," or, by extension, "fat or greedy." *In 1980, during a campaign stop at an Iowa farm, (candidate for the Democratic presidential nomination) Senator Ted Kennedy stood near a pigpen in which two hogs happened to be mating; for a few moments, the press corps cameraman— the nation's "eye"— ignored Kennedy to focus on the porcine activity.*

THE WIZARD OF OZ VOCABULARY BUILDER

"It's not a great way," he answered **congenially**[3], **doffing**[4] his hat. "Take the road to the South and you'll soon reach it."

They walked past **idyllic**[5] fields and across pretty bridges until they spotted a beautiful Castle. Walking closer, they saw,

---

[1] **cherubic** A *cherub* is an angel, or other celestial being, portrayed in art as a winged child with a chubby, rosy face (Cupid, for example). To describe a person as *cherubic* (or to refer to a person, especially a child, as a *cherub*) is to say that he or his face is angelic, sweet, innocent, or chubby. *In his review of the 1987 film* Planes, Trains and Automobiles, *journalist Hal Hinson said, "[Actor] John Candy is so exuberantly cherubic that his feet never seem to touch the ground."*

[2] **rubicund** To describe someone's complexion as *rubicund* is to say that it has a healthy rosiness; it's ruddy, reddish, full-blooded, etc. *Twenty-two years before writing (the set of four violin concertos known as)* The Four Seasons *(1725), Italian baroque composer Antonio Vivaldi (1678–1741) entered the priesthood; because of his red hair and rubicund complexion he was known as "The Red Priest."*

[3] **congenial (congenially)** A person described as *congenial* is pleasant and easy to get along with; he's friendly, agreeable, good-natured, personable, sociable, etc. A relationship described a *congenial* is friendly, pleasant, etc. *Actress Katharine Hepburn and actor Spencer Tracy, who appeared in nine films together, had a particularly congenial off-screen relationship.* To describe a thing (an occupation, home, surroundings, etc.) as *congenial* is to say that it's well-suited to one's needs or nature; it's pleasant, agreeable, etc. *Scottish novelist Robert Louis Stevenson (1850–1894) was a tuberculosis sufferer who traveled extensively in search of a congenial climate.*

[4] **doff (doffing)** To *doff* a hat is to tip it or remove it (as in greeting). To *doff* an article of clothing is to remove it; take it off. *In a 1985 New York Times advertisement, (upscale men's clothing store) Brooks Brothers referred to hats as "the classic finishing touch, a confident statement of your personal good taste," then reminded readers that "the well-dressed man still doffs his hat."*

[5] **idyllic** An *idyll* (pronounced the same as *idol*) is a poem or short narrative that describes something charmingly simple, especially a rural scene. To refer to something (a place, setting, vacation, etc.) as *idyllic* (pronounced with accent on the second syllable) is to say that it's simple, carefree, picturesque, pleasing, etc. *In 1891 French artist and stockbroker Paul Gauguin (1848–1903) abandoned his business career, family, and country to live in the idyllic South Pacific island of Tahiti, where he painted some of his finest works (his series of paintings depicting the beauty of Polynesian women, for example).*

garrisoned[1] at the gate, a young, pretty, blonde-haired soldier girl in a red uniform. Attached to her belt was a long sword with a **gilded**[2] **hilt**[3]. As Dorothy approached, the soldier said to her, "Why have you come to the Land of the South?"

"To see the Good Witch who rules here," Dorothy answered, staring at the golden **haft**[4] and deciding that it must be a **harbinger**[5]

---

[1] **garrison (garrisoned)** As a noun, a *garrison* is a soldier or soldiers assigned to provide protection or keep watch (as at a fort); a guard, lookout, etc. As a verb the word has two senses: to *garrison* a thing (a fort, town, etc.) is to provide it with such soldiers; to *garrison* people (soldiers) is to place them on guard or lookout duty (as at a fort). *During the war for Texan independence from Mexico (1835–1836), a garrison of about 180 Texans defending the Alamo (a San Antonio chapel-fort) was massacred by an army of several thousand Mexicans.*

[2] **gild (gilded)** As a verb, to *gild* (something) is to cover it with a thin layer of gold or a gold-colored substance, or to give it a superficially or deceptively bright or pleasing appearance. A related word is *gilt*, which as an adjective means "covered with a thin layer of gold or gold coloring; gilded" (as in *gilt bronze statuettes*) or "gold in color; golden," and as a noun means "the gold or other material used in gilding." *In 1986, speaking of a legendary European café, Gourmet magazine said, "Here, seated on red velvet [benches] at marble-topped tables, one can't help wonder what sights these smoky, gilded mirrors have reflected for more than 250 years."*

[3] **hilt** The handle of a weapon or tool, especially a sword or dagger, is known as a *hilt*. *The well-known Japanese Samurai sword has a long, single-edge blade set in a long hilt.* Note: The phrase "to the hilt" means "to the maximum extent or degree; completely; fully."

[4] **haft** The handle of a knife, sword, or dagger is known as a *haft*. *While all fencing swords have protective hand guards (between blade and handle), they are all shaped differently: The foil's is small and circular; the epee's is bell shaped; and the sabre's is arched (it curves around the knuckles and attaches to the top of the haft).*

[5] **harbinger** Anything (a natural phenomenon, for example) that foreshadows or signals a future event is known as a *harbinger* (of that event). *Cirrus clouds (high, wispy clouds) that become thicker over time are sometimes a harbinger of a hurricane.* A person referred to as a *harbinger* is a forerunner (that is, he foreshadows or is influential in bringing about a future trend or event). *Beginning with his Third Symphony (Eroica, 1803), German composer Ludwig van Beethoven (1770–1827) broke from the strict formalities of (late 18th-century) Classicism to become the harbinger of (19th-century) Romanticism (which stressed passion, experimentation, and freedom of form).*

of hope. "Will you take us to her?"

"Give me your names and I'll ask Glinda if she'll see you," answered the girl. Dorothy explained who they were, and the soldier went into the Castle.

While they waited, the Tin Woodman decided that if they received a denial, he would use his **ingratiating**[1] charm to **inveigle**[2] the girl into letting them through the gate; so he prepared a few **blandishments**[3], just in case. The Scarecrow, in a similar vein, decided that if they were denied he would devise a clever scheme to sneak them into the Castle. But neither **cajolery**[4] nor **subterfuge**[1]

---

[1] **ingratiate (ingratiating)** To *ingratiate* yourself is to (often by deliberate effort) bring yourself into the favor or good graces of someone else. The adjective *ingratiating* means either "charming, agreeable, pleasing, etc.," as in *an ingratiating manner*, or "meant to please or win favor," as in *an ingratiating smile*. *In 1975 singer John Denver (1943–1997), famous for his pageboy haircut, granny glasses, and ingratiating stage presence, was named Entertainer of the Year by the Academy of Country Music.*

[2] **inveigle** To *inveigle* someone (into doing something that he doesn't want to) is to induce, entice, or convince him (to do it) by means of flattery, coaxing, slick talk, etc. To *inveigle* a desired object (a free pass to something, for example) is to obtain it (from someone) by means of charm, sweet-talk, flattery, etc. *In Carlo Collodi's* Adventures of Pinocchio *(1883), a lazy, mischief-making boy named Lampwick inveigles Pinocchio into skipping school and running away with him to Playland (where there are "no schools, no teachers, no books!").*

[3] **blandishments** Flattering or insincere statements intended to coax or convince someone into doing or believing something are known as *blandishments*. *In 1987 National Conference on Soviet Jewry chairman Morris Abram said that Soviet leader Mikhail Gorbachev's implied promises that thousands of Jews would soon be allowed to leave the Soviet Union are "blandishments and soft soap" intended to cover up a repressive policy on Jewish emigration.*

[4] **cajole (cajolery)** To *cajole* (someone) is to urge or persuade (him) by persistent flattery, gentle teasing, repeated appeals, etc. The noun is *cajolery*. *In January 2000 Defense Secretary William Cohen said that he had recently visited Beverly Hills to cajole such film stars as Julia Roberts, Tom Cruise, and Robert De Niro into making TV commercials praising service in the armed forces.*

was required, for after a few moments the soldier came back to say that Dorothy and the others were to be admitted at once.

They followed the soldier girl into a **commodious**[2] room where the Good Witch Glinda sat upon a throne of rubies. She was both young and **ethereally**[3] beautiful to their eyes. From her **tiara**[4]-adorned, rich red hair, flowing ringlets fell over the shoulders of her pure-white dress. Her **limpid**[5] blue eyes gazed kindly upon the little girl. "What can I do for you, my child?" she asked in a

---

[1] **subterfuge** A *subterfuge* is a devious or underhanded means to achieve an end; a scheme, a trick, etc. *In 1986 President Ronald Reagan said that members of Congress who use "subterfuge or backroom deals" to stop passage of military aid to Nicaraguan Contras (rebels) will set back the cause of peace and "hand down a verdict of shame on us all."*

[2] **commodious** To describe something (a home, ship, harbor, etc.) as *commodious* is to say that it's spacious, roomy, ample, etc. *During his Presidency (1909–1913), William Howard Taft (all 350 pounds of him) threw out the first ball of a major league baseball game from a specially built, extra-commodious box seat.*

[3] **ethereal (ethereally)** Depending on the context, this word (derived from the Greek word for "upper air") can mean "light, airy, insubstantial," "delicate, highly refined," "heavenly, celestial," or "otherworldly, spiritual." *Art Garfunkel's ethereal harmonies helped (folk/rock duo) Simon and Garfunkel achieve major success in the late 1960s.*

[4] **tiara** A small, often semicircular, ornamental (often jeweled) crown or headpiece worn by women on formal occasions (or by queens, princesses, or beauty pageant winners) is known as a *tiara*. *With the official rhinestone tiara threatening to fall, the new Miss America steadied it with her hand as she began her tear-filled stroll down the runway.*

[5] **limpid** To describe an object or substance (water, air, crystal, etc.) as *limpid* is to say that it admits light through it; that is, it's clear, transparent, see-through, etc. To describe writing or speech as *limpid* is to say that it's transparently clear in style; that is, it's understandable, direct, unambiguous, etc. *In 1981, speaking of Florida's Cypress Swamp, journalist Anne Oman said, "Spring rain is plopping into the limpid pools, marring the mirror image of the bald cypress trees that merge into a cathedral ceiling 150 feet overhead."*

mellifluous[1], flutelike tone that carried with it its own musical accompaniment.

---

[1] **mellifluous** To describe a voice, sound, or phrase as *mellifluous* (a word derived from the Latin word for *honey*) is to say that it's sweet-sounding, smooth, flowing, pleasing, etc. *In September 1993, when 50 radio talk show hosts were assembled at the White House to hear administration officials' views on health care reform, journalist Howard Kurtz alliteratively described the scene as "a sea of spin, a mélange [mixture] of mellifluous voices, a tangle of talkmeisters."*

Chapter 28 "The Return Home"

Dorothy told Glinda her entire story, starting with the cyclone and ending with the Hammer-Heads. "My greatest wish now," Dorothy finished, "is to get back to Kansas, for Aunt Em will surely think something dreadful has happened to me." As Dorothy spoke that last sentence, an invisible **exudation**[1] of all her **toils**[2] and **torturous**[3] sufferings drifted slowly upward from her body and condensed into a beautiful **translucent**[4] radiance that filled the entire room.

---

[1] **exude (exudation)** Technically, when something (sweat through pores in the skin, for example) *exudes*, it oozes out. But to say that someone *exudes* a particular feeling (anger, self-satisfaction, joy, etc.) or personality trait (sincerity, confidence, charm, shyness, etc.) is to say that he exhibits it in abundance; it seems to flow out of him. The noun is *exudation*. *Speaking of actress Marilyn Monroe (1926–1962), the* Reader's Companion to American History *said, "In most of her films she exuded a blatant yet attractive sexuality that set her apart from the other screen personalities of her time."*

[2] **toils** Laborious tasks (especially those involving continuous or exhausting exertion) are collectively known as (one's) *toils*. The word is often seen in the phrase "toils and tribulations" (troubles, distress, suffering). *In his June 1940 "Their Finest Hour" speech (delivered four days after the Nazis entered Paris), British Prime Minister Winston Churchill said of his country's war efforts, "If final victory rewards our toils, [France] shall share the gain— aye, freedom shall be restored to all."*

[3] **torturous** This is the adjective form of the word *torture*. To refer to something (a situation, ordeal, difficulty, etc.) as *torturous* is to say that it's characteristic of torture; that is, it's intensely agonizing or painful. *During World War II, Nazi official Adolf Eichmann was responsible for the torturous treatment and outright killing of millions of Jews.*

[4] **translucent** To describe something (frosted glass, for example) as *translucent* is to say that it permits light to pass through, but that objects on the other side are not distinctly visible; it's semi-transparent. Note: An object that permits no light to pass through is said to be *opaque*. *In 1987 journalist Paula Span said of a chocolate-covered cherry, "[It's] elegant to look at, inelegant to eat— as soon as you bite into its shell, the cherry-flavored liquid begins oozing stickily onto your fingers; another bite, and the maraschino cherry inside is squishing into a translucent pulp."*

THE WIZARD OF OZ VOCABULARY BUILDER

The Good Witch leaned forward and kissed the sweet, upturned face of the **prepossessing**[1] little girl. "Bless your dear heart," she said, fully aware that they were all standing at the very **denouement**[2] of Dorothy's **epic**[3] adventure. "I'm sure I can tell you of a way to get back to Kansas."

"How?" asked Dorothy, a little drop of brightness forming in the corner of each eye.

"Your Silver Shoes will carry you home," replied Glinda. "If you had known their power you could have gone back to your Aunt Em the very first day you came to this country. One of the most curious things about the Silver Shoes is that they can carry you to

---

[1] **prepossessing** To refer to someone as *prepossessing* is to say that he impresses favorably; he's naturally appealing, engaging, pleasant, etc. *In its review (1977) of a book entitled* Underwater Wilderness: Life Around the Great Reefs, *the* Washington Post *said, "The coral, undeniably one of nature's least prepossessing animals, is one of its most impressive and durable builders, as generation succeeds generation to create reefs, islands, and atolls wherein thrive the numerous subjects of this book."*

[2] **denouement** As a dramatic or narrative device, a *denouement* (pronounced with the last syllable accented and nasalized, as in French) is the ending of (or especially the resolution or clarification of the intricacies of) a film, play, or novel. *During the denouement of the 1960 film* Psycho, *a psychiatrist explains that Norman Bates had dressed in his dead mother's clothes and had "become" his mother.* But in general usage, the word can refer to the final outcome (ending, result, conclusion) of any (doubtful) series of events. *In the stunningly dramatic denouement of the 1980 American League pennant race, George Brett slammed Goose Gossage's 100-mile-per-hour fastball into the third deck of Yankee Stadium to win the Kansas City Royals the league championship.*

[3] **epic** As a noun, an *epic* is an extended (often poetic) narrative that (usually in elevated style) describes or celebrates the adventures or feats of a heroic figure. (Homer's *Odyssey* is an example of an *epic* poem). But the word can also denote any story or series of events that resembles an *epic* in scope, subject matter, etc. (as in *war epic, space epic,* etc.). As an adjective, the word describes anything suggestive of an *epic;* that is, anything heroic or impressive in quality (as in *epic events*), or anything unusually grand in size or scope (as in *epic proportions*). *American filmmaker Cecil B. De Mille (1881-1959) was known for his spectacular epic productions, including* The Greatest Show on Earth *(1952) and* The Ten Commandments *(1956).*

anyplace in the world in three steps, and each step will be made in the wink of an eye. All you have to do is click the heels together three times and command the shoes to carry you wherever you wish to go."

"If that's so," said the child, staring down at the scintillating[1] Shoes and wondering why the Good Witch of the North hadn't been aware of that salient[2] fact, "I'll ask them to carry me back to Kansas."

She couldn't bear to think of leaving her friends, but that pain was palliated[3] by the thought of returning to Aunt Em. First she turned to the Lion. Looking tenderly into his eyes, she said, "I

---

[1] **scintillate (scintillating)** To refer to something (a surface, for example) as *scintillating* is to say that it emits flashes of light; it sparkles or shines. By extension, to refer to a person (or his mind, wit, conversation, etc.) as *scintillating* is to say that he's brilliant and animated. *In his review of the April 1988 opening of the New York City Ballet's American Music Festival at the New York State Theater, journalist Alan Kriegsman said, "Glitter and glitz galore marked the gala opening, along with some scintillating flashes of genuine glamour and the troupe's accustomed virtuosity."*

[2] **salient** To refer to something (a fact, trait, feature, etc.) as *salient* is to say that it's noticeable and often consequential; it's prominent, conspicuous, important, striking, remarkable, etc. *A November 1986 op-ed piece in the* Washington Post *said of that paper's article criticizing ABC for beginning Monday night football games so late, "[It] appears to have overlooked the single most salient point: the time-zone factor— while a Monday night game begins at 9 p.m. here on the East Coast, it is telecast at 6 p.m. in the West (of course, your average Western Joe doesn't get home from the office until around 6, and would miss the first quarter of a game begun any earlier than 9 p.m.")*.

[3] **palliate (palliated)** To *palliate* something (pain, discontent, conflict, etc.) is to make it less severe; to alleviate, ease, or calm it. As a noun, a *palliative* is something (especially a drug or medicine) that palliates. *The Missouri Compromise (1820–1821), which admitted Missouri as a slave state and Maine (formerly part of Massachusetts) as a free state, palliated the conflict between abolitionists and slavery's defenders.*

know you'll find a way back to that beautiful, **serene**[1] forest where you've been proclaimed King and that you'll be happy there." She handed the Golden Cap to Glinda, then threw her arms around the Lion's neck and kissed him, gently patting his big head. Inwardly he **harbored**[2] a surge of pent-up feelings, but his **indomitable**[3] bravery forbade him from displaying them.

Then she turned to the Tin Woodman, who was weeping in a way most dangerous to his metal joints. "You mustn't cry or you'll rust your joints again," she said with just a hint of **reproach**[4]. "Will you be going back to the Land of the West to rule over the Winkies?" Not trusting his voice to speak, he merely nodded. Dorothy kissed his hot metal cheek and a look of tenderness and devotion welled up in his eyes.

---

[1] **serene** To describe something (a setting, mood, climate, etc.) as *serene* is to say that it's peaceful, quiet, calm, tranquil, still, etc. The noun is *serenity*. *In 1970 a Christian Science Monitor article entitled "Parks of Paris" noted, "Appreciation, gratitude, affection— these are the qualities Parisians bestow on their parks; beauty, serenity, majesty— these are the rewards they reap in return."*

[2] **harbor (harbored)** As a verb, to *harbor* a feeling or thought is to keep or hold it in your mind. *According to the* Reader's Companion to American History, *"Beneath a usually friendly manner, [President Harry Truman (1884–1972)] harbored a thick layer of aggressiveness that occasionally discharged itself in angry outbursts."*

[3] **indomitable** To refer to something (a warrior, pride, courage, valor, etc.) as *indomitable* is to say that it can't be overcome or subdued; it's unconquerable, invincible, unyielding, strong, etc. *According to a 1976 book entitled* Winning Is Everything and Other American Myths, *tennis star Jimmy Connors (noted for his indomitable need to win) once said, "People don't seem to understand that it's a damn war out there."*

[4] **reproach** As a verb, to *reproach* someone is to criticize, scold, or blame him. As a noun, a *reproach* is an act or expression or disapproval, criticism, or blame. *After the 2000 presidential election (between George W. Bush and Al Gore) ended in a virtual tie and remained unresolved even after several Florida recounts, journalist Gene Weingarten said, "So now everyone hates the electoral college system; well, not me— the electoral college was a product of our Founding Fathers, who, being giants of history, are beyond reproach (even though they wore stockings and, as historical manuscripts suggest, lisped a little)."*

THE WIZARD OF OZ VOCABULARY BUILDER

Finally she turned to the Scarecrow, her first friend in Oz, the one she knew best of all. She touched his arm, and an enormous, overwhelming rush of fondness for the girl swept over him, **prevailing**[1] over every other sensation. She gave him a little **conspiratorial**[2] smile and said **sub rosa**[3], "I think I'll miss you most of all."

But he made no response. He just stood there as if permanently paralyzed, with one hand over his eyes and the other dangling lifelessly at his side.

"Scarecrow!— "

---

[1] **prevail (prevailing)** If one thing *prevails over* another, it's more powerful, influential, or significant (than the other). *During the War of 1812, American warships frequently prevailed over British vessels.* If someone *prevails on* (or *upon*) another, he influences or moves the other to do or accept something. *In 1939 a group of scientists who had received evidence that the Nazis were planning to build an atomic bomb to use against the U.S. prevailed upon physicist Albert Einstein to write to President Franklin D. Roosevelt and urge that the United States develop one first.* If someone or something simply *prevails* (without a following preposition), then, depending on the context, it (1) achieves success; wins (as in *the Yankees prevailed*), (2) is widespread or current (as in *the prevailing viewpoint*), or (3) appears as the most important or frequent feature of something (as in *a painting in which greens prevail*). *In a 1983 speech to the UN General Assembly after the Soviet downing of a Korean passenger plane, President Ronald Reagan said, "The founders [of the United Nations] hoped that a world of relentless conflict would give way to a new era, one where freedom from violence prevailed; but the awful truth is that the use of violence for political gain has become more, not less, widespread in the last decade."*

[2] **conspire (conspiratorial)** When two or more people *conspire*, they secretly agree to act together (often to some unethical or illegal end). To describe something (a wink, smile, whisper, etc.) as *conspiratorial* is to say that it sends the message "this is just between us." *As the waiter surprised Jack with a piece of cake with a birthday candle in it, he gave Jack's wife a conspiratorial wink.*

[3] **sub rosa** In ancient times a rose was hung over meetings as a symbol of the sworn secrecy of the participants. Today, to say that something is done *sub rosa* (which in Latin literally means "under the rose") is to say that it's done secretly, privately, confidentially, etc. *According to journalist James L. Rowe, Jr., the 1979 campaign to bail out the struggling Chrysler Corporation (with a loan of over a billion dollars under the U.S. Loan Guarantee Act) was waged sub rosa on Capital Hill for months before it was ever argued in the open.*

THE WIZARD OF OZ VOCABULARY BUILDER

Tears spilled through his fingers and dripped onto his feet. He made no sound. His whole body was shaking with his effort not to give way. But it was no use. "Don't cry! There's nothing to cry about," Dorothy said, gently patting his back, her eyes glazing over. She felt her throat swell into an unbearably **turgid**[1] lump, nearly suffocating her. Violent sobs suddenly broke from her, convulsing her narrow shoulders. She desperately flung her arms around the soft, stuffed body of the Scarecrow and kissed his painted face.

He tried to speak, but the words clung to the straw lining of his throat. "I'm sorry," he finally said, in a strangled croak that brought with it a few strands of straw. "I'll be all right... I'll be all right." He wiped a sleeve across his painted eyes.

As Glinda stepped down from her throne to give the little girl a good-bye kiss, **fulgent**[2] patterns of sunlight crisscrossed the room. Dorothy, composing herself as well as she could, thanked the good Witch for her kindness. Glinda's smile deepened, emphasizing the lines of kindness around her eyes. Now Dorothy took Toto solemnly in her arms and said, "I'm ready now." Then, waving good-bye to them all, she clicked her heels together three times and said, "Take me home to Aunt Em!"

Instantly she was whirling through the air so swiftly that all she

---

[1] **turgid** To describe something (a bodily organ, for example) as *turgid* is to say that it's swollen, enlarged, bloated, etc. To describe writing or speech as *turgid* is to say that it's overly embellished or complex; it's inflated, overblown, etc. *As U.S. ambassador to the United Nations (1953–60), Henry Cabot Lodge, Jr., said (of the UN), "The fact that the talk may be boring or turgid or uninspiring should not cause us to forget the fact that it is preferable to war."*

[2] **fulgent** If something is *fulgent*, it's shining, dazzling, radiant, etc. *In 1988, speaking of a north woods area of Lake Michigan, journalist Colman McCarthy said, "The waters are turquoise-green, Caribbean clear, and syringe-free; plant life 20 feet deep is visible, [and] the growth, rising out of light sand, is healthy and fulgent, delivering the message that once-sewery Lake Michigan is back to life."*

could hear was the **sibilant**[1] wind rushing past her ears. The Silver Shoes took but three steps and then stopped so suddenly that Dorothy rolled over upon the grass several times. Then she sat up and looked around her.

"Good gracious!" she cried, for she was sitting on the broad Kansas prairie, and just before her was the new farmhouse Uncle Henry built after the howling **holocaust**[2] had devastated the old one. Dorothy stood up and found she was in her stocking feet. The Silver Shoes, her only **tangible**[3] evidence of her fantastic adventure, had fallen off during her flight through the air and were lost forever. After taking only a few steps toward the house, she felt comfortably **acclimated**[4] to her wonderfully **mundane**[1] existence.

---

[1] **sibilant** To describe something as *sibilant* is to say that it makes a hissing sound (like that of the letter *s* or the letters *sh*). *In 1990 journalist Joan Reinthaler observed, "[Classical] guitar audiences are really quite wonderful— where others cough and rattle things and whisper sibilantly through the music, guitar audiences sit, quiet and [engrossed], even through the breaks between movements."*

[2] **holocaust** When spelled with a capital *H*, the *Holocaust* denotes the mass extermination of European Jews by the Nazis during World War II. When spelled with a small *h*, the word denotes any great or complete devastation or destruction (especially by fire) or any great disaster (war, rioting, storms, epidemic diseases, etc.). *In the 1983 film* WarGames, *a young computer whiz, trying to hook into a game manufacturer's computer, almost begins a thermonuclear holocaust when he accidentally connects with a government military computer.*

[3] **tangible** If something (an object, for example) is *tangible*, it can be touched; that is, it has material existence; it's real or actual (as opposed to imaginary, spiritual, or visionary). *According to a July 2000 op-ed piece in the* Washington Post, *"An invisible barrier blocks Middle East peace as surely as the tangible obstacles of Jerusalem, the Golan Heights, or Israeli settlements on the West Bank; the unseen barrier is an Arab political system dominated by authoritarian and frequently corrupt rulers."*

[4] **acclimated** To become *acclimated* to something (a new environment, climate, or situation, for example) is to become accustomed or adjusted to it. *To maintain an acceptable state of health in space, astronauts (in addition to needing air, food, hygiene facilities, and exercise) require a proper balance between work and rest periods and sufficient time to become acclimated to a weightless environment.*

THE WIZARD OF OZ VOCABULARY BUILDER

Aunt Em had just come out of the house to water the flowers when she looked up and saw Dorothy running toward her. "My darling child!" she cried, folding the little girl in her arms and **effusively**[2] kissing every part of her face. "Where in the world were you?"

Aunt Em's **wan**[3] face suddenly began to regain its natural, **robust**[4] color, and Dorothy stared into the **maudlin**[1] eyes that sat

---

[1] **mundane** To describe something (an activity, work of art, etc.) as *mundane* is to say that it's commonplace, ordinary, routine, uninteresting, etc. (as in *such mundane activities as doing the laundry and walking the dog*). The word also describes what refers to the actual world, as opposed to things heavenly or spiritual (as in *beyond the realm of mundane existence*). *In January 2001 the* Washington Post *printed the following letter to the editor from a recently engaged woman: "After years of constant neglect in favor of its more useful counterpart, my left hand has come into its own; sure, the right does the writing and dials the phone, but lately, as it performs these mundane tasks, my left hand has been basking in my admiring gaze— the left hand is wearing the ring."*

[2] **effusive (effusively)** If you say that something (a greeting, praise, an acceptance speech, an apology, etc.) is *effusive*, you mean that it's excessively or unduly emotional; it's unrestrained, gushy, profuse, overflowing, etc. *According to journalist Mary McGrory, in May 1984 "our aging, macho President met a young andro-rock star on the White House's South Lawn; President Reagan was effusive in his greeting and praise of Michael Jackson, who came to his shoulder and glittered like a Christmas tree."*

[3] **wan** To describe someone's face or complexion as *wan* (rhymes with *gone*) is to say that it lacks color; it's unnaturally pale, pasty, etc. The implication is that the paleness has been caused by illness, stress, weariness, or unhappiness. To describe something other than one's complexion (a movie, a smile, sunlight, etc.) as *wan* is to say that it's weak, feeble, ineffective, incompetent, etc. *In his review of ABC's six-hour historical documentary entitled "The Beatles Anthology" (1995), critic Tom Shales said, "It's a long and winding road that sometimes seems a wan and whining drone."*

[4] **robust** A person described as *robust* is strong, healthy, vigorous, etc. A thing described as *robust* is either strong and healthy (as in *robust economic growth*) or rich and full-bodied (as in *a robust wine*). *Academy Award–winning actor Anthony Quinn (1916–2001) is best remembered for his role as the robust title character of the 1964 film* Zorba the Greek.

at its center. How could she possibly explain her **preternatural**[2] adventures? She knew she couldn't. "In a faraway land," she answered simply, tears of joy running down her cheeks. "And here is Toto, too. And oh, Aunt Em, there's no place like home!"

---

[1] **maudlin** To describe something (a movie, song, etc.) as *maudlin* is to say that it's overly or tearfully sentimental; it's tear-jerking, sappy, syrupy, etc. *The maudlin songs of the mid-'60s girl group the Shangri-Las ("Leader of the Pack," for example) invariably revolved around some kind of teen trauma.*

[2] **preternatural** Things that are *preternatural* (pronounced with the accent on the third syllable) are beyond the normal course of nature; they're otherworldly, unearthly, supernatural, irregular, strange, extraordinary, etc. *In his 1986 biography of television pioneer and NBC founder David Sarnoff (1891–1971), Kenneth Bilby said, "[He] had come to view [television] as a force of nearly preternatural dimensions, life-transforming in its impact."*

Index

INDEX

INDEX

INDEX

INDEX

INDEX

INDEX

INDEX

INDEX

INDEX

INDEX

INDEX

INDEX

metamorphose, 70
metaphor, 113
mete, 82
meticulous, 90
métier, 256
mettle, 89
miasma, 89
mien, 287
milquetoast, 110-111
mince, 329
minion, 84
minister, 236
minuscule, 125
minutiae, 232
mire, 242
misanthrope, 332
miscreant, 227-228
misogyny, 112
missive, 173
mitigate, 106
modicum, 227
moil, 185
mollify, 231
moniker, 233
monolithic, 161
moot, 147
morass, 307
morbid, 83
moribund, 318
morose, 171
mortification, 29-30
mote, 68-69
motley, 162
mottled, 2
mount, 57
mufti, 209
mulct, 217
multitudinous, 87
mummery, 252
mundane, 370-371
munificent, 223
musings, 270
myopic, 140
myriad, 68

nabob, 145
nadir, 284
napery, 100
nascent, 206
natty, 25
nebulous, 172
nefarious, 170
nemesis, 170
neophyte, 195
niggardly, 174
niggling, 182
nimbus, 93
nocturnal, 316
noisome, 317
nomadic, 204
nominal, 222
nonplussed, 213
novice, 265
noxious, 78
nubile, 109
nullify, 340
nuptials, 345
obdurate, 352
obeisance, 84
obfuscate, 121
obliterate, 5
oblivious, 183
obloquy, 242
obscurantism, 142
obsequious, 100
obstinate, 152
obstreperous, 98
obtrude, 168-169
obtuse, 279
obviate, 95
occlude, 37
odious, 82
odyssey, 201
oeuvre, 259
offal, 317
officious, 101
ominous, 2
omnibus, 263
omnipotent, 129

INDEX

INDEX

INDEX

INDEX

INDEX

INDEX

INDEX

INDEX

INDEX